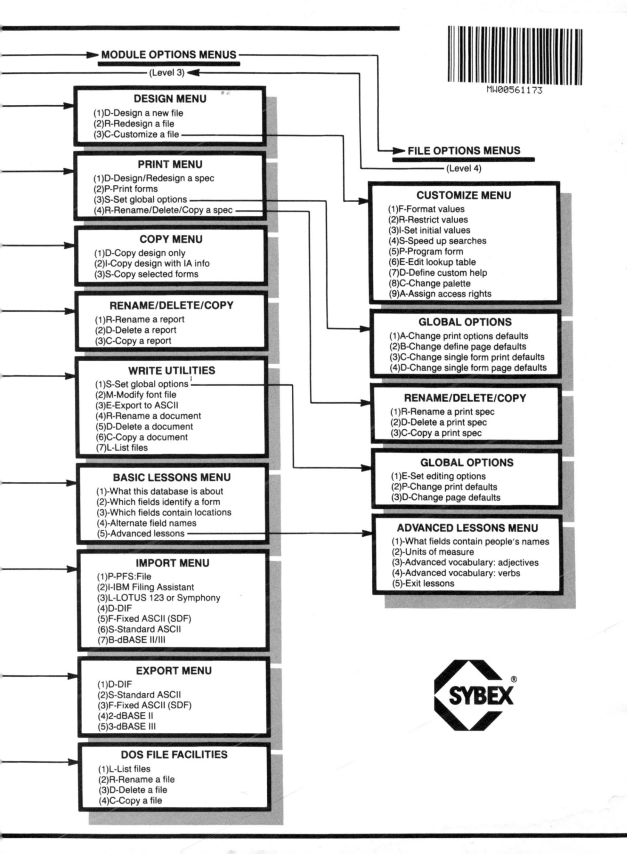

MW00561173

**MODULE OPTIONS MENUS**
(Level 3)

**DESIGN MENU**
(1)D-Design a new file
(2)R-Redesign a file
(3)C-Customize a file

**PRINT MENU**
(1)D-Design/Redesign a spec
(2)P-Print forms
(3)S-Set global options
(4)R-Rename/Delete/Copy a spec

**COPY MENU**
(1)D-Copy design only
(2)I-Copy design with IA info
(3)S-Copy selected forms

**RENAME/DELETE/COPY**
(1)R-Rename a report
(2)D-Delete a report
(3)C-Copy a report

**WRITE UTILITIES**
(1)S-Set global options
(2)M-Modify font file
(3)E-Export to ASCII
(4)R-Rename a document
(5)D-Delete a document
(6)C-Copy a document
(7)L-List files

**BASIC LESSONS MENU**
(1)-What this database is about
(2)-Which fields identify a form
(3)-Which fields contain locations
(4)-Alternate field names
(5)-Advanced lessons

**IMPORT MENU**
(1)P-PFS:File
(2)I-IBM Filing Assistant
(3)L-LOTUS 123 or Symphony
(4)D-DIF
(5)F-Fixed ASCII (SDF)
(6)S-Standard ASCII
(7)B-dBASE II/III

**EXPORT MENU**
(1)D-DIF
(2)S-Standard ASCII
(3)F-Fixed ASCII (SDF)
(4)2-dBASE II
(5)3-dBASE III

**DOS FILE FACILITIES**
(1)L-List files
(2)R-Rename a file
(3)D-Delete a file
(4)C-Copy a file

**FILE OPTIONS MENUS**
(Level 4)

**CUSTOMIZE MENU**
(1)F-Format values
(2)R-Restrict values
(3)I-Set initial values
(4)S-Speed up searches
(5)P-Program form
(6)E-Edit lookup table
(7)D-Define custom help
(8)C-Change palette
(9)A-Assign access rights

**GLOBAL OPTIONS**
(1)A-Change print options defaults
(2)B-Change define page defaults
(3)C-Change single form print defaults
(4)D-Change single form page defaults

**RENAME/DELETE/COPY**
(1)R-Rename a print spec
(2)D-Delete a print spec
(3)C-Copy a print spec

**GLOBAL OPTIONS**
(1)E-Set editing options
(2)P-Change print defaults
(3)D-Change page defaults

**ADVANCED LESSONS MENU**
(1)-What fields contain people's names
(2)-Units of measure
(3)-Advanced vocabulary: adjectives
(4)-Advanced vocabulary: verbs
(5)-Exit lessons

**SYBEX** ®

# MASTERING
# Q&A

# MASTERING
# Q&A™

*Second Edition*

## GREG HARVEY

San Francisco • Paris • Düsseldorf • London

Series design by Julie Bilski
Chapter art by Suzanne Albertson
Screen reproductions produced by XenoFont

To Shane

# ACKNOWLEDGMENTS

I wish to express a deep appreciation to all of the talented people whose hard work helped to make this book a reality.

To Kathy Johnson, the Director of Product Support at Symantec, who not only contributed her considerable writing skills to this project, but also her deep concern for the users of Q&A and her tremendous knowledge of the program. Without her dedication and help in updating, revising, and, most importantly, expanding this book, my efforts just wouldn't have done justice to Version 3.0.

To Lev Liberman, copy editor, whose outstanding editing job and tireless attention to every detail contributed so much to the consistency and flow of the final published work.

At SYBEX, I want to thank Dianne King, acquisitions editor; Joanne Cuthbertson, supervising editor; Bob Myren, word processor; Winnie Kelly, typesetter; Maria Mart, proofreader; Sonja Schenk, screen producer; Suzanne Albertson, designer and pasteup artist; and Anne Leach, indexer.

And, finally, I would like to thank Symantec Corporation for their support in sending me copies of Q&A Version 3.0 and the Network Pack, making Q&A Version 3.0 all that it is, and for having people like Kathy Johnson on staff.

# CONTENTS AT A GLANCE

# TABLE OF CONTENTS

# CHAPTER 2: Q&A WRITE   36

# CHAPTER 3: Q&A FILE 104

# CHAPTER 4: ADVANCED WORD PROCESSING APPLICATIONS 190

# CHAPTER 6: THE INTELLIGENT ASSISTANT 272

# CHAPTER 7: MACROS

# CHAPTER 8:
# ADVANCED DATABASE APPLICATIONS     378

# CHAPTER 9: USING Q&A ON A NETWORK 454

# INTRODUCTION

## *Q&A*

Very rarely do programs of Q&A's caliber come along. Here, you have a completely integrated system that offers full-featured word processing combined with advanced data management and report-writing capabilities. As if this weren't enough, you have at your fingertips a program with which you can converse in English.

This natural language interface, called the Intelligent Assistant, makes it possible to retrieve information stored in a database by simply asking for it in the same way you would ask a fellow employee. This question-and-answer ability is one of Q&A's more exciting aspects—not just because it's so amazing to be able to converse with a computer in your own language instead of computer lauguage, but because it is so practical. With it, the new database user is able to get at the information in his or her database and explore relationships that exist there without first having to learn the intricacies of a formal query language.

Beyond the basics, Q&A offers you plenty of extra features that you will come to appreciate—like macro commands and automated program control and calculations in data entry forms, to name but a few. Perhaps the best part of Q&A is its superior user interface, which manages to protect you from most errors without seeming to get in your way. All in all, Q&A provides a versatile package with a full range of practical, easy-to-use features to meet almost all of your word- and data-processing needs.

## *WHO SHOULD READ THIS BOOK*

If you have already purchased Q&A Version 3.0 and are just learning your way around it, this book is perfect for you. Even if Q&A is your first software product or you have never used a word processor or data manager before, you need not worry. This book will lead you through every step of mastery, from the most basic to fairly advanced techniques and applications. Each topic is introduced with a complete discussion of each new concept and feature, followed by step-by-step instructions to exercises that will quickly get you started using all of Q&A's features.

If you have not yet purchased Q&A but are curious about how it works and want to see if it will fit your business needs, you will find that this book can work well as a decision-making guide. Throughout, you will find abundant screen illustrations that will give a real feel for the way Q&A works and how it interfaces with the user. From the wide range of business applications covered in each chapter, you should also be able to assess the program's relative strengths as they pertain to your own needs and applications.

If you have been using Q&A Version 3.0 for some time and have already mastered the basics, you will still find this book to be a solid resource, full of hints and advanced applications that will help you get the most out of Q&A's diverse, sophisticated functions. You may even find, in the first few introductory chapters, valuable techniques that you had previously overlooked or had not fully understood. In any case, you will undoubtedly find information important to your work in the chapters covering more advanced topics, such as using the Intelligent Assistant without "teaching" it about your database, creating macros, automating your data entry forms, and sharing data between Q&A and other popular software products.

## *NOTE TO USERS OF OLDER VERSIONS OF Q&A*

This book was written specifically for Q&A Version 3.0. If you are using an earlier version of Q&A, I urge you to upgrade to Version 3.0 today. This latest version offers substantial new features for the word processor and database manager. These new features not only give you extra capabilities, but also make Q&A even easier to use.

Symantec's upgrade policy is as follows. If you purchased Q&A on or after February 1, 1988, you are entitled to a free upgrade. To get this upgrade you should send in your registration card, noting the date of purchase or attaching a copy of your sales slip or invoice. If you purchased Q&A before February 1, 1988, you can upgrade to Version 3.0 for $69.95 plus $3.50 for shipping and handling. Write your request for the upgrade on your company letterhead and be sure to include the serial number for your copy of Q&A. If you have mislaid your serial number, you can send in one of your original disks or the title page of your manual along with your letter requesting the upgrade.

When ordering your upgrade, specify whether you want the program disks in 5¼- or 3½-inch format. Symantec will send you a complete disk set in the format you specify, along with a complete set of the documentation for Version 3.0. Send all orders to:

Symantec Corporation
1021 Torre Avenue
Cupertino, CA 95014
Att'n: Upgrades

If you need to use this book with an older version of Q&A, you can do so. However, be aware that the presentation of the menu system as well as some of the menu options talked about in the text and shown in the figures will differ somewhat from your version. You will have to be especially careful when following the step-by-step instructions for a particular exercise, because the program prompts or menu options described may be different from those in your version.

Although you will be able to do most of the exercises in this book, you will encounter some that rely on Version 3.0 features that your version doesn't have. In particular, you won't be able to do the exercises in Chapter 4 on producing mailing labels and setting up a document printing queue. Nor will you be able to do the exercises in Chapter 8 on the external lookup feature, which enables you to retrieve data that has been stored in a separate database into the database file you are working on.

## *HOW TO USE THIS BOOK*

This book is organized by major sections progressing from an overview of Q&A and its capabilities to advanced topics and techniques. Each new topic is introduced by a discussion of the relevant features and commands and how they work. This is followed by practical exercises that give you the opportunity to apply the techniques just introduced. Step-by-step instructions are included to guide you through each tutorial. It is suggested that you perform each of these exercises to gain valuable hands-on experience with Q&A; however, if you don't have the time (or are not at your computer) you should still be able to follow what is being described by reading the instructions and studying the accompanying illustrations.

The main idea of each chapter and its major topics are summarized below:

Chapter 1    Overview of Q&A and its capabilities. Here, you will find instructions on how to install Q&A and customize it to your computer, as well as how to get around the Q&A menu system.

Chapter 2    Introduction to Q&A Write. In this chapter, you will learn all of the basic features of Q&A's word processor, including how to edit, format, save, and print the documents you create. You will also learn how to enhance your text.

Chapter 3    Introduction to Q&A File and designing and building databases. In this chapter, you learn techniques for setting up the database entry form, adding and editing data, searching and sorting, and printing data. All of these are applied to a sample database application for tracking personnel information which you will create.

Chapter 4    Introduction to some specialized word processing features offered by Q&A Write. The topics covered in this chapter include how to use the mail merge facility to prepare form letters using data in your Q&A database files; addressing envelopes; preparing mailing labels; and exchanging documents between Q&A and other software programs.

Chapter 5    Introduction to Q&A Report. In this chapter, you will learn how you can use the report writer to organize, format, and print all types of reports using the data stored in your Q&A database files.

Chapter 6    Introduction to Q&A's Intelligent Assistant, which provides a natural language interface that can be used to retrieve data from your database. Here, you learn how to prepare your database files for English language queries. After preparing your sample database you will get practice in all the various types of queries you can make with it, including ad hoc queries and producing reports.

Chapter 7    Introduction to creating and using macros in Q&A. The exercises in this chapter show how macros enable you to customize many aspects of the program. Here you will learn how to construct practical macros for word processing, working with your database, and producing reports.

Chapter 8    Introduction to some specialized data processing techniques. This chapter acquaints you with methods for controlling data input into the database, relating data from two different database files, and maintaining your data files as they grow in size. Finally, you learn how you can use Q&A with other popular software programs like Lotus 1-2-3 and dBASE III.

Chapter 9    Introduction to using Q&A on a network. In this chapter, you will learn the benefits of using Q&A on a multi-user system. In addition, you will learn how Q&A works in a multi-user environment. Techniques covered in this chapter include how to install the Network Pack, how to set your Network ID and personal path, and how to password-protect your database files.

## THE FAST TRACKS

The Fast Track section at the beginning of each chapter summarizes the chapter's contents, lists the steps or keystrokes needed to complete specific tasks, and points you to the page where you can find a tutorial presentation or more detailed explanation. In some cases, the Fast Track entry will be all you need to get going. In other cases, you can use the Fast Track to pick out the points you are interested in and then go directly to the information you need. Also note that Fast Tracks cover the chapters' primary topics; they do not cover every option, exception, or caveat discussed in the text.

# CHAPTER

1

# INTRODUCTION
# TO Q&A

# Fast Track

**To install Q&A on a two-drive system,**        9

    format five 5 ¼" (or three 3 ½") disks with the DOS format command and then copy each of your original disks. Label each one as it is labeled on the original, and store your originals in a safe place.

**To install Q&A on a hard disk system,**        10

    create a directory named QA into which you can copy the Q&A program files by entering **md c:\qa**. Next, make this new directory current by typing **cd\qa**. Then copy each of the original program disks, making sure that you copy disk 5 (the Dictionary disk) last.

**To start Q&A on a two-drive system,**        11

    place your DOS disk in drive A:, turn on your computer, and respond to the date and time prompts (if necessary). Replace the DOS disk with your working copy of disk 1 (labeled *Q&A Startup Disk*), and then enter the startup command **qa**.

**To start Q&A on a hard disk system,**        11

    change the directory to QA by entering **cd\qa** after turning on your computer and enter the startup command **qa**.

**To select a menu option from Q&A's Main Menu,**        12

    use the cursor keys to move the highlight bar to that option and press the ↵ key. You can also choose an option by typing its number (not shown on screen) as indicated in the menu map on the front inside cover of this book.

**To install your printer,**  14

select the Utilities option (**u** ⬅ or 5) and then select the Install Printer option (**p** ⬅ or 3). Highlight the letter of the printer (A–E, as you can install up to five printers) and press Return. Highlight the printer port that this printer uses and press Return. Highlight the name of the printer from the printer list and press Return. Indicate any special printer functions and press Return to complete installation.

**To set the default drive and directory**  18

for your Q&A Write documents and Q&A File databases, select the Utilities option (**u** ⬅ or 5) and then select the Set global defaults option (**s** ⬅ or 5). Type in the complete path name for the directory that will contain your Q&A Write files, and then indicate the one that will hold your Q&A database files. Press F10 to exit this screen and save your changes.

# WHAT IS Q&A?

Q&A is an integrated system offering a full-featured word processor with an electronic file and report manager for the IBM PC and compatible computers. Created by Symantec Corporation, the package includes many advanced features throughout, though none is so extraordinary as its ability to deal with queries in plain English through a module called the Assistant. Q&A's Assistant introduces microcomputers to a branch of artificial intelligence called *natural language interface* that allows you to retrieve specific data and create reports without having to learn a highly specialized and programming-like query language.

The package consists of five modules: Q&A Write, Q&A File, Q&A Report, the Assistant, and Utilities. Each of these is tied together and accessed through Q&A's Main Menu. As you will soon discover, Q&A's menu system is exceptionally straightforward and easy to use, and the program has plenty of context-sensitive help available to guide you at almost every step of its operation.

## Q&A WRITE

Q&A Write is an easy-to-learn word processor that allows you to create and edit all sorts of documents containing up to about 80 pages of text. This maximum varies, depending upon the amount of memory you have installed in your computer. Because Q&A Write uses a memory-based system whereby the entire document is kept in RAM at all times, it is not possible to create much longer documents in one file. You can, however, get around this limitation very easily by breaking up your document into several files, each containing a section of the document. At print time, these can then be combined by using Q&A's join and print facilities.

The word processor offers you all the standard editing and formatting features you will need to create a wide variety of document types. On-screen editing matches the final printed output as much as possible. This includes showing most special print effects, a ruler line containing your current margin settings, the white margins and edge of the paper, as well as any headers and footers you may have defined. This makes for a "what you see is what you get" word processing system that you can easily adapt to, regardless of the extent of your previous word processing experience.

Advanced features include an online spelling checker (with a dictionary of 100,000 words), an extended search-and-replace feature, on-screen line drawing for creating boxes, and use of up to nine different fonts in each document with laser and Postscript printers. Q&A can even prepare the envelope for a letter automatically just by scanning the letter's text, locating the address within it, and then spacing the address appropriately for a business-size envelope when printing.

Perhaps even more important to most users are Q&A's merge print and mailing label features. The easy-to-use merge print feature permits you to create form letters with Q&A Write and then merge in selected data from any of your data files maintained with Q&A File. Built-in mailing label formats make creating a label very simple, and labels can be printed up to eight across.

## Q&A FILE AND Q&A REPORT

Q&A File offers you a sophisticated electronic filing system for storing and retrieving all types of data that you might need to keep. With it, you can create huge databases of information. Its data files can contain a maximum of 16 million forms, each containing up to 2,182 fields or 16,780 bytes, making for a maximum data file size of 256 million bytes.

To set up a data file, all you have to do is create a screen input form for it, using the same editing features available to you when using Q&A Write. You then assign field types to each field within the form and input your data. When designing your form, you can even use the word processor's line drawing feature to add boxes or center fields. The only drawback to this kind of forms-oriented system is that you cannot have more than one form for each data file you create. If you should want to use an alternate screen form for presenting the data, you have to copy all of the information into a new data file containing that form. However, should you need to make modifications to any of your data files, all you have to do is edit the screen input form attached to the data file.

Advanced features include merging information from multiple Q&A data files into your current input form, programming your form for automatic math and financial functions, and multi-user operations. If you need to share information via network, Q&A File offers a complete multi-user environment for accessing the data files you have created. Several persons can access the same data file at the same time without a conflict.

Q&A File allows you to sort and retrieve data by simply entering appropriate codes into the fields. Once you learn these codes, you will find it relatively easy to search for and retrieve the data you desire. If you have no experience with database managers or have little desire or time to learn to use these specialized codes, Q&A offers the perfect alternative. You can use the Assistant to retrieve your data. To use the Assistant, you first set up a glossary of the words you will use and then simply enter your requests for specific data in the form of questions phrased in everyday conversational English.

Q&A's report manager (Q&A Report) permits you to set up a wide variety of report formats that control the printing of selected information from your data files. These reports can contain headers and footers, or breaks on columns with subtotals and totals. You can also set up new columns whose results are derived from calculations made on fields in the form, or retrieve information from another Q&A data file. Again, you set up all of this by using the screen input form attached to the data file and by entering the appropriate codes into it. Once you have set up the report specification as you want it, you can save and reuse it as often as you like. Unlike the screen input form, you can create and use up to 100 different report specifications with a single data file.

For those applications such as filling in a pre-printed form, Q&A gives you an alternative to using the report module. In such a case, you can quickly create a print specification from within Q&A File that lets you choose the fields to be used and control their final layout on the printed page.

## THE INTELLIGENT ASSISTANT

Through the Intelligent Assistant (also known as the Assistant), Q&A offers a direct interface with both its File and Report modules.

You can use it to locate or update the data in specific fields of the form or to obtain reports from your data files, all by typing statements in plain English. Unlike most other data management software, Q&A does not require you to learn a special "query language" with rigid and peculiar syntax in order to retrieve the information you need from your data files. As you will see, Q&A's Assistant is amazingly adept at handling all types of inquiries entered in ordinary English.

In order to use Q&A's Assistant with your data file, it must first be taught some of the terms you will be likely to use when referring to specific fields or characteristics of the data file. This process of "teaching" the Assistant about your database is required only once (though it may have to be refined as you use the Assistant later).

Whenever you make a request of the Assistant, it analyzes each of the terms in your English sentence. As soon as it has evaluated all of the terms, it shows you its understanding of the request (translated into database logic) and asks for your approval to carry out the task. If it cannot understand some part of your request, it will stop at whatever term is giving it trouble and ask you for clarification. Once the trouble is cleared up and you give the go-ahead, the Assistant quickly responds to your inquiry by bringing the appropriate data to the screen.

## WHAT Q&A CAN DO FOR YOU

Q&A gives you two of the most-needed tools for conducting today's business. The first is word processing, which is fast replacing the typewriter in businesses of all sizes. The primary strength of word processing lies in giving you the ability to revise and edit your documents without requiring you to completely retype them or do a messy cut-and-paste edit. Another of its prominent benefits is that it can cut down on the amount of typing required to produce standard documents. Because a word processor allows you to easily incorporate standard paragraphs (often called stands or boilerplate) from other saved documents, it makes producing contracts and other similar documents a lot less time-consuming. Q&A Write provides you the means to do all of these things and more. With it, you will be able to produce almost all of the correspondence, memos, and reports that your office now does with either a typewriter or another word processor.

The second software tool included in the Q&A package is an electronic file manager. This type of software allows you to organize and maintain collections of related data in a systematic order. Accurate, up-to-date record-keeping is one of the most important functions of an office, regardless of the nature of the business. With Q&A's file manager, you will be able to keep most all of the types of records necessary to the success of your business.

Though it may not eliminate all of the paper from your office, Q&A File will make it much simpler to maintain control over the different bodies of information vital to your concern. Further, by giving you the ability to quickly and thoroughly locate, update, and cross reference the information on hand, it will make it so much easier to analyze and understand the implications of your data.

Coupled with Q&A's file manager is a powerful and flexible report generator that facilitates isolating and relating specific data and presenting data however you wish in printed form. If your business requires preparing formal reports with set formats, you'll appreciate the power that Q&A Report gives you over the final output of your information in written form.

## SUGGESTED APPLICATIONS

As you gain experience with Q&A, you will find it well suited for countless applications unique to your particular business. To help you at this stage, listed here are a few of those commonly needed by all professions.

For word processing:

- Business letters, memos, outlines, annual reports, policy and training manuals, formal contracts, and proposals.

- Mass mailings for marketing and advertising campaigns and business announcements.

- Articles and research reports that do not require extensive indexing and footnotes.

For data management:

- Keeping personnel, insurance, and salary review records on the office staff.

- Keeping lists of client contacts, suppliers and vendors, customers, and sales leads.

- Maintaining a filing system for the corporate library or for tracking magazine and newspaper subscriptions.

- Maintaining a filing system for monitoring the use and reordering of office supplies, renewing service contracts, and keeping track of the frequency of repair and maintenance of office machines.

- Maintaining a schedule of business and personal appointments and meetings.

- Maintaining directories, catalogs, and mailing lists.

- Tracking product and research data, marketing trends, expense and travel reports.

- Maintaining simple financial records.

## *LIMITATIONS OF Q&A*

While Q&A is quite adept at a great number of business and personal applications, there are some things that it is not at all well suited for. For one thing, because its word processor does not include indexing and footnoting features, it is a poor choice for applications such as research papers and dissertations that require such capabilities. It contains most of the other advanced word processing features that you will require for normal business applications.

In the area of file management, there are other limitations. Q&A is a file manager as opposed to a relational database management system. Products such as dBASE, R:BASE, and Paradox fall into this latter category. They are known as application development systems because they include built-in programming languages that allow you to create specialized business applications such as a medical billing system or a general ledger accounting system. Q&A, however, offers some multi-file, multi-user, programming, and macro features which make some application development possible.

The Lookup programming feature in Q&A allows you to create applications that would typically be considered relational. To illustrate some of the benefits that this Lookup feature can offer, consider the following simplified example. A company keeps track of its customers' addresses and credit histories in a data file separate from the one that generates the invoice showing each customer's purchases and credit terms. Each file is itself a database. At times, some of the data from one file must be related to data in another file—for example, when invoices are prepared. At such times, it would be ideal if the database manager could get the customer name and address from the customer data file and merge it in the appropriate places with the rest of the billing information entered in the invoice file.

In the past, a relational database system would have been required in order to do this, but Q&A makes it possible with a simpler-to-use file manager. Q&A cannot, however, automatically update the information in another file, or store the information in only one place. When you update the information in one file, you have to update it in the second to keep all of the data current and accurate.

If your needs tend in the direction of specialized menus and application development with relations between your data files at all times, you will probably find that Q&A File is not adequate.

# GETTING STARTED

Before you begin using Q&A to do the practice exercises coming up in the chapters ahead, you should take the time to read the following sections on the hardware requirements for running Q&A and on how to make backup copies of your program disks and install the printer you are using with the program. Here, you will also receive an introduction to Q&A's menu system and some basic practice in getting around the Q&A modules.

## HARDWARE REQUIREMENTS

The hardware requirements to run Q&A are the IBM Personal System/2 and the IBM PC, XT, AT, and Compaq families of personal computers or compatible computers running PC-DOS or MS-DOS version 2.0 or higher (DOS 3.3 required for PS/2 models) with two floppy disk drives (or one floppy drive and a hard disk) and at least 512K of RAM. Because it takes a lot of memory to run Q&A's Assistant with the rest of the program modules, 640K of RAM is highly recommended. Q&A can also access memory beyond 640K, so it can take advantage of extended memory boards such as AST's Rampage or Intel's Above Board.

If you run Q&A on a two-disk-drive system, you will be required to swap disks from time to time. This is especially true if you plan to spell-check your word processing documents, which requires replacing the startup disk with one containing the spelling dictionary. Whenever Q&A requires another program disk to carry out your commands, you will be instructed as to which disk to replace in drive A:. Running Q&A on a two-disk system is not only a little less convenient than on a hard disk, but it also makes the program run somewhat slower.

Q&A supports many types of dot-matrix and letter-quality printers as well as the HP LaserJet printer. The program comes configured for what it refers to as a vanilla-type printer. This allows you to print documents and reports without the benefit of any special print enhancements like boldface type or underlining. To install your printer with Q&A, refer to the section on printer installation.

## MAKING BACKUPS

Q&A requires little preparation to use. All you have to do is make backup copies of the five program disks included in the package. Q&A employs no copy-protection scheme, so you can make as many working copies of the program disk as you need. This also means that you can copy Q&A onto your hard disk and run it directly from the C: drive without having to insert a startup disk each time you begin work.

To make working copies of your program disks, you will have to first format at least five 5¼-inch disks or three 3½-inch disks using your DOS FORMAT command. To do this, get out five (or three, if you are using 3½-inch disks) double-sided, double-density disks and then do the following:

1.  Put your PC-DOS (or MS-DOS) disk in drive A: and one of your blank disks in drive B:. Turn on your computer. Enter

the date and time or press Return twice to bypass these entries.

2. At the A> prompt, type **format b:** and press Return. Press Return a second time to begin the formatting process.

3. Once DOS has finished formatting, you will be asked if you wish to format another disk. Type **y** and replace the newly formatted disk with a second unformatted one. Press Return to format it.

4. Repeat this process three more times to format the third, fourth, and fifth disks. Then type **n** to end the formatting process.

5. Replace the DOS disk in drive A: with the Q&A disk numbered 1 (the startup disk).

6. If you are new at copying with your computer, make sure that the side notch on the startup disk has been covered with a write-protect tab. Next, type the command **copy \*.\* b:** and press Return. After the copying is complete, remove your new working copy of the Q&A startup disk from drive B: and label it "Q&A Startup Disk" with a felt-tip pen.

7. Copy the information from the remaining program disks. (You may also copy the last two disks containing the tutorial and sample files in the same way.) Each time you finish making a copy of a Q&A program disk, be sure and label the copy as soon as you remove it from drive B:.

If you will be using Q&A on a computer with a hard disk, you need only create a subdirectory for the program files and then copy each of the program files there. The only precaution is that you must copy program disk #5 (containing the spelling dictionary) onto your hard disk last. To make sure that you don't mix up the order, it is probably a good idea to arrange the first five in numerical order and then just copy them one by one. You can then copy the last two disks containing the sample files and tutorial on your hard disk if you wish. (Or you can omit this step and use them from drive A: if you are short on storage space on the hard disk.) To install Q&A on a hard disk, do the following:

1. Turn on your computer. When you are asked for the date and time, enter them or press Return twice to bypass these steps. Then type **mkdir c:\qa** and press Return.

2. Enter the command **cd\qa** and press Return. Now you are ready to copy the Q&A original disks onto drive C: in ascending numerical order. Put disk #1 in drive A:, type **copy \*.\* c:**, and press Return.

3. Once the copy has been made, remove disk #1 from drive A: and replace it with disk #2. Repeat this copy command a second time and repeat this entire step until you have copied both disks #3 and #4 onto the hard disk. Remember that disk #5 must be copied last in order for the program to work correctly.

4. If you wish, you may then copy disks #6 (Samples and Font Files) and #7 (Tutorial) onto drive C:. You can copy these files into a subdirectory attached to your new Q&A subdirectory. To create it, type **cd\** and press Return. Then enter **mkdir qa\tutor** and press Return. Make this directory current by typing **cd qa\tutor** and then copy these last two disks on drive C: as you did before with the other program disks.

## STARTING UP Q&A

1. To start Q&A, put your PC-DOS (or MS-DOS) disk in Drive A: and then turn on your computer.

2. Enter the date and time in response to the prompts (if your computer does not have a battery-operated clock/calendar).

3. When you see the A> prompt, remove the DOS disk and replace it with your working copy of disk #1 (which should also be marked "Q&A Startup Disk"). Type **qa** at the A> prompt and press Return.

With a hard disk system that is logged onto the root directory of the C: drive, you must first change to your Q&A directory by entering

**cd\qa** and pressing Return before entering this startup command. Notice that the startup command does not require you to enter the product's name as q&a. All you need to type is **qa**.

## Q&A'S MENU SYSTEM

As soon as you press Return, a screen containing the Q&A logo appears. In the center at the bottom of this screen, notice that the word *loading* is flashing on and off. This lets you know that Q&A is still busy loading all of the necessary program files into memory. You will see that Q&A is very good about letting you know when it is busy and you must stand by. As soon as the program is loaded, the screen will change and you will see the Q&A Main Menu as shown in Figure 1.1.

Six menu choices are associated with the Main Menu. The first five allow you to choose between the different Q&A modules, while the sixth quits Q&A and takes you back to the operating system. Presently, the cursor (the flashing underline) is located on the F for File, which is highlighted. To choose one of the menu choices, you can either type the letter indicated or use the ↓ and ↑ keys located on your numeric keypad to highlight your selection. After choosing your selection, press the Return key (often marked as ←). Each letter choice, except for that of the Exit command, is the same as the initial

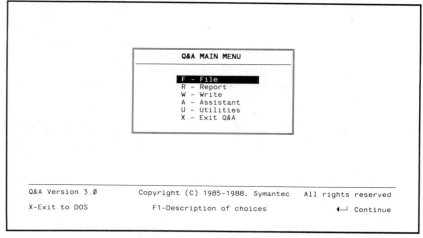

*Figure 1.1:* The Q&A Main Menu

letter of the module's name. Thus, you type **r** and press Return to access Q&A's Report module, or **w** and Return to access the word processor.

Q&A also provides a shortcut to having to type the letter and then press the Return key. You can type the number of the choice instead. Though there are no numbers shown on the Main Menu, the menu choices are numbered consecutively from 1 to 6 as far as Q&A is concerned. To start the word processor this way, simply type **3** (with no Return); to start the Assistant, type **4**.

To get help at any point in Q&A, press the function key marked F1. Try it now and you will get a Help screen describing all the menu choices on the Main Menu, just like the one shown in Figure 1.2. Notice that in addition to a brief description of the function of each module, this Help screen also lists the exact pages in your manual where you can get more specific information about each function. This is a common feature of Q&A's on-line help. On the last line of the screen at the left edge, Q&A lets you know that the Escape key (marked Esc on your keyboard) works as a cancel key. If you press it from this Help screen, the program will return you immediately to the Main Menu. You will find as you use Q&A's menu system that the Escape key always takes you back to your previous position.

| CHOICE | DESCRIPTION | VOLUME |
|--------|-------------|--------|
| File | Create, fill out, and work with forms of information. | 1 |
| Report | Take information from your forms, sort and arrange it, print results in a table. | 1 |
| Write | Write and print documents. | 2 |
| Assistant | Teach your Intelligent Assistant (IA) about your forms then ask questions, generate reports, or change information using ordinary English. | 1 |
| Utilities | Set-up your printer, import/export data from other programs, DOS file facilities, etc. | 2 |

**CAUTION:** Sudden loss or interruption of power can damage a data file. Never turn your machine off or reboot the system UNLESS you are at one of the main Q&A menus. If a power loss does occur, however, you can probably recover the file (see pg. U-65). Make frequent backups (pg. F-187).

Esc-Cancel

*Figure 1.2:* Q&A's first Help screen

## INSTALLING YOUR PRINTER

At this point (if you have not already done so) you should go ahead and install the printer you will be using with Q&A. You do this from the Utilities Menu.

1.  To select it, type **u** and press Return (or type **5**).

Once you have done so, the Utilities Menu will appear as it does in Figure 1.3. There are six menu selections available here. The one you want to use is number 3, Install Printer.

2.  Select it by entering **3** or by typing **p** and pressing Return.

Figure 1.4 shows you the next screen, labeled Printer Selection, that will appear.

Q&A allows you to install up to five different printers at the same time. The first thing you must do is select a printer that has not yet been installed. This way you can assign Printer A as your Epson printer, for example, and Printer B as your laser printer if you have both.

3.  To select the first printer, make sure Printer A is highlighted, then press Return.

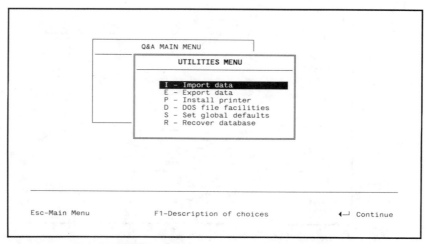

*Figure 1.3:* Q&A's Utilities Menu

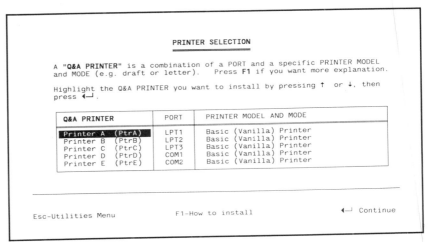

PRINTER SELECTION

A "Q&A PRINTER" is a combination of a PORT and a specific PRINTER MODEL and MODE (e.g. draft or letter). Press **F1** if you want more explanation.

Highlight the Q&A PRINTER you want to install by pressing ↑ or ↓, then press ◀┘ .

| Q&A PRINTER | PORT | PRINTER MODEL AND MODE |
| --- | --- | --- |
| Printer A  (PtrA) | LPT1 | Basic (Vanilla) Printer |
| Printer B  (PtrB) | LPT2 | Basic (Vanilla) Printer |
| Printer C  (PtrC) | LPT3 | Basic (Vanilla) Printer |
| Printer D  (PtrD) | COM1 | Basic (Vanilla) Printer |
| Printer E  (PtrE) | COM2 | Basic (Vanilla) Printer |

Esc-Utilities Menu        F1-How to install        ◀┘ Continue

*Figure 1.4:* The Install Printer Selection screen

The next thing you must do is tell Q&A which port it is attached to. The first three choices are marked LPT followed by their number. As you can see in Figure 1.5, LPT1 is currently highlighted as the default choice. LPT stands for *line printer*; it indicates that the printer has a parallel interface. If your printer uses a parallel interface, you will choose one of these ports. Most likely, your printer will be attached to LPT1.

The next two selections are marked COM followed by a number. This stands for *communications*; it indicates that the printer uses a serial interface. This is the same type of interface that a modem uses, so if you have a modem and a serial printer hooked up to your computer, you may not know which is connected to COM1 and which is connected to COM2. If you are not sure and have no one to ask, go ahead and try COM1. If your printer doesn't work with Q&A, you can always come back and change this to COM2.

Notice that the printer selections to the right of these port abbreviations and numbers are currently all listed as Basic (Vanilla) Printer. As soon as you indicate the proper port to use, you will change these to list your actual printer.

4. To select the appropriate port, press the space bar until the port is highlighted; then press Return.

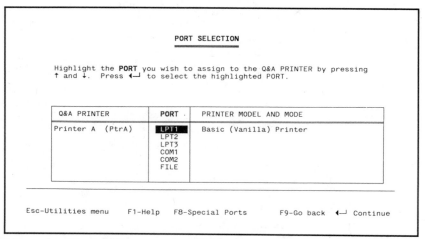

PORT SELECTION

Highlight the **PORT** you wish to assign to the Q&A PRINTER by pressing
↑ and ↓.  Press ↵ to select the highlighted PORT.

| Q&A PRINTER | PORT | PRINTER MODEL AND MODE |
|---|---|---|
| Printer A  (PtrA) | LPT1<br>LPT2<br>LPT3<br>COM1<br>COM2<br>FILE | Basic (Vanilla) Printer |

Esc-Utilities menu      F1-Help      F8-Special Ports            F9-Go back    ↵ Continue

***Figure 1.5:*** The Install Printer Port Selection screen

Once you have selected the correct port by pressing Return, the
first screen containing a list of printers appears, as illustrated in Figure 1.6. As you can see by the instructions at the end of the right
column, you press the Page Down key (marked PgDn and located on
the cursor pad) to see the other possible printer selections. If your
printer is not listed on this first screen, press PgDn and check the rest
of the list. If your particular printer is not listed as one of the choices
on any of these screens, check your printer manual to see if it emulates any of those that are listed. If not, you can still print with Q&A,
though you will have to use the Basic (Vanilla) selection and will not
be able to use any of the print enhancements supported.

5. As soon as you locate your printer, use the arrow keys to
   highlight it and select it by pressing Return.

Figure 1.7 illustrates what happens once you select a particular
printer. In this case, the Citizen MSP-10 and MSP-15 printers were
selected.

6. To confirm your printer selection, simply press F10.

If the printer you actually select here cannot reproduce some
printed effect supported by Q&A Write, you will be informed of this
with a message.

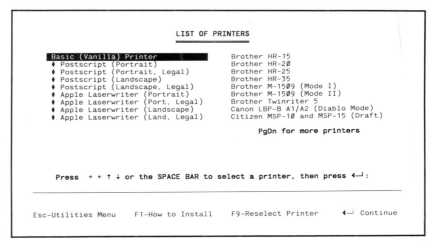

*Figure 1.6:* Q&A's first Printer Selection screen

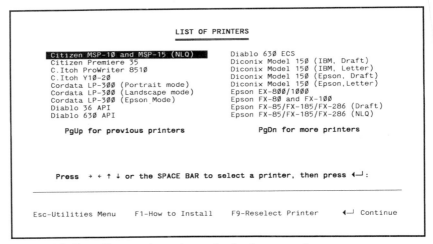

*Figure 1.7:* Installing a printer (second selection screen)

Once you have selected a particular printer, you will come to the Special Printer Options screen, as seen in Figure 1.8. You only need to change things on this screen if you have problems with your printer. Here you can change the way Q&A communicates with your printer by telling Q&A not to check if the paper has run out, not to check for a signal from your printer when it's ready and online, etc. There are also places for inserting special printer codes for printing

```
                      SPECIAL PRINTER OPTIONS
                      ──────────────────────

        Use this screen if you have problems with your printer or want
        to use a cut sheet feeder.

        Check for printer timeout?......:   ▶Yes◀   No

        Length of timeout (in seconds)..:    15

        Check for printer ready signal?.:   ▶Yes◀   No

        Check for paper out?............:   ▶Yes◀   No

        Formfeed at doc end?............:    Yes   ▶No◀

        Bin 1 setup code.:
        Bin 2 setup code.:
        Bin 3 setup code.:
        Eject page code..:
        Font File Name...:
       ─────────────────────────────────────────────────────────────

     Esc-Cancel installation        F9-Reselect printer          F10-Continue
```

*Figure 1.8:* Special Printer Options

with bins or cut sheet feeders if your printer requires this. These codes can be found in your printer manual. Most often you will not need to worry about any of these additional settings.

If you have more than one printer attached to your computer, you can go ahead and answer **yes** to ''install another'' and simply repeat the above procedure for your second printer. Often, an office will have both a high speed dot-matrix printer to produce rough drafts of documents and reports, and a letter-quality printer for final print-outs. If this is the case for you, be sure and tell Q&A about each printer and to which port it is connected. Then, to switch between final and draft quality, all you have to do is tell Q&A which one you want to use at print time.

## *SETTING THE DEFAULT DRIVE AND DIRECTORY*

While you are at the Utilities Menu, there is one more thing you might want to do before beginning to use Q&A to produce your work. This is to set the default drive and directory with the Set global defaults option (number **5** if you prefer not to have to both type the letter **s** and press Return). This is an especially good idea if you have a hard disk and want to keep your data files in a separate subdirectory from the one containing the Q&A program files. By using this option, you can tell Q&A which subdirectory to make current each time you start up the program. To access this option, type s and press Return (or type 5).

Figure 1.9 shows the case in which the subdirectory named FILES attached to the QA directory (which contains all the program files) is being made the default for both the word processing and the database files produced with Q&A. As you can see, Q&A allows you to set a default directory for your word processing document files which is different from that holding your database files. Often, you will want to keep these files separate.

To set a new default directory, simply type in the complete path name of the new default directory. To edit the current contents of the line, move the cursor to the characters you need to change by holding down → until it is in the proper position, and then type over the text that is there. You can also use the space bar to delete a character at the cursor position. To take the cursor directly to the end of the line of text that appears, hold down the Control key (marked Ctrl on your keyboard) and press → one time. Once you have edited the path name for the document files, press Return. Then do the same for the directory in which you wish to contain your database files.

To confirm your default directories and have Q&A save them as they are now entered, you cannot use the Return key as you did when installing your printer. It merely moves the highlighting to the

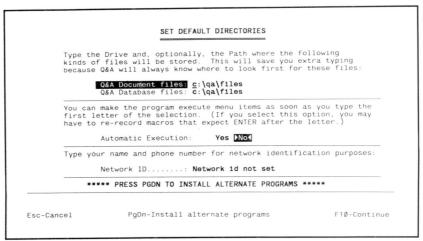

*Figure 1.9:* Q&A's Set Default Directories screen

next choice on the screen. To confirm your choices here, press the function key marked F10. As you can see in the bottom-right corner of the screen in Figure 1.9, F10 is referred to as the Continue key. Q&A often uses this key to have you confirm a menu choice and continue to another part of the program. In this case, pressing F10 saves your default directory choices and takes you back to the Utilities Menu. If you had pressed Esc instead, you would have been returned to this menu, but your new defaults would not have been saved.

You can always override these default settings and save your files in different directories (or on a different drive) by typing in the drive and directory names as part of the file name just before you save the file.

The additional options available from the Set Default Directories screen will be discussed in Chapter 8. If you are now at the Utilities Menu, press Esc to back up to the Main Menu level before reading on.

## A QUICK TOUR OF Q&A

You have already gained a little experience with how Q&A's menu system works. You know that to select a particular menu option, you type the first letter of the option and then press Return. There are always alternatives to this. As you saw earlier, you can speed up the menu selection process by typing in the number of the option or by using the ↓ and ↑ keys to highlight the option. On a Q&A menu, options are numbered consecutively down the columns. In addition, you know that to back up to the Main Menu level from a second-level menu like the Utilities Menu, all you have to do is press the Esc key one time.

Before going on and learning how to use the specific features of each of Q&A's modules in the chapters ahead, this is a good place to stop and take a look at how Q&A's complete menu system is organized and learn a little about what each menu option does. In the front of your book is a chart that shows you the organization of Q&A's menu system. Refer to it as we go along.

As you can see from this chart, four possible menu levels can be accessed in Q&A. The chart shows that the Q&A menu system is organized as a hierarchy sometimes likened to a tree that branches at particular places. In this hierarchy, some menu choices lead you directly to more choices on a new menu, while others do not.

At the Main Menu (or root level of the tree), choosing any of the first five menu choices presents you with a new menu, each with its own options. Only the sixth option, that for exiting the program, has no menu attached to it. If you type **x** and press Return, you are returned immediately to your computer's operating system. There are no more decisions to make at that point from within Q&A.

You have already seen and used some of the options on the Utilities Menu when you installed your printer and set up the default data file directories. You get to all of the other second-level menus and their options by selecting them from the Main Menu, just as you did when accessing the Utilities Menu earlier.

## NAVIGATING THE MENU LEVELS

Refer to the menu organization chart and look at the File Menu. Notice that if you select the Design file option, you will get a new menu with three options on it. Further, if you then choose the Customize a file option on this menu, you will be presented with another menu with nine choices on it. Try going down to this Customize File Menu on the fourth level by taking the following steps:

1. Place a copy of your sample file disk in drive B: (or drive A: if you didn't copy these sample files to your hard disk).

2. With the Main Menu on the screen, make sure File is highlighted and press Return (or type **1**).

3. With the File Menu on the screen, press Return to select Design, and press Return (or type **1** again).

4. With the Design Menu on-screen, type **c** and press Return (or type **3**). Q&A now needs to know the name of the file that you wish to customize. You can only make these changes to an existing database, but you can use one of the sample files that Symantec gives on the sample disk. To see what files are there, change the drive letter to correspond with the location of your sample disk (if need be) and press Return. Q&A now shows the names of the two existing data files on your sample disk. Press ↓ to highlight the file called EMPLOYEE.DTF, and press Return to select it. (Figure 1.10 shows you the screen at this point.)

5. After the file is loaded into memory, the Customize File Menu will appear. Type **c** and press Return to choose the Change palette option (or type **8**). The form associated with this sample employee database now appears. If you wish, press F8 a few times to see what effects can be associated with this form.

6. When you have finished experimenting with modifying the screen palette, press Esc. You are then returned to the Customize Menu, where you could make other adjustments to this database. (Because you pressed Esc instead of F10 previously, none of your changes to the screen palette will be saved.)

7. Press Esc again. This time you will be returned to the File Menu. Note that from the Customize Menu, Q&A takes you back directly to the File Menu (on the second level) instead of to the Design Menu (on the third level). This is the only place where Q&A skips a menu level when backing up toward the Main Menu.

8. Press Esc a third time. You should now be back at the Main Menu of Q&A.

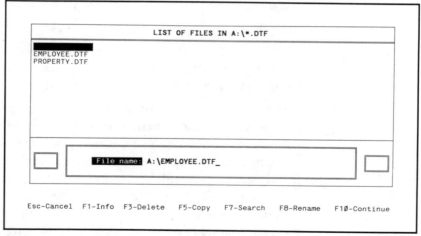

*Figure 1.10:* Getting a directory of existing database files

You will soon get used to going up and down the menu tree in this fashion. From doing this exercise, you should have gotten a feel for how easy it is to skip around the various levels. Remember that if you choose a menu option in error, you can always back out of the menu and get back to a previous level just by pressing Esc. If you are unsure of the functions of the options listed on a particular menu, online help is also available; to access it, press the F1 function key.

You will get a lot more practice in navigating Q&A's menu system as you do the exercises in the chapters ahead. Right now, let's examine briefly the major functions of each of the menus in Q&A. For now, don't worry if there are functions you don't understand; use this section as an overview and come back to it later for reference.

## *THE FILE MENU*

Figure 1.11 shows you the File Menu as it appears on the screen. You use the first option, Design file, to create a new database form or modify an existing one. Attached to this option is a submenu called the Design Menu. Three choices are available there: Design a new file (by creating a new form); Redesign a file (by making changes to the form); and Customize a file. This last option is attached to a submenu called the Customize File Menu. The options on this menu allow you to make various types of changes that mostly affect data entry and its presentation on the screen. You can add on-line help messages, set initial entry values, restrict the types of entries to be made, create lookup tables, and even automate form entry. The one option you have already examined on this menu is called Change palette. This allows you to change the on-screen presentation of a form by choosing among one of several ways to highlight the various fields.

The second option on the File Menu is Add data. You use it to add data to your forms once you have designed them by using the first menu option.

The third choice is Search/Update. You will use this to locate specific forms in the database. You can also place instructions in specific fields of the form that will update their values. (You can also do these things from within the Assistant module.)

The fourth option on the File Menu is Print. Choosing this leads to a Print Menu with three new choices. You can first fill out a Print

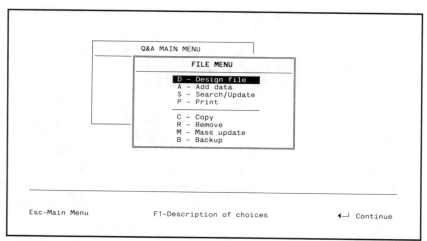

*Figure 1.11:* Q&A's File Menu

Specification form that tells Q&A which of the forms in a database file to print, and then use the second option on this menu to print them out. The third option is used to reach another menu where you can set up page and printing defaults. The fourth option on the Print Menu is attached to yet another menu with its own three choices. This latter menu is used when you want to either rename, delete, or copy one of the Print Specifications you created earlier.

The fifth File Menu option is Copy. You can make three types of copies of database files. You can copy just the design itself (which is the same as copying the form), copy the form design along with the information you have taught your Assistant, or you can copy some or all of the forms in a database (which is the same as copying all of the data in fields). This option is attached to a Copy Menu that gives you a choice of these functions.

The sixth File Menu option is Remove. You use it to delete records (forms that have been filled in) from a database file. This is faster than deleting each form one at a time.

The seventh option is called Mass update. You will use it to update data in a specific field in selected forms of your database. Using this option saves you from having to go in and change each of the values in a particular field or fields by hand. Any update that affects the entire database can be automated by using this Mass update option.

The eighth and last option on the File Menu is Backup. You use this option to back up your database either to a floppy disk or to another place on your hard disk. This is an important function, since making routine backups of your data files can save you a great deal of time in the event that you need to restore lost or damaged data.

## THE REPORT MENU

There are only four choices on the Report Menu, shown in Figure 1.12. The first is called Design/Redesign a report. You use it to define the fields and their layout in your printed form. As the name suggests, you can also use it to redefine a Report Specification after you have defined it.

You use the second option, Print, to print your report once you have defined a Report Specification for it.

The third option is called Set global options. Attached to this option is a submenu. Here, there are four additional selections for design of reports. The first is Set column headings/widths. Use this to change the name and size of the headings for your reports. The second is Set format options, where you can change formatting specifications such as the space between columns and rows. Set print options is the third selection. You will use this to indicate the type of

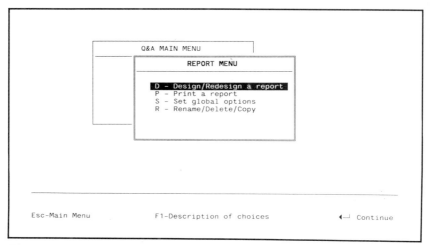

*Figure 1.12:* Q&A's Report Menu

paper you are using and where you would like the report printed. The fourth and last option on the submenu is Set page options. Use this to change the dimensions of your printed report and set the headers and footers.

The fourth option, Rename/Delete/Copy, is attached to another menu with three options. It allows you to either rename, delete, or copy a Report Specification. It works just like the Rename/Delete/Copy Menu attached to the Print Menu under the File Menu.

## THE WRITE MENU

The Write Menu contains all of the word processing functions in Q&A. Figure 1.13 shows this menu as it appears on the screen. The first option here is Type/Edit. You use it to create a new document or make editing changes to an existing one. To use this option for editing an existing document, you must first load the document into memory from a data disk. To do this, you use the fifth option on this menu, called Get. It loads the document file into memory after you supply the file name. Then you choose the Type/Edit option and make your changes.

To save a document, you use the sixth option on this menu, called Save. Q&A Write does not automatically save your document on disk after you have initially created it or made some editing changes.

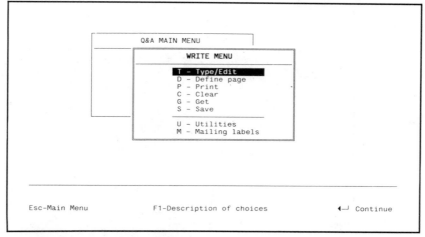

*Figure 1.13:* Q&A Write Menu

Before you exit the program, you must use this option to make a permanent copy of your information and any changes you have made to it. If you try to escape to the Main Menu without having used the Save option, Q&A will warn you that your edits have not been saved. When you give the Save command, Q&A then asks you to name the file.

The third option on this menu is Print. You use it to send your document file to the printer and obtain a hard copy of it.

The second option, Define page, is a formatting command. It allows you to set up or redefine the page parameters. As you will see when you begin to work with the word processor in the next chapter, Q&A stores default values for all of these parameters and uses them automatically unless you change their values here.

You use the Clear option, number four on this menu, to clear the computer's memory of whatever document it currently contains. You will use this option most often to delete a document that you do not wish to save before starting a new one. You can also use it to abandon changes you make to a document that you have already saved on disk. Before you use this option, make sure you have already saved the document you have been editing before clearing your changes and starting a new document.

The seventh option on this menu is Utilities. Attached to this option is a submenu called Write Utilities. From this submenu you can perform several functions. The second option is Modify Font File, which is used only if you have a printer that supports fonts. The third option is Export to ASCII. You use it to make a copy of your document file in ASCII code. Q&A files are not automatically stored in ASCII code, so you must use this command whenever you need to have a copy of your document file in ASCII code. The uses for ASCII files and the need for conversion are discussed in Chapter 8. The fourth through sixth options are Rename, Delete, and Copy a document, and they work just like the other rename/delete/copy options in Q&A. The seventh option is List files, which is used to see a directory listing of all the files you have previously stored.

The first option, called Set global options, has yet another submenu attached to it with three additional selections; Set editing options, Change print defaults, and Change page defaults. These options are used to set up standard page layouts, printing selections, and editing criteria (such as insert versus overtype mode).

If you are on the Global Options menu now, press Esc three times to return to the Q&A Main Menu. Type **a** for Assistant and press Return.

## THE ASSISTANT MENU

As you can see in Figure 1.14, the Assistant Menu has only three options attached to it. The first is Get acquainted. When you choose this option, Q&A gives you some introductory material explaining what the Assistant is and a little about how it works. You should explore this option on your own some time before reading Chapter 6 and trying to do the exercises contained there.

The second option, Teach me about your database, is attached to a Basic Lessons Menu with five options of its own (shown in Figure 1.15). After defining a database from the File Menu, you will use this option to tell Q&A's Assistant about your database. You will only have to go through the Basic Lessons Menu one time to tell it about your database, but you must go through this process before you will be able to use the Assistant to retrieve information from it.

As you can see in Figure 1.15, the Basic Lessons Menu options are numbered. From the titles of these option choices, you get a feel for the types of things you must define for the Assistant. Basically, you will be instructing it in the grammar of your database by telling it

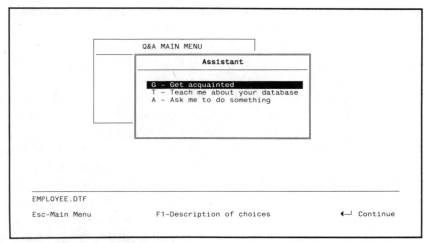

*Figure 1.14:* Q&A's Assistant Menu

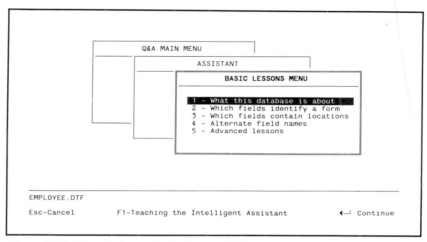

*Figure 1.15:* The Assistant Basic Lessons Menu

what your database is about, which fields contain places, and any synonyms you wish to use when referring to a field. Though going through these options might seem like it will involve a great deal of work now, you will probably find that using the Basic Lessons Menu is really quite easy and a lot of fun. The last option, number 5, takes you to the Advanced Lessons Menu (shown in Figure 1.16). Here you teach the Assistant which fields contain people's names, places, and units of measure, and you also define for it any adjectives and verbs you might use in describing your database. It's not necessary to use this advanced menu in order for the Assistant to answer most questions you will ask about your database.

The third option on the Assistant menu, Ask me to do something, is the one you will use when you want to make inquiries into your database or give some other type of command in English. You can use this option at any time after you have used the Teach option and have gone through the options on the Basic Lessons Menu. Here, you get to type in your requests in plain, conversational English. You will get a lot of practice with the Assistant when you go through the exercises in Chapter 6.

## *THE UTILITIES MENU*

You have already met and used two of the six options on the Utilities Menu (shown in Figure 1.17). Besides the Install Print and Set global

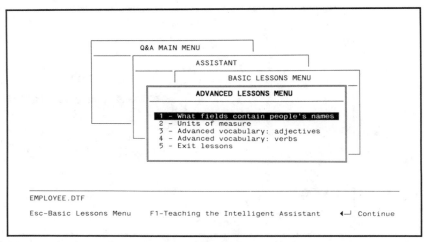

*Figure 1.16:* The Advanced Lessons Menu

defaults options with which you are already familiar, there are options for Import, Export, DOS file facilities, and Recover database.

The first option, Import, is attached to an Import Menu with seven options of its own. You use this menu to convert files created by other software programs into a format that Q&A can use. The first two options on the Import Menu allow you to bring in pfs:File and IBM Filing Assistant files and use them as Q&A database files. The third option allows you to bring in parts of Lotus 1-2-3 worksheets and incorporate their data in Q&A databases that you have already set up. The fourth option, DIF, allows you to do similar things with spreadsheets like VisiCalc and SuperCalc3 that use the DIF (Data Interchange File) format. The fifth and sixth options, Fixed and Standard ASCII, allow you to take data stored in ASCII formats into your Q&A database files. The seventh option is dBASE II/III and it allows you to import dBASE II or III datafiles into a Q&A database. All of these options will be discussed and explained in Chapter 8.

You can export as well as import data with Q&A. The next choice on the Utilities Menu is Export. It is attached to a submenu with only five choices: DIF, Standard and Fixed ASCII, and dBASE II and III. If you want to send data stored in your Q&A data files to a spreadsheet program, you would use the DIF option. Lotus 1-2-3 as well as many other popular spreadsheets can read DIF format files. If you want to send your data to another database program or use it with a program created

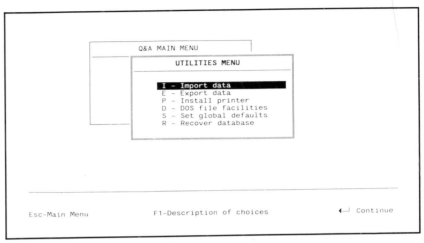

**Figure 1.17:** Q&A's Utilities Menu

in a programming language like BASIC or COBOL, you would export it as an ASCII file using the Standard ASCII option on this menu. The dBASE II and III options would be used if you wanted to transfer your Q&A data to a dBASE II/III format.

The DOS file facilities option is attached to a menu with four options. All of them are file commands that allow you either to get an alphabetical listing or to rename, delete, or copy your Q&A files between disks. The first option, called List files, is explained in Appendix C of this book, ''Using Q&A's List Manager.''

The last option on the Utilities Menu is Recover database. This option is only used if your Q&A database has been damaged in some way and you need to have Q&A try to recover the data.

## SUMMARY

Now that you have become briefly acquainted with Q&A's many features, it is time to begin to learn how to use them. In the next chapter, you will begin to work with Q&A's word processor. Learning about its features and functions will also help prepare you for Q&A File, where you will use many of the same features to create and lay out your database forms.

# CHAPTER

2

# Q&A WRITE

# Fast Track

# CONTINUED

**To perform block operations,**                               **76**

press the appropriate block operation key sequence and then mark the block. To copy a block, press F5 to begin the block operation. To move a block, press Shift-F5. To copy a block to a new document, press Ctrl-F5. To move a block to a new document, press Alt-F5. To delete a block of text, press F3, use the cursor movement keys to mark it, and then press F10 to delete it.

**To add a header to your document,**                          **80**

press F8 to access the Options Menu, type **h**, and press Return. Then enter the text of your header and press F10. To add a footer, repeat this procedure, but this time type **f** instead of *h*. To add a page number to a header or footer, type #.

**To add a user-defined page break,**                            **82**

position the cursor on the first line you want shifted to the next page, press F8 to access the Options Menu, and type **n**. The program inserts a double-line right corner symbol to mark the position of the page break. To remove a user-defined page break, position the cursor on this symbol and delete it.

**To add a soft hyphen**                                             **83**

(one that isn't printed if the word is no longer at the end of a line), position the cursor on the letter that the soft hyphen is to precede and press Alt-F6.

**F7 is the search-and-replace key.**                             **86**

To search for a string in the document, you enter a search string and leave the replace string blank. To perform an advanced search, where you can perform case-sensitive searches, press the PgDn key after pressing F7. To abandon a search or search-and-replace operation, press the Esc key.

**To do line drawing in a document,** 91

press F8 to access the Options Menu; then type **d** and press Return, or type **8**. Then use the cursor movement keys on the 10-key pad to draw the lines. To draw double lines, hold down the Shift key as you draw. Press F8 again to erase lines. Press Esc to leave draw mode.

**To spell-check** 93

the entire document, press Ctrl-Home and Shift-F1. To spell-check just a single word, position the cursor somewhere on the word and press Ctrl-F1.

**To print your document,** 96

press F2 and change any of the print settings on the Print Options as required, then press F10 to begin printing. To stop printing, press the Esc key.

**To rename, delete, or copy a document** 100

from within Q&A, type **r** and press Return, or type **7** from the Q&A Write Menu. To rename a document, type **r** and press Return again, or type **1**. To delete a file, type **d** and press Return, or type **2**. To copy a document to a new disk or directory, type **c** and press Return, or type **3**.

## WORD PROCESSING WITH Q&A

When you create a new document with Q&A Write, you use Type/Edit, the first option on the Write Menu. To follow along with the discussion and exercises in this chapter, you should now turn on your computer and start up Q&A if you don't already have the program loaded into memory.

1. At the Main Menu, choose the Write option by typing **w** and pressing Return (or by typing **3**).

2. At the Write Menu, Type/Edit is already highlighted, so you can just press Return (or type **1**).

Once you have done this, your computer screen should match the one shown in Figure 2.1.

You will see this screen whenever you begin a new document in Q&A Write. The program indicates that you are working on a new document by giving it the temporary name Working Copy, shown at the extreme left of the status line. In addition to supplying the name of your document, the status line gives you a lot of important information to help you with your editing.

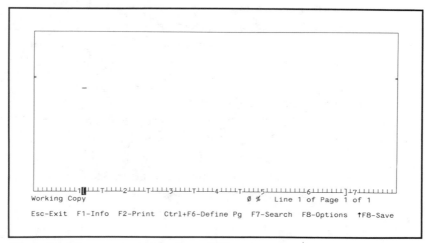

*Figure 2.1:* Components of the Type/Edit screen

## *Q&A WRITE AND YOUR COMPUTER MEMORY*

Slightly to the right of center on the status line you will see the memory-used indicator. Currently it reads 0%. This indicator shows the amount of computer memory currently taken up by your document as a percentage of the total available to the system. How quickly this indicator changes as you enter text is determined primarily by how much memory you have installed in your computer. As a rule of thumb, you can enter about 80 pages of single-spaced text using the program's default settings if you have 640K of memory. As soon as this percentage reads about 65% or so, you should evaluate how best to proceed with your writing. If you still have about a quarter of the document's text to enter, you should probably find an appropriate place to end the current document file and then continue entering the remaining text in a new file.

If you are almost finished entering all of your text but anticipate many future editing changes that could include insertion of a lot of new text, you might also need to consider breaking the document into smaller pieces. As stressed earlier, it is probably better to enter large documents as smaller sections stored in separate files. This prevents your having to worry about being hampered by a lack of sufficient memory when editing.

## *MONITORING THE CURSOR'S POSITION IN THE DOCUMENT*

To the immediate right of the memory-used indicator, Q&A lets you know where you are in the document you are creating or editing. The line and page number appear on the status line, and a block highlighting the cursor's column position appears on the ruler line directly above. Within the body of the text, the cursor position is indicated by a flashing underline. As you can see, the cursor starts out in column 1, line 1 on page 1 when you first bring up the Type/Edit screen. The cursor position tells you where the characters you type from the keyboard will be entered or where your editing commands will take effect. As you will see shortly, there are many ways to move the cursor through your document in Q&A Write.

## *WORD PROCESSING*
## *FUNCTION KEY ASSIGNMENTS*

Below the status line, some of the function key assignments in Q&A Write are shown. As in all the Q&A modules, Esc appears first. Pressing this key takes you immediately back to the Write Menu. The next function key listed is F1 for help. If you press it when you are using Q&A Write, you will get a full listing of the word processing commands available to you in Type/Edit mode and a brief description of the function of each.

Five other function key assignments are listed on this line. As you can see, they include F2, F7, F8 both shifted and alone, and F6 used with the Ctrl key. Q&A mostly uses only the first ten function keys either alone or in combination with the Shift key. (If your keyboard has F11 and F12, they are not used.) There are several cases in which a function key is used with either the Ctrl or Alt key as a special kind of shift key. This use of the ten function keys alone or shifted is quite consistent throughout all of the Q&A modules, though assignments given to a particular function key are not always the same in each module. The function key template supplied with your program lists those function key assignments that are consistent throughout all of Q&A.

Whenever you need to give a command that uses a shifted function key, you hold down either the left or right Shift key (or Ctrl or Alt) while you press the particular function key one time. The list of word processing function key assignments shown on the screen is only partial. Table 2.1 gives a complete list.

As you can see, Q&A uses the function keys to carry out all of its major word processing commands. If you ever need to refresh your memory about what a function key does, press F1 for help. If you ever press a key in error, press Esc to cancel the command. It is also very handy to keep in mind that in addition to using F1 as the help key and F10 as the confirm and continue key, Q&A consistently in all its modules uses F2 as the print key, F4 to delete a word, and Shift-F4 to delete a line.

*Table 2.1:* Q&A Write function key assignments

| Assignments for the function keys used alone: | |
|---|---|
| F1 | Get online help. |
| F2 | Print document (same as choosing the Print option on the Write menu). |
| F3 | Delete a block of text (by marking with cursor highlight). |
| F4 | Delete an entire word and trailing space if cursor is at the first letter; otherwise, delete from cursor position to word's end and leave trailing space. |
| F5 | Copy a block of text within a document (by marking with cursor highlight). |
| F6 | Set a temporary indented left or right margin or clear temporary indent. |
| F7 | Search-and-replace text in a document. Press PgDn for advanced search options. |
| F8 | Access the Options Menu to add headers or footers, center or uncenter a line, set tabs on ruler, insert text from a separate document file, add a page break, or use the line drawing set (draw mode). |
| F9 | Scroll down document window. |
| F10 | Confirms command selection and tells Q&A to carry it out. |
| **Assignments for the function keys used with the shift keys:** | |
| Shift-F1 | Spell-check the entire document. |
| Shift-F2 | Define a macro sequence, record keystrokes or word processing commands, or save or load a new macro file. |
| Shift-F4 | Delete the line containing the cursor. |

*Table 2.1:* Q&A Write function key assignments (continued)

| | **Assignments for the function keys used with the shift keys: (continued)** |
|---|---|
| Shift-F5 | Move a block of text (by marking with cursor highlight). |
| Shift-F6 | Define print enhancements such as underlining, boldface, italics, superscripts, and subscripts, or return text to normal. |
| Shift-F7 | Undo key to bring back the text just deleted before making any further deletions or copying or moving a block of text. |
| Shift-F8 | Save document in memory (same as Save option on Write Menu). |
| Shift-F9 | Scroll up document window. |
| | **Assignments for the function keys used with the Ctrl Key:** |
| Ctrl-F1 | Spell-check the word containing the cursor. |
| Ctrl-F2 | Print only the block of text defined with the cursor highlight. |
| Ctrl-F3 | Display document statistics. |
| Ctrl-F4 | Delete from the cursor to the end of the line. |
| Ctrl-F5 | Copy a block of text defined with the cursor highlight into a new document file. |
| Ctrl-F6 | Define a page (same as Define a page option on Write Menu). |
| Ctrl-F7 | Go to a specified page or line. |
| Ctrl-F8 | Export the document to ASCII. |
| Ctrl-F9 | Assign fonts to the current document. |

*Table 2.1:* Q&A Write function key assignments (continued)

| Assignments for the function keys used with the Alt Key: | |
|---|---|
| Alt-F5 | Move a block of text defined with the cursor highlight into a new document file. |
| Alt-F6 | Add a soft hyphen. |
| Alt-F7 | List the field names of the associated merge datafile. |
| Alt-F8 | Print mailing labels. |
| Alt-F9 | Calculate a row or column of numbers. |

## Q&A'S ON-SCREEN PRESENTATION OF YOUR TEXT

The Type/Edit screen represents the physical borders of the sheet of paper. Within it, two square brackets display the left and right typing margins. The top and side edges of the paper are represented by the box drawn on this screen. The lower edge of the box contains a ruler line showing margins, tab stops, and tick marks representing each column position. Every tenth tick mark on this ruler is indicated by a number from 1 to 7, so there are 80 columns from the left to the right edge of the box. Each column (within the margin settings) can contain a single typed character.

Because your monitor is capable only of displaying text in a uniform 10 characters per inch (often abbreviated *cpi*), this ruler demarcated in tenths never varies. Depending on what printer you have, you can change this 10 cpi (pica) default pitch to compress or expand the type, which changes the number of characters in a line. Pitches of 12 cpi (elite), 15 cpi, and even 17 cpi are common. Some dot-matrix printers, like the Epson models, support an expanded print font that can also be used by Q&A. It is important for you to understand that when you use other pitches for printing, you should change the margin settings if you want to see on the screen how your lines will break when printed. You will learn how to do this in the discussion on formatting your documents later in this chapter.

Q&A Write always assumes that you will be printing your document on a 8½ x 11-inch sheet of paper unless you tell it otherwise. The ruler line, however, only displays a total of 79 characters (columns), which at 10 characters per inch equals a total on-screen page width of just slightly over 7⅞ inches. The mapping of the printed page to the screen representation of the text is not exact. This means that there is a discrepancy of ⅝ inch between the on-screen display of your page and the actual width of your paper that is added to your left and right margins on the printout. For example, when using the program default settings, the on-screen display shows a one-inch left margin (or 10 columns) with a full line of text extending across 5⅞ inches (from 10 to 68 or 58 columns wide) and a right margin of 1 inch (column 68 to 78, another 10 columns).

When you print the document, this line actually has a left margin of 1¼ inch, a line of text measuring 5⅞ inches, and a right margin of 1⅜ inches. This means that you may still have to do some calculations when setting up your margins to take into account the difference between what you see on the screen and what you get in the printout, as you will see later in this chapter.

You can experiment until you find a format that is suitable for most of the documents you work with. Then save a blank document (or one containing a ''reminder'' line of text, such as ''invoice form'') in this format and use it as a template for subsequent documents you create.

The space at the top of your page for top margin is indicated by a double tick mark at the left and right borders of the box representing your page. The default setting for line spacing is single space, which translates into 6 lines per inch (often abbreviated *lpi*). This top border is exactly equivalent to 6 lines of text or one vertical inch. There is another corresponding marker at the bottom of the page (not yet visible on your screen) indicating the bottom margin of the page. When you add a header or footer to these margin areas, the header and footer are displayed on the screen exactly as they will be printed on the page. This feature is extremely useful when you create longer documents containing page numbers in either the header or footer. You will learn how to work with these in the section on advanced editing a little later in this chapter.

# *BASIC EDITING FEATURES*

Now it is time to get some hands-on experience with Q&A Write and explore a few of its basic editing features. Q&A Write accepts any printable character typed from the keyboard. As you type, the cursor automatically stays ahead of the typing. As with all word processors, you need not worry about carriage returns. Any text that extends beyond the right margin is automatically wrapped around to the next line. You use the Return key as a carriage return only when you want to signal a paragraph's end.

Because no text has yet been entered in your document, you have few choices for manually moving the cursor at this point. You can only press the space bar to add a blank space or press the Tab key to move the cursor to the first tab stop. The Tab key is marked on many keyboards with two arrows pointing in opposite directions. It is usually located below the Esc key on your PC keyboard.

## *CREATING YOUR FIRST DOCUMENT*

For practice, enter this line of text:

**It seems like only yesterday that word processing replaced the electronic typewriter in our office.**

If you make a mistake while entering this line, use the Backspace key (the gray key marked ← above Return) to delete. Even if you didn't make a mistake, you should try using this key to delete a couple of characters at the end of the sentence and then retype them. Watch how the Backspace key deletes any character it contacts as it moves the cursor one space to the left. Notice that Q&A Write used word wrap to put the rest of the sentence after the word replaced on the second line to make it conform to your margins. Figure 2.2 shows your document at this point. As you can see, there was no need to use a carriage return when you came to the end of the first line.

### *DELETING SINGLE CHARACTERS*  Next, change the word *electronic* to *electric*. To do this, you must move the cursor back across the words *typewriter in our office* without deleting them. You cannot

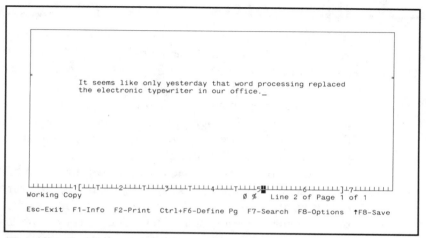

```
        It seems like only yesterday that word processing replaced
        the electronic typewriter in our office._




Working Copy                              Ø %   Line 2 of Page 1 of 1

Esc-Exit  F1-Info  F2-Print  Ctrl+F6-Define Pg  F7-Search  F8-Options  ↑F8-Save
```

*Figure 2.2:* Entering text in a new document

use the Backspace key because it would erase all the correct characters as it moved the cursor to the left. Instead, use the ← key located on the numeric keypad. It moves the cursor left one space nondestructively. (You can hold the ← key down to move the cursor quickly, rather than having to press the key repeatedly.)

1. Move the cursor until it is beneath the letter *o* in *electronic*. (If you overshoot the letter, use the → key to move the cursor back into position.)

2. Then press the Delete key (marked Del) twice to delete the characters *on*.

Using Del erases any character above the cursor, as well as removing the space it occupies.

### *CHANGING FROM OVERTYPE TO INSERT MODE*    Now change *word processing* to read *word processor* in the line above.

1. To move the cursor up to line 1, press the ↑ key one time. Then use the → key to move to the *i* in *processing*, and press the Del key three times.

2.  Next, type in **or** and press the space bar.

You now have *processor* entered correctly, but not without having done damage to *replaced*. Because Q&A Write stays in overtype mode (sometimes called typethrough mode) unless you press the Insert key (marked Ins), it has rubbed out the *re* in *replaced* instead of inserting the necessary spaces before the word.

3.  To rectify this, press the Ins key one time.

Once you do so, the cursor changes shape from a flashing underline to a flashing rectangle to let you know that you are now in insert mode. Notice too, that the word "Insert" has now appeared on the status line next to the memory-used indicator (as shown in Figure 2.3).

4.  Type **re** and watch as the program inserts these characters by pushing the rest of the word to the right.

To get back to overtype mode, all you have to do is press Insert a second time. This key toggles back and forth between insert and overtype mode each time you press it.

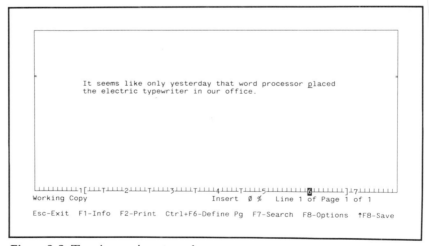

```
It seems like only yesterday that word processor placed
the electric typewriter in our office.
```

```
LllllllllllL1[LllLTLlllL2LlllTLlllL3LlllLTLlllL4LlllLTLlllL5LllllllllllL6LllllllllL]L7LlllllllL
Working Copy                         Insert  Ø %   Line 1 of Page 1 of 1

Esc-Exit  F1-Info  F2-Print  Ctrl+F6-Define Pg  F7-Search  F8-Options  ↑F8-Save
```

*Figure 2.3:* Turning on insert mode

***MOVING THE CURSOR A WORD AT A TIME***   Next, you will want to add the word *the* before the word *processor*.

1.   This time, hold down the Ctrl key and depress the ← key to move the cursor to the beginning of each word.

This is a faster way because it moves the cursor a word at a time across a line of text. (Pressing the Ctrl and → keys works just like this, only it moves the cursor to the space after each word to the right.) The first time you hold down Ctrl and depress the ← key, the cursor moves to the first letter in *replaced*.

2.   Press this combination two more times until the cursor is located at the beginning of *word*. Type **the**.

Notice that the addition of this new word has caused *replaced* to be wrapped to the second line. In Q&A Write, you do not ever have to give a special command to reformat the text within the margins of a paragraph after inserting or deleting text. This is always done automatically for you.

***INDENTING A PARAGRAPH***   To get to the beginning of the line, press the Home key (top left on the cursor pad). The End key works as the opposite of the Home key. If you pressed it now, the cursor would jump to the end of the first line. In insert mode, you can indent a paragraph by pressing Tab. All of the text will move to the right to the first tab stop. Try this now by pressing the Tab key one time.

***DELETING AND RESTORING TEXT***

1.   To remove the paragraph indent, press Home and then press Del four times.

You can also use the delete-word key, F4, as a faster way to remove the spaces inserted by pressing Tab.

2.   Try this method by pressing Tab, then Home, and then F4. Press F4 a second time to delete the word *It*.

With Q&A Write's Undelete function, you can restore any word you just erased by pressing Shift-F7.

3. Try this: hold down the Shift key and depress F7 one time to restore the first word of this paragraph.

4. This works with larger blocks of text also. Go ahead and delete the entire first line by pressing Shift-F4.

5. Now bring it back by pressing Shift-F7 again.

Q&A will warn you if a block marked for deletion is too big to be restored. The only thing to keep in mind is that you must restore your deleted text before you go on and do any more deletions in the document. Save yourself needless retyping: use the Undelete function in time.

You can also use Ctrl-F4 to delete text from the cursor location to the end of the line. This makes deleting an unnecessary piece of text very simple.

6. Move the cursor to the space between the words *typewriter* and *in*. Now delete the text to the end of the line by pressing Ctrl-F4.

7. Now bring it back again by pressing Shift-F7.

### MOVING THE CURSOR AROUND THE SCREEN

1. Move the cursor to the end of the first line by pressing the End key; then press End again. This positions the cursor at the end of the second line.

2. Press Home twice. Notice that it takes the cursor from the beginning of the second line up to the beginning of the first.

If you had entered an entire screen of text or more, pressing the End key twice would have taken the cursor to the end of the last line on the screen (which is line 2 in this case), just as then pressing the Home key twice in a row would have positioned it at the very beginning of the screen. Table 2.2 summarizes the cursor movements possible in Q&A Write.

***Table 2.2:*** Cursor movements in Q&A Write

| | |
|---|---|
| ↑ | Up a line |
| ↓ | Down a line |
| → | One character to the right |
| ← | One character to the left |
| Ctrl-→ | One word to the right |
| Ctrl-← | One word to the left |
| Home    1st time | To the beginning of the line |
| 2nd time | To the top of the screen |
| 3rd time | To the top of the page |
| 4th time | To the beginning of the document |
| Ctrl-Home | To the beginning of the document |
| End    1st time | To the end of the line |
| 2nd time | To the bottom of the screen |
| 3rd time | To the bottom of the page |
| 4th time | To the end of the document |
| Ctrl-End | To the end of the document |
| PgUp | To the top of the previous screen |
| Ctrl-PgUp | To the top of the previous page |
| PgDn | To the top of the next screen |
| Ctrl-PgDn | To the top of the next page |

3. Take Q&A Write out of insert mode by pressing Ins, and then press Tab a couple of times.

In overtype mode, pressing Tab does not disturb the text by pushing it over to the next tab stop. In this mode, you can use Tab as another means to move the cursor quickly across a line.

4. Now put Q&A Write back into insert mode (press Ins) and press Home to move the cursor to the beginning of the line. This time, press Return to open a new blank line and move the paragraph down.

5. Press Return a second time, as you will need two blank lines before the start of your first paragraph.

6. Now press the Home key twice more to move the cursor up two lines to the new beginning of this document.

## CENTERING A LINE

1. Enter a heading for this document by typing

   **The Benefits of Word Processing**

2. You will want to center this title on the page. To do this, access the Options Menu by pressing F8.

Q&A inserts the Options Menu right in the middle of your screen, just as it is shown in Figure 2.4. There are many important word processing commands attached to this vertical menu. For now, you only want to use the fourth option, Center line.

3. Type **c** and press Return.

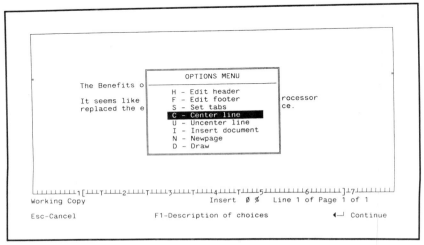

*Figure 2.4:* Q&A Write's Options Menu

As always in Q&A, instead of typing the first letter of the command and pressing Return, you can type the option's number. In this case, you would type **4**. As soon as you give this command, the menu disappears and the text of the line containing the cursor is centered between the document's margins. If you change the margin settings, this centered line will also be adjusted. If you edit a centered line, it will also adjust according to whether you deleted or inserted text.

You can return the line to left justification by using the Uncenter line option on the Options Menu. Try it now: press F8, type **u**, and press Return (or type **5**). Q&A Write does not have to be in insert mode to center a line. Test this out: press Ins, press F8, and this time just type **4** to center the title again.

## USING PRINT ENHANCEMENTS

Next, you will want to emphasize the word *yesterday* in the first line by having it printed in boldface type.

1. To access print enhancements like boldface, underlining, italics, and the like, press Shift-F6.

Before you add print enhancements to your text, you will want to position the cursor at the start of the word or words to be included.

2. Move the cursor down to the first line of the paragraph, press Home, and then press Ctrl-→ four times to position the cursor at the beginning of *yesterday*.

3. Now hold down one of the Shift keys and press F6.

Q&A presents you with a new horizontal menu of print enhancement choices, as shown in Figure 2.5. To select a particular enhancement, all you have to do is type the letter preceding its name. There is no need to press the Return key.

4. Type **b**, and the Print Enhancements Menu disappears.

It is replaced by your edit screen, which now contains a message about how to proceed. Your screen should now match the one shown in Figure 2.6. On the line below the status line is the message to use

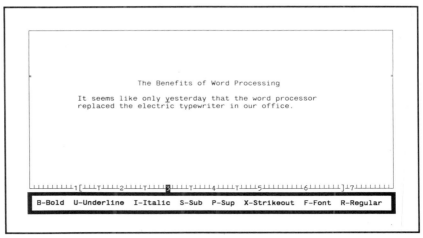

*Figure 2.5:* The Print Enhancements Menu

the arrow keys to select the text to be set off in boldface type. Q&A Write always places its messages about how to proceed on this line. Notice too, that the first letter in *yesterday* is now highlighted. If you pressed F10 now, only the *y* would be emboldened. To highlight the entire word, you could press Ctrl-→. Another method is to press the space bar. This differs from the previous option in that it will extend the highlight to include the space trailing the last letter of the word.

5. Press the space bar.

6. Because you only want to embolden the word *yesterday*, press ← and then press F10 to continue.

The word *yesterday* now appears in double intensity on the screen and the word ''Bold'' is now displayed to the right of the words ''Working Copy'' on the status line.

All of the other print enhancements work in this same way, including the Regular option, which puts any text marked for enhancements back to normal. First you position the cursor at the start of the text to be included, then choose from the menu the print enhancement you want, then highlight all of the text to be affected, and finally press F10 to confirm and give the command. You can select and

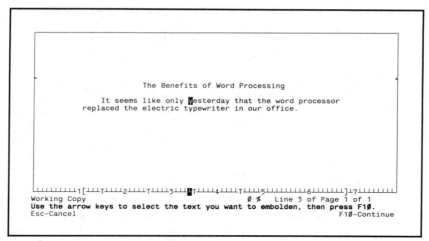

*Figure 2.6:* Selecting text to boldface

highlight large areas of text quickly by using any of these methods:

- Press the space bar to highlight the next word. In the previous example, pressing the space bar with the cursor on the first *y* of *yesterday* would highlight the entire word (just as pressing Ctrl-→ did) plus the space after it.

- Press a letter key to highlight to the next occurrence of that letter in the text. In this example, typing the letter **w** would have extended the highlighting from the first *y* in *yesterday* to the *w* in *word*.

- Press Return to highlight from the cursor's position to the end of the paragraph. Pressing Return a second time then extends the highlighting to include the next paragraph, and so on.

Another type of print enhancement, called a *font*, is also available in Write. The actual font must be purchased separately from Q&A, and your printer has to support the use of fonts as well. Font description files, files with the extension .FNT, are provided with Q&A. You can assign a font to a particular piece of text in your document, and Q&A uses the information contained in the font file when it prints your document. For a more detailed description of the use of fonts, please refer to Appendix F.

Now that you have some experience with the basic editing features of Q&A Write, it should be easy for you to go on and enter some more of this report on the transition to word processing in the office. Figure 2.7 shows you the rest of the first paragraph and the beginning of the second paragraph. When you finish entering the last sentence of the first paragraph, press Return to mark the end of that paragraph and the beginning of a new one. When you press Return, the cursor moves down a line and over to the left margin. Press the Tab key to indent the new paragraph, and then type in the text as shown in Figure 2.7.

```
                        The Benefits of Word Processing

              It seems like only yesterday that the word processor
         replaced the electric typewriter in our office.  While the
         transition from mechanical to electronic media was not
         without its ups and down, there is not a single secretary
         or clerk in any of our departments who would willingly
         give up his or her computer and go back to the "good old
         days" of the typing pool!
              At the close of this past fiscal year, we have in
         place a total of 15 personal computers dedicated primarily
         to word processing throughout our five departments.  The
         benefits reported by our managers and supervisors as a
         result of this transition can be summarized as follows:_

└┴┴┴┴┴┴┴┴┴┴1[┴┴┴T┴┴┴2┴┴┴T┴┴┴3┴┴┴T┴┴┴4┴┴┴T┴┴┴5┴┴┴┴┴┴┴┴6┴┴┴┴]┴7┴┴┴┴┴┴┴┴
Working Copy                                Ø %    Line 14 of Page 1 of 1

Esc-Exit  F1-Info  F2-Print  Ctrl+F6-Define Pg  F7-Search  F8-Options  ↑F8-Save
```

*Figure 2.7:* Text of sample document

## FORMATTING YOUR DOCUMENTS

Up to now, the program's default settings for tabs and margins have worked just fine for this document. Whenever you start a new document in Q&A, it will set the left margin at column 10, the right margin at column 68, and four tab stops starting at column 14 and at intervals of 10 spaces.

The other defaults that come into play are a ragged-right margin (as opposed to right justification) and single spacing. Changes to either right justification or larger spacing cannot be shown on the screen. You see the result of these modifications only in your printed copy of the document. Both of these are changed from the Print Menu and affect the entire document to be printed.

## USING THE DEFINE PAGE COMMAND

To change the margin settings in a document, you must use the Define Page option. You may remember from your quick tour of Q&A that this is one of the choices on the Write Menu. However, you do not need to escape back to this menu just to make changes to the margins of a document. Q&A gives you an alternative command, Ctrl-F6, that can be given from the Type/Edit screen. To see what this option includes, hold down the Ctrl key and press F6 one time.

Figure 2.8 shows you this screen, where you can see the preset values for a document page. The first line of this screen contains the values that determine the width of the left and right margins. These are both expressed in the number of columns. In this case, the left margin is in column 10 and the right in column 68. Because the page width is set at 78 (expressed in columns also), the right margin is also 10 columns. With the pitch of 10 characters per inch, this makes both margins an inch wide.

The second line has the values for the top and bottom margins. These are currently set at 6, which stands for six lines per inch, equaling an inch at both the top and bottom of the page. The third line

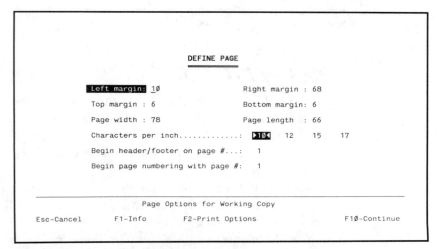

*Figure 2.8:* The Define Page screen

contains the page width and length settings. The page width is expressed in the number of columns visible on the screen. Remember that the standard width of 8 ½ inches is equivalent to 85 columns on the screen at 10 characters per inch. Q&A Write uses a default setting of 78 columns simply because of its appearance on the screen. At this value, you can see all of your text and still get a fair idea of how the margins will look when the document is printed. The minimum value for page width is one inch or 10 columns, and the maximum is 14 inches or 140 columns.

Page length is listed here as 66 and is given in the number of lines. At six lines per inch, 66 lines is equivalent to a total length of 11 inches. With a top and bottom margin of six lines each, this leaves 54 lines of text on each page. Notice that you cannot change the line spacing setting from the Define Page screen. This is done from the Print screen just before you print your document. There you can choose only between single or double spacing of the entire document. The minimum page length is one inch or 6 lines, and the maximum is 32 inches or 192 lines.

The next line on the Define Page screen determines the characters per inch. The default is 10 cpi, which is commonly called pica type. The next choice is 12 cpi, referred to as elite type. The third choice, 15 cpi, is a smaller type available only on daisywheel printers equipped with the correct wheel. Be aware that when you use this small font, you may have to adjust the number of lines per page because 15 cpi uses less space between lines than either 10 or 12 cpi. The last choice is 17 cpi, which is used only with dot-matrix printers like the Epson FX series. It prints your page in what is called compressed type. See your printer manual for a sample of this size. As with 15 cpi, you need to adjust the lines per page setting if you want to fill up the entire page when printing with this option.

The last two lines of the screen allow you to define the first page to contain any headers and footers or page numbers that you may have defined for the document. You set up automatic page numbering by placing a special code in either a header or footer. The default value is page 1, which you will want to use most of the time. If you are printing a report with a title page that you do not want to number or to contain a continuous heading, you would set this value to 2. You will learn how to define and use headers, footers, and page numbers later in this chapter.

## ADJUSTING THE MARGIN SETTINGS

When you change the margin settings in a document, there are two things to keep in mind: the overall width of the page and the characters per inch setting. Because it is often difficult to determine the proper margin settings in columns, Q&A allows you to give these values in inches. When you do, you must type a quotation mark (") after the value and express any fractions of an inch in decimal form. For instance, to set a left margin of 1 ¼ inches in inches instead of columns, you would type **1.25"** in place of the 10 now shown. Whenever you change the settings on the Define Page screen, you must press F10 to have your document reformatted to the new values. When you save your document to disk, these new settings are saved with it.

To see how this works, you will now make the changes to the formatting of your word processing benefits document as shown in Figure 2.9. Change the default values so that you have a 1 ½ inch left margin, a 1-inch right margin, and a page width of 8 ½ inches (the true width of your paper). To do this, take the following steps:

1. Press the → key to move the cursor one space to the 0 in 10. Then type **.5"** and press Return.

2. Type **1"** over the 68 in the Right margin setting and press Return three times until you are at the Page width setting.

3. Type **8.5"** over the 78; then press F10.

After pressing F10, you will see the status message ''formatting'' flashing. As soon as Q&A is finished reformatting your document to the new margin and page width settings, you will be taken back to the document at the Type/Edit screen. It should match the one shown in Figure 2.10. Using these new settings, you cannot now see the right margin on the screen. To see the effects of changing from pica (10 cpi) to elite (12 cpi) using a left and right margin of one inch with the same page width setting, make these changes:

1. Press Ctrl-F6 to get to the Define Page screen.

2. Press → one time and type ". Then press the space bar twice to delete the .5", and press Return.

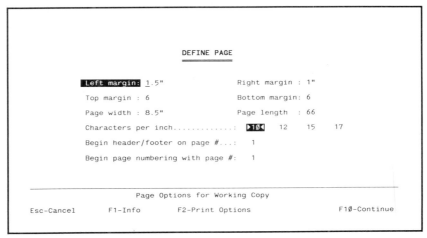

***Figure 2.9:*** Changing the margin settings

```
                    The Benefits of Word Processing
              It seems like only yesterday that the word processor
        replaced the electric typewriter in our office.  While the
        transition from mechanical to electronic media was not
        without its ups and down, there is not a single secretary or
        clerk in any of our departments who would willingly give up
        his or her computer and go back to the "good old days" of
        the typing pool!
              At the close of this past fiscal year, we have in place
        a total of 15 personal computers dedicated primarily to word
        processing throughout our five departments.  The benefits
        reported by our managers and supervisors as a result of this
        transition can be summarized as follows:
```

```
Working Copy                                  Ø %    Line 15 of Page 1 of 1
Esc-Exit  F1-Info  F2-Print  Ctrl+F6-Define Pg  F7-Search  F8-Options  ↑F8-Save
```

***Figure 2.10:*** Sample document with new margins

3. Press ↓ three times until the cursor highlight is located on the Characters per inch option. Press the → key once to change the setting from 10 to 12; then press F10 to confirm this new choice.

Figure 2.11 shows you the effect of this change. Notice that at 12 cpi the on-screen look of the document is very different. Not only

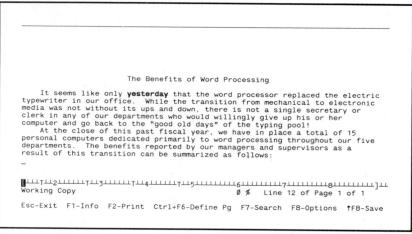

*Figure 2.11:* Sample document at 12 characters per inch

have the paragraphs been reformatted to new margin settings but the left margin is no longer visible. Because the program cannot really show you elite type on the screen, it has to adjust the ruler and the right margin. The right margin is now set at column 90 so that you can see how much text will fit on a line at the more condensed pitch of 12 characters per inch. Previously, the first line of your document ended with *word processor*. Now it includes the next three words of the sentence.

Q&A Write will always adjust the screen presentation of your text as best it can, given the limitations of your monitor display, when you make changes to the page characteristics of a document. Any changes you make are saved with the document when it is saved on disk.

Now you will want to change these settings back to their original values, but instead of expressing them in numbers of columns and lines, use inch equivalents:

1. Press Ctrl-F6 to access the Define Page screen.

2. Press the ↓ key twice until you are at the Top margin option. Type **1"** and press Return. Now type the same thing for the Bottom margin setting.

3. At Page width, type **7.8"** and press Return.

4. At Page length, type **11″** and press Return.

5. At Characters per inch, press the ← key to set it to 10. Then press F10 to confirm these settings.

The margins and formatting of the text of your document should now appear as they did originally before making any of these changes. Refer back to the screen shown in Figure 2.7 if you are unsure.

## TAB SETTINGS

You do not modify the tab stops on the ruler from the Define Page screen. This is done from the Options Menu, which you already used when you centered the document's heading. Press F8 now to bring up this menu; then type **s** and press Return (or type **3**) to select the Set tabs option. Once you have selected Set tabs, you can edit the ruler line, adding or deleting tab stops anywhere within the margins.

Q&A Write provides several ways for you to move quickly back and forth across the ruler. You can use the End key to go directly to the column just before the right margin setting and Home to go directly to the column just after the left margin setting. Pressing Ctrl-← or Ctrl-→ moves the cursor five columns in either direction. Pressing Tab will take you to the next preset tab. You can also press Shift-Tab; it works like a Backtab key, taking the cursor to the previous tab stop to the left of its present position.

To set a new tab stop, you move the cursor to the desired position on the ruler and type **t**. You can also set up decimal tab stops by typing **d** instead of **t**. A decimal tab differs from a textual tab in that it right-justifies all the characters you enter until you type a period. After the program detects the presence of a period, all further characters are left-justified. You usually use decimal tabs to align numerical data in columns of tables. To remove an existing tab, move to the tab to be deleted and then press the Del key or the space bar.

For practice, you will now add the new tab settings that you will need to indent the next section of text for your sample document.

1. Press Tab and then Ctrl-→, which takes the cursor to column 20. Then press ← one time and type **t** to set a tab stop in column 19.

2. Press End to take the cursor to the end of the ruler line. Next, press Ctrl-← one time; then press ← twice and type **t** to set another tab stop in column 60.

3. Press F10 to confirm and return to editing.

## *SETTING TEMPORARY MARGINS*

There are times when you will need to set temporary margins in your document. The most common application for this is outlining. When you outline, you need to set up varying temporary left margins, each corresponding to a new level in the outline and each level indented further. This effect is sometimes referred to in word processing as a hanging indent. Once you set a temporary left margin, all text that you enter conforms to this new margin until you give the command to clear it and return to your regular left margin.

Q&A allows you to do this kind of indenting by setting up either temporary left or right margins. You will practice using this technique to set off the numbered points that list the benefits of word processing from the rest of the text in the second paragraph of your document. If your cursor is now on line 13 right after the colon, press Return two times to skip a line. Then press Tab and type **1.** to number the first point; then press Tab again. It is here that you will set a temporary left margin. You will also want to indent the right margin slightly from its current setting.

1. Press F6. The Set Temporary Margin Menu appears (shown in Figure 2.12). Select the left option by typing **l**. The menu disappears and a greater-than symbol (>) appears on the ruler line in column 19 to let you know that there is now a left indent set there. (You do not need to press Return when selecting options from horizontal menus.)

2. Press the Tab key four times until the cursor is located in column 60. Press F6 again and choose the right option by typing **r**. The cursor immediately returns to its previous position in column 19. A less-than symbol (<) appears on the

ruler line in column 60 to let you know that there is now a right indent set there.

3. Type in the text for the first point as shown in Figure 2.13. Press Return after you have finished entering that sentence.

4. Press F6 and type **c** to return to the normal margins. Press Return; then press Tab and type **2**. Then press Tab again.

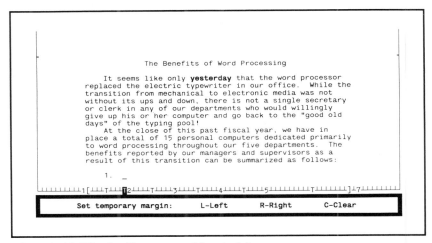

*Figure 2.12:* The Set Temporary Margin Menu

*Figure 2.13:* Adding text with hanging indents

5. Repeat the steps to set up a temporary left margin in this column: press F6 and type **1**. Set a temporary right margin in column 60: press F6 and type **r**. Then enter the text for the second point as shown in Figure 2.13.

6. Press Return to enter a blank line. Press F6 and type **c** to clear the temporary margins. Then press Return. Repeat this entire process when adding the text for the third point shown in Figure 2.13. When you are done, press Return and F6; then type **c** to return to the normal margin settings.

## JUSTIFYING SECTIONS OF TEXT IN A DOCUMENT

Q&A allows you to format text with either ragged-right or right-justified margins. As mentioned earlier, right justification, which is selected from the Print Menu, cannot be shown on-screen, although it affects the entire document. There are times when you may want to mix ragged-right margins and right justification within a single document. For instance, it would be very effective to right-justify the text listing the three points you entered with hanging indents. To have only these right-justified in the document, you must enter embedded commands that tell the program where the right justification begins and ends. Though embedded commands are visible in the document on the screen, they are not printed.

You set off all Q&A embedded commands by typing an asterisk (*) before and after the command. To turn justification on, you type **\*JUSTIFY Y\*** right before the text you want justified. To turn it off, type **\*JUSTIFY N\*** right after the place in the text where you want to go back to ragged-right margins. These commands can be abbreviated to **\*JY Y\*** to turn justification on, or to **\*JY N\*** to turn it off. You do not have to capitalize the commands, but be sure that you have added an asterisk before and after them to let Q&A know that this text represents an embedded command.

You can add these commands to any line already containing text. Be sure to turn on insert mode (by pressing Ins) before adding them in front of any existing text, or you may end up typing over some text. You can also add these codes to any blank lines that occur before and after the text to be justified. Be aware that these codes will not be printed, so you will have to add another blank line to keep your original spacing.

Figure 2.14 shows the embedded commands for turning justification on and off added to the document. Their placement is such that only the numbered list of benefits will be right-justified. As you can see, they have no visual effect on the on-screen formatting of this text. To add these commands to your document, enter them as follows:

1. Press ↑ to move the cursor up to the blank line above your first indented sentence (line 15) and press Home to go to the beginning of the line.

2. Type **\*Justify Y\***.

3. Put Q&A in insert mode by pressing Ins (the cursor will appear as a flashing block), and press Return to add a new blank line.

4. Press ↓ to move the cursor down to the first blank line immediately below the last line (line 29).

5. Type **\*Justify N\***.

6. Press Return twice and turn insert mode off by pressing Ins again.

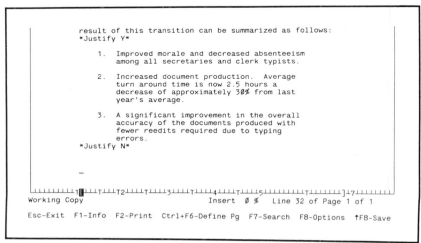

*Figure 2.14:* Using selective justification

## USING EMBEDDED
## PRINTER CODES IN A DOCUMENT

As well as being able to add embedded command codes to turn on and off right justification, you can use other embedded commands that control the printing of special effects in your documents. The format for these embedded commands is the same as for Justify Yes and No. The code always begins and ends with an asterisk. The biggest difference is that all of these codes are prefaced with the word *Printer* instead of *Justify*, followed by the printer-specific codes.

Unfortunately, what codes you can use and how they affect your document differs greatly from printer to printer. You must also involve yourself with entering escape and control codes in their ASCII code equivalents. While almost every printer manual contains some information about what codes are supported, what they do, and how to use them, this whole area can be intimidating to the new user. Trying out a new printing effect generated by entering an embedded printer code can also involve a lot of experimentation before everything proceeds as planned.

Nevertheless, you can make Q&A Write a much more versatile writing tool by using these codes to get the full benefit of all of the printing effects supported by your particular printer. For instance, you can use embedded codes with certain dot-matrix printers to do shadow printing, use double-width characters, or even change to italics. You can also use the codes with almost any type of printer to change from single to double spacing within the same document.

(You may not want to take the time now to learn to use embedded codes, but you can come back to this section later when you feel more comfortable with the basics of the program. For now, you can turn to the next section, "Saving Your Document," if you want to continue with program basics.)

The first thing to know about these printing codes is that you can represent all printable letter and punctuation keyboard characters (and many that are not printable) by numerical equivalents in what is called the ASCII Code (American Standard Code for Information Interchange). A chart containing this code is shown in Appendix D of this book.

The second thing is that many printer codes are preceded by the escape character. For instance, with most IBM and Epson dot-matrix printers, Esc-E turns on shadow printing (also called emphasized), while Esc-F turns it off. But when entering this code as an embedded printing command in Q&A Write, you must convert both Esc and E into ASCII code number equivalents.

Refer to Appendix D and see that the ASCII code numbers run from 000 to 127. Go down the column and find number 027, the decimal number equivalent of pressing the Esc key. Then find the capital letter *E*. Its code number is 069. Notice, too, that lowercase *e* has a different number, 101. The codes are case specific. For embedded printer codes in Q&A, you will always use the ASCII value for the uppercase letter listed in your printer manual.

If you have an IBM or Epson dot-matrix printer and you want to enter the code to start emphasized printing in your document, turn on insert mode, move the cursor to the place just before the text you want to emphasize, and then enter

    *Printer 27 69*

To turn it off again, move the cursor to the place just after the last character to be enhanced with emphasized print, and enter

    *Printer 27 70*

This code is equivalent to entering Esc (027) F (070), the code that turns off this effect on the IBM and Epson dot-matrix printers. Notice that you do not have to enter a zero before the code number in the Q&A embedded printer command, even though the chart gives it to you with the zero. You may also abbreviate the word *Printer* as **p** when entering an embedded printer command in Q&A Write.

## *CHANGING FROM SINGLE TO DOUBLE SPACING*

As you remember, Q&A Write only supports single or double spacing of the entire document. There may be many times when you want to mix these in the same document. For instance, in your sample report you might very well want to have the majority of the text double spaced, yet use single spacing for the indented section that enumerates the three most prominent benefits of word processing.

To change to double spacing and then back to single spacing, you must enter the embedded code **∗Ls 2∗** before the text that is to be double spaced, and the code **∗Ls 1∗** before the text that is to be single spaced (*Ls* stands for *Linespacing*; you do not have to spell it out).

If you were to use these codes in your sample document, you would enter this first embedded code to turn on the double spacing on the very first line of the first paragraph below the heading. The code should be entered on a line of its own. You would place the cursor on this line and then press the Home key to move it to the first column. You would then press the Ins key to get into insert mode. You would press Return to enter a blank line, and then you would move the cursor up to it. There you would enter the command **∗Ls 2∗**. Though this code is now on a line of its own, it will not add a beginning blank line to your document.

To print the three points in single spacing, you would then move the cursor down to the blank line right above the one containing the text of the first point in the list. There you would enter the code **∗Ls 1∗**. To turn off single spacing and go back into double spacing, you would move the cursor to the line below the one containing the embedded command to turn the justification off, and enter the embedded code again. You can also use this embedded command to do even larger spacing by merely entering a number between 1 and 9 in place of the 1 or 2 in these examples. For example, to do triple spacing, you would enter the embedded code as **∗Ls 3∗**.

## ───── *SAVING YOUR DOCUMENT* ─────

It is now time to save your document on disk. Thus far, the only copy of your text that exists is in your computer's memory. If you were to have a power failure, you would lose this copy and have to reenter it. To guard against losing any of your edits, you should develop the habit of frequently saving your text on a data disk. A data disk is simply a blank diskette that you have already prepared using the DOS FORMAT command (see your DOS manual for formatting instructions). You should always have several data disks on hand when working with Q&A. Save your work often during an editing session. The more often you save, the smaller the amount of text that could be lost because of a power interruption. That translates into a smaller amount of work you would have to redo.

Before you learn how to save a document, you should become aware of a safety feature built into Q&A Write. Try to exit the word processor without first saving this document on disk: press Esc twice. When you try to escape back to the Main Menu from the Write Menu, you receive the warning shown in Figure 2.15. You do not want to override this warning and return to the Main Menu without saving (although you can if you really don't want to save a document), so press Return to accept the default answer of No. You will receive this warning message any time you attempt to exit the word processor without having saved your original document or your editing changes. Once you have given your document a name when saving it the first time, its name will replace Working Copy whenever you encounter this warning message. Seeing the name as Working Copy is a clue that you have never saved this document before.

You are now at the Q&A Write Menu. If you use the program on a two-drive system, you should put your new data disk in drive B: before continuing the save procedure. If you are using Q&A on a hard disk system and you want to save your file on a floppy disk rather than on the hard disk itself, you should put your data disk in drive A: at this point.

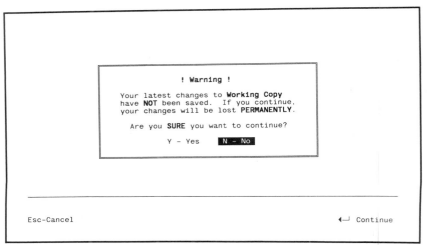

*Figure 2.15:* Q&A's Not Saved warning message

To access the Save option, type **s** and press Return (or type **6**) now. The cursor then drops down to a data entry line after the Document prompt. It is here that you give the file a name. This line will already contain the letter of the drive and the name of the subdirectory that you set as the default in Chapter 1. You can override the default by simply typing in a new drive and subdirectory (if you use them) followed by the file name. In Figure 2.16, you see an example in which the default drive is C: and the subdirectories are \qa\files\. The cursor is located after the last backslash. It is here that you would type in the file name.

File names must be unique and must obey the DOS naming conventions. This means that your file name must not be longer than eight characters. Do not use spaces in file names. You may also add a three-letter extension to a file name. It should come after the eighth (or last) character and be separated by a period. Q&A Write does not give automatic file name extensions to document files.

For this sample document, you will enter a file name that describes the content in abbreviated form, lists the revision, and uses a file extension describing its type. Because the content describes the benefits of word processing in the office, you can call it *wpbene*. It is the first draft, so you can add the number *1* to it. For a file extension,

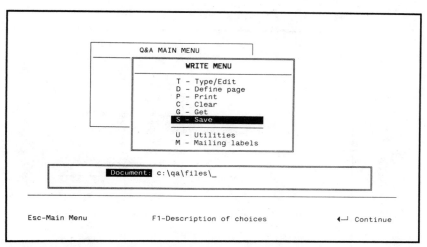

*Figure 2.16:* Saving the sample document on disk

you can add the abbreviation .*rpt* to list it as a report. Now, enter the complete file name:

**wpbene1.rpt**

Press Return to save the file on disk. You will then see the word "Saving" flashing for a few seconds to let you know that Q&A is busy saving an exact copy of your document on your data disk. As you are editing a document, you can save the new text and any changes as often as you like from within Type/Edit. To see how this works, press Return, since Type/Edit is already highlighted, to go back to the document. Now press Shift-F8 to save the document a second time (this command is listed at the bottom of your screen).

Figure 2.17 shows you the screen at this point. This time, Q&A suggests that the document be saved under the name you originally gave the file after the "Save as" prompt. In this case, it lists the file name WPBENE1.RPT. Because you do not wish to change the file name, you simply press Return to save it again. If you had made any further edits since you saved the document the first time, these would then be saved on disk. When you want to change a file name, you simply move the cursor to the beginning of the file name and type in a new name, which results in two differently-named files containing the same document.

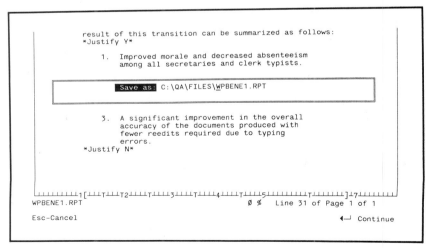

*Figure 2.17:* Saving the document in Type/Edit

You can use this technique effectively to keep disk files containing earlier versions of the same document for reference. For instance, let's say you had already worked ahead and typed in the rest of the text in the report and were now ready to save this more complete version of the document to disk. You would press Shift-F8 and, instead of accepting the name WPBENE1.PRT by pressing Return, you would change the name to WPBENE2.RPT. You would then have two files on disk, WPBENE1.RPT and WPBENE2.RPT, containing different versions of this report.

## ADVANCED EDITING FEATURES

Many advanced editing features are included in Q&A Write. Chief among these are block operations, headers and footers, page breaks, soft hyphens, search-and-replace, and calculate. Q&A also offers you an on-screen line and box drawing capability that is very easy to use. This feature makes creating forms for the office both efficient and enjoyable.

To gain practice in using these features, you will have to add some more text to your word processing report. The rest of the text you will need to enter is shown in Figure 2.18, and the formatting settings you will use are shown in Figure 2.19. Go ahead and enter the text now if

```
The Departments and Personnel Affected

     The five departments involved in this transition to word
processing are: Personnel, Accounting, Marketing and Sales,
Engineering, and Research and Development.  Each department has
assigned to it a different number of secretaries and clerk
typists responsible for producing all required written documents.
The total number affected is 27.  Table 1 gives their breakdown
by department:


                              Table 1


                        No. of               No. of
          Department      Secretaries          Clerk Typists

          Personnel           2                   5

          Accounting          1                   2

          Marketing &         3                   6
          Sales
```

*Figure 2.18:* Text of the sample document

```
        Engineering          2               4

        R&D                  1               2

Computers, Printers, and Software

     The computers purchased numbered 25 and were all IBM PCs and
XTs.  All secretaries were equiped with their own IBM XT with a
10 MB hard disk and 640K RAM.  The remaining 16 computers
purchased for the clerk typists were IBM PCs with two disk drives
and 512K RAM.  These machines are shared among the 18 clerk
typists.
     The printers purchased are of two types:  Epson FX/100
dot-matrix printers and IBM Quietwriter letter-quality printers.
From a total of 25 printers, five are letter quality and 10 are
dot matrix.  Each department is equipped with its own letter-
quality printer attached to the senior secretary's computer.
     The software purchased consists of WordStar 2000 and Q&A, an
integrated program offering a word processing, mail merge, and
data file management.  Five units of WordStar 2000 were purchased
along with 20 units of Q&A.

Background of the People

     The word processing background of the personnel affected by
this transition varied greatly.  A questionnaire polling their
experience and comfort level with computers and word processing
was sent to all.  A copy of this questionnaire is included in
Appendix A of this report.  From this, it was determined that
over 75% of our staff had no prior experience with computer
technology or word processing. Of the other 25%, only 2 people
had any extensive experience with either.  Both of these are in
the Research and Development department.  Interestingly, all
polled showed a great willingness to make the transition from
secretary to word processing operator.

Training

     All personnel affected by this transition were given 28
hours of computer and software-specific training. Eight hours
were alloted to an introduction to the IBM PC and DOS. Eight
hours were alloted to WordStar 2000 training and 12 hours were
devoted to Q&A.  All training was conducted by an independent
training center at their facility.
```

*Figure 2.18:* Text of the sample document (continued)

you plan to do the exercises that accompany the discussion of these editing features. Don't bother to correct any spelling errors you come across in the text (especially *equiped*), because they are there to provide you with practice in using Q&A's spelling checker later on.

To enter the table, you will want to add new tab settings in columns 29, 34, 49, and 53, as shown in Figure 2.19. You may delete the other existing tabs beyond the first one in column 14 if you wish. Remember, to modify tabs, you press F8, type **s**, and press Return. Then move the cursor to the column where you want to add a new

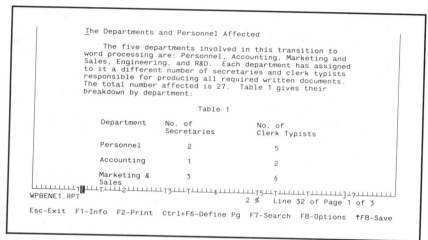

*Figure 2.19:* Tab settings for the sample document

tab and type **t** at each position. To delete an existing tab, you can use the space bar or the Del key to blank it out. Center the title, *Table 1*, by pressing F8, typing **c** and then pressing Return.

Press Return after entering each line of the table, because you do not want the lines of the table to wrap, as with a regular paragraph of text. As soon as you enter the figures for the Engineering department, your cursor will automatically move to the beginning of a new page. Note that Q&A uses a double line to indicate a page break on the screen. After you enter enough text to see the page break line, look at the status line. It will indicate that you are on the first line of Page 2.

When you have finished entering all of the text, save the document again under the same name by pressing Shift-F8 and pressing Return. Then move the cursor to the beginning of the document by pressing Ctrl-PgUp until the cursor is on Line 1 and Page 1.

## BLOCK OPERATIONS

There are many block operations that you can do with Q&A Write. You can copy or move a block of text within a document or copy or move a block of text to a new document. All of these operations require that you first define the limits of the block before you carry out the operation. You do this by highlighting with the cursor all of the text to be included.

You already did this kind of selection when you boldfaced the word *yesterday* in your document. You can use the same methods for quickly extending the highlighting as listed near the end of the section on using print enhancements. In addition, you can enlarge the highlighted area in increasingly larger steps by pressing the function key or keys a number of successive times.

For instance, if you press F5 (to start the copy operation) a second time, Q&A highlights the word containing the cursor. If you press it again, the entire sentence is highlighted. The fourth time you press F5, it selects the entire paragraph, the fifth time the entire page, and the sixth time the whole document. This method works the same way for all of the block operations. You can think of the F5 function key as the block operations key in Q&A Write. To copy a block in a document, you press F5 alone. To move a block, you press Shift-F5. To copy a block to a new document file, you press Ctrl-F5, and to move a block to a new document, you press Alt-F5.

***USING THE BLOCK MOVE*** To see how a block operation works in practice, you will move the two paragraphs under the heading *Background of the People* from their present position in the document to a position immediately before the section *Computers, Printers, and Software*.

1. Press the PgDn key to scroll through the document until you locate the heading *Background of the People* (as shown in Figure 2.20).

2. Press Shift-F5 to begin the block move operation. You will then receive the message shown in Figure 2.20 telling you to select the text to move.

3. Press ↓ until you have extended the highlighting to include all of the lines down to line 37. Then press the End key to extend the highlighting to the end of this line.

4. Press F10 to confirm this block. Press PgUp and then use ↑ to position the cursor at the beginning of the heading *Computers, Printers, and Software*.

5. Make sure the cursor is located in the first column on the *C* of *Computers*, and then press F10 to move the selected block to this position in the document.

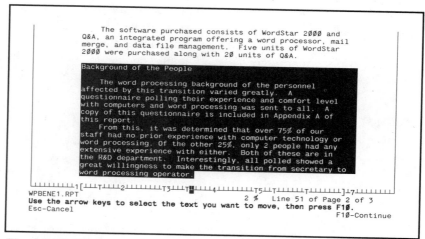

The software purchased consists of WordStar 2000 and
Q&A, an integrated program offering a word processor, mail
merge, and data file management.  Five units of WordStar
2000 were purchased along with 20 units of Q&A.

Background of the People

    The word processing background of the personnel
affected by this transition varied greatly.  A
questionnaire polling their experience and comfort level
with computers and word processing was sent to all.  A
copy of this questionnaire is included in Appendix A of
this report.
    From this, it was determined that over 75% of our
staff had no prior experience with computer technology or
word processing. Of the other 25%, only 2 people had any
extensive experience with either.  Both of these are in
the R&D department.  Interestingly, all polled showed a
great willingness to make the transition from secretary to
word processing operator.

WPBENE1.RPT
                                        2 %    Line 51 of Page 2 of 3
**Use the arrow keys to select the text you want to move, then press F10.**
Esc-Cancel
                                                        F10-Continue

*Figure 2.20:* Marking a block of text for copying

6. Press ↓ to move the cursor to the repositioned heading *Computers, Printers, and Software.* Turn on insert mode if necessary and press Return to add a blank line between the heading and the preceding paragraph.

7. Press the PgDn key and locate the heading *Training.* See that there are now two blank lines between the last line of the preceding paragraph and this heading. Move the cursor to one of them and press Shift-F4 to delete the extra blank line.

**COPYING BLOCKS**   If you had wanted to copy this block of text rather than move it in the document, you would have used the same procedure. The only difference would have been in the way you issued the command. To copy a block, you press F5 instead of Shift-F5.

**COPYING A BLOCK TO A NEW DOCUMENT**   To copy a block of text to a separate document, you use Ctrl-F5 to start the operation. Practice this block operation by making a copy of *Table 1* and saving it in a new file:

1. Press the PgUp key a few times to move to the table. Then press ↑ until you have positioned the cursor on the line containing the title, *Table 1.*

2. Press Ctrl-F5 to start the block copy operation. Press ↓ or Return until all of the table is highlighted on the screen.

3. Press F10 to confirm the block. You will receive the prompt "Copy to what document?". Type the name of the new file as **table1** and press Return. You will see the flashing message "Copying . . ." on the screen.

If you wish to see this new document to verify that it contains a copy of Table 1, save WPBENE1.RPT again before exiting Type/ Edit. Remember that you have not yet saved the block move you made earlier. This time, save the new version under a different name, WPBENE2.RPT. To do this, press Shift-F8, move the cursor to the 1, and type **2** in its place. Then press Return. You now have the two versions of the document saved as separate files.

After saving the document, press Esc and then type **g**. Enter the filename as **table1** and press Return. You will see an exact copy of Table 1 at the beginning of this document. To return to editing your word processing report, press Esc, type **g**, enter **wpbene2.rpt**, and press Return.

***INSERTING A BLOCK FROM ANOTHER DOCUMENT*** Now that Table 1 is stored as a separate document, you can easily insert it into any other document where it might be needed, thus eliminating the need to retype it. To do this, you would open your document and first locate the cursor at the place in the text where you want to insert a copy of Table 1. Then you would press F8 and select the Insert Document option by typing **i** and pressing Return. Q&A would then ask for the file name, at which point you would type **table1** and press Return. A copy of Table 1 would then be inserted at the cursor's position.

This technique is very useful when you deal with standard paragraphs of text that you need to incorporate into many different documents on a regular basis. Save each paragraph in a separate file and then use the Insert Document option to insert it wherever you need it.

***DELETING BLOCKS OF TEXT*** To delete a block of text, you press F3 and then highlight the block. Once you press F10, the block is erased. You can restore it again by pressing Shift-F7. You can use this delete and restore procedure as an alternate way of moving text in your document. Once you have deleted your block as described above, move the cursor to the place where you want the text to be moved and then press Shift-F7 to have it restored in this new position in the document.

## ADDING HEADERS, FOOTERS, AND PAGE BREAKS

The word processing report you are creating could use a header and footer to identify each printed page. Headers are headings that are printed on each page in the top margin of the document. Footers are headings that are printed on each page in the bottom margin. You can add page numbers that are automatically numbered by Q&A Write in either a header or footer of the document. For this report, you will have the page numbers appear at the bottom of the page in a footer.

Headers and footers in Q&A can consist of more than one line. They cannot, however, be longer than the number of lines specified for the top and bottom margins. If you need to, you can make these margins bigger on the Define Page screen. As you have seen on this menu, you can also have the header or footer begin printing on a page other than the first, or begin the page numbering with a number other than one.

This latter option is very useful when you must chain-print documents stored in separate files, each containing a successive section of the same report. After final editing is complete on one section or file, use this option on the Define Page screen to set a new beginning page number for the next document to be printed. Set this to begin with the next number higher than the number displayed in the header or footer on the last page of the previous document.

**ADDING A HEADER TO THE DOCUMENT**   You will now add a header to your word processing document that identifies the document's subject matter.

1. Go to the top of the document by pressing Ctrl-Home. Then press F8, type **h**, and press Return to edit a header.

2. The cursor moves up to the beginning of the first line in the top margin area now demarcated by a double line. Press Return twice to start the header down two lines.

3. Type **The Transition to Word Processing**. Press F8, type **c**, and press Return to center the header on the line.

4. Press F10 to end editing the header. The cursor returns to its original position in the document.

The header *The Transition to Word Processing* is now visible on the screen in the top margin. Q&A always displays your headers and footers on the screen as they will be printed.

Before you go on and add a footer, delete the centered heading *The Benefits of Word Processing*. To do this, make sure that the cursor is on line 1 of the document and then press Shift-F4. Replace this heading by entering **History** in the first line. Do not bother to indent it, but do add a new blank line to separate it from the text in the first paragraph. Remember that you must be in insert mode to add a new blank line when you press Return.

***ADDING A FOOTER TO THE DOCUMENT*** You will now add a footer that will contain the page number centered at the bottom of the page. To do this:

1. Press F8, type **f**, and press Return. The cursor moves down to the first line of the bottom margin demarcated by a double line on the screen.

2. Press Return twice to skip two lines. Type **Page #** to enter the page number. (The symbol # will be replaced by the appropriate number.)

3. Press F10 to finish editing the footer. The cursor then returns to its original position in the document.

To see your footer, press PgDn until you can see the bottom margin on the screen (as shown in Figure 2.21). Notice that in place of the pound symbol (#) you entered, Q&A now displays Page 1. You can also see your header at the top of the second page that is now in view.

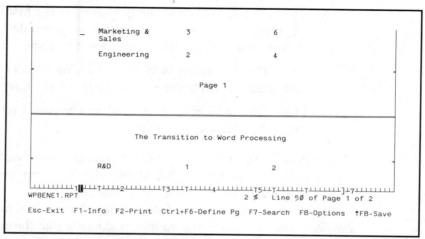

```
         Marketing &        3              6
         Sales
         Engineering        2              4


                           Page 1



         ─────────────────────────────────────────────

                   The Transition to Word Processing


         R&D                1              2

   1        2        3        4        5        7
WPBENE1.RPT                              2 %   Line 5Ø of Page 1 of 2
Esc-Exit  F1-Info  F2-Print  Ctrl+F6-Define Pg  F7-Search  F8-Options  ↑F8-Save
```

***Figure 2.21:*** Header and footer in sample document

You can edit the content or format of the headers and footers you add to a document, or even delete them entirely, by using the same options you used to create them. For example, to delete a single-line header you would press F8, type **h**, and press Return. Then you would move the cursor to the line containing the text, press Shift-F4, and press F10 to return to the body of your document.

**ADDING PAGE BREAKS TO THE DOCUMENT**  Table 1 in this document will not be printed all on one page as the document is now paginated. To rectify this, you must add a page break at the start of the table.

1. Press ↑ until the cursor is positioned on the line containing the centered heading *Table 1*.

2. With the cursor anywhere on this line, press F8, type **n** (for *Newpage*) and press Return.

3. The screen display will change so that the first part of Table 1 is repositioned below the on-screen page break and now appears at the beginning of Page 2.

Notice the double-line right corner symbol that now appears below the last line of the paragraph ending with "Table 1 gives their breakdown by department:''. This is there to let you know that the page break that follows it was user-defined.

As you experienced when you originally entered this table, Q&A Write automatically pages the document as you are typing. The program supplies a page break whenever it calculates that a sufficient number of lines have been entered (54 in this case), according to the size of the top and bottom margins and lines-per-page setting. When you override this paging system as you did here, your page will be short by the number of lines placed on the following page. If you ever need to delete a page break that you have defined, you simply move the cursor to the corner symbol and erase it with the Del key.

Press Ctrl-PgDn (to take you to the first line of the next page) and examine what effect putting the entire table on Page 2 has had on the rest of the paging of your document. Now the heading *Training* is split off from its paragraph description beginning on Page 3. In word processing terminology, *Training* is referred to as an *orphan* because it is a single line separated from the text it accompanies by the page break. This will often happen to the first or last line in a paragraph.

To take care of the orphan in your document, you can add a page break on the line containing the heading *Training*. Use the ↑ key to move the cursor on this line (the cursor can be located anywhere on it) and press F8 to access the Options menu. Type **n** and press Return (or just type **7**). The heading is now rejoined with its paragraph as the start of Page 3. You will see the user-defined page break symbol located on its own line below the last paragraph on Page 2.

## *SOFT HYPHENS*

Q&A allows you to add soft hyphens to your documents. They are called soft hyphens because if your margins change or you reformat your paragraph and the hyphenated word is no longer at the end of the line, Q&A will automatically remove the hyphen. If you use soft hyphens, you will prevent long words at the end of lines from wrapping to the next line and leaving a large empty space.

***USING SOFT HYPHENS IN YOUR DOCUMENT*** To see how soft hyphenation works, you will hyphenate the word *purchased* in the second paragraph of your document.

1. Press ↓ until the cursor is on the word *purchased* in the second paragraph.

2. Now press → three times until the cursor is positioned on the letter *c*. This is where you want to insert the hyphen.

3. Press Alt-F6 to insert a soft hyphen. Notice that *pur-* automatically moves to the previous line and that the paragraph is reformatted accordingly.

Q&A will always remember that you want this word hyphenated instead of wrapping it to the next line and causing an empty space. So, even though in the course of editing the word may no longer require hyphenation, the hyphen will reappear automatically when necessary.

## SEARCH-AND-REPLACE

Q&A's Search-and-Replace feature makes it easy to locate specific text within a document. You can use it to replace words or phrases, to locate a particular area in the document that you have marked for revision, or even to locate patterns like telephone and social security numbers.

Q&A Write has two levels of search-and-replace: simple and advanced. Simple search allows you to search for text and does not distinguish between case differences when searching for a specific word or phrase. In other words, if you want to locate the word *Transition*, you can enter it as **transition**, **TRANSITION**, **Transition**, or any other combination of upper- and lowercase letters. If you want to distinguish between upper- and lowercase in the search, the advanced search level gives you this option.

Searches can include what are known as *wildcard characters*. This is handy when you don't remember the exact spelling or when you want to locate groups of words that are all spelled slightly differently. There are two kinds of wildcards: the question mark (?), which stands for a single character, and two periods (..), which stand for an indeterminate number of characters. A great number of possible combinations can be generated, as shown in Table 2.3.

*Table 2.3:* Q&A searches with wildcard characters

| YOU ENTER: | Q&A LOCATES: | EXAMPLES: |
|---|---|---|
| a? | A two-letter word beginning with *a* | At, an, as, etc. |
| a?? | A three-letter word beginning with *a* | and, All, etc. |
| a.. | Any word beginning with *a* | A, as, all, another, etc. |
| ?s | A two-letter word ending in *s* | is, as, us |
| ???s | A four-letter word ending in *s* | Less, mass, hers, etc. |
| ..s | Any word ending in *s* | is, Let's, famous, etc. |
| ?s.. | Any word with *s* as its second letter | us, assume, isn't, etc. |
| ..s? | Any word with *s* as its second to last letter | ask, last, amass, etc. |
| a..s | Any word beginning with *a* and ending in *s* | As, arises, amounts, etc. |
| a.. s.. | Any phrase in which the first word begins with *a* and the second word begins with *s* | As shown, a sample, any such, etc. |

When using the Replace feature, you have the option of giving approval for replacement on a case-by-case basis (Manual), having Q&A replace all occurrences and show you each replacement without your approval (Automatic), or have Q&A replace all occurrences and not show you while it's being done (Fast Automatic).

Whenever entering a replacement, Q&A is case-sensitive. It will replace the word or phrase entered exactly as it is typed after the Replace prompt. You can use one type of wildcard character when doing replacements. The double-period global character (..) can be used to completely remove the word or phrase searched for.

**USING SEARCH-AND-REPLACE IN THE DOCUMENT**   To
practice using the Search-and-Replace feature, you will locate the
occurrences of *R&D* in the document and replace them with *Research
and Development* on a case-by-case basis.

1. Locate the cursor at the beginning of the document by pressing Ctrl-PgUp. Begin the search-and-replace operation by
   pressing F7.

2. You will see the Search-and-Replace screen as shown in Figure 2.22. The cursor will be positioned after the prompt
   "Search for:". Type **R&D** (or **r&d**) and press Return.

3. Type the replacement string **Research and Development**
   (exactly as shown) and press Return. All Q&A editing functions are available if you need to correct typing errors.

4. Accept the default, Manual, for manual replacement by
   pressing F10 to begin the search-and-replace.

The first occurrence of *R&D* is located on Line 35 of Page 1. The
entire word is highlighted on the screen. At the bottom of the screen
(shown in Figure 2.23), Q&A gives you both the message indicating
that it has found your search string and information on how you may
proceed. To have this occurrence replaced, you press F10. To go on

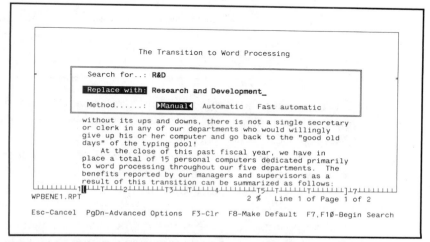

*Figure 2.22:* Search-and-Replace screen

to locate the next occurrence without replacing this one, you press F7. If you want to abort the search-and-replace operation at this point, you press Esc.

5. Press F10 to replace this occurrence. Q&A will then make the replacement, re-form the margins, and display a new message telling you that the occurrence has been replaced and to press F7 if you wish to continue the search.

6. Press F7 at this point to continue.

The second occurrence is in Table 1. If you replace *R&D* here, you will disturb the layout of the table.

7. Press F7 to bypass this replacement and continue the search.

8. The third occurrence in the second paragraph under *Background of the People* should be changed, so press F10 here.

Q&A will then continue its search to the end of the document, display the message that the search-and-replace is completed, and return the cursor to its original position in the document.

Try another search-and-replace in the document. This time, locate the number *15* and replace it with *25*. There is a discrepancy in your document as to the stated number of computers involved in word processing.

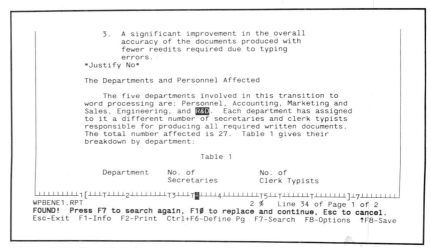

*Figure 2.23:* Locating the first occurrence of the search string

1. To rectify it, press F7. See that the previous search string, *R&D*, is still displayed.

2. Type **15** over it and then blank out the final letter by pressing either Del or the space bar.

3. Press Return and then type **25** for the replacement string.

4. Press Return again and accept the Manual option by pressing F10.

5. Press F10 again to replace the first (and only) occurrence that Q&A locates. Then press Esc to abort the operation.

You can experiment with using wildcard characters to locate various words and phrases in this document. For instance, locate the occurrences of *Personnel* in the document by typing the search string as **p..l** and pressing Return. Do not type anything after the "Replace with:" prompt, just press Return. Begin a case-by-case search by pressing F10.

Whenever you do not give a replacement, Q&A does only a Search operation. As before, you have the options to continue by pressing F7 or to abandon the search at any time by pressing Esc. After you are finished, save this document again by pressing Shift-F8 and Return.

***USING THE ADVANCED SEARCH LEVEL***   To use the advanced level of Search-and-Replace, you will locate all the words in your document which end in the letters *ed*. You don't want to replace them here, since doing so would incorrectly change the content of the document. You could, however, use this feature to change tense in one of your own documents.

1. Place the cursor at the beginning of the document by pressing Ctrl-Home. Begin the search-and-replace operation by pressing F7. You will see the Search-and-Replace screen appear.

2. Now press PgDn to expand to the Advanced Search-and-Replace screen as shown in Figure 2.24.

3. The cursor will be positioned after the prompt "Search for:". Type **ed** and press Return.

4. Type the replacement string **ing** and press Return.

5. Accept the default, Manual, since you don't really want to change from past tense in your document.

6. Now change the Type of search to Text instead of Whole Words by pressing the → once.

7. Press F10 to begin the search-and-replace. The first occurrence of a word containing the text *ed* is the word *replaced* in the first sentence.

8. Press F7 to search again and leave the word as is. Next, Q&A finds the word *dedicated*. As you can see, the search-and-replace function is now locating any word that contains the text string *ed*, regardless of whether it is a whole word or not.

9. Press Esc to cancel the search-and-replace.

The advanced level search box also has an option to make the search case-sensitive, which will allow you to change text from upper- to lowercase and vice versa. Occasionally search-and-replace functions are used to count the number of words in a document; however, Q&A has a built-in function key assignment which will give you this information.

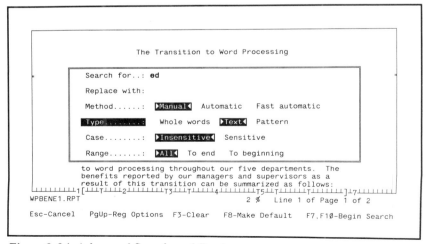

*Figure 2.24:* Advanced Search-and-Replace

The Document Statistics key is Ctrl-F3, and it can be used anywhere within your document. To view the statistics in your document, try the following:

1. Press Ctrl-Home to position the cursor at the beginning of the document.

2. Now press Ctrl-F3. A box containing the statistics will appear as shown in Figure 2.25. The statistics include the number of words, lines, and paragraphs both before and after the cursor, as well as the totals for the entire document.

## LINE AND BOX DRAWING

Q&A Write offers you an amazingly easy way to draw lines and boxes in your documents by using IBM's graphics characters. Once you access Q&A's Draw option, you use the keys on the cursor pad to draw lines wherever you want them to appear on the page. You must be a little careful when drawing, because it is easy to draw over existing text in overtype mode. In insert mode, you must be even more careful when drawing on a line containing text. Inserting new graphics characters can end up destroying the format of text on that and succeeding lines. As a general rule, take Q&A Write out of insert mode before you begin using its Draw option.

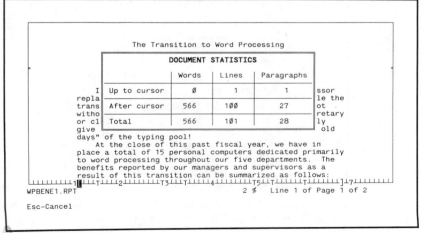

*Figure 2.25:* Document Statistics

Unfortunately, not all printers are able to print the graphics characters as they appear on the screen in a document. None of the letter-quality printers are capable of producing these effects, nor are all of the dot-matrix printers. Some of the older Epson models and their clones will not correctly print any of the graphics characters. With some printers, you cannot get the corners of your boxes to print, although straight lines will print as shown. Q&A allows you to create double-line drawings by shifting the cursor key in draw mode. Though this works fine on the screen, even those printers that have no trouble with single-line graphics cannot print the double-line variety as displayed. In such a case, all double-line characters are printed as single lines.

Experiment with your printer's capabilities by doing the following exercise, which draws a box around Table 1 in your document and separates the headings from the data with vertical lines. This effect is shown in Figure 2.26. To create it:

1. Move the cursor to the top of Page 2. Turn on insert mode (if off) by pressing Ins; press Return to move the entire table down a line. Press Ins again to take Q&A out of insert mode.

2. Press F8 and type **d** (for *Draw* ). Press Return (or type **8**). Press and hold down → to draw a horizontal line above *Table 1*. Continue to hold down → until you reach column 68 containing the right margin.

3. Press and hold down ↓ to draw a vertical line down the right side of the table. Keep the key depressed until you reach Line 17 below the last line of data in the table.

4. Press and hold down ← to draw a horizontal line from column 68 to column 10 containing the left margin.

5. Press and hold down ↑ to draw a vertical line up the left side of the table. Keep the key depressed until you reach Line 1 containing the first horizontal line you drew.

6. Press ↓ until you reach Line 3. Then press and hold down → to draw a horizontal line beneath the title, *Table 1*. Keep the key depressed until you reach column 68 and connect the line to the right side of the box.

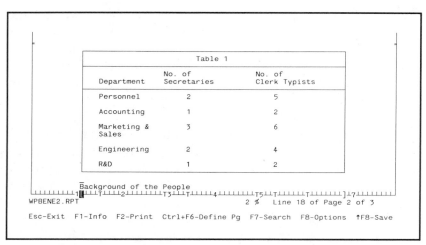

*Figure 2.26:* Line and box drawing

7. Press ↓ again until you reach Line 6. Then press and hold down ← to draw a horizontal line below the headings and above the first line of data. Keep the key depressed until you reach column 10 and connect the line with the left side of the box.

8. Press Esc to take Q&A out of draw mode.

9. Move the cursor to line 5 and position it exactly under the *D* in the word *Department*. Retype it here just as it appears above. Then move the cursor up to line 4 to the *D* in the word *Department* and delete it by spacing over it (press the space bar 10 times).

Pressing F8 again after you are already in draw mode allows you to erase any lines you drew by mistake. Once you press F8, movements made with the cursor keys will erase any graphics characters in the cursor's path. To get back to drawing, you merely press F8 again. You'll try printing this box at the end of the chapter.

In addition to drawing straight lines as you did here, you can draw diagonal lines by using the keys at the four corners of your cursor pad. Home draws a diagonal up to the left, PgUp up to the right, PgDn down to the right, and End down to the left.

You can use line and box drawing when creating screen entry forms for your database files. You will get more practice with using draw mode when you get to the section on designing input forms in the next chapter.

## SPELL-CHECKING DOCUMENTS

Using a spelling checker program to check your document for typographical errors and spelling mistakes is a mixed blessing. While it is easy to overlook an obvious mistake on the screen, having the spelling checker find errors for you seldom involves just locating bona fide spelling errors and typos. Spelling checkers, whatever the size of their dictionaries (Q&A's contains 100,000 entries), do not include proper nouns, which usually populate your document.

This means that you must take the time to tell the spelling checker to ignore all of the personal, corporate, and product names that you use in correspondence on reports. While you would probably end up adding to the dictionary the name of your company and all of the products you are involved with, this is just not practical for all of the proper names you are likely to use intermittently.

If you have a two-drive system, using Q&A's spelling checker means having to deal with even more disk swapping (you have already experienced a great deal of this just in using Q&A Write). To stop and have the program check a single word means having to replace the installation disk with the spell disk. Once you have finished checking the word, you then have to replace the spell disk with the program disk. Given the trouble, chances are that you will use the spelling checker program only to check entire documents once they are completely finished.

On a hard disk system, this is not a problem. Q&A can call up the spelling program and check the dictionary without requiring any disk swapping. This makes its feature for checking just the word at the cursor practical. Despite the drawbacks, Q&A's spelling checker does provide a means for you to be confident that the documents you produce will not be littered with unsightly typos and unnoticed transpositions. To check the spelling of just a single word, you locate the cursor somewhere within the word and press Ctrl-F1. To spell-check the whole document, you take the cursor to the beginning and press Shift-F1.

. Before you go on and print the final version of your sample document, you should use the spelling checker to make sure it is free from any spelling errors.

1. First, take the cursor to the beginning of the document by pressing Ctrl-Home.

2. Then press Shift-F1 to start (you will have to replace your program disk with the spell disk if you have two floppy drives).

If you entered the document exactly as shown without any unplanned typos, the first word it should flag will be *equiped*, which was purposely misspelled, and your screen should look like Figure 2.27.

There you can see that *equiped* is highlighted and that Q&A gives you five options on how to proceed. You can check its dictionary listing for possible spellings, ignore the word and go on, add the word to the dictionary and go on, add the word to the dictionary and stop the operation, or edit the word and then recheck its spelling.

3. Choose the default, List possible spellings, by pressing Return. You will then see the possibilities as displayed in Figure 2.28.

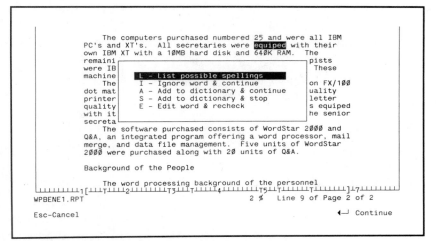

*Figure 2.27:* Spell-checking the sample document

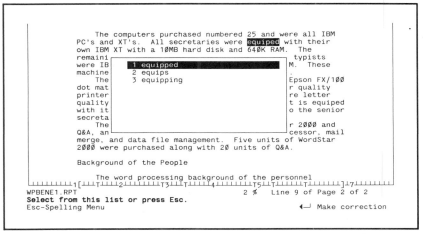

*Figure 2.28:* Q&A's suggested spellings

    4. Q&A's spelling checker lists the correct spelling as the first option. Because the word is already highlighted, press Return to have Q&A make the replacement.

The second word flagged is *MB*. The abbreviation for *megabyte* is not in Q&A's dictionary. If you plan to create a lot of computer-oriented documents, you might want to add it to the dictionary.

    5. At this point, move the cursor down to "Ignore word & continue" and press Return.

    6. Next, *FX* is flagged as misspelled. Continue to choose the same option to ignore and go on. Do the same as the spelling checker finds the brand name *Quietwriter*.

The next word flagged by the spelling checker should be *alloted*, which was also purposely misspelled.

    7. This time, press Return to check the possible spellings. The fourth one on the list is *allotted*, which is the correct spelling.

    8. Press the ↓ three times until the correct spelling is highlighted, and press Return to have Q&A make the replacement.

After you have finished checking your document, save it again to store the latest revisions on disk by pressing Shift-F8 and Return.

# PRINTING DOCUMENTS

You can access the command to print your document from within Type/Edit by pressing F2, or escape back to the Q&A Write Menu and access it by typing **p** and pressing Return. Either way, once you give this command, you will be presented with the Print Options Menu as shown in Figure 2.29. Because you are currently in the document you want to print, press F2 now to get to this screen.

## Q&A WRITE'S PRINT OPTIONS

The first line of information controls how much of the document is to be printed. In this case, the entire document from Page 1 to Page 3 is listed as the default. If you want to do selective printing in the document, you indicate both the starting and ending page numbers here. As you can see on the second line of this screen, you can also have Q&A print multiple copies of a document. The default value for copies is always 1.

To the right of Number of copies is Print offset. Print offset has a default value of 0. You will change it only if you need to adjust the position of the printhead before it begins to indent for your left margin. Most of the time you will adjust this manually. You can enter a positive number which will adjust where it begins to the right. Remember, the

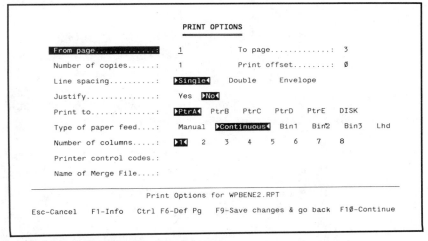

*Figure 2.29:* The Print Options Menu

left margin setting already controls how many spaces the printhead will move right from the left edge of the paper before printing.

The third line of the Print Options screen highlights the line spacing default of Single. To change this to double spacing, you would use → to move the highlight to Double. The third option here, Envelope, is used with letters to have Q&A automatically print the address found in the letter on an envelope. You will learn how to use this option in Chapter 8. The next print option, Justify, controls right justification of the entire document. As it stands, you want to leave the highlight on No. That way Q&A will only justify those paragraphs in the document that are indicated by the embedded justify commands. The rest of the document will be printed with ragged-right margins.

The Print to option listed on the fifth line of the screen allows you to change the printer and subsequently the associated port to be used. Remember, in Chapter 1 you not only chose your printer from a list but you also associated it with a particular printer port. At that time, we indicated that you could have several printers installed, even assigned to the same port. Here, you indicate which printer you want to use. If you have two printers installed as PrtA and PrtB—a dot-matrix and letter-quality printer, for example—you could print rough drafts by using PrtA and then print a final copy by changing this to PrtB. For now, use PrtA to print this first copy of your document.

You use the final option on this line, Disk, to make a copy of your document in ASCII code for use with other word processors or with other types of programs. This option does not use your printer at all. It merely translates your document into ASCII code and saves it in a new disk file. You will learn about the uses of this method in Chapter 4 in the section on exporting files.

The following option, Type of paper feed, is used to choose between continuous-feed paper, single sheets, and additional bins on your printer. If your printer has a tractor feed and you are using fan-folded continuous-feed paper, leave the highlight on Continuous. If you have only a friction feed and use single sheets, use the ← key to move this highlight to Manual.

You can also have the printer pause at a particular place in the document by inserting a **\*STOP\*** embedded code in the document itself. Just as with other embedded codes, you should place it on its own line in the document. Whenever the program encounters this embedded code, it will pause the printing until you press the Return key. During this pause, you can change the wheel or ribbon on your printer or make any other kind of manual adjustment you need to.

You only need to use the Bin1, Bin2, Bin3, or Lhd (letterhead) options if your printer has additional bins used for feeding multiple sheets of paper. The Number of columns option allows you to reformat your document into columns at print time. This change to the number of columns cannot be seen on the screen in Type/Edit.

The Printer control codes option allows you to enter special printer codes that affect the entire document. You enter these codes in their ASCII equivalents, just as you practiced earlier in this chapter in the section on using embedded printer codes. The only difference is that here you neither preface the code numbers with an asterisk and the word *Printer* nor terminate the command with a second asterisk as you would when embedding commands within the body of the document. For example, if you use an older Epson dot-matrix printer like the MX-80 or MX-100, you turn on italics with Esc-4 and turn them off with Esc-5. To print the document all in italics with this type of printer, you would enter the numbers **27 52** after this prompt. Remember that all codes, including Esc, must be expressed in ASCII code numbers. Refer to the ASCII chart in Appendix D and your printer manual when experimenting with using this option.

The last option on the Print Options screen is used only when you are using Q&A's merge print feature to print out form letters or reports. You give the name of the Q&A database file that will supply the data to be merged into each letter or report to be printed. You will learn all about this feature in Chapter 8.

## PRINTING OUT YOUR PRACTICE DOCUMENT

Check over the values listed on this screen and make sure they are correct. You can use ↑ to move up to a prior option if you see something that is still not set correctly. As soon as you are satisfied that you have set up all the options to work with your printer, make sure your printer is turned on and that you have sufficient paper. Then press F10 to begin printing. As soon as Q&A finishes printing, it will return you to the document, because you issued this command from within Type/Edit.

If you ever need to abort a printing job, just press Esc one time. Printing will be suspended as soon as your printer buffer is emptied of the last characters sent by Q&A just before you pressed Esc. You will then be presented with a menu that allows you to cancel the printing completely or continue. As Q&A prints, it lets you know the status of the print job by keeping you informed of its progress in terms of the page and line number. If, once Q&A starts printing, you find that something you set on the Print Options screen is not right, press F2 to abort the print job and return immediately to the print options. You can change the necessary values and then press F10 to begin printing again.

Examine your printout carefully. On Page 1, did both the header and footer print correctly? Did your printer boldface the word *yesterday* in the first paragraph? Is the list containing the three benefits correctly indented on both the left and right sides and is it right-justified? Did justification turn off in the following paragraph?

Next, examine Page 2. How did your printer do with printing the box around Table 1? Is the pagination correct with Table 1 at the top of Page 2 and the Training section at the top of Page 3?

If you experienced any problems, go through the document and make sure that you have entered everything exactly as described. If *yesterday* was not boldfaced, move the cursor to it and examine the status line. Make sure that it indicates BOLD. If some other print enhancement is listed here, return the text to normal by pressing F8, typing **r**, and selecting the text with the space bar. Then repeat the procedure to embolden again. If you are having trouble with right justification, examine your embedded codes. Make sure they begin and end with asterisks (*) and that Justify Yes and Justify No are spelled as two words.

If your box did not print correctly, you will probably have to remove it. Your printer is not capable of supporting the IBM graphics characters. To erase the box, you can use draw mode as an eraser. Press F8, type **d**, press Return, and then press F8 a second time. Now, trace over the box with the arrow keys and then press Esc. If you had pagination problems, check to see that your page breaks are marked with the double-line corner.

If the printing problems persist, you should go back to the Utilities Menu and choose the Install printer option. Then experiment with installing a different printer that might work like yours. Return to the Q&A Write Menu and try printing the sample document again with the newly installed printer setup.

# MANAGING
# YOUR DOCUMENT FILES

As you create more and more of your own document files with Q&A Write, there will come times when you need to do some disk housekeeping. Q&A Write provides you with three useful utilities that allow you to copy your document files between disks, delete unneeded files, or rename files. These are found on the submenu Write Utilities. To get to this menu, press Esc to get back to the Write Menu and then type **u** and press Return (or type **7**).

## COPYING A DOCUMENT FILE

Most often you will use the Copy a document option to make backup copies of all your document files. Using Q&A's Copy a document option is easier than having to make copies from the DOS operating system by using its COPY command. Figure 2.30 shows a

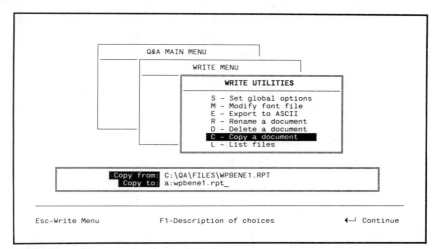

*Figure 2.30:* Copying a document file

situation in which the first version of your word processing report, WPBENE1.RPT, is located on a hard disk in a directory called \FILES. A copy of this file is being made on a floppy disk in drive A:. If you have a two-disk drive system, you would use the drive letters A: and B: before the file name. Just make sure that you use the correct letter for the file to copy from.

## *DELETING A DOCUMENT FILE*

To delete an unwanted file and make new space on your disk, you can use the Delete a document option. Figure 2.31 shows you a situation in which WPBENE1.RPT on drive C: (previously copied to a floppy disk in drive A:) is about to be deleted. As you can see, Q&A displays a rather large warning message when you press Return to go ahead and delete a file. It gives you a last chance to back out. If you find yourself about to destroy a file in error and have not yet pressed Return after typing the file name, press Esc to cancel the deletion. If you have already pressed Return, press Return again to select the No option suggested by Q&A. If you want to continue with the deletion, press ← and Return. Q&A will then delete your file from whatever disk and drive are indicated in the file name.

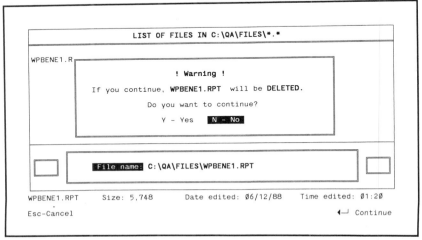

*Figure 2.31:* Deleting a document file

## *RENAMING A DOCUMENT FILE*

The fourth option available on this menu is to rename your file. Figure 2.32 shows a situation in which WPBENE1.RPT on drive C: is about to be renamed WPBENE.BAK. Remember that WPBENE1-.RPT is already an older version of the practice document. It is being renamed with the .BAK extension to show that it is now a backup file to be used only if WPBENE2.RPT were inadvertently destroyed. Because WPBENE2.RPT is now the final version of the practice document, it could justifiably be renamed WPBENE.RPT. You would still have two versions of the same report stored on the same disk, only under less confusing names.

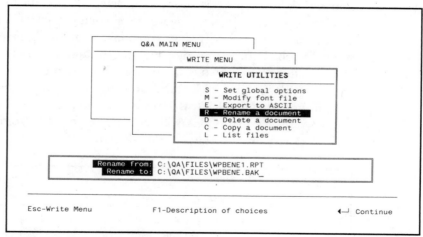

*Figure 2.32:* Renaming a document file

## SUMMARY

You are now ready to go on to create and edit documents of your own. As you will soon discover, much that you have learned about Q&A's word processor will be used when you begin to create database files in the chapter ahead. Using the database will provide you with an excellent opportunity to put into practice much of what you know at this point.

# CHAPTER

3

# Q&A FILE

# *Fast Track*

**To select a new palette for the display form**      135

which determines its foreground and background attributes, select the Design file option on the File Menu by typing **d** and pressing Return (or by typing **1**); select the Customize a file option by typing **c** and pressing Return (or by typing **3**); and then specify the name of the file and press Return. Then select the Change palette option by typing **c** and pressing Return (or by typing **8**). Press F8 to see the next palette or F6 to see the previous palette. Press F10 to select the one you want to use.

**To enter data into a blank form,**      142

type the information in each field. Use the Tab or the Return key to move the cursor to the next field. When finished, press F10 to save the form and move on to a new blank form. Press Shift-F10 to save the data and return to the File Menu.

**To retrieve forms from a database,**      143

select the Search/Update option on the File Menu by typing **s** and pressing Return (or by typing **3**), enter the name of the file to use and press Return. Enter your search conditions in the Retrieve Spec that appears, and press F10 to have the program locate the matching records.

**To view the records in your database**      144

in a column and row format called a Table view, press F6 from the Retrieve Spec screen. To make editing changes to the data in a particular record, move the cursor highlight to record and press F10 to return to normal Form view.

**To sort the records in a database,**            **160**

press F8 from the Retrieve Spec screen. This takes you to the Sort Spec screen. Fill out this form, indicating the order of the fields by number. Use **as** to designate ascending order or **ds** for descending, separated from the order number by a comma. Press F10 to perform the sort.

**To redesign a database,**            **161**

select the Design file option on the File menu by typing **d** and pressing Return (or by typing **1**), select the Redesign a file option by typing **r** and pressing Return (or by typing **2**), and specify the name of the file and press Return. You can edit the fields and add new fields to the form as well as modify the field types. Always make a backup of the original database before you do any redesigning.

**To select forms in a database for printing,**            **174**

select the Print option on the File menu by typing **p** and pressing Return (or by typing **4**), specify the name of the file and press Return. Then select the Design/Redesign a Spec option on the Print menu by typing **d** and pressing Return (or by typing **1**). Enter the name you want to assign to the Print Spec, fill out a Retrieve Spec, a Field Spec, the Print Options, and, if required, the Page Options, and press F10. Press Return to have the selected forms printed.

## ADVANTAGES OF USING Q&A FILE

Q&A File allows you to easily record and track all kinds of information necessary to the success of your business. It is based on the design concept of storing related information as forms, not at all unlike the paper forms you already use. Because Q&A is forms-based, it allows you to get up and running with the program very quickly. If you currently keep essential data on standard forms, you have only to make on-screen replicas of these, define some basic information about the type of entries that will be made within each, and you are ready to start filling them in.

### EASIER FORMS REVISION

You may wonder what the advantages are of maintaining an electronic filing system with Q&A rather than the more traditional paper files. First, it is easier to edit and update the design of your basic forms. Q&A File offers you an online editing system almost identical to that of Q&A Write. As long as you use a little care, you can later modify the layout of a Q&A form even after you have added data to the file. If you find you must track some new data that is not provided for on the original form, you can simply add new entry blanks to contain that information. It will not disturb the data that has already been entered into your existing forms.

### REDUCING DATA INPUT ERRORS

Another advantage over traditional record-keeping is that you can set up a form in such a way that Q&A File actually helps direct and aid the operator who is filling in entries in the forms, thus cutting down on input errors. You can do this by restricting the kinds of values that can be entered, setting ranges of acceptable values, and setting initial entry values that can be brought forward and used in new forms. You can even create your own online help messages to which the operator can refer when in doubt about how to proceed with a specific entry. You will learn how to put all of these features to good use in Chapter 8, in the sections on advanced techniques.

## FASTER DATA RETRIEVAL

As you are well aware, you store your paper forms according to an orderly file system that makes locating and retrieving them as quick and easy as possible. You need to retrieve particular forms and specific data within them for a wide variety of reasons. For example, you need to check that they are filled out correctly and completely as well as updating the information in them to make it current. At times, you also need to clean up your files to make more room by archiving older forms or even deleting some of them. Perhaps the most frequent need for locating and retrieving specific data is to apply that information to other uses. For example, you may need to verify data in order to make policy decisions, or you may need to compile and produce an analytical or statistical report using part of the data.

Whatever the need, maintaining records with Q&A File gives you a more efficient way to retrieve data than is possible manually. With Q&A File you can locate the records you need without having to worry about how current your filing is. Once a record is added, it is available for recall regardless of the order in which it was entered. Not so with paper forms. Until they have been filed according to your system, they are difficult, if not impossible, to locate. However efficient you are with filing, you can't beat the data access offered by Q&A File.

Q&A File also allows you to easily review, update, or even delete specific forms or entries within forms. Better yet, it makes it easy to select the specific data you need, ordering it exactly as you require. Used with its counterpart, Q&A Report, File enables you to create both standardized and one-of-a-kind reports containing all of the information or whatever part you see fit.

## REDUCING YOUR PAPERWORK?

You may also wonder whether using Q&A File to store your forms will cut down on the amount of paperwork in your office or perhaps even make it altogether unnecessary to keep paper forms. While it is true that electronic filing systems can reduce some of the paperwork involved in maintaining your data files, it is very unlikely that you will experience a dramatic decrease in this area.

By and large, you will find electronic filing to be much more of a time saver than a paper saver. For one thing, you will always have to maintain the filled-in paper forms you use to input the data in your Q&A forms. You may also find yourself generating more printed reports from your Q&A data files than you ever did from your paper files. Using an electronic filing system will save you so much time and will help you stay so organized that you may find yourself starting to track even more information online than ever before. Though this will put you more on top of the information essential to the health of your business, the end result may be that you find yourself awash in paper reports generated from all of this data.

## APPLICATIONS FOR Q&A FILE

The applications for Q&A File are quite numerous. Think about all of the forms required in your profession to stay on top of the information flow. Just some of the many forms required by businesses include those for tracking data on personnel, customers and clients, sales leads, marketing campaigns, business expenses, insurance claims, product development and quality assurance, appointments and meetings.

Along with these more generalized applications, there are others more specialized and unique to the business you are in. For instance, in the medical profession these could include patient case histories and insurance claims forms. In real estate, you might use forms to carry property listing descriptions. In more sales-based professions, you may need shipping and inventory forms as well as forms containing vendors and sources of supply information.

You can maintain all of these forms with Q&A File. And to do so does not require that you significantly alter the way you input and keep your data. In fact, one of the nicest things about Q&A File is its versatility and flexibility in forms design.

## THE COMPONENTS OF A Q&A DATABASE

To use Q&A File successfully, you do not have to learn a lot of new terminology and concepts about electronic data files. Because you are already familiar with how to set up forms and maintain them, you will be quite comfortable with the way Q&A File works. There are, however, a few specialized terms that you should be acquainted with as you begin to use this program.

## DATABASE OR DATABASE FILE

The first term is *database* or *database file*. It is used to describe all of the Q&A File forms that are stored together in a single disk file. Just as you probably keep all related forms or forms of a single type filed together physically, you will do so electronically.

For example, personnel forms containing information on all of your employees are usually kept in file folders arranged alphabetically and stored together in one file cabinet. In Q&A File, you would likewise try to keep all of your personnel data stored in one database file. One difference is that in your paper files, each folder on a particular employee contains many different forms, such as an original employment application, W-2, salary and review history, and so forth. All of these forms are related to one another primarily by the fact that they pertain to one particular employee.

A Q&A database, however, can contain only one form design. Because this one form can consist of many screen pages (up to 10 screens or 210 lines), you could design it to hold all of the required data related to the subject of the database file. In the personnel file example, you would try to include all of the data that you keep on each employee in the personnel file even if you currently keep that data in several individual paper forms. In other words, the Q&A File database form would hold within it all of the entry blanks required to generate several different kinds of forms (reports).

While designing Q&A database files this way can cut down significantly on the amount of data entry required, it is not always practical. You may find that designing such a super form results in a database file too large to be efficiently maintained. The larger the database, the slower the retrieval and updating. There are times when keeping redundant data (like an employee's name and Social Security number) in several database files as opposed to trying to maintain all necessary data in one large form is too difficult.

## FIELDS IN A DATABASE

The second term commonly used to describe an essential component of electronic databases is *field*. Each blank on a paper form is referred to as a field in a Q&A File form. Using the above example of a personnel database, the entries for the employee's name, Social Security number, address, home phone number, and so on, are all separate fields in a Q&A database. The number of fields that you can put in one Q&A form is very large. It will allow up to 2,182 fields.

In addition to standard fields where you enter the data manually, you can also set up fields in a Q&A database that are calculated and filled in automatically by the program. This is especially nice in forms that require totaling of individual entries. Q&A can perform this function for you by adding the appropriate formula in a special field. Fields that are calculated from the values entered in other fields in a form are called *derived fields*.

## FIELD NAMES

Each entry blank in a standard paper form is preceded by a label such as ''Last Name:'' in front of the blank where you fill in an employee's surname. In database terminology, this is called a *field name*. With Q&A File, you can give the fields any descriptive name you wish. Unlike field names in many other database programs, this field name can contain spaces between the words, as in *Social Security Number:* instead of *SSN* or some other cryptic abbreviation. This allows you to follow the labels you use in your paper forms as closely as you want to.

With Q&A File, you can also change the field names used in your form design even after you have added many records to the file. The only restraint on field names is that they must be terminated with the proper symbol—either a colon (:) or a less-than sign (<)—so that Q&A File is able to recognize what immediately follows the colon as a bona fide database field. You can even add titles and other descriptive text to your forms as long as you do not terminate them with a colon or less-than symbol. If you did, Q&A would require a field entry to follow it.

## DATABASE RECORDS

The last term used to describe electronic databases is *record*. It is really just an alternate term for a filled-out Q&A File form. Using the word *record* instead of *form* helps to avoid any possible confusion. *Form* is used to refer to the form design (the one shared by all of the filled-in forms in the database) as well as to each form containing the actual data input into the database file. Although you use only one form design, you can have up to 16 million filled-in forms (records) in a single Q&A database.

Q&A keeps track of how many forms are in your database as you add data to it. At the bottom of the screen, you will see the number of the form displayed along with the total number of forms in your database. For instance, when you begin to add data to the fourth form in a new database, you will see "Form 4 of 4" displayed at the bottom center of your screen. You now know that we could just as well refer to this as adding the fourth record to a database consisting of only four records.

## DESIGNING YOUR FIRST DATABASE

There are a few basic considerations to take into account when you begin to design a new database with Q&A File. One of the first is whether you wish to try to make an exact on-screen replica of the paper form you are currently using or whether you wish to make some improvements to it. You could use a slightly different layout, more descriptive labels, or even include more or fewer separate fields.

The second might be whether to combine the data kept on several individual paper forms into one database file. As discussed previously, this is an important consideration. Referring back to the personnel file example, you would have to decide whether you were going to include a section containing information like date hired, starting and current salary, review dates, degrees held, schools attended, and so on, along with a section containing essential information like name, sex, Social Security number, home address and telephone number, who to contact in an emergency, and so forth, on each employee in the database file.

Deciding how much of this data to include in the design of one Q&A form depends on a couple of factors. To begin with, it depends on how large the staff in your office is at present and how large you anticipate it will grow. This consideration determines how many records you can expect to maintain in the database file. If you have a staff size of even 500 employees in your office, you will be dealing with a much more manageable personnel database that can easily contain more data on each employee than if you have a staff of 5000 employees, notwithstanding anticipated growth. By "manageable" is meant how long a delay you experience when performing routine maintenance operations like editing, updating, and retrieving records from the data file.

## COMPUTER STORAGE AND DATABASE DESIGN

A crucial limit to the maximum amount of data you can have in a single database is determined by the kind and amount of storage space available in your computer. With a two-disk system on an IBM PC or XT or laptop, a single 5¼-inch data disk will hold only up to 360K bytes of data while a 3½-inch disk will hold about 730K bytes of data. With an IBM PC/AT or PS/2, a single 5¼-inch data disk will hold up to 1.2 MB (roughly four times the amount of data offered by a standard IBM PC) while a 3½-inch disk will hold up to 1.44 Mb. Because you need to keep all of the data in a single database on the same data disk, you may find that the storage available on your data disks is the primary factor limiting how many fields you can design into one form. You may have to reduce the number of fields in a file in order to be able to store all of the records that you need.

Of course, if your computer is equipped with a hard disk, the amount of storage required by your database is much less of a design concern. In this case, you only have to be sure that you have sufficient storage space for the Q&A programs and all of the database files you create to reside on the fixed disk. The factors determining this are the overall size of the hard disk (30 or 40 MB is standard) and how many other application programs and data files you also need to keep on it (for example, you might only use Q&A and a spreadsheet program). With a fixed disk system, you can back up your database files on as many floppy disks as you need, as long as you use the original file on the hard disk when retrieving and updating your data.

## COMPUTER MEMORY AND DATABASE DESIGN

Another limitation on how large a form you can design for your database is tied to the amount of memory available in your computer. The Q&A program requires 470K of memory to run. If you have the fairly standard 512K of RAM, the minimum required to use Q&A, you have very little memory space available in which to design your database form. Remember, part of your available 42K is used up when you first load your version of DOS into memory upon starting up the computer.

Under these circumstances, you may find it impossible to design the kind of multi-page form containing all of the fields you would like to include. Your original form design, just as when creating a document in Q&A Write, must fit entirely into the computer's memory in order for you to save it on a data disk. Though the program's maximum limit on a database form is 10 screen pages, you may find in practice that you are limited to designing much more modest forms, given the amount of memory installed in your system. As in Q&A Write, File keeps you informed of the percentage of memory still available for designing by displaying an identical memory-used indicator on the screen.

If you have 640K of RAM or expanded memory, Q&A will automatically take advantage of this additional memory and, therefore, the possible size of your database design will increase.

## ASSIGNING FIELD TYPES IN YOUR DATABASE

Once you have decided which fields to include and have settled on a general idea of how you want them laid out on the screen, you have to think about one more design consideration—which data type to assign each field. There are seven distinct field types supported by Q&A File. This gives you quite a bit of flexibility when designing your form. Table 3.1 shows each one and describes how it is used.

*Table 3.1:* Field types

| FIELD TYPE | HOW INPUT | DESCRIPTION AND USE |
|---|---|---|
| Character | **T** (for Text) | Alphanumeric characters; all types of punctuation, such as commas, dashes, periods, etc. |
| Numeric | **N** (for Number) | Numeric characters, commas, plus and minus signs, and |

*Table 3.1:* Field types (continued)

| FIELD TYPE | HOW INPUT | DESCRIPTION AND USE |
|---|---|---|
| | | periods only. Used primarily in fields that are subject to arithmetic calculation. Cannot be used with phone or Social Security numbers that require dashes and other punctuation to be input in the field. |
| Currency | **M** (for Money) | Formats numeric input into standard dollar-and-cents display; e.g., 125 becomes $125.00, while 1.25 becomes $1.25. |
| Date | **D** (For Dates) | Treats input as date indicating day, month, and year. You can enter the parts of the date separated by dashes (2-15-49), forward slashes (2/15/49), or in standard form (February 15, 1949). You can control the way date entries are displayed, and perform date arithmetic with them. |
| Time | **H** (for Hours) | Treats the input as time indicated by hours and minutes. You enter the time, separating hours and minutes with a colon. Time can be input using am/pm or on a 24-hour clock (3:45 pm or 15:45). Default displays time entries on a standard 12-hour clock terminated with am or pm (3:45 pm). |

*Table 3.1:* Field types (continued)

| FIELD TYPE | HOW INPUT | DESCRIPTION AND USE |
|---|---|---|
| Logical | **Y** (for Yes/no) | Accepts only logical entries indicating a positive or negative condition. Positive entries can include only Yes, True, Y, or 1. Negative entries can include only No, False, N, or 0. Can be used very effectively to set up automatic conditions within the form. |
| Keyword | **K** (for Keywords) | Allows you to enter words or phrases (separated by semicolons) that can be used as keywords to retrieve a particular form from the database. Will accept all alphanumeric characters and punctuation except the semicolon within the keyword entry. |

**TEXT VERSUS NUMERIC FIELDS**   When you set up your database, assigning the correct data types to each of the fields is important. If you assign the wrong type to a particular field, Q&A File then might not accept all of the characters you wish to enter in it. For instance, in a telephone number field, it is common practice to separate the area code from the rest of the number by enclosing it within parentheses, while a dash is used to separate the three-digit prefix from the rest of the number. Assigning a numeric data type to a telephone number field would therefore effectively prevent you from being able to add any of the punctuation symbols that help make it easier to read. A numeric field will accept only the digits 0 to 9, commas, the plus and minus signs, and the period.

Another less obvious example is the zipcode field. Here, it would seem all right to make it a numeric field because zipcodes are composed only of numbers and in their short form use no punctuation. Nevertheless, the zipcode field should always be assigned a text field type. This is because you never want a zipcode that begins with zero to have the leading zero removed (which would occur if it were defined as a numeric field). And later, if you needed to expand your zipcode entries to include the last four extra digits separated by a dash, Q&A File would not allow the dash unless the field is of the text type. A good general rule to follow is to assign the text type to any field that you know will not be used in arithmetic calculations, even if the entries in this field will be composed only of numbers.

**CURRENCY FIELDS**    Q&A File offers you choices among some specialized field types that you can use to good advantage in the database. A currency field, called a Money field by Q&A, automatically formats all numeric input into the common dollars-and-cents display, preceding each entry with a dollar sign and using two places after the decimal point. If you have a field that will contain only monetary figures, this formatting relieves the data entry operator from having to enter both the dollar sign and the zeros for whole numbers. To enter $575.00 into such a field, you just type *575*. It is then displayed as $575.00 in the form as soon as you press Return to go on to the next entry.

**DATE FIELDS**    Q&A File also provides a special date and time field. Any field in the database that will hold only date information should be assigned the Date field type rather than Text. The reason for this is that Q&A can then perform arithmetic calculations using the date entry, which is not possible with a text field. For instance, you could have Q&A subtract 30 days from a date field and enter this new date in a report.

Using the Date type also gives you maximum flexibility in how the date can be input in the field. For example, you could enter the date **January 11, 1955** just like this in a birthday field, or enter it as **1/11/55**,

**1-11-55**, or **55-1-11**. Any of these alternatives will be accepted by Q&A File. The default display for a date field would result in "Jan 11, 1955" being shown in the field. This too can be changed to any of six different date display formats. You can use this feature to date-stamp each form with the date it is input. Q&A will automatically input the current date (as entered by you at the DOS prompt when starting up your computer or by a clock/calendar card) into a date field using the @DATE function as the initial value.

*TIME FIELDS* Though used less frequently, Q&A File also provides a time data type that it refers to as Hours. This allows you to enter the hours and minutes into a field in a couple of ways. You can enter the time as **1:15 pm** just like this or simply as **13:15** using the so-called military or 24-hour clock. Q&A gives you a choice of displaying the entry either way in the field, regardless of how it was input. Just as with the current date, you can have the program supply the current time (the time set at the operating system level at startup of the computer) into an hour field by using the @TIME function as the initial value. Using this feature provides, in essence, an on-screen clock for the data entry operator.

*LOGICAL FIELDS* The next data type is commonly referred to as a *logical field*, although your Q&A documentation gives it the more descriptive name of a *Yes/No field*. A field containing a logical data type can only indicate whether or not a particular condition is true or false. Nevertheless, it represents a powerful field type that can help you when selecting particular forms from a database or setting up certain conditions within a form. You have a wide choice of the way you can indicate a positive or negative condition in a logical field. You can enter **Yes**, **y**, **True**, **t**, or **1** for positive conditions and **No**, **n**, **False**, **f**, or **0** for negative conditions.

For example, you might add a logical field to a personnel data file indicating if an employee were due for a salary review. You could then quickly retrieve all of the forms for people requiring reviews just by asking for only those whose salary review field contained a Yes entry. You could also add a procedure so that a reminder message like "Salary Review Now Due!" would automatically display in a different field on the screen if the salary review field were given a Yes entry. You could even further automate this whole process so that the salary review field would be filled out as a result of a formula that would calculate the difference between the current date and the last review date. If this result were more than six months, the salary review field would be given a Yes entry and the reminder message would be displayed on the screen. If it were less than six months, this logical field would hold a No entry and no message would appear. You will learn how to make such use of a logical field later, in Chapter 8.

**THE KEYWORD DATA TYPE**   The last field type supported by Q&A File is called a *Keyword field*. This very interesting field type gives you a great deal of flexibility both when entering data into it and when using it to retrieve particular forms in the database. You use this kind of field when you need to add a series of entries in a single field. Any one of the series can then be used as a key in retrieving the form.

For example, your company might want to track all the foreign languages spoken by its employees. It is, of course, quite possible that many of your employees may speak more than one foreign language. Instead of having to add individual fields for each language (especially since you don't know how many might be required), you would set up one field called Foreign Languages. There, you could list as many foreign languages as are appropriate. A list of whatever length (as long as it fits in the blank on the form) could be entered in any order. Individual entries are indicated by separating them with semicolons.

Then, any time you need a list of those employees who speak Spanish, you can get it by listing Spanish in the Foreign Languages field. The only catch is that you must use the same term and spell it consistently to retrieve all of the forms. For instance, you could not use *Spanish* as the keyword for that language in one form and *Español* in another and expect Q&A to retrieve both.

## LAYING OUT A DATABASE FORM

Now that you have a theoretical understanding of the basics of a Q&A database, it is time to put it into practice by setting up a sample form. If need be, turn on your computer and load Q&A. At the Main

Menu, choose File by pressing Return (or simply type **1**). You will then see the File Menu as shown in Figure 3.1. There are eight options listed on this menu.

### NAMING YOUR DATABASE FILE

The first option listed, D for Design file, is the one you want here. Press Return to access it, since it is already highlighted. Choosing the Design file option leads you directly to the Design Menu (shown in Figure 3.2). There are three designing options on this menu. Choose the first, Design a new file, by pressing Return again. The cursor drops down to the line containing the prompt "Data File". Unlike with Q&A Write, you are required to name a new database file before you can design it. The name of the sample database you are going to design is Personnel. Unfortunately, DOS file names can only have eight characters and there are nine in Personnel, so you must abbreviate it a bit. Enter the file name as **personel** and press Return. Capitalize the *p* in *personel* if you wish. Q&A File will later change it to all uppercase letters on the file directory, regardless of how you entered it. If you make a mistake when typing, you can use the Backspace key to delete letters, just as with the word processor. To completely delete a file name on this line, you can press Shift-F4 or simply press the space bar.

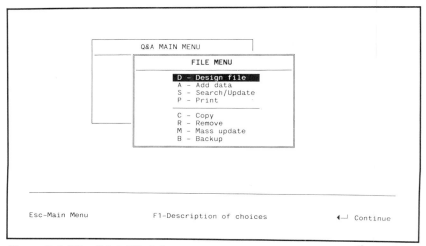

*Figure 3.1:* The Q&A File Menu

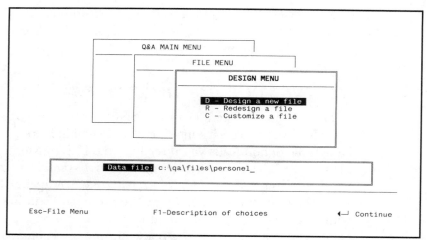

*Figure 3.2:* The Q&A Design Menu

After you press Return, Q&A renames this file PERSONEL.DTF and flashes the message "Working . . ." on the screen. Q&A File always automatically appends the file name you enter with the three-letter extension .DTF (for *data file*). You must not try to give your database file names extensions or to rename the .DTF extension as something else. Q&A File needs to see this particular extension to locate and load your database.

## THE FORM DESIGN SCREEN

As soon as Q&A has finished loading the necessary programs for designing a new data file into the computer's memory, the display will change to an almost entirely blank screen showing only a ruler line, a status line, and a line listing the Esc and three function key assignments (as shown in Figure 3.3). Except that the borders of the screen are missing, this display is very similar to the Type/Edit screen in Q&A Write.

Notice that here the ruler line extends across the screen with every tenth tick mark numbered from 1 to 8, indicating that there are 80 columns displayed on this ruler. Eight tab stops have been preset, starting at column 5 and at every tenth column thereafter to column 75. Unlike the Type/Edit screen, this screen contains no square brackets to indicate left and right margin settings. The maximum

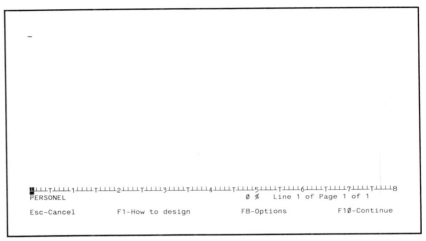

```
PERSONEL                                      Ø %   Line 1 of Page 1 of 1

Esc-Cancel            F1-How to design       F8-Options        F1Ø-Continue
```

***Figure 3.3:*** Q&A File's Design a New Form screen

width of a Q&A form is 80 columns. There is no way to extend your
form beyond the screen width. There are 21 lines available for entry
on this screen. As indicated earlier, your form can consist of up to 10
of these screens, or a maximum length of 210 lines.

The line directly beneath this ruler is identical to that of the Type/
Edit screen. Notice that in the left-hand corner the name of the database
is displayed (without the extension assigned by the program). You must
keep in mind that Q&A File works in a way slightly different from Q&A
Write. Even though the file name is now displayed here, this file and
anything you add to it is not yet saved on disk.

In Q&A Write, you learned that the program assigns the temporary file name Working Copy to your document until you give it a
permanent file name when saving it on disk. When you see a file
name in this screen position, you might think that the document had
been saved on disk at least one time. However, this is not so when
using Q&A File. As you work here, a copy of the layout of your form
and all of the field names you enter into it exists only in the computer's memory. Your form is not safe from loss due to a power interruption until you save it using the F10-Continue option.

As promised in the previous chapter, you already know from your
experience with the word processor how to use many of Q&A File's
features for laying out your form on the screen. Do not be intimi-
dated by the rather sparse screen display. You can move the cursor,

**124    MASTERING Q&A**

CH. 3

enter and delete text, go between insert and overtype mode, set tabs, and even use centering and line and box drawing just as you do in Q&A's word processor.

Press F8 now to examine the options available to you when designing a form. As you see, there are fewer options on this menu than there are in Q&A Write. You can only set tabs, center and uncenter a line, and use line and box drawing. All of these options work exactly as they do in the word processor.

## ENTERING THE DATABASE FIELDS

Figure 3.4 shows you all of the fields to be added to this personnel form. Notice that a few of the fields like MI:, State:, Sex:, and Exempt: are followed by a right angle bracket (often referred to as the *greater-than symbol*). You use this symbol whenever you want to limit the length of the entry in a particular field. Normally, a field's length is limited only by the placement of the next field name or character to the right on the same line. If it is the only field on a line, its length extends to the end of the line itself. For example, though Social Security numbers consist of only 11 characters, Q&A File would accept more than that in the first field. You can enter as many characters in this field as there are spaces following its colon up to the *D* in *Department*.

```
    Social Security No.:              Department:

    Last Name:              First Name:              MI:    >

    Address:
    City:                      State:    >  Zip Code:

    Home Phone:            Sex:  >        Birthdate:

    Position:             Job Title:

    Exempt:  >  Date Hired:            Supervisor:

    Work Phone:           Ext:

                  In Case of Emergency, Notify -

          Name:                      Phone:_

    PERSONEL                        2 %   Line 19 of Page 1 of 1

    Esc-Cancel      F1-How to design     F8-Options     F10-Continue
```

*Figure 3.4:* Fields in the sample database

But because of the placement of the greater-than symbol after the middle initial field (abbreviated MI), this field will accept only two characters, even though there are seven spaces available until the end of this line (to column 80). The middle initial should consist of only two characters, the initial itself and a trailing period. The field's width is limited to help the data entry operator. Should he lose his place on the paper form and try to enter more data in this field, this restriction would help alert him to the error. Whatever else he tried to type, only two characters of it would go in.

All the rest of the fields are restricted in length only by the occurrence of the next field name or, in the case of the Address field, the end of the line in column 80. You can set up fields consisting of more than one line in your forms. You can even set these up so that the data is aligned. You will get a chance to add just such a field in a later exercise in this chapter.

Notice the heading *In Case of Emergency, Notify* - in line 17 of the form. This heading is there only to help identify the content of the following fields. Note that a dash was substituted for the more normal colon following *Notify*. Because it is not a field name, you must avoid using a colon. The colon means only one thing in Q&A File: that the characters preceding it are a field name and that the blank spaces following it will contain data for that field.

Go ahead now and enter the field names for this form as follows:

1. Press Return to skip a line. Press Tab so that the cursor is located in column 5 on line 2. Type **Social Security No.:**, making sure that you add a colon after *No.*

2. Press Tab three times and type **Department:** in column 45; then press Return.

3. Press Return to skip a line. Press Tab so that the cursor is located in column 5 of line 4. Type **Last Name:**.

4. Press Tab two times and then press → twice. With the cursor in column 37, type **First Name:**.

5. Press Tab two times and then press → three times. With the cursor in column 68, type **MI:**. Press → to move right three

more spaces to column 74, and type > (press Shift and period). (To get the middle initial field to accept only two characters, you must place the greater-than symbol at least four spaces to the right of the colon. This is because Q&A leaves the first of three spaces between the colon and the > blank.)

6. Press Return twice and Tab once. Type **Address:** in column 5 of line 6 and press Return.

7. Press Tab and type **City:** in column 5 of line 7. Then press Tab three times and press → to move the cursor to column 42. Type **State:** and press → four times; then type > in column 52. Now press → two times and type **Zip Code:** starting in column 55. Then press Return.

8. Press Return and Tab once to start in column 5 of line 9. Type **Home Phone:** and press Tab two times more. Type **Sex:**, press → two times, and type >. Press → until the cursor is in column 50 and type **Birthdate:**.

9. Press Return twice and Tab once. In column 5 of line 11, type **Position:**. Press Tab twice and → eight times. Type **Job Title:** beginning in column 33. Press Return.

10. Press Return and Tab once. In column 5 of line 13, type **Exempt:**. Press → twice to reach column 14; then type >. Press → twice more and type **Date Hired:**. Press Tab and → eight times. Type **Supervisor:** beginning in column 43 and press Return.

11. Press Return and Tab one time. Type **Work Phone:**. Press Tab two times more and type **Ext:**. Press Return.

12. Press Return. At the very beginning of line 17, type **In Case of Emergency, Notify -**. Press F8, press ↓ once, and press Return to center this heading on the line (see Figure 3.5).

Notice that you center a line of text in a form very much as you do in Q&A Write.

13. Press Return. Press Tab and → seven times. Then type **Name:**. Press the Tab key three times, type **Phone:**, and press Return.

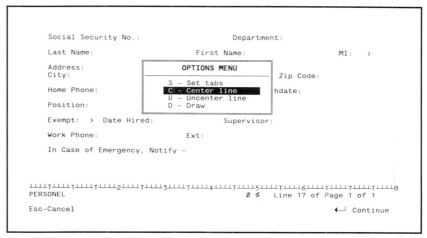

*Figure 3.5:* Centering a line in the form

## ENHANCING THE FORM
## WITH A LINE DRAWING

Your on-screen form should now look like the one shown in Figure 3.4. Look at Figure 3.6, showing the final input screen form. It was created by using the same line drawing feature that you encountered when learning about Q&A Write. That feature works the same way in Q&A File. In fact, even if you can't make effective use of line and box drawings in your word processing documents because your printer doesn't support graphics, you can still make use of them when designing your database screen forms. Because these forms do not represent a printed version of your data, there is no reason not to use line drawings in them.

Contrast the visual effect of the completed screen form in Figure 3.6 with the version on your screen (or in Figure 3.4). See how bordering different sections of the form helps you quickly identify the components and how they relate to one another. This form has been designed with an eye toward aiding in retrieval of the information rather than inputting information. It is assumed that the ordering and layout of the fields on the screen follow rather closely, if not exactly, the paper form from which the data will be taken.

The information on the form consists of four sections that are all bordered in some way to delineate them. The first, in the very top

```
┌─────────────────────────────────────────────────────────────────┐
│ ┌───────────────────────────────────────────────────────────┐   │
│ │ Social Security No.:                  Department:          │   │
│ │ Last Name:              First Name:              MI:   >   │   │
│ │ Address:                                                   │   │
│ │ City:                        State:    >  Zip Code:        │   │
│ │ Home Phone:             Sex:   >     Birthdate:            │   │
│ ├───────────────────────────────────────────────────────────┤   │
│ │ Position:               Job Title:                         │   │
│ │ Exempt:  >  Date Hired:              Supervisor:           │   │
│ │ Work Phone:               Ext:                             │   │
│ │     ┌─────────────────────────────────────────────┐        │   │
│ │     │       In Case of Emergency, Notify -         │        │   │
│ │     │  Name:                      Phone:           │        │   │
│ │     └─────────────────────────────────────────────┘        │   │
│ └───────────────────────────────────────────────────────────┘   │
│ └┴┴┴┴T┴┴┴┴1┴┴┴┴T┴┴┴2┴┴┴┴T┴┴┴3┴┴┴┴T┴┴┴4┴┴┴T┴┴┴5┴┴┴┴T┴┴┴6┴┴┴T┴┴┴7┴┴┴┴T┴┴┴┴8│
│ PERSONEL                          2 %    Line 21 of Page 1 of 1  │
│                                                                   │
│ Esc-Cancel       F1-How to design     F8-Options    F10-Continue  │
└─────────────────────────────────────────────────────────────────┘
```

*Figure 3.6:* Final form with line drawing

row, is composed of two particularly important fields in this personnel form—the Social Security number (used as the employee number in this case) and the department in which the employee works. While it is possible to have many employees with the same last name (and maybe even with the same first name), none will ever have identical Social Security numbers. The department is prominent in the form (and key to the database) because so many personnel reports are organized by department.

The second section, starting with the name and ending with the date of birth fields, is concerned with personal data about the employees, their names, where they live, how to contact them at home, their sex, and their dates of birth. The third section below this, starting with current position in the company and ending with work telephone extension, is concerned with more business-related data: job held, job title and classification, date of hire, supervisor, and how to contact the employee on the job.

The last section is centered and bordered by itself to make it the easiest information in the form to locate. It contains the name and telephone number of the person to contact in the event of an emergency on the job. Should this information ever be needed, it is prominently displayed so that the computer operator can make quick use of it once the proper form is retrieved.

As you are designing your own forms, you should experiment with using Q&A's line and box drawing to make your forms easy to read when they are on the screen. As a general rule, you will want all of your screens to remain uncluttered and appear clean, while still making it easy to pick out prominent data. Remember, your database will eventually contain hundreds of identical forms, many bearing almost identical data. It is important to make them as legible as possible.

To finish designing your screen form, you still need to draw the lines in your form. To do this, follow these steps:

1. Press the Home key twice until the cursor is located in column 1 of line 1. Now press F8, use the ↓ to highlight Draw, then press Return. (You are now in draw mode. Any movement you make with the arrow keys will draw a line. If you make a mistake and need to erase, press F8 a second time. Then your cursor will act like an eraser.)

2. Depress and hold down → to draw a line from column 1 to column 80.

3. Depress and hold down ↓ to draw a line from line 1 down to line 3.

4. Depress and hold down ← to draw a line from column 80 to column 1 across line 3.

5. Depress and hold down ↑ to draw a line from line 3 up to the upper-left corner of the form (column 1, line 1).

6. Depress and hold down ↓ until you reach column 1, line 10.

7. Depress and hold down → to draw a line from column 1 to column 80 across line 10.

8. Depress and hold down ↑ to draw a line from column 80, line 10, to line 3.

9. Depress and hold down ↓ to draw a line from line 3 down to line 21 in column 80.

10. Depress and hold down ← to draw a line from column 80 across line 21 to column 1.

11. Depress and hold down ↑ to draw a line from line 21 up to line 10 (completing the box). Press F10 (or Esc) to take Q&A out of draw mode.

12. Move the cursor to column 10 in line 16. Press F8, type **d**, and press Return to begin drawing again. Depress and hold down → to draw a line from column 10 to column 70 across line 16.

13. Depress and hold down ↓ to draw a line from line 16 down to line 20.

14. Depress and hold down ← to draw a line from column 70 to column 10 across line 20.

15. Depress and hold down ↑ to draw a line from line 20 up to line 16 (completing the box). Press F10 to get out of draw mode.

## DEFINING FIELD TYPES

The last step in creating a form in Q&A File is to define the field type for each of the fields placed on the screen. Now that you have exited from draw mode by pressing F10, you can proceed to this step by pressing F10 again. As soon as you press it, you will see the flashing message "Saving design . . ." while Q&A File saves the layout and content of your form on disk. When it is done, you will see a new screen entitled Format Spec (see Figure 3.7).

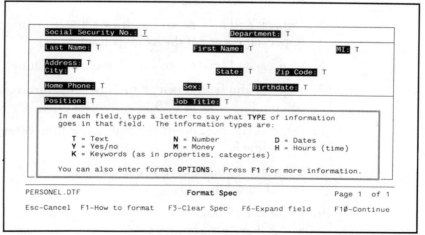

*Figure 3.7:* The Format Spec screen

Notice that all of the field names still visible on this screen are now highlighted and contain capital T's. The T stands for Text. Q&A File uses the Text field as its default and automatically assigns this type to all of the fields in your database once you have saved the design. You can now go in and change the fields that should not be text to any of the other field types available. Q&A File always provides this help screen enclosed in a box to remind you of the different field types available and their abbreviations.

***FORMAT OPTIONS FOR FIELD ENTRIES*** As the Help screen indicates, you can also enter format options along with the field type. To see what options are available, press F1 to get the Help screen shown in Figure 3.8. You can control the on-screen justification of all of the seven different types by using the abbreviations jr, jc, or jl. The abbreviation jr will right-justify an entry (as long as it does not take up the entire blank) and jc will center it. jl, or left justification, is the default for all entries regardless of type.

In addition to setting the justification, you can also have Text, Keyword, and Yes/no (logical) field entries automatically converted to uppercase by adding **u**. This is quite handy in fields that contain the state, where you usually use the post office two-letter abbreviations in all caps. By entering **t,u** in the field, the data entry operator

```
┌─────────────────────────────────────────────────────────────────────────┐
│  ┌──────────────────────────────────────────────────────────────────┐    │
│  │          HOW TO FORMAT: THE FORMAT SPEC       pg. F-22, 107        │    │
│  └──────────────────────────────────────────────────────────────────┘    │
│   In each field, enter an information TYPE followed optionally by format   │
│   OPTIONS:              •                                                  │
│     ┌───────┬──────────┬────────────────────────────────────────────┐     │
│     │ TYPE  │ MEANING  │              FORMAT OPTIONS                  │     │
│     ├───────┼──────────┼────────────────────────────────────────────┤     │
│     │  T    │ Text     │  JR = Justify Right        U = Uppercase     │     │
│     │  K    │ Keyword  │  JC = Justify Center                         │     │
│     │  Y    │ Yes/No   │  JL = Justify Left                           │     │
│     ├───────┼──────────┼────────────────────────────────────────────┤     │
│     │  N    │ Number   │  JR, JL, JC                                  │     │
│     │  M    │ Money    │  0-7 = # of decimal digits (for N only)      │     │
│     │       │          │  C   = insert commas                         │     │
│     ├───────┼──────────┼────────────────────────────────────────────┤     │
│     │  D    │ Date     │  JR, JL, JC                                  │     │
│     │  H    │ Time     │                                              │     │
│     └───────┴──────────┴────────────────────────────────────────────┘     │
│    Examples:   N,2,JR,C  =  This field contains numbers, and they should have │
│                             two decimal digits, be right justified, with commas.│
│                T,U       =  This field contains text, in uppercase.        │
│   Esc-Cancel                                                               │
└─────────────────────────────────────────────────────────────────────────┘
```

*Figure 3.8:* Help screen with options for the Format Spec

can input the state abbreviation in lowercase and let Q&A automatically convert it to its correct format.

In numeric fields, you can control the display of decimal places in the entry by adding a number between 0 and 7. If, for instance, you wanted to suppress the display of decimal points in a numeric field, you would add a zero after the N (**N,0**). In both currency and numeric fields, you can have commas automatically added in these fields by typing **c**. For example, if you typed **m,c** in a salary field, Q&A would display an entry of 35000 as $35,000.00 in the field. Press Esc now to return to the Format Spec screen.

**CHANGING FIELD TYPES IN THE SAMPLE FORM**    Before you begin to modify some of the field types, press the Caps Lock key. To edit a particular field type, you just type over the existing letter. To put Q&A File in insert mode, you must press the Ins key just as you do in Q&A Write. To move from field to field, you can press Return or the Tab key. To move the cursor back to the previous field, hold down one of the Shift keys and press Tab. This acts as a Backtab key.

The first field to be modified of those currently displayed in the Format Spec is the middle initial field (MI:). You should leave the type as Text but add the U option to convert the data automatically to uppercase. To move to the cursor to this field, press Return (or Tab) four times. Now press → to move the cursor over one space; type **u**. The use of a comma between T and U is optional.

You should now do the same thing in the State field. Press Return until the cursor is located in it, press → one time and type **u**. Next, you will want to add the uppercase conversion to the sex field. Press Return to move the cursor to it. Because this field has space for only one character entry, it is too short to accept TU within it.

Whenever you want to add codes to a field that is too short to accept them, you must use the F6 key make more room. Notice that F6 is listed at the bottom of the screen as the Expand field key. When you press it, the cursor is automatically repositioned in the left corner of a line right below the last line of the form's border. The status line has moved down a line and the prompt ''Long value: T'' is now displayed right above the name of your database file. Your cursor should now be located on the T in this line. Press → once, type **u**, and press Return. As soon as you press Return, a → symbol replaces the T after the Sex: field name. It is used to indicate that the codes assigned to this field are too long to be displayed within it. Whenever you position the cursor on such a field, its contents will be shown after the ''Long value'' prompt.

You now need to modify the Birthdate: field from a text field to a date field. Type **d** to replace the T entry in it and press Return. The entries in your Format Spec should now match those shown in Figure 3.9. Press Return two times to leave the next two fields as they are and to continue your modifications.

Q&A then automatically changes the Format Spec screen display as soon as you press Return at the Job Title: field. Your screen should now look like the one shown in Figure 3.10. This figure shows you the other changes that should be made to your field types. The Exempt: field should be made a logical or Yes/no field. Here, you indicate whether or not an employee is salaried—that is, exempt from overtime pay. Type **y** there and press Return.

The last modification you want to make is in the next field. Change the Date Hired: field from a Text to a Date field. Check over your form and make sure that it is identical to that in Figure 3.10. Then press F10 to continue.

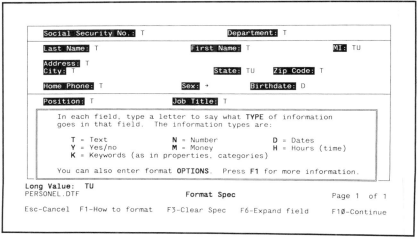

*Figure 3.9:* Assigning field types to the first 14 fields

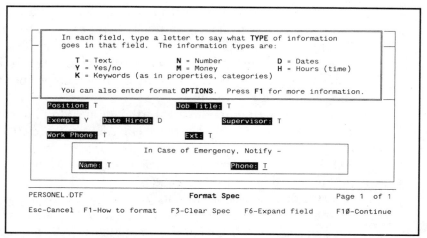

In each field, type a letter to say what **TYPE** of information
goes in that field.  The information types are:

   **T** = Text             **N** = Number           **D** = Dates
   **Y** = Yes/no           **M** = Money            **H** = Hours (time)
   **K** = Keywords (as in properties, categories)

You can also enter format **OPTIONS**.  Press **F1** for more information.

Position: T               Job Title: T

Exempt: Y    Date Hired: D        Supervisor: T

Work Phone: T          Ext: T

In Case of Emergency, Notify –

Name: T                 Phone: T

PERSONEL.DTF              **Format Spec**           Page 1  of 1

Esc-Cancel  F1-How to format   F3-Clear Spec   F6-Expand field    F10-Continue

***Figure 3.10:*** Assigning field types to the last seven fields

Q&A File now displays a new screen (shown in Figure 3.11) showing the global formatting options in effect for any currency, numeric,
date, or time fields you have just assigned in the Format Spec. They
are global in the sense that any fields of the particular type will be formatted as currently highlighted. For example, all date fields in the
form, the Date of Birth and Date Hired fields, will be converted
to the format *Jan 20, 1989* (with the name of the month abbreviated,
the number of the day and a comma, and then all four digits of the
year). To change the format, you have only to use the arrow keys to
move the highlighting to a new choice.

You can choose the placement of the currency symbol; a space
between the symbol and number; the European method of showing
decimal points with a comma or the American method of using a period in currency and numeric fields; twenty different ways of displaying the date in date fields; and the 12-hour clock with the am/pm
convention or the military 24-hour clock in time fields. You can easily modify these format options later, even after you have added data
to your database, by choosing the Redesign option on the Q&A File
Design Menu. For now, use the default options listed here and con-
clude the design of your sample database by pressing F10. Q&A File
will now save your database design, including the field names, their
layout, and field types on disk.

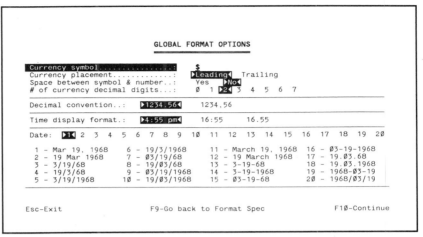

*Figure 3.11:* Global Format Options screen

## ADDING DATA TO FORMS

Q&A takes you back to the File Menu. From here, choose the Add Data option by typing **a** and pressing Return (or by typing **2**). Q&A supplies the name of the file you just used and locates the cursor at the beginning of its name. In this case, it suggests PERSONEL.DTF. If you want to add data to another database file, you can blank out the suggested file name by pressing the space bar. Then you can type in the name of the file or press Return to get a listing of existing database files. Press Return to select your sample database.

### CHANGING THE FORM
### DISPLAY FROM THE CUSTOMIZE MENU

Q&A now displays your form without any of the format codes or brackets limiting the length of the data entry. All of the field names are highlighted just as they were in the Format Spec screen. You can change the way your field names and data are displayed on the screen by using the Customize a file option on the Design Menu. To see how this works, press Esc to back up to the File Menu.

Now choose the Design file option by typing **d** and pressing Return (or by typing **1**). Choose the Customize a file option by typing **c** and pressing Return (or by typing **3**); then specify which file you wish to customize. The option to modify the screen display is called Change palette on this menu. Type **c** and press Return (or type **8**) to access this menu. Figure 3.12 shows you the screen that now appears. Notice that it says Palette 1 of 7 at the bottom of the screen. There are seven different predefined palettes from which to choose. Palette 1 (Figure 3.12) is the default automatically assigned to any new database file, although the figures in this book use Palette 2 to present the material more clearly.

You can review each of the seven palettes in numerical order. You can even enter dummy data in the fields to see how entries are displayed by each palette. Press the F6 key to select the previous palette and F8 to select the next. When you locate the palette you wish to use with your screen form, you press F10 to assign it to the database. If you have a computer running off a monochrome card or a color/graphics card with a monochrome monitor, not all of the effects of some of the palettes will be visible to you. Some of these have been designed for use with color monitors. Table 3.2 lists the attributes of each of the palettes available.

After you have finished examining the visual effect of the various palettes on your monitor, go to Palette 2 and press F10 if you want your forms to match those shown in this book. Otherwise, press Esc

```
┌──────────────────────────────────────────────────────────────────┐
│                                                                    │
│   Social Security No.:                    Department:              │
│   Last Name:                 First Name:                 MI:       │
│   Address:                                                         │
│   City:                       State:      Zip Code:                │
│   Home Phone:                 Sex:        Birthdate:               │
│   Position:                   Job Title:                           │
│   Exempt:    Date Hired:                  Supervisor:              │
│   Work Phone:                 Ext:                                 │
│          ┌────────────────────────────────────────────┐           │
│          │      In Case of Emergency, Notify -         │           │
│          │   Name:                     Phone:          │           │
│          └────────────────────────────────────────────┘           │
│                                                                    │
│   PERSONEL.DTF            Palette 1 of 7           Page 1 of 1     │
│   Esc-Cancel      F6-Previous palette   F8-Next palette  F10-Continue │
└──────────────────────────────────────────────────────────────────┘
```

*Figure 3.12:* Palette 1

*Table 3.2:* Palettes

| | |
|---|---|
| Palette 1 (default palette for Q&A File) | All field names in the form are highlighted (a reverse effect of light background with black letters). The current field is also indicated by such highlighting. Data entered in the field is displayed in blue on black background (on color monitors) or underlined (on monochrome monitors). |
| Palette 2 | All field names in the form are highlighted. The current field is indicated by a blinking underline cursor. Data entered in the field is displayed in normal single intensity (light letters on black background). |
| Palette 3 | All field names in the form are shown in double intensity. The current field is indicated by highlighting. Data entered in the field is displayed in normal single intensity. |
| Palette 4 | All field names in the form are shown in single intensity. The current field is indicated by highlighting. Data entered in the field is displayed in blue (on color monitors) or underlined (on monochrome monitors). |
| Palette 5 | All field names in the form are shown in double intensity. The current field is indicated by a blinking underline cursor. Data entered into a field is displayed in blue (on color monitors) or underlined (on monochrome monitors). |
| Palette 6 | All field names in the form are highlighted. The current field is indicated by a blinking underline cursor. Data entered into a field is displayed in blue (on color monitors) or underlined (on monochrome monitors). |
| Palette 7 | All field names in the form are highlighted. The current field is indicated by a blinking underline cursor. Data entered into a field is displayed in double intensity. |

twice to return to the File Menu and to leave the palette for your sample database as Palette 1. From this menu, select the second option, Add data, by typing **a** and pressing Return. Select your file name and press Return.

## FILLING OUT YOUR FIRST FORM

When you add data to your forms, the cursor always starts out in the first field at the top of the screen. You type the data in the field using the same cursor movement and editing options that were available when designing the form. Once you are finished with the first entry, you can press Return to move the cursor to the next field. As you press Return, Q&A File automatically advances the cursor from left to right across a line, down each succeeding line of the screen form.

You are not, however, forced to enter data in each field according to this order. Q&A provides a number of ways to navigate the cursor throughout the screen form. Table 3.3 summarizes these options.

Figure 3.13 shows you the data for the first record in your database. You will now be walked through the data entry of this and the second record. Appendix A at the end of this book contains all of the data for all 20 records that are part of this database. After inputting the first two records here, refer to it if you wish to complete the data entry for this database. These records will be used in subsequent exercises on how to edit, retrieve, and print specific records from the personnel database in this chapter. The data will also be used in exercises in the next two chapters for generating reports with Q&A Report and retrieving information using the Intelligent Assistant.

The cursor is now at the beginning of the first field of what is listed as Form 1 of 1. Type in the Social Security number as shown in Figure 3.13. Because this is a text field, it will accept numbers with dashes between them. Press Return (or Tab) to move the cursor to the next field once you have finished entering the number. If you make a mistake, use the Backspace key as you did with the word processor to erase the character to the left.

In the Department field, enter **Accounting** and press Return. The cursor automatically advances to Last Name field at the beginning of the second line. Enter the last name as shown and press Return.

*Table 3.3:* Cursor movements in Q&A File

| | |
|---|---|
| ↑ | Up a line in the form. |
| ↓ | Down a line in the form. |
| → | Next character right in the current field. Beginning of next field to the right if cursor is at the very last blank in the field. |
| ← | Next character left in the current field. Beginning of previous field to the left if cursor is at the very first blank in the field. |
| Ctrl-→ | End of the next word right in the current field. Will not move cursor to the next field even if at the very end of the blank. |
| Ctrl-← | Beginning of the previous word left in the current field. Will not move cursor to the previous field even if at the very beginning of the blank. |
| Home | First time pressed—beginning of the current field. Second time pressed—first space of the first field on the current screen page. Third time pressed—first space of the first field in the form. |
| End | First time pressed—first space of the current field. Second time pressed—beginning of the last field on the current screen page. Third time pressed—beginning of the last field of the form. |
| Ctrl-Home | Beginning of the first field of the form. |
| Ctrl-End | Beginning of the last field of the form. |

Then enter the first name, type **d.** (lowercase) in the middle initial field, and press Return again. Notice that Q&A automatically converted this entry to *D*.

Enter the street address and city as shown, pressing Return (or Tab) after each entry. In the State field, type **il** and press Return.

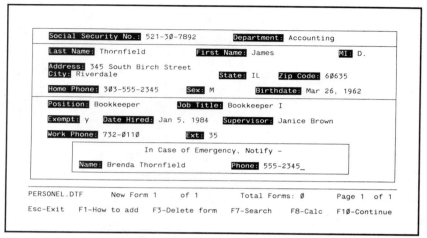

*Figure 3.13:* First record in sample database

This is also automatically converted to *IL* by Q&A. Type in the zip-code and press Return again.

In the home phone field, you have a choice of how you want to enter and display the telephone number. You can enter it as shown in Figure 3.13, separated only by dashes and no spaces, or you can enclose the area code in parentheses as (303). Press the space bar and then enter the rest of the number as shown. Q&A will accept either entry because the field type is Text. Type the sex entry as **m** (lowercase) and verify that Q&A converts this to *M* once you press Return.

## CORRECTING ERRORS

In the next field for the birthday, make a deliberate data entry error. Instead of entering 3/26/62, enter **3/56/62** and press Return. Q&A immediately responds by giving you an error message (shown in Figure 3.14) and does not advance the cursor to the next field. It tells you that 3/56/62 cannot be reformatted to a valid date (you are using the default format that will display the correct date as Mar 26, 1962). It is programmed with a table telling it how many days each month contains and which abbreviation to use for the number entered for the month. You would have received an identical error message if you had input the date as 13/26/62, because there is no month abbreviation for the number 13 in Q&A's lookup table.

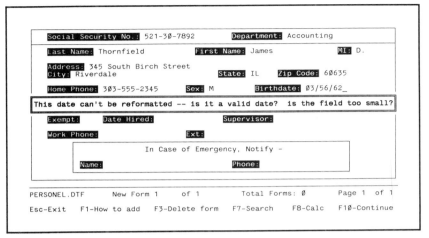

*Figure 3.14:* Date entry error message

The last part of this error message questions whether the field is too small. You will also receive this error message if the format you have selected for the date display is too long for the width of the field. In such a case, you would have to either choose a different, smaller date display or lengthen the field by using the Redesign option on the Design Menu.

Use → to move the cursor to the *5* in *56*. As soon as you press it, the error message disappears. Type in **2** and press Return. You do not have to be at the end of a field to enter your data in it. Now complete the entries for the Position and Job Title fields as shown in Figure 3.13.

At the Exempt field, you are restricted in the type of entry you can make. Because you defined this as a logical field, you can only indicate positive or negative conditions. As you restricted the width of the field to one character, you can only input **y/n**, **t/f**, or **1/0**. Try making another type of entry here. Type **a** in the Exempt field. Q&A gives you a new error message (''This doesn't look like a yes/no value''). Then type **y** here. The error message disappears. Press Return and notice that this entry is not converted to its uppercase equivalent because you did not format this field to convert data to uppercase. You can change this later when you redesign and add to this form.

You do not have to enter the date as numbers separated by slashes. You can enter it in a variety of ways. As long as it is a legal date that will fit in the width of the date field, Q&A will accept it. Try a variation here in the Date Hired field. Enter this as **84-1-5** (you could just as well type **January 5, 1984**, too) and press Return. The date displayed should still read Jan 5, 1984.

## INPUTTING THE REST OF THE RECORDS

Now go ahead and type in the data for the rest of the remaining fields. Press Return or Tab after each entry. When you reach the last field on this screen page (and currently the last field in the form), press Return. The cursor returns to the first field on this page. You must press F10 to save this record on disk and advance to the next form. By the way, if you press Esc at this point, you will receive a warning message from Q&A telling you that if you continue, your data will not be saved. Press F10 now to go to the next form.

Your previous entries in the first form are blanked out and a clean form is displayed on your screen. Notice on the status line that this is New Form 2 of 2 and Total Forms: 1. The screen still reads "Page 1 of 1" because your form currently consists of only one screen page. You are now ready to enter the data shown in Figure 3.15 for the second record in the Personnel database.

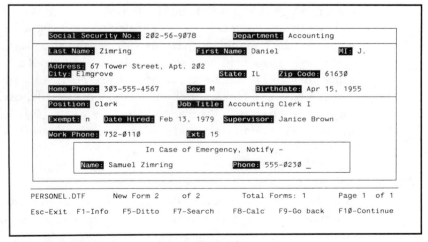

*Figure 3.15:* Second record in sample database

Type in the Social Security number displayed and press Return. Notice that the department is Accounting, the same as it is for the first record. You do not have to retype the department name here. You can always use the F5 key to bring forward the data entry recorded in the same field in the previous form to the field you are currently inputting. Press F5 to see how this works. The cursor does not advance to the next field; this allows you to make any editing changes necessary. When you have the data, press Return to enter it in the field. This permits you to bring forward similar data that you can then modify. This technique can sometimes save you many keystrokes.

You can use this feature to good advantage in filling out this form. You can press F5 and Return to fill in the State, Sex, Supervisor, and Work Phone fields in this form. Go ahead and input all of the data for this second record as shown in Figure 3.15. When you are finished, press Shift-F10. Then you can refer to Appendix A and input the remaining 18 records by using the same techniques outlined here. When you are finished filling in all of the forms, press Shift-F10 to return to the File Menu.

## *EDITING DATA IN FORMS*

To edit the data in any of the records input in a database, you use the Search/Update option on the File Menu. This is the third option listed there. Type **s** and press Return (or type 3). Q&A File then moves the cursor to the File Name prompt, where it supplies the name of the previously used data file, PERSONEL.DTF, as the default. Press Return to select it.

### *THE RETRIEVE SPEC*

Q&A now presents you with a screen displaying a blank form just like the one you used when adding new records to the file (shown in Figure 3.16). Notice, though, that here the status line reads Retrieve Spec instead of indicating the number of the form. You use the Retrieve Spec to tell Q&A which record to locate and display on the screen. When it is retrieved, you can either just review the information in the form or make editing changes to it.

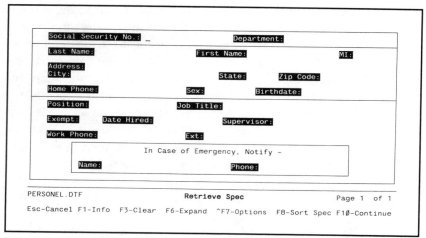

*Figure 3.16:* The Retrieve Spec

Press the F10-Continue key now. When you press F10 without filling in any of the fields in the form, Q&A File automatically retrieves all of the records in the database and displays the very first one in it. In this case, it is that of James Thornfield. Look at the function key assignments listed on the second line below the status line on this form. The function of F6 is listed as Table, F7 as Search, and F8 as Calc. Pressing F6 gives you a tabular view of the database, displaying the data in the first few fields of the form. To clear the screen of the current record displayed and return to a new Retrieve Spec form, you press F7. There you can specify which record or records to retrieve next. To perform the calculations specified in any of the fields in the form, you use F8 (you will learn how to set up calculations in fields in Chapter 8).

## USING THE TABLE
## VIEW TO RETRIEVE RECORDS

Press F6 now to get a table view of the database. Figures 3.17 and 3.18 show you the data displayed in this view from the 20 records that have been input. This table is only partial for each record displayed. The first five of the 21 fields in this database are displayed in each row. There is no way to scroll more fields into view; Q&A File can only show five fields of any database you design in this tabular form.

Nevertheless, if you design your database so that unique and key identifying fields always come first in the form, this table will help you quickly locate a specific record for review or editing.

Notice that the first record is highlighted. The status line below reads "Form 1". The function of F10 is now listed as Show form. If you pressed this key now, it would retrieve the complete form and display it on your screen. You can move this highlighting up and down to the

| Social Security | Department | Last Name | First Name | MI |
|---|---|---|---|---|
| 521-30-7892 | Accounting | Thornfield | James | D. |
| 202-56-9078 | Accounting | Zimring | Daniel | J. |
| 360-31-5633 | Accounting | Freels | Jessica | B. |
| 567-21-3456 | Accounting | Parish | Katherine | A. |
| 501-11-4523 | Engineering | Bennett | Kelly | T. |
| 234-57-8908 | Engineering | Rosner | Owen | M. |
| 225-88-3421 | Engineering | Peterson | Monica | L. |
| 672-01-9942 | Engineering | Graydon | Ronald | F. |
| 456-71-0034 | Marketing | Johnson | Jeffry | G. |
| 781-15-0632 | Marketing | Gibbon | Faith | H. |
| 586-03-3187 | Marketing | Burke | Lisa | A. |
| 985-41-112 | Sales | Burgoyne | Mark | T. |
| 606-33-0915 | Sales | Thompson | Ann | M. |
| 892-44-5591 | Sales | Rush | Del | B. |
| 453-02-2285 | Sales | Shepard | John | G. |
| 553-04-0126 | Marketing | Johnson | Alice | M. |
| 399-75-2205 | Personnel | Schumacher | Keri | A. |

PERSONEL.DTF          Retrieved form 1      of 20           Total forms: 20

Esc-Exit              ( ↓ ↑ Home End PgUp PgDn )-Navigate          F10-Show form

*Figure 3.17:* Table view of database (first screen)

| Social Security | Department | Last Name | First Name | MI |
|---|---|---|---|---|
| 399-75-2205 | Personnel | Schumacher | Keri | A. |
| 901-77-3351 | Personnel | Raye | Jennifer | R. |
| 448-35-9622 | Administration | Brown | Janice | F. |
| 589-11-3276 | Administration | Chang | Edward | A. |

PERSONEL.DTF          Retrieved form 17     of 20           Total forms: 20

Esc-Exit              ( ↓ ↑ Home End PgUp PgDn )-Navigate          F10-Show form

*Figure 3.18:* Table view of database (second screen)

other entries on the table to select a specific record by using the ↑ and ↓ keys.

Q&A can only display fields for 17 records in one table display. To move to the next screen, you press the PgDn key. Press it now to see the rest of the table as shown in Figure 3.18. Notice that the last record on the previous screen (Form 17) is now the first record on this screen. This is done to help you keep your place as you scroll from screen to screen in the table. To get back to the first screen, press the PgUp key.

You can change which five fields are displayed on the Table View anytime you wish. The default is the display of the first five fields on your form, but this may not always contain the most useful information for quickly identifying the record you need. To change which fields are displayed, do the following:

1. Press Esc to return to the File Menu. Then press **s** and Return to Search the database again.

2. Press F10 on the Retrieve Spec to retrieve all the forms in your database.

This time, before you press F6 to display a Table View of all the forms in your database, change which fields will be displayed.

3. Press Shift-F6 and your screen will change to the Table View Spec.

Notice that the first five fields are numbered from one to five (see Figure 3.19). The middle initial field is numbered as the fifth column for your Table View. Instead of this field, however, the field Position would provide more useful data.

4. Press the Tab key four times until you reach the MI field. Press the space bar once to erase the number 5.

5. Press the Tab key until the cursor is in the Position field, and type **5**. Press F10 to save the new Table View Spec.

Notice when the Table View is displayed that the last column has now changed to the Position field as shown in Figure 3.20.

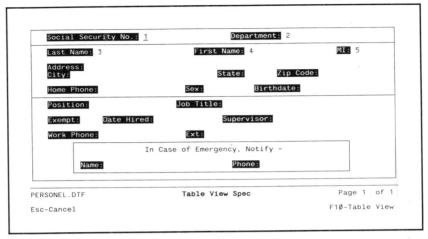

**Figure 3.19:** The Table View Spec

| Social Security | Department | Last Name | First Name | Position |
|---|---|---|---|---|
| 521-30-7892 | Accounting | Thornfield | James | Bookkeeper |
| 202-56-9078 | Accounting | Zimring | Daniel | Clerk |
| 360-31-5633 | Accounting | Freels | Jessica | Accountant |
| 567-21-3456 | Accounting | Parish | Katherine | Secretary |
| 501-11-4523 | Engineering | Bennett | Kelly | Drafter |
| 234-57-8908 | Engineering | Rosner | Owen | Drafter |
| 225-88-3421 | Engineering | Peterson | Monica | Engineer |
| 672-01-9942 | Engineering | Graydon | Ronald | Engineer |
| 456-71-0034 | Marketing | Johnson | Jeffry | Artist |
| 781-15-0632 | Marketing | Gibbon | Faith | Director |
| 586-03-3187 | Marketing | Burke | Lisa | Vice President |
| 985-41-112 | Sales | Burgoyne | Mark | Sales |
| 606-33-0915 | Sales | Thompson | Ann | Sales |
| 892-44-5591 | Sales | Rush | Del | Sales |
| 453-02-2285 | Sales | Shepard | John | Vice President |
| 553-04-0126 | Marketing | Johnson | Alice | Secretary |
| 399-75-2205 | Personnel | Schumacher | Keri | Secretary |

PERSONEL.DTF     Retrieved form 1     of --     Total forms: 20

Esc-Exit     ( ↓ ↑ Home End PgUp PgDn )-Navigate     F10-Show form

**Figure 3.20:** New Table View with Position field

## *MAKING EDITING CHANGES TO A SPECIFIC RECORD*

Now you can get practice in selecting a specific form from the table.

1. Press ↓ until Form 6, that of Owen Rosner, is highlighted.
2. Press F10 to select it and display the complete form.

3. Here you want to change the position from Drafter to Designer. To do this, press ↓ five times until the cursor is located in the Position field. Press → once and type **esigner** over the existing letters.

4. Because this is the only change you need to make to this record, press F10 to save this edit.

Q&A advances you to the next record in the database, Form 7 for Monica Peterson. Here you want to change the Position from Engineer to Junior Engineer and the Job Title from Product Engineer I to Engineer I.

1. Press Ins to get into insert mode, type **Junior**, and add a space with the space bar right before *Engineer*.

2. Press Return to advance to the Job Title field and press F4 to delete *Product*.

3. Now press F10 to save these changes and advance to the next record.

4. Move the cursor down to the Position field in this record for Ron Graydon by pressing ←. Change this entry from Engineer to Senior Engineer in the same way. You must press Ins again because Q&A File automatically takes you out of insert mode when you advance to the next field. Now type **Senior**, press the space bar, and then press F10 to save this edit.

5. Press F6 to return to the table view of your database.

The next editing change you are going to make is in Form 16, that of Alice Johnson. When the table is displayed again on your screen, the highlight is still on Form 9, the one you were on when you pressed F6.

1. Move the highlight down to Form 16 on this screen and press F10 again to select it.

2. Press Tab to advance to the Job Title field. Here you will change the job title from Clerk/Typist II to Clerk/Typist III. To do this, press the End key to get to the end of the entry; then type **I**.

3. Press F10 to save this change.

## USING THE RETRIEVE SPEC
## TO EDIT A SPECIFIC RECORD

The last editing change to make to your sample database is in Ed Chang's record. Instead of returning to the table to locate this record, press F7 to let Q&A locate it for you. Once you press this key, you are presented with a blank form (labeled Retrieve Spec). Move the cursor down to the Last Name field and type Chang there. Press F10 to have Q&A find and display the form in which the last name is Chang. If you knew that there was more than one Chang in the company, you could further restrict the search by filling in the first name before pressing F10 to locate the record.

You should now have Ed Chang's record on your screen. Here you want to modify the next-to-last field by adding Chang to Janet Fielding, the person to contact in case of an emergency.

1. To get the cursor there quickly, press the End key twice, once to advance it to the end of the first field and a second time to advance it to the last field on this screen page.

2. Now hold down one of the Shift keys and press Tab to move to the previous field.

3. Press End to move to the end of the entry; then press the space bar and type in **Chang**.

4. Now press F10 to save this change. Once you do, you receive the message "No more forms."

5. Press Esc to exit or F9 for the previous form.

6. Press Esc to return to the File Menu.

## RETRIEVING
## FORMS FROM A DATABASE

As you saw when editing these records, you can use the Search/Update option to retrieve all of the forms in a database and then locate the particular ones you want by selecting them in the table view of the database. In the last example, you also learned that you can retrieve one particular record for editing by entering an identifying piece of data in a specific field, as you did to locate Ed Chang's record for updating.

You can also use Q&A's Retrieve Spec to identify and locate groups of records that fall between certain ranges that you specify in this form. For instance, you could identify all of the records for those employees living in zipcodes between 61000 and 62000, or locate only those who were hired prior to 1977. Q&A gives you a great deal of flexibility when you are setting up the search criteria by which groups of records are located. Depending upon the criteria used, it may locate hundreds, one, or even no matching records in your database.

To set up your criterion (or multiple criteria) for retrieval, you place codes along with the required value in the appropriate field or fields of the Retrieve Spec. Table 3.4 gives you these codes and examples of how they are used.

*Table 3.4:* Examples of search criteria in the Retrieve Spec

| EXAMPLE | MEANING |
| --- | --- |
| **Exact matches (can be used with all types of fields):** | |
| = Accounting | Retrieves all records in which the Department is Accounting. Use of the equal symbol in the field is optional. |
| /Accounting | Retrieves all records in which the Department is not Accounting. |
| = | Retrieves all records in which the field containing an equal sign (followed by no input) is empty. |
| / = | Retrieves all records in which the field containing / = contains some data. (Locates all records in which this field is not empty.) |
| **Selective matches (can be used with all field types except for Yes/No [logical] fields except where indicated):** | |
| >10 | Retrieves all records in which the entry for the field is greater than 10. |

*Table 3.4:* Examples of search criteria in the Retrieve Spec (continued)

| EXAMPLE | MEANING |
|---|---|
| **Selective matches (can be used with all field types except for Yes/No [logical] fields except where indicated): (continued)** | |
| > = 10 | Retrieves all records in which the entry for the field is greater than or equal to 10. An alternate form, 10.., can be used except in Text and Keyword fields. |
| <10 | Retrieves all records in which the entry for the field is less than 10. |
| < = 10 | Retrieves all records in which the entry for the field is less than or equal to 10. An alternate form, ..10, can be used except in Text and Keyword fields. |
| >10..<15 | Retrieves all records in which the entry for the field is more than 10 and less than 15 (e.g., numbers between 11 and 14). |
| 10..<15 | Retrieves all records in which the entry for the field is greater than or equal to 10 and less than 15 (e.g., numbers between 10 and 14). |
| >10..15 | Retrieves all records in which the entry for the field is more than 10 and less than or equal to 15 (e.g., numbers between 11 and 15). |
| 10;15;20 | Retrieves all records in which the entries are 10, 15, or 20. |
| 10..15 | Retrieves all records in which the entry for the field is between 10 and 15 (e.g., any number 10 through 15). Cannot be used in Text or Keyword fields. |

*Table 3.4:* Examples of search criteria in the Retrieve Spec (continued)

| EXAMPLE | MEANING |
|---------|---------|
| **Statistical matches (can be used with all field types except for Keyword and Yes/No [logical] fields):** | |
| MAX1 | Retrieves the record whose field contains the highest value in the database (e.g., MAX1 in a salary field would return the record of the highest-paid employee in the company). |
| MIN2 | Retrieves the two records whose fields contain the lowest values in the database (e.g., MIN2 in a salary field would return the records of the two lowest-paid employees in the company). |
| **Wildcard matches in Text and Keyword fields only:** | |
| b.. | Retrieves all records in which the entry for the field begins with the letter *b*. |
| ..n | Retrieves all records in which the entry for the field ends in the letter *n*. |
| b..n | Retrieves all records in which the entry for the field begins with the letter *b* and ends in the letter *n*. |
| ..ben.. | Retrieves all records in which the entry for the field contains the letters *ben* within it in that order. |
| **Special matches in Keyword fields only:** | |
| BA;MA | Retrieves all records in which the entry for the Keyword field contains either *BA* or *MA*. Can also include the relational operators > or < (e.g., <10; >15, meaning less than 10 or greater than 15). |

*Table 3.4:* Examples of search criteria in the Retrieve Spec (continued)

| EXAMPLE | MEANING |
|---|---|
| **Special matches in Keyword fields only: (continued)** | |
| &MA;PhD | Retrieves all records in which the entry for the Keyword field contains *MA* and *PhD*. |
| **Special match in Date fields only:** | |
| ]????/02/?? | Finds all dates with the month 02 or February. |
| ]1978/??/15 | Matches all dates in the year 1978 and the day of 15 for any month. |
| **Special matches in all the information types:** | |
| /.. | Retrieves all incorrectly formatted values. |

## USING SEARCH CRITERIA IN THE SAMPLE DATABASE

You will now practice setting up search criteria and retrieving matching records in your sample database.

1. Choose the Search/Update option on the File Menu by typing **s** and pressing Return to select your Personnel database.

2. The first search you are going to do is to locate all of the records in which the Department begins with the letter *a*. To do this, press the Return key twice to move the cursor to the Department field and type **a..** (the letter *a* and two periods).

3. Now press F10 to have Q&A retrieve these records. Once the program has finished working, James Thornfield's record will appear on your screen.

4. To see how many other matches were made during this search, press F6 to get a table view (this always gives you a quick view of the number and types of records retrieved by the search).

Figure 3.21 shows you these records. See that there are six records in which the name of the department begins with *a*—four in Accounting and two in Adminstration.

You can further restrict this search. To do so, first press F10 to display the first record on the screen and then press F7, the Search key.

Q&A now displays the Retrieve Spec screen again. Notice that your previous criterion is still listed in the Department field. You could delete it and start over or add to it, but leave it alone for now.

For your second search, move the cursor to the Date Hired field. Enter > 1/1/80. This means ''retrieve the records for those employees hired after January 1, 1980.'' But because you have not deleted the ''a..'' criterion in the Department field, this search is further restricted. Q&A will retrieve only those records in which the department starts with *a* and the date hired is after January 1, 1980.

1. Press F10 to have Q&A perform this search. Again, it displays James Thornfield's record.

| Social Security | Department | Last Name | First Name | Position |
|---|---|---|---|---|
| 521-30-7892 | Accounting | Thornfield | James | Bookkeeper |
| 202-56-9078 | Accounting | Zimring | Daniel | Clerk |
| 360-31-5633 | Accounting | Freels | Jessica | Accountant |
| 567-21-3456 | Accounting | Parish | Katherine | Secretary |
| 448-35-9622 | Administration | Brown | Janice | Supervisor |
| 589-11-3276 | Administration | Chang | Edward | President |

```
PERSONEL.DTF          Retrieved form 1    of 6          Total forms: 20

Esc-Exit         { ↓ ↑ Home End PgUp PgDn }-Navigate         F10-Show form
```

*Figure 3.21:* Records in which departments begin with *a*

2. Press F6 again to see the table. It should match the one shown in Figure 3.22.

3. This time, there are only three records that meet these criteria. Press F10 and then press F7 to do another search.

4. This time, delete the criteria listed in the Department and Date Hired fields by moving the cursor to them and pressing the Del key (you can also use Shift-F4 to delete an entire entry in a field).

5. Next, move the cursor to the State field, type /il, and press F10. This means "retrieve those records in which the state is not Illinois." There is only one record in your sample database where Illinois is not the state. When finished with the search, Q&A will display the record of Lisa Burke, who lives in Gary, Indiana.

6. Press F7 to get back to the Retrieve Spec. Delete the /il criterion in the State field and move the cursor to the Birthdate field. Here, enter the criterion **MIN1** and press F10.

This tells Q&A to locate the record with the minimum date in the Birthday field. This will be the oldest person in the company—that is, the one with the earliest date of birth. If you use MIN in fields containing numbers or currency, Q&A will return the record holding the

| Social Security | Department | Last Name | First Name | Position |
|---|---|---|---|---|
| 521-30-7892 | Accounting | Thornfield | James | Bookkeeper |
| 360-31-5633 | Accounting | Freels | Jessica | Accountant |
| 567-21-3456 | Accounting | Parish | Katherine | Secretary |

PERSONEL.DTF     Retrieved form 1     of 3          Total forms: 20

Esc-Exit          { ↓ ↑ Home End PgUp PgDn }-Navigate          F10-Show form

***Figure 3.22:*** Records in which departments begin with *a* and employees were hired after 1/1/80

smallest number or lowest amount of money in that field.

The oldest person in your sample database is the president, Ed Chang, born August 12, 1947, and Q&A displays his record on your screen. You can use the MAX or MIN functions with numbers other than 1. For instance, if you replaced MIN1 with MAX2 in the birthday field, Q&A would retrieve the records of the two youngest employees in the firm.

## *USING EITHER-OR CRITERIA*

You can also set up either-or criteria in fields in the Retrieve Spec.

1.  To see how this works, delete the MIN1 entry in the Birthdate field and move the cursor to the Last Name field.

Q&A uses the semicolon to indicate an OR condition. Here, locate the records where the last name is either Parish or Burgoyne.

2.  To do this, enter **Parish;Burgoyne** in the Last Name field and press Return.

3.  Press F10 and see that the first record retrieved by Q&A is that of Katherine Parish.

4.  Press F10 again and see that it has also retrieved that of Mark Burgoyne.

5.  Now press F7 to return to the Retrieve Spec. This time, you will enter a numerical criterion in the Social Security Number field.

6.  First, return the cursor to the Last Name field and delete the previous criterion.

7.  Press ↑ and enter **580..<800** in the Social Security field. This tells Q&A to retrieve those records in which the Social Security number is greater than or equal to 580 and still less than 800.

8.  Press F10 to process this request. Q&A will display Ronald Graydon's record on your screen.

9.  Press F6 to see what other records have been retrieved in this search.

Figure 3.23 shows you these records. There are five records in which the Social Security numbers (at least the first three digits) are greater than or equal to 580 and less than 800. Q&A is able to process numerical comparisons even though the field is a Text field and contains dashes.

## SEARCHING ACROSS FIELDS

Q&A is set to use the AND as the operator when it searchs across fields. For example, if you wanted to find the employees who are in the Sales department and who hold the position "secretary," you simply type these two criteria in the appropriate field and Q&A will retrieve the forms. However, what if you wanted anyone in Sales or anyone who has the position of secretary? In order to perform this type of search you need to change Q&A's search logic.

To see how this works, press Esc until you return to the File menu. Now type **s** to search, and press Return. On the Retrieve Spec, first change Q&A's search logic before typing in any search criteria.

1. Press Ctrl-F7. Q&A displays the Search Options box as shown in Figure 3.24.

| Social Security | Department | Last Name | First Name | Position |
|---|---|---|---|---|
| 672-01-9942 | Engineering | Graydon | Ronald | Engineer |
| 781-15-0632 | Marketing | Gibbon | Faith | Director |
| 586-03-3187 | Marketing | Burke | Lisa | Vice President |
| 606-33-0915 | Sales | Thompson | Ann | Sales |
| 589-11-3276 | Administration | Chang | Edward | President |

PERSONEL.DTF        Retrieved form 1      of 5          Total forms: 20

Esc-Exit        ( ↓ ↑ Home End PgUp PgDn )-Navigate        F10-Show form

*Figure 3.23:* Records in which the Social Security number begins with numbers between 580 and 800

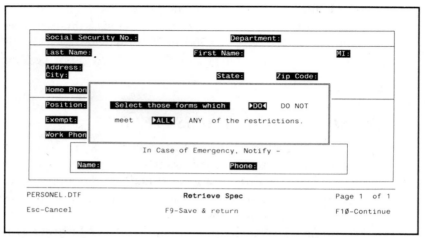

*Figure 3.24:* Q&A's Search Options box

2. To change Q&A's logic to an OR across fields search, press the ↓ once, then the → to highlight the word ANY. Press F10 to save the Search Options box.

Now Q&A will find ALL the records that match ANY of the search criteria. For example, Q&A will be able to retrieve anyone in the PERSONEL.DTF file who is a secretary or who works in the sales department.

## USING WILDCARDS

As your final practice in searching the database, you will use the question mark wildcard character. As you remember from the searches you did in Q&A Write, this character is used to make an exact match of the number of characters in an entry without regard to their content. Mark Burgoyne's Social Security number is lacking a final digit. It consists of only 10 instead of the standard 11 characters. To correct this mistake, you can locate his record by using this wildcard character in the Social Security Number field rather than using an exact match in the Last Name field.

1. First, delete the current AND condition in this field by pressing Shift-F4.

2. Now enter ?????????? (10 question marks) in this field and then press F10.

3. When Q&A displays Mark Burgoyne's record, press End and type **8** at the very end of the number to make this entry correct.

4. Press F10 to save this edit. Q&A responds by displaying a message that there are no more forms. It is letting you know that only Mark's record met the 10-character criterion in this field.

5. Press F7 to return to the Retrieve Spec.

## SORTING RECORDS IN A DATABASE

You can also use the Search/Update function in Q&A to sort the records in your database. As you saw earlier when you retrieved specific records in a file, Q&A presents them on the screen or in a table view in the same order as they were originally entered. You entered the records in the personnel database roughly by department, although not even the department was in strict alphabetical order. Many times you may prefer to see the employees listed in alphabetical order by last name when looking at them in a table view or when browsing through complete records on the screen.

To do this, you change the order of records from the way they were entered by having Q&A File sort them according to an order designated by a specific field. This field is then referred to as a *primary key*. The order can be either ascending (a to z and 0 to 9) or descending (z to a, 9 to 0). Q&A then arranges the records according to the data you have entered in the primary key field. For instance, to sort the personnel database alphabetically by last name, you tell Q&A to use the Last Name field as the primary key and do the sort in ascending order.

Q&A File allows you to refine the sort further by using more than just one key. You can also designate other key fields and their precedence in the sort. For instance, you could designate the Department field as a secondary key along with the Last Name field as the primary key in the same sort operation. Then if Q&A finds two last names that are identical in the database, it will order those two records by the order of the name of their departments.

As a general rule, you do not need to use more than one key field in a sort if that field contains only unique data (no duplicate entries). In your personnel database, the Social Security Number field is such a field. If you wanted the database sorted by Social Security number, you would use only this field as the key. However, the more general the data in the primary key, the more duplicate entries you will find in it, which will require you to use other keys to refine the sort further. For instance, because each department in the database is duplicated for many of the employees, using it as the primary sort key will not result in a very complete sort of the records. In that case, you could use the Last Name field as a secondary key so that employees would be listed first by department and then alphabetically by last name. Because there are employees with the same last name in the database, you would then designate a third key, probably the First Name field, to order these duplicate records.

## USING THE SORT SPEC

To see how easily this is done in Q&A, you will now sort the records in your database according to these criteria. First press F8, listed at the bottom of the screen as the Sort Spec key. Q&A now shows you a new screen called Sort Spec. To designate which fields are primary, secondary, and third, you place the number *1*, *2*, or *3* in the appropriate fields. If you need to use more than three key fields, you just go on adding the next highest number in other fields. To tell Q&A the type of order, ascending or descending, you then place either *as* or *ds* in all of these fields, separated from their number by a comma.

Figure 3.25 shows you how to fill in this Sort Spec. Move the cursor to the Department field and type **1,as**. Then press Return to advance the cursor to the Last Name field, and enter **2,as**. Finally, press Return again to move to the First Name field, and type **3,as**.

You use *as* for ascending because you want all of these fields to be ordered alphabetically from a to z. If you had wanted any of these records arranged in descending order, you would have typed *ds* instead of *as* in the key field. You can mix ascending and descending order of the various keys you're using in a sort as you see fit.

## RESULTS OF THE SORT

Press F10 to have Q&A perform the sort. When it is finished, it will display the first record—that of Jessica Freels in the Accounting

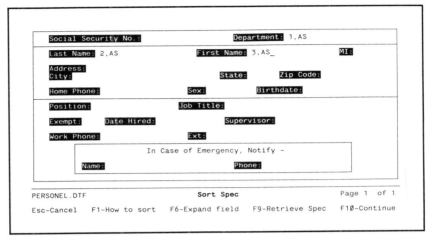

```
┌─────────────────────────────────────────────────────────────────┐
│  ┌───────────────────────────────────────────────────────────┐  │
│  │ Social Security No.:           Department: 1,AS            │  │
│  │                                                           │  │
│  │ Last Name: 2,AS          First Name: 3,AS_        MI:     │  │
│  │                                                           │  │
│  │ Address:                                                  │  │
│  │ City:                        State:      Zip Code:        │  │
│  │                                                           │  │
│  │ Home Phone:            Sex:        Birthdate:             │  │
│  │                                                           │  │
│  │ Position:              Job Title:                         │  │
│  │                                                           │  │
│  │ Exempt:     Date Hired:          Supervisor:              │  │
│  │                                                           │  │
│  │ Work Phone:            Ext:                               │  │
│  │      ┌────────────────────────────────────────────┐      │  │
│  │      │        In Case of Emergency, Notify -       │      │  │
│  │      │   Name:                    Phone:           │      │  │
│  │      └────────────────────────────────────────────┘      │  │
│  └───────────────────────────────────────────────────────────┘  │
│  PERSONEL.DTF              Sort Spec              Page 1  of 1   │
│                                                                   │
│  Esc-Cancel   F1-How to sort   F6-Expand field   F9-Retrieve Spec   F10-Continue │
└─────────────────────────────────────────────────────────────────┘
```

***Figure 3.25:*** Defining a Sort Spec

department—on your screen. Press F6 to get a table view of the database. Yours should match the screen shown in Figure 3.26. Notice that not only are the departments listed in alphabetical order, but so are each of the last names for every person within a particular department. Look at the order of the Johnsons in Marketing. There they are arranged alphabetically by first name.

You can resort the records in your database as often as you like. Just be aware that the larger the database, the more time-consuming

```
┌─────────────────────────────────────────────────────────────────┐
│  ┌─────────────┬──────────────┬────────────┬────────────┬───────────────┐ │
│  │Social Security│ Department  │ Last Name  │ First Name │  Position     │ │
│  ├─────────────┼──────────────┼────────────┼────────────┼───────────────┤ │
│  │360-31-5633  │Accounting    │Freels      │Jessica     │Accountant     │ │
│  │567-21-3456  │Accounting    │Parish      │Katherine   │Secretary      │ │
│  │521-30-7892  │Accounting    │Thornfield  │James       │Bookkeeper     │ │
│  │202-56-9078  │Accounting    │Zimring     │Daniel      │Clerk          │ │
│  │448-35-9622  │Administration│Brown       │Janice      │Supervisor     │ │
│  │589-11-3276  │Administration│Chang       │Edward      │President      │ │
│  │501-11-4523  │Engineering   │Bennett     │Kelly       │Drafter        │ │
│  │672-01-9942  │Engineering   │Graydon     │Ronald      │Engineer       │ │
│  │225-88-3421  │Engineering   │Peterson    │Monica      │Engineer       │ │
│  │234-57-8908  │Engineering   │Rosner      │Owen        │Drafter        │ │
│  │586-03-3187  │Marketing     │Burke       │Lisa        │Vice President │ │
│  │781-15-0632  │Marketing     │Gibbon      │Faith       │Director       │ │
│  │553-04-0126  │Marketing     │Johnson     │Alice       │Secretary      │ │
│  │456-71-0034  │Marketing     │Johnson     │Jeffry      │Artist         │ │
│  │901-77-3351  │Personnel     │Raye        │Jennifer    │Director       │ │
│  │399-75-2205  │Personnel     │Schumacher  │Keri        │Secretary      │ │
│  │985-41-112   │Sales         │Burgoyne    │Mark        │Sales          │ │
│  └─────────────┴──────────────┴────────────┴────────────┴───────────────┘ │
│  PERSONEL.DTF       Retrieved form 1     of 20      Total forms: 20 │
│                                                                   │
│  Esc-Exit       { ↓ ↑ Home End PgUp PgDn }-Navigate      F10-Show form │
└─────────────────────────────────────────────────────────────────┘
```

***Figure 3.26:*** Table view of the sorted database

sorting it becomes. Having this ability to change the order means you don't have to worry about the order in which records are entered. Q&A will always preserve the original order of entry in the database file saved on disk. Press Esc now to return to the File Menu before going on.

# REDESIGNING A DATABASE

You can redesign a Q&A database at any time, even if you have entered data in the fields. You must, however, be careful that you do not alter any of the fields containing data in a way that could damage the data. For example, if you shorten a date field too much, your dates will become unrecognizable. During a redesign, Q&A allows you to rearrange the layout of existing fields, change their length, delete them, or even add new fields. You can also modify the field type and format for any existing field.

## MAKING BACKUPS OF YOUR DATABASE FILES

Before redesigning any of your databases, you should make a backup copy of them on a data disk. That way, even if you make a change that damages some of the data, you will have a copy that is still intact. You can use the DOS COPY command to make this backup, or the Backup option on the File menu. If you use DOS COPY, you will have to copy two files for each database, but if you use the Backup selection, Q&A will copy both for you. Q&A automatically makes a file with the extension .DTF and a second with the extension .IDX. There are always two files required to use a database. For your sample database, they are PERSONEL.DTF and PERSONEL.IDX. Do not forget to copy both on a backup diskette. You can do this very easily by giving the COPY command as

COPY PERSONEL.* A:

at the B > or C > prompt, and pressing Return. To do this, however, you must exit Q&A (from the Main Menu). An easier method is to choose Backup from the File Menu. Place the backup data disk in drive A: (in place of your Q&A system disk, if you have a two floppy drive computer). Choose the .DTF file you wish to back up from the list of files and press Return. Press Shift-F4 to erase the drive letter on the Backup To: line and type **A:** and the name for your backup file.

Go ahead and make a backup copy of your sample database before going on to this next exercise. Once you have done so, replace the backup disk with the Q&A program disk and boot up the program again. Choose File at the Main Menu and then Design file from the File Menu.

## REDESIGNING YOUR SAMPLE DATABASE

You are now going to redesign your sample database, first by modifying two of the existing fields and then by adding some new fields to a second screen page. Choose the Redesign a file option by typing **r**. Q&A then asks you the name of the database. Type **personel** and press Return, or simply press Return if that file is already listed before the cursor.

Q&A will then show you your form just as it appears in Figure 3.27. All of the fields now contain two-letter codes. These codes are very important to your database. You must always be careful not to

```
┌─────────────────────────────────────────────────────────────────┐
│   ┌─────────────────────────────────────────────────────────┐    │
│   ┤  Social Security No.:AA            Department:AB          │    │
│   │ Last Name:AC              First Name:AD          MI:AE >  │    │
│   │ Address:AF                                                │    │
│   │ City:AG                       State:AH  >  Zip Code:AI    │    │
│   │ Home Phone:AJ         Sex:AK>       Birthdate:AL          │    │
│   │ Position:AM           Job Title:AN                        │    │
│   │ Exempt:AO> Date Hired:AP          Supervisor:AQ           │    │
│   │ Work Phone:AR              Ext:AS                         │    │
│   │     ┌───────────────────────────────────────────────┐    │    │
│   │     │      In Case of Emergency, Notify -            │    │    │
│   │     │   Name:AT                 Phone:AU             │    │    │
│   │     └───────────────────────────────────────────────┘    │    │
│   └─────────────────────────────────────────────────────────┘    │
│ ▐┴┴┴T┴┴┴┴T┴┴┴┴1T┴┴┴┴T┴┴┴2┴T┴┴┴┴3┴┴┴┴T┴┴┴┴4┴┴┴┴T┴┴┴5┴┴┴┴T┴┴┴6┴┴┴┴T┴┴┴┴7┴┴┴┴T┴┴┴┴8
│ PERSONEL                            2 %   Line 1 of Page 1 of 1    │
│ Esc-Cancel        F1-How to design        F8-Options      F10-Continue │
└─────────────────────────────────────────────────────────────────┘
```

*Figure 3.27:* The sample form as it appears during Redesign

alter or delete them when making changes to the fields. If you move a field to a new place in the form, you must make sure that you move the code along with it. If you don't, Q&A will not be able to locate the data that you have already entered in the database for this field.

If you should alter one of these codes by mistake, reenter it exactly as it appears on the screen. To make a hard copy of this screen that you can have at your side as you make changes here, turn on your printer and hold down one of the Shift keys and then press the Print Screen key (marked PrtSc).

***EDITING AN EXISTING FIELD***   Whenever you make changes to a form in Redesign, all of the same editing features are available that you had when you first designed the form. The first change you are going to make is to the field name Birthdate. You want to change it to read Date of Birth. Press ↓ eight times until the cursor is on the line containing Birthdate. Next, press Ctrl and then press → four times to reach the *B* in Birthdate. Finally, press ← four times and type **Date of Birth** from this position. Part of this new field name will be typed over the existing Birthdate.

***ADDING NEW FIELDS***   Now you want to add some new fields on a second page of the form. To do this, press the PgDn key. You will then see a blank screen marked Page 2 of 2. Here you will add salary data and information on the employee's educational background. These fields and their layout are shown in Figure 3.28.

The last two fields, for listing job-related courses taken and comments, differ slightly from the other fields you have entered in this form. The data entry for both can consist of multiple lines of information. Furthermore, they are set up so that these lines will be both left- and right-justified after their field names. To do this, you enter the left angle bracket (or less-than symbol) instead of the regular colon after the field name. You then indicate how far to the right and how far down the field is to extend, by entering a right angle bracket (or greater-than symbol). You have already used the right angle bracket to show the end of the field in lines containing more than one field.

You can also create fields with multiple-line entries by using the standard colon after the field name and then a right angle bracket to show where the field ends. If you set a field up this way, your data will

*Figure 3.28:* Adding new fields to Page 2 of the form

not be left-justified on succeeding lines. It will instead extend all the way to the left margin during word wrap. When you set up multiple-line fields, you can't have any other characters on the line containing the field name or any of the succeeding lines until after the > marking the end of this field. This is the reason that the border drawn with the line drawing feature does not include these two fields.

To create this new screen page and add all of these new fields, take the following steps:

1. Move the cursor down to line 2, press Tab, and type **Hourly Rate:**.

2. Press Tab twice and → twice to position the cursor in column 37. Type **OT Authorized?:**. Then position the cursor in column 55 and type >.

3. Press → to move the cursor to column 58. Type **Total Hours:**.

4. Press Return and then Tab; type **Fulltime?:**. Press the → key until the cursor is in column 18; type >.

5. Press Return and then Tab and type **Total Hours:**.

6. Press Tab twice and then → twice to position the cursor in column 37; type **OT Rate:**.

7. Press the Tab key to move the cursor to column 55; type **OT Total:**.

8. Press Return twice to locate the cursor on line 6. Press Tab and type **Commission?:**. Press → to move to column 20; type >.

9. Press → to move to column 24 and type **Class:**.

10. Press Tab and then → twice to position the cursor in column 37. Type **Rate:**.

11. Press → to move the cursor to column 50; type **Yearly Quota:**.

12. Press Return; then press Tab and type **Base Salary:**.

13. Press Tab three times; then press → once until the cursor is in column 46. Type **Commission Total:**.

14. Press Return twice to locate the cursor on line 9. Press Tab and type **Current Salary:**.

15. Press Tab twice and then use the → key to move the cursor to column 37. Type **Starting Salary:**.

16. Press Tab twice and then use the → key to move the cursor to column 67. Type **%:**.

17. Press Return twice to move the cursor down to line 11. Then press Tab and type **Date of Last Review:**.

18. Press Tab and then use the → key to move the cursor to column 41. Type **Evaluation Codes:**.

19. Press Return twice to move the cursor down to line 13. Press Tab and type **Total Years of School:**.

20. Press → to move the cursor to column 33. Type **College Attended:**.

21. Press Return, then Tab, and type **Degree:**.

22. Press Tab twice and the → key once to move the cursor to column 26. Type **Other:**.

23. Press Return and then Tab. Type **Foreign Languages:**.

24. Press Return twice to move the cursor down to line 17. Type **Job Related Courses**<. Press Tab six times and the ↓ key to move to the next line. Then press → four times to move to column 79. Type >.

25. Press Return and type **Comments**< at the beginning of line 19. Press ↓ twice to go down to line 21, press Tab seven times, and then press → four times to go to column 79. Type >.

26. Press the Home key twice to move the cursor to column 1 of line 1. Press F8, type **d**, and press Return.

27. Press → and move the cursor to column 80 in line 1.

28. Press ↓ and move the cursor down to line 16.

29. Press ← and move the cursor to column 1.

30. Press ↑ and move the cursor up to line 1 to complete the outside border.

31. Press → and move the cursor to column 35.

32. Press ↓ and move the cursor down to line 10.

33. Press → and move the cursor to column 80.

34. Press ↑ and move the cursor up to line 5.

35. Press ← and move the cursor to column 1.

36. Press ↓ and move the cursor to line 8.

37. Press → and move the cursor to column 80.

38. Press ↓ and move the cursor to line 12.

39. Press ← and move the cursor to column 1 to complete the line drawing.

40. Press F10 to exit draw mode, and check your screen against the one shown in Figure 3.28. If everything checks, press F10 again to save your design.

**EDITING FIELD TYPES IN EXISTING FIELDS**   After you save this new design, Q&A presents you again with the Format Spec for Page 1 (notice that now the indicator shows that this is Page 1 of 2). Here, you will change the format of the Exempt field to convert the yes or no input to uppercase. First, press the Caps Lock key and then press ↓ six times to move the cursor to the *Y* in the Exempt field. Press → two times and type **u**, just as it is shown in Figure 3.29. You do not need to make any more changes to the Format Spec on this page.

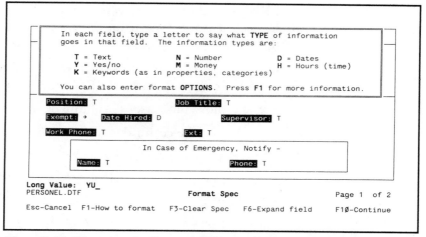

*Figure 3.29:* Changing the Exempt field to uppercase

When working with your own database files, you may find that you need to change not only the formatting characteristics of a field but its field type as well. To do this, you simply move the cursor to the field and type in the new code letter. If your field is too small to accept the new field and formatting codes, press F6 to move to the data entry line at the bottom of the screen. Always be careful when modifying field types if you have already entered data into the database. Changing a field from Numeric or Date to Text type would do no harm to your data, while changing a field type from Text to Money or Numeric would.

***DEFINING FIELD TYPES FOR NEW FIELDS*** Press the PgDn key to define the field types for the new fields you have added to your sample database. Figures 3.30 and 3.31 show you the field types for each of these. Go ahead and type in the codes as shown there. Press Return after typing in the code letters for each.

As you can see, here you will be using some new field types not used in the fields on Page 1 of the form. The first field on this screen page contains the hourly rate for non-exempt employees. This should be a Money field, though the amounts you enter here will be too small to require formatting with commas. The same is true of the overtime rate you will enter in the OT Rate field. The rest of the Money fields will

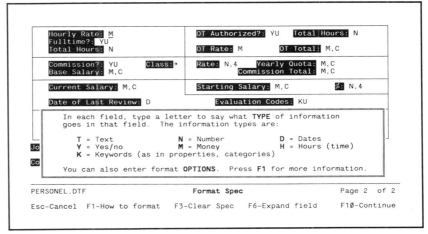

*Figure 3.30:* Assigning field types to the first 18 fields of Page 2

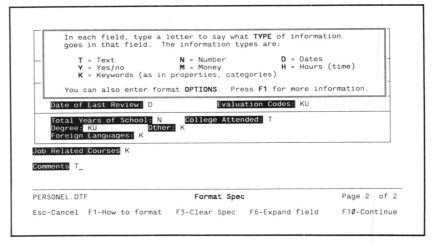

*Figure 3.31:* Assigning field types to the last seven fields of Page 2

have entries large enough to require the use of commas in the figures, so use the C code after M for the Money type.

The Rate field will contain the commission rate for all sales employees who are paid a commission on their total sales. This will be defined as a numeric field with four decimal places (N,4). The same is true of the % field that will show the percent of increase between the starting and current salary figures of the exempt employees. Later, in Chapter 7, you will customize these fields so that their values are automatically multiplied by 100. You will also learn how to have Q&A perform the calculation between the starting and current salary and enter the appropriate value in the % field.

Look at the Evaluation Codes field. It will contain standard codes and numerical ratings from the last review given to each employee. The field type is Keyword because this allows you to enter these codes separated by commas and later do searches on any one of them. This makes it possible, for instance, to find all of the employees who were rated substandard in attendance or excellent in accuracy. The Keyword field type is also used in the Degree, Other, Foreign Languages, and Job Related Courses fields. Each of these fields can contain several entries in the same field.

Go ahead and assign these field and format codes to those in your database. As soon as you type **k,u** in the Evaluation Codes field and press Return, your screen will automatically change to match the one shown in Figure 3.31. When you have finished and have checked that the fields are correct, press F10. You will then be presented with the Format Options screen that you saw when first designing this database. Do not make any changes here; just press F10 to complete your redesign. This will take you back to the File Menu.

## ADDING DATA
## TO YOUR REDESIGNED DATABASE

To add data to the new fields you just added, you use the Search/Update option rather than the Add data option. You use the Add data option only to add new records to your database (Form 21 in your Personnel database). Here, you want only to add new information to the existing 20 records in your database on Page 2. Type **s** and press Return to select the database to update. Press F10 to retrieve all of the records (they all need to be updated).

Q&A will then bring up on your screen Page 1 of the first form in your database, that of James Thornfield. Notice that even though you changed the formatting of the Exempt field to have its entry automatically converted from lowercase to uppercase, this field still shows a lowercase *y*. Q&A cannot go back and reformat all of the entries already made in the existing records to the new format, though from now on it will do so in all new records you add to this database. You will have to retype all of the entries in the existing 20 records to have them displayed in uppercase.

Move the cursor down to this field and type **y**. It will now be displayed as an uppercase letter. Then press the PgDn key to move to the second page of this form. You always must press the PgDn key to go to succeeding pages of a Q&A form. You do not automatically advance to the next page when you press Return at the last field of the page.

Figure 3.32 shows the filled-in Page 2 for James Thornfield's record. To fill it out as shown, press ↓ three times to reach the Commission field; type **n**. Then press ↓ twice to reach the Current Salary field; type **25500**. You do not need to add the dollar sign, comma, or period here. Press Return and then enter **23500** in the Starting Salary field. Press Return twice to advance to the Date of Last Review field. You can enter this date as **1/20/86** and press Return.

Then enter the evaluation codes as shown and press Return. Be sure and type the semicolons as shown. They designate each code as a separate Keyword field entry. Enter **16** in the Total Years of School field, and press Return to advance to the College Attended field. Type **University of Illinois** and press Return. Enter **ba** in the Degree field. Next, press ↓ to go to the Foreign Languages field. Enter **German** and press Return to advance to the Job Related Courses field.

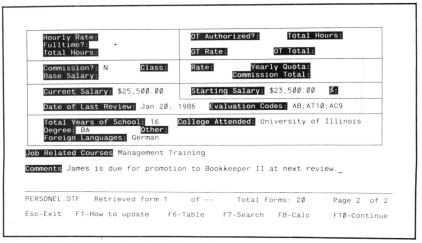

*Figure 3.32:* Data for Page 2 of Form 1

Enter **Management Training** and press Return. Here, the cursor advances to the next line of this field rather than to the Comments field. This is because this is a multiple-line field. If a word at the end of a line in such a field extends beyond column 80, word wrap would automatically place it on the next line. There is no need to press Return at the end of the line unless you want to separate part of the entry on different lines. Press Return again and type in the comment as shown in the Comments field. Then press F10 to save this record and advance to the next record in the database.

Figure 3.33 shows you the data for Page 2 of the second form in your database, that of Daniel Zimring. Because of Daniel's non-exempt status, you will fill in the information in the first part of this page. You need only type **9.5** in the Hourly Rate field. Type **y** in the OT Authorized and Fulltime fields. Enter the OT Rate as **14.25**. All of the rest of the fields are input just as you did for James Thornfield. When inputting the comments in the Comments field, let Q&A word wrap the lines as shown.

The rest of the data for Page 2 of the remaining 18 forms are shown in Appendix A of this book. Refer to it now and enter the rest of the data just as you did with these first two forms before doing the printing exercises in the next section of this chapter.

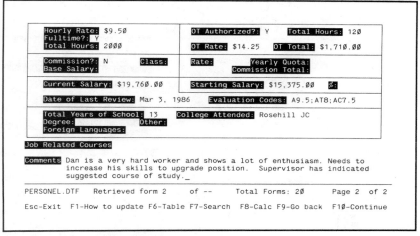

*Figure 3.33:* Data for Page 2 of Form 2

# PRINTING FORMS IN A DATABASE

Q&A File offers you many printing options that do not require the use of Q&A Report. You can print copies of your entire forms, or particular information from each one. You can generate mailing labels or limited reports, and you can print data on preprinted forms. However, Q&A File does not allow you to do subtotals and totals or to add other calculated fields in your reports. That job is left to Q&A Report, which is covered in Chapter Five.

To print information from your database using Q&A File, you must set up a Print Specification. You can create as many of these as you want for a particular database file. They are saved on disk and can be reused whenever you need to print a new report. When you set up a Print Spec, you can use a Retrieve Spec to limit the records used, and a Sort Spec to change the order of the printing as well as to indicate which fields are to be printed.

## PRINTING THE
## ENTIRE DATABASE AS ENTERED

To obtain a hard copy of all of the records and of all of the fields in each record, you merely press F10 at the Retrieve Spec prompt and then F10 again at the Field Spec prompt. Q&A also allows you to choose to print these records either with or without their field names. (The data lists in Appendix A are examples of using this method with field names printed.) This allows you to store a hard copy of all the data in your entire database exactly as it was entered at any stage of its growth.

## CONTROLLING THE ORDER
## OF THE FIELDS IN PRINTING

To create more limited printouts, Q&A gives you two methods for specifying where the fields should be printed on each page. You can use either what the documentation refers to as a *free-form* method or a *coordinate* method. With a free-form report, you merely indicate in the Fields Spec form the order and spacing of each field by first typing a number indicating its order, followed by either a plus ( + ) or x to indicate whether or not to start a new line. Typing + after the number in a field tells Q&A to print the next field one space after it on the same line, while typing **x** after the number indicates that the next field should be printed at the beginning of the following line. If you do not wish to rearrange the fields in a different order from the way they appear on the screen, you merely type + or **x** to indicate where to start a new line.

With the coordinate method, you specify the line and then the column number indicating where the printing of each field is to begin. This method gives you greater control over the output, though it is harder to set up initially. You will use this method most often to create a Print Spec for printing on preprinted forms.

***CREATING AND PRINTING A PHONE LIST FROM THE SAMPLE DATABASE***   As your first practice with printing forms, you will create a phone list using the sample Personnel database. At the File Menu, type **4** and press Return to select PERSONEL.DTF. The Print Menu now appears. It has four options. The first, Design/Redesign a spec, is where you set up your print specifications. You can always modify an existing Print Spec by using the same menu option. After creating a Print Spec, you can use the second option, Print forms, to actually print them. As you will see, Q&A also allows you to print your report right after defining a Print Spec from within the first option. The third choice, Set global options, is used to set up print specifications as defaults for all future reports. The last option, Rename/Delete/Copy, is used to rename, delete, or copy existing print specification files.

To get started, press Return (or type **1**). You are asked to give a name to the Print Spec. Type the name **phonelst** and press Return. You are then presented with a Retrieve Spec on Page 1 of 2 of your Personnel database. The Retrieve Spec here works exactly as it did when searching the database earlier. Notice that the F8 option to sort the database is still available from this screen. Because you want to print out the telephone numbers and extensions for all the employees, you do not need to limit the search by entering criteria in the Retrieve Spec.

You will, however, want to sort the database alphabetically for this Print Specification. Press F8 to go to the Sort Spec. Move the cursor down to the Last Name field and type **1,as** and press Return. In the First Name field, type **2,as** and press Return again. This will sort the records alphabetically by last name and first name without regard to department. Press F10 to sort the records and continue defining the Print Spec.

You now should see a new screen marked Fields Spec for PHONELST, similar to the one shown in Figure 3.34. Here you will specify the fields to include and their order for the final printed report. Fill it out exactly as it is shown in Figure 3.34.

In the phone list you want to have first name, middle initial, and last name on the first line. The second line will start with the name of the department, followed by the position. The third and final line will list the telephone number followed by the extension. These are the only fields that need to be included in this phone list report.

To mark them, you must give each one a number indicating the order of their printing, as well as entering either a + or **x** to indicate where the next field will be printed. To do this, take the following steps:

1. Move the cursor to the First Name: field, type **1 +** , and press Return.

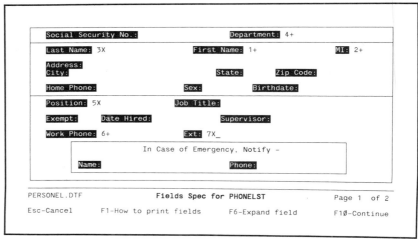

***Figure 3.34:*** Fields Spec screen for PHONELST

2. Type **2 +** in the MI: field and press Shift-Tab twice to move the cursor back to the Last Name: field.

3. Type **3x**. (This indicates that the field marked 4 will start on a new line.)

4. Press the ↑ key and then press Return to get to the Department: field. Type **4 +** and then press Shift-Tab to return to the first field.

5. Press the ↓ key to move the cursor to the Position: field. Type **5x** there.

6. Press the ↓ key to move to the Work Phone: field, type **6 +** and press Return.

7. Type **7x** in the Ext: field and press F10 to finish the definition of the Fields Spec.

You can optionally control the spacing of your printed form by adding a whole number after the *x* or + on the Field Spec. For example, **1 + ,2** would print the field as the first field of the report and then leave two spaces. **3x,5** would print the field as the third on the report followed by five carriage returns.

The next screen you will see is the Print Options screen shown in Figure 3.35. The first option on this screen allows you to tell Q&A to which printer it should send your Print Spec file. You can also print the file to disk by choosing that option. It allows you to create an ASCII file containing the data specified (see Chapter 8 for details on using ASCII files). You can also choose the SCREEN option to preview the report on the screen before sending it to the printer for a hard copy. This is useful because it allows you to make sure that you have arranged everything correctly before printing a large report.

The next option tells Q&A what type of paper feed you require. You would change the default of Continuous to Manual if you were printing on single sheets of paper. The Printer offset option works just as it does in the word processor. You change it from 0 to a positive number to move the position of the print head relative to the beginning of the page. The next option, Printer control codes, also works just like it does in Q&A Write. Here, you can enter escape codes to have your printer produce special printing effects.

```
                         FILE PRINT OPTIONS

        Print to.....:    ▶PtrA◀  PtrB   PtrC   PtrD   PtrE   DISK   SCREEN

        Type of paper feed............:   Manual  ▶Continuous◀  Bin1   Bin2   Bin3

        Printer offset................:   Ø

        Printer control codes.........:   _____

        Print field labels?...........:   Yes  ▶No◀

        Number of copies..............:   1

        Number of forms per page......:   15

        Number of labels across.......:   ▶1◀  2   3   4   5   6   7   8
       _____
  PERSONEL.DTF            Print Options for PHONELST

  Esc-Cancel         F8-Define Page          F9-Go back            F10-Continue
```

*Figure 3.35:* Print Options screen for the PHONELST Print Spec

The fifth option allows you to have the field names as part of your report. Most of the time, as with your phone list, you will not want the field names to be printed as part of the report. If you do, you change this option from No to Yes.

The next two options on this page control the number of copies to be printed and the number of records to be included on a single printed page. You set this last option according to the number of lines you have specified in the report. If you were printing an entire page of a screen form, you could set this number to 3, as three 21-line screens will fit on a single 66-line printed page. If you are printing fewer lines from a page, as you are in the phone list, you can set this number higher. In this case, you can get 15 records on a single printed page.

The last option allows you to print in columns or multiple labels across in the case of mailing labels. If you use the Print Spec to design an address label, this option will allow you to print up to eight labels across the page.

At this point, go ahead and set up your Print Options screen as it is shown in Figure 3.35. Then press F10 to save your Print Spec on disk. You will then receive a boxed message indicating that your Print Spec has been saved and giving you the option of now printing the forms. If you press Return at this point, Q&A will return you to the Print Menu. From there, you can later print the phone list by choosing the Print forms option and supplying the name of your Print Spec, PHONELST. Q&A will then give you a chance either to make any last-minute changes to this Print Spec before using it, or to go ahead and print your report.

If you want to get a printout of your phone list now, press the ← key to change the option to Yes, turn on your printer, and then press Return. Q&A will keep you informed of its progress by displaying a box indicating progress first in scanning the records and then in printing them. You can press Esc during the printing to abandon printing and return to the File Menu. When Q&A has finished printing your report, you will be returned to the Print Menu.

Figure 3.36 shows you the first five records as they would appear if you had selected the SCREEN option from the Print Options screen and then had instructed Q&A to go ahead and print the report. Notice that the order is alphabetical by last name, but because you indicated that the last name was to be printed third on the first line, the names now appear in standard first name, last name order in the phone list.

**CREATING AND PRINTING MAILING LABELS FROM THE SAMPLE DATABASE** Next, you will set up a Print Spec to print mailing labels using the home address of each employee. Choose the

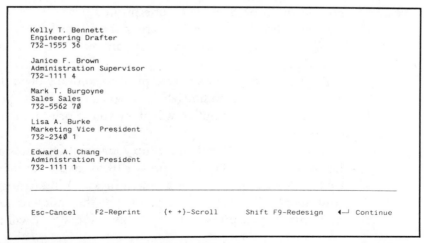

*Figure 3.36:* Phone list printed to screen

Design/Redesign option by typing **d**, and press Return to use the PERSONEL.DTF file. Give the Print Spec the name MAILABEL, when you are prompted to name it. Just as with the previous print spec, you will want to use all of the records in the database, so you need not fill out the Retrieve Spec. You will want to sort the records again, this time first by zipcode and then by last name.

Press F8 to sort the database and then move the cursor to the Last Name: field. Type **2,as** and press Return. Now press the ↓ key to move the cursor to the line containing the Zip Code field and then press Return twice to locate the cursor in it. Type **1,as** and then press F10 to go on to the Fields Spec.

Figure 3.37 shows you the Fields Spec for this report. It will include only the first and last name (in first name, last name order) on the first line. The second will have only the street address, and the third line will include city, state, and zipcode, in that order. Go ahead and fill out your Fields Spec as shown in Figure 3.37. When you have finished, press F10 to go on to the Print Options screen.

To print mailing labels properly, you must leave the Number of forms per printed page set to 1, and also change the number of lines per page. To do this, press F8 at this screen to access the Define Page options. Figure 3.38 shows you this screen with the proper settings for printing using this Print Spec with $1\frac{1}{2} \times 4$-inch continuous-feed mailing labels. Because Q&A will print one label per page, the page

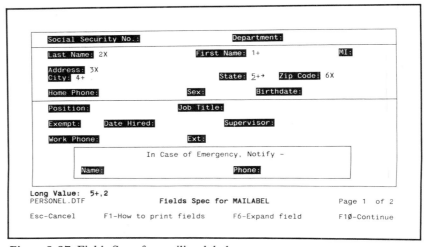

*Figure 3.37:* Fields Spec for mailing labels

length had to be changed from the default of 66 to 8 lines (a 1½-inch-long label measures slightly under 9 lines). Because the label is only four inches wide, the page width was modified from the default of 140 (for 14-inch-wide paper) to 40 columns.

The top margin was left at its default of 3 to center the printing of the three lines vertically on the label. Setting the left margin to 4 assures that the printing will be indented and centered horizontally on the label. If you use mailing labels of other sizes, you will have to experiment with these settings until you have them just right for the size of labels you use.

If you have 1½ × 4-inch labels and want to try using this Print Spec to print them out, set the values of your Define Page screen to match those shown in Figure 3.38 and then press F10 to save this Print Spec. You can then have Q&A print the labels by answering Yes to the prompt asking if you want to print the forms now.

If you do not have mailing labels but want to see how these labels will look printed, leave the default values alone and then press F9 to return to the Print Options screen. Set the number of forms per printed page to 15. You can then change the Print to option to SCREEN if you don't want to send them to the printer; then press F10. Answer Yes when you are prompted about printing the forms now. Figure 3.39 shows how the first screen of this Print Spec should look.

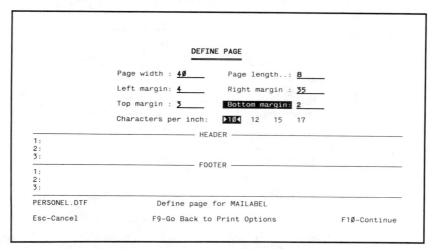

*Figure 3.38:* Define Page options for the MAILABEL Print Spec

```
        John Shepard
        9Ø034 Deerfield Road
        Olympia Fields IL  60355

        Ronald Graydon
        67Ø Glen Way, Apt. 7Ø1Ø
        Chicago IL  6Ø6Ø1

        Keri Schumacher
        8Ø5 Lake Shore Drive, Apt. 56Ø2
        Chicago IL  6Ø6Ø1

        Jessica Freels
        7823 Chase Plaza, Apt. 345
        Chicago IL  6Ø635

        James Thornfield
        345 South Birch Street
        Riverdale IL  6Ø635
```

```
  Esc-Cancel    F2-Reprint    (← →)-Scroll    Shift F9-Redesign   ◄┘ Continue
```

*Figure 3.39:* Mailing labels printed to screen

### CREATING AND PRINTING A SIMPLE REPORT FROM THE SAMPLE DATABASE

As a final exercise, you will set a Print Spec that will generate a report indicating all of those employees who are now due for an evaluation review. To create this report, type **d** to design a third Print Spec and press Return to select the personnel database. Give it the name **review** and press Return to get to the Retrieve Spec.

Here, you will want to set up a condition to retrieve only those records in which the date of the last review is January 1, 1986 or earlier.

1. Press the PgDn key to get the second page of the screen and then press ↓ until the cursor is located in the Date of Last Review: field.

2. There, enter **..1/1/86**. The two periods before 1/1/86 mean "less than or equal to." Q&A will retrieve only those records in which the entry for the last review is either January 1, 1986 or before.

3. Press F8 next to sort the database. Move the cursor to the Department: field. Enter **1,as** and then press the PgDn key to advance to the second page of the form.

4. Move the cursor down to the Date of Last Review: field and type **2,as**.

5. Press F10 to advance to the Fields Spec. Figures 3.40 and 3.41 show how it is to be filled out. The first line of the report will include the department, first name, last name, position, and job title, in that order. The second line will include the date of the last review, the current salary, and the evaluation codes given at that review, in that order.

6. Go ahead and fill out your Fields Spec just as it is shown in Figures 3.40 and 3.41. When you have entered **5x** in the Job Title: field, press the PgDn key to get to the next screen. Once you have finished filling it out, press F10 to save this Print Spec on disk.

7. At the Print Options screen, change the Number of forms printed per page to **25**.

8. Press F8 to access the Define Page screen. On this screen, you will enter a left margin setting of **5** and widen the top and bottom margins from 3 to **6** lines.

9. Then press ↓ until Header is highlighted. Here you will enter a header to appear in the top margin of the report. Type **Personnel Due for Review as of November 25, 1986.**

10. Press the Home key and then the Ins key. Then press the space bar until you have this line almost centered on the

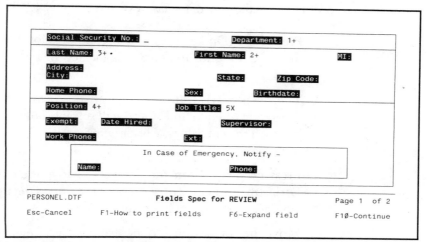

*Figure 3.40:* Page 1 of the Fields Spec for the review report

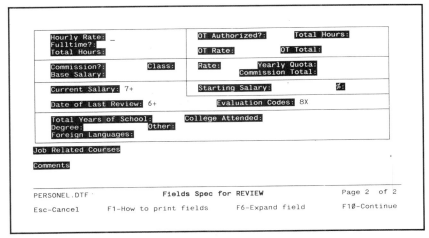

*Figure 3.41:* Page 2 of the Fields Spec for the review report

screen. (You will learn in the next chapter how to automatically center a header or footer from the Define Page screen.)

11. Press Return and enter the footer, **Page #**.

12. Press Home and the Ins key again. Press the space bar until the *P* of *Page* is aligned below the first *e* of *Review* in the header. Figure 3.42 shows you how this will appear.

13. Press F10 to save this Print Spec. If you want, answer Yes to have the report printed now. Figure 3.43 shows you how the records in this report appear when printed to screen.

14. When you have returned to the Print Menu, press Esc to return to the File Menu once again.

## *PRINTING FIELDS ON PREPRINTED FORMS*

To use preprinted forms with your Q&A databases, you must use the coordinate method, telling the program where to print each field on the form. This involves specifying first the number of the line and then the number of the column for each field you wish to use. The line number is separated from the column number by a comma.

A fast way to determine the column and line number for each entry is to put one of your preprinted forms in a typewriter and count

```
                          DEFINE PAGE
                          ──────────

          Page width : 240        Page length..: 66

          Left margin: 5          Right margin : 240

          Top margin : 6          Bottom margin: 6

          Characters per inch:   ▶10◀   12   15   17
─────────────────────────── HEADER ───────────────────────────
 1:
 2:          Personnel Due for Review as of November 25, 1986
 3:
─────────────────────────── FOOTER ───────────────────────────
 1:                          Page #_
 2:
 3:
───────────────────────────────────────────────────────────────
PERSONEL.DTF              Define page for REVIEW

Esc-Cancel          F9-Go Back to Print Options        F10-Continue
```

*Figure 3.42:* The Define Page screen for the REVIEW Print Spec

```
Accounting Katherine Parish Secretary Clerk Typist IV
Jan 5, 1985 $20,800.00 A7.5;AT5;AC8

Accounting Jessica Freels Accountant Senior Accountant II
Dec 12, 1985 $35,500.00 A10;AT9;AC10

Administration Janice Brown Supervisor Administrative Assistant
May 24, 1985 $39,800.00 A8;AT6;AC8

Engineering Ronald Graydon Engineer Head of Engineering
Nov 15, 1985 $45,000.00 A10;AT10;AC10

Marketing Alice Johnson Secretary Clerk/Typist II
Jan 1, 1986 $30,680.00 A10;AT8.5;AC9.5

Sales Ann Thompson Sales Central Account Executive
Oct 10, 1985 $27,600.00 A10;AC7
───────────────────────────────────────────────────────────────


Esc-Cancel   F2-Reprint   **** END OF PRINT ****   Shift F9-Redesign  ◀─┘ Continue
```

*Figure 3.43:* Review report printed to screen

off the number of lines and columns for your field entries. You can
have Q&A begin printing the field anywhere after the form label. If
you wish to leave two spaces after the colon in the label, be sure and
count them as part of the column number.

For example, suppose you are using a preprinted form that has the
label Social Security Number: followed by a blank line, and you want
Q&A to print this number from your personnel database. You would

put the form in the typewriter and press Return until you reach the line containing this entry. Say it occurs on the eighth line down from the top of the form. You would then count the number of spaces it takes to reach two spaces beyond the colon on your form. Say this count comes to 30. You then create a Print Spec using the Design/ Redesign a print spec option. In the Social Security Number: field in the Fields Spec, you would enter **8,30**. You would use the same method to determine and define each of the fields to be printed on your form.

Getting each and every field placed properly on your form may take some experimentation, but the time is well worth it. Once you have defined it, you can use the Print Spec over and over again without any modification unless you change the preprinted forms you are using. You can also copy this Print Spec so that it can be used with other database files that use the same preprinted forms.

## *SUMMARY*

Q&A File offers you a sophisticated database management tool. As you have seen, there are many features to this program, all of which are very easy to use. By way of a general review of things you have learned about Q&A File, keep the following steps in mind when creating and using your own database files:

- When designing a new database, first determine all of the different types of information you want to keep in it.

- Each piece of information will become a field of the new database, and each one must be given an identifying label called a field name.

- After deciding upon the number of fields and their field names, start to think about their layout on the screen. If you will be doing data entry from a printed form, you should probably design the screen form to look as much like it as possible. Your database entry form can consist of up to 10 screen pages, each containing 21 lines.

- After laying out the fields and their field names on the screen, you will have to decide which field type to assign each of them. The field type determines not only what kind of data that field can contain but also the way it will be formatted on the screen.

- After assigning field types and saving the database on disk, enter a few records to see if you need to make any modifications either to the layout or to the field type and format.

- If you need to make any changes using the Redesign option, be careful not to disturb the letter codes Q&A places in each field. Always make a backup copy of your database before changing its structure.

- You can retrieve all the records from your database by pressing F10. To change the order in which the records are displayed, you can sort the database, using as many key fields as you need to refine the order. You can then press F10 to browse through each complete record or use F6 to get a table view of the first few fields of each record.

- To retrieve groups of records or a specific record from the database, you restrict the search by entering a condition that must be matched in the appropriate fields. Not all of Q&A's conditional statements can be used with every field type in the database. You will receive an error message referring you to a specific page in your manual if you try to enter a search condition that Q&A cannot perform.

- To print records from the database, you must first set up a Print Spec. This includes filling in a Retrieve Spec that tells the program which records to use (identical to the ones you use when searching the database). It also includes filling in a Fields Spec, which indicates what fields to print.

- When you are finished using Q&A File, always exit back to the Main Menu before turning off your computer. If you have a power interruption or if you fail to exit through the menu system, you may not be able to access your database file again.

While the print options available as part of Q&A File are fine when printing very simple reports or items like mailing labels, they are not adequate for producing all of the kinds of reports that you will need to generate from your databases. In Chapter 5, you will learn how to use Q&A Report, a printing tool that goes far beyond the abilities of the Print Spec in Q&A File. As before, you will find using Q&A Report very easy because so many of its options are just like those you have used in this chapter.

CHAPTER

4

# ADVANCED
# WORD PROCESSING
# APPLICATIONS

*Fast Track*

**To merge-print using data from a Q&A File database**      **194**

into a Q&A Write document, prepare the standard document in Q&A Write. To indicate where you want data from the database to be merged in the letter or form, locate the cursor in the document where you want a field's data inserted. Then press Alt-F7 and enter the name of the database to use (you only need to designate the file the first time you press Alt-F7). A field list will appear; use the ↑ and ↓ arrow keys to highlight the name of the field you wish to use, and press Return. The program will insert the field name enclosed in a pair of asterisks at the cursor's position. Continue this procedure to insert all of the fields you wish to use in the merge.

**To quickly locate a field name in the field list**      **197**

which appears when you press Alt-F7 (after specifying the name of the file), just type the first letter of the field name. Once it is highlighted in the list, press the Return key to insert the field name enclosed within a pair of asterisks into the document.

**To merge-print,**      **199**

press F2 (the Print Options screen will already contain the name of the database file that you specified the first time you pressed Alt-F7 to insert the first field name) and change any print settings that need modification, then press F10. Fill out the Retrieve Spec, press F10 and then fill out the Sort Spec. Finally, press F10 again to start the merging. Press Return when prompted to print the merged documents.

**To format the data merged from the database,**                    203
add the code **(T)** between the field name and the final asterisk to
have any data in that field that has been entered on two lines
printed on a single line in the merged document. Add the **(L)**
code to left-justify data, or the **(R)** to right-justify.

**Q&A Write will automatically address envelopes**                  205
using the inside addresses entered below the line containing the
date in the letter. To print envelopes, press F2, then change
the line spacing from Single to Envelope. Check that the correct
database is listed on the Name of Merge File line and then press
F10. You will be prompted to put an envelope in the printer.
After you position it, press F10 to have it printed. Continue this
procedure until all of your envelopes have been addressed.

**To create mailing labels for your merge letters,**               206
select the Mailing labels option on the Q&A Write menu by
pressing **m** and return (or by typing **8**). Select the correct size of
label for your printer from the list that appears and press
Return. Change any field names on the label form by inserting
the new field name (press Alt-F7, specify the database file,
highlighting the field name to be inserted, and press Return)
and deleting any unwanted field names from the label. Use the
Define Page options (Ctrl-F6) to make any changes to the format (such as 12 cpi). Press F10 to advance to the Mailing
Labels Print Options screen, and then F10 again to print the
labels.

**To chain-print individual documents as one long document,**    **210**

use the **JOIN** embedded command (which can be abbreviated
to **j**) enclosed in a pair of asterisks. Indicate the file name of the
document (along with the drive and directory path) before
the final asterisk, as in *JOIN A:\LETTER1*. Continue to enter
**JOIN** commands, each on its own separate line, for each document that is to be chain-printed. Then, press F2 and print the
document containing these codes as you would any other.

**To establish a print queue**    **211**

that batch-prints a group of separate documents in the order
specified, use the **QUEUE** embedded command enclosed in a
pair of asterisks. Indicate the file name of the document (along
with the drive and directory path) before the final asterisk, as in
*QUEUE A:\REPORT1*. Continue to enter **QUEUE** commands, each on its own separate line, for each document that is
to be batch-printed, in the order in which you want it printed.
Then, press F2 and print the document containing these codes
as you would any other.

**To include data from a Lotus 1-2-3 worksheet**    **211**

in a Q&A Write document, enter the **SPREADSHEET** embedded command (which can be abbreviated to **ss**) enclosed in a
pair of asterisks. Indicate the file name of the worksheet (along
with the drive and directory path) before the final asterisk, as in
*SPREADSHEET C:\123\ACCOUNTS.WK1*. To import and
print just a range of cells, enter the cell addresses of the range or
the range name after the worksheet file name before the final
asterisk. Then, press F2 and print the document containing
these codes as you would any other.

**To insert a graph from a Lotus 1-2-3 worksheet**                    212
    in a Q&A Write document, enter the **GRAPH** embedded command (which can be abbreviated to **g**) enclosed in a pair of asterisks. Indicate the file name of the graph file (along with the drive and directory path) before the final asterisk, as in **∗SPREADSHEET C:\123\ACCOUNTS.PIC∗**. Then, press F2 and print the document containing these codes as you would any other.

**To import an ASCII file into Q&A Write,**                    214
    use the Get option on the Write menu by typing **g** and pressing Return (or by typing **5**) and specifying the name of the document file. Q&A will then automatically display the Import Document screen. Select the Special ASCII option (**2**) to have the text brought in with word wrap for any words that extend beyond the right margin.

**To export a Q&A Write document in ASCII format,**                    216
    press F2, select the Print to DISK option on the Print Options menu, and press F10. Then select either the IBM ASCII or Macintosh ASCII option, enter the file name you want to give to the ASCII file, and press Return. You can also export a Write document to an IBM ASCII file format by pressing Ctrl-F8, entering the file name, and pressing Return.

## OVERVIEW

In this chapter, you will explore more advanced features of using the word processor in Q&A. You will learn techniques for integrating Q&A Write and File, including methods for producing mailing labels and envelopes as well as using Q&A Write documents with other software programs.

You will begin by learning how to use Q&A's merge-printing facility, which allows you to bring data from your database files into word processing documents. As you will see, merge-printing can also be used to print envelopes and to chain together separate document files so that they are printed as one long document.

In addition, you will learn about transferring documents from other software to Q&A Write. These operations can include importing into Q&A Write documents which have been prepared in word processors like WordStar, or spreadsheets and graphs prepared in programs like Lotus 1-2-3.

At other times you may need to transfer out your Q&A Write documents for use with other software programs. This involves exporting the document to an ASCII format which can be read by any number of programs. As you will learn, Q&A provides a simple facility for creating an ASCII document.

## MERGE-PRINTING

The most common application for merge-printing involves using Q&A Write to merge various items which have been stored in a separate data file into a word processing document. This procedure is commonly referred to as mail merge. During mail merge, the program takes a document like a form letter and prints several individualized copies of it at one time. Every printed letter contains a common body of text, although each is individually addressed by substituting the appropriate names and addresses from a single data file where they are stored. In Q&A, this data file is a database, just like your sample personnel file. Substitutions are made in the document from specific fields in the database.

Merge-printing is extremely easy in Q&A. All you have to do is prepare the standard text of the letter, using Q&A Write. Wherever data substitutions must be made, you place the name of the database field containing that information. All that is required is that the field name be enclosed in a pair of asterisks (*). This is similar to the embedded printer commands used in Chapter 2. However, for mail merge documents, Q&A Write automatically places field names surrounded with asterisks wherever you tell it to.

## *PREPARING AN EMPLOYEE LETTER FOR MAIL MERGE*

To see how this is done, press Esc to return to the Main Menu (if you are doing this exercise right after finishing Chapter 3), and then choose the Write option and press Return. Choose the Type/Edit option from the Write Menu, and press Return to display the new document screen. You will now enter the text for the employee letter (shown in Figure 4.1), announcing a new credit union plan to all of the employees. Instead of addressing it to one particular employee, you will use Q&A's mail merge facility to send every employee a personally-addressed letter.

Now that you have completed the body of the letter, you can add in the field names where the data from the personnel file will be printed. Whenever you merge-print a letter, it always contains both

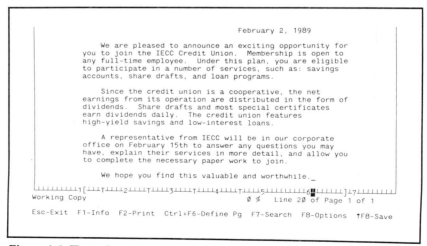

*Figure 4.1:* Text of employee letter

standard text and items that will be supplied from a database (sometimes called *data variables*). In this case, the first name, middle initial, last name, address, city, state, and zipcode of each employee will vary from letter to letter.

Add the name and address merge fields to your employee letter so that the correct data can be retrieved form the personnel database.

1. Place the cursor at the end of the first line, just past the date. Press the Ins key to change to Insert Mode, and press Return three times to insert blank lines.

2. Press Alt-F7. Q&A will prompt you for a data file name. Type in **personel** as shown in Figure 4.2, and press Return.

You will now see a list of the field names from your personnel file. Notice in Figure 4.3 that the field names are listed for you in alphabetical order. This makes it easy to locate the fields you would like to add to your mail merge letter.

3. Use the ↓ key to move down the list until you highlight the First Name field, and press Return.

The field First Name will be placed in your document exactly where the cursor was positioned.

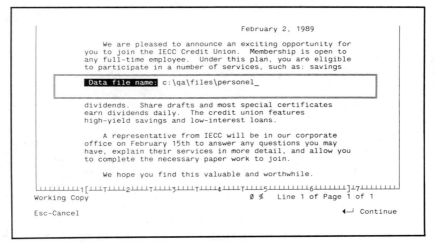

*Figure 4.2:* Naming the Q&A merge database

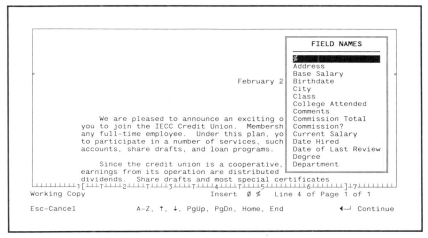

*Figure 4.3:* List of field names from the merge database

4. Now press the space bar once and then press Alt-F7 to see the list of fields again. This time choose MI for *Middle Initial*, and press Return to insert it in the document.

In order to speed up selection of the field names, Q&A allows you to skip to field names beginning with a specific letter. If you type the letter **p**, for example, you will advance to the first field name beginning with *p*. Try this method for the next merge field.

5. Make sure the cursor is positioned correctly in your letter and then press Alt-F7. Now type the letter l. Notice that the highlighted bar moves quickly to the field Last Name, which happens to be the only field beginning with the letter *l*. Press Return to have it inserted in the document.

6. Press Return to move to the next line. Then use Alt-F7 to see the list of field names, and insert Address on this line. Continue the same procedure for the final address line by inserting the City, State, and Zip Code fields.

Notice in Figure 4.4 that the third line of the address contains the standard comma that separates the city from the state. There are also two spaces after the state and before the zipcode. When you place any required spaces between data variables, treat the asterisks as if they were actual alphabetical characters.

```
                                        February 2, 1989

        *First Name* *MI* *Last Name*
        *Address*
        *City*, *State*  *Zip Code*

        Dear *First Name*,_

            We are pleased to announce an exciting opportunity for
        you to join the IECC Credit Union.  Membership is open to
        any full-time employee.  Under this plan, you are eligible
        to participate in a number of services, such as: savings
        accounts, share drafts, and loan programs.

Working Copy                          Insert  Ø %   Line 8 of Page 1 of 1

Esc-Exit  F1-Info  F2-Print  Ctrl+F6-Define Pg  F7-Search  F8-Options  ↑F8-Save
```

*Figure 4.4:* Employee mail merge letter

7. After the Zip Code field, press Return twice to insert a blank line. Now you need to add a salutation to the letter.

8. Type the word **Dear** and press the space bar. Use Alt-F7 to insert the First Name field, and follow it with a comma. Your letter should now look like the one shown in Figure 4.4.

To close the letter, add **Sincerely,** then three blank lines. Now type **Jennifer Raye** and her title, **Director of Personnel**, below. This will end the document.

In Q&A, the field names entered in your document do not have to be identical to the corresponding field names in the database. You have a great deal of latitude in this area. For instance, if you created a field in your database without a name or field label, you could enter a name for the purpose of a mail merge when preparing the letter. At printing time, you would then get a chance to associate this name with the actual field to ensure that the letter is printed correctly. This is done by typing the mail merge field name into the corrected field via an Identifier Spec, which only appears if you need it. In your employee letter the Identifier Spec is not required.

In designing your own database files for form letters or mailing labels, keep in mind the ways in which data items are used by mail merge. For example, if the full employee name was stored in one field it would be impossible to use the first name only, as you did in the salutation. Remember that you can also add a field that contains a person's title—like Mr., Ms., or Mrs.—in such a database. It could then be used in letters that require a more formal greeting like "Dear Mr. Smith." Again, this is only possible if you have the person's name split up into different fields so that you can enter **Dear \*Title\* \*Last Name\*** in the letter. If you kept the full name in one field, the best you could do would be to enter **Dear \*Title\* \*Name\***, which would result in a rather stilted greeting like "Dear Ms. Joan J. Smith."

You will find that you get an unwanted space in the printout if the field that supplies one of the data variables is blank in one or more of the records in the database. Because Q&A does not provide a code that will suppress the space caused by a corresponding blank field, you will have to set up two documents to handle this situation. For instance, if you are using the full name including the middle initial in the first line of your letter's address, and if there exist in the database some records in which you have not entered a middle initial for an employee, the letter will have an unnecessary space between the first and last name.

To get around this, you would first print letters for only those employees whose MI field was not empty. You do this by placing the code / = (for *not empty*) in the MI field in the Retrieve Spec you fill out prior to merge-printing. Then you modify the employee letter by removing the \*MI\* data variable from it, and use merge-printing again, this time placing the code = (for *empty*) in the MI field in the Retrieve Spec.

## *MAIL-MERGE PRINTING*

Now that you have prepared the credit union letter, you should save it under a name. Press Shift-F8, enter a new file name, **22credit.ltr**, and press Return. (This file name includes the date, 2/2, the subject of the letter, and the type of document as the file extension, all in abbreviated form.)

You are now ready to print the letter. In mail-merge printing, you use the same Print Menu as you do when printing a word processing document. Press F2 to access the Print Menu. Figure 4.5 shows you

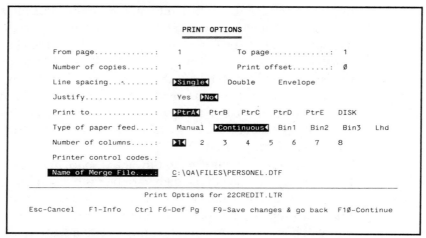

*Figure 4.5:* Print options for mail merge

how to fill out this screen. If you do not use continuous-feed paper with your printer, be sure and change Type of paper feed to Manual. Notice that the database PERSONEL.DTF has already been added to this screen as the Name of Merge File. Q&A transferred the name here during the Alt-F7 operation to assign the merge fields to your letter.

Once you have confirmed the correct selections on the Print Options screen, press F10 to continue. The next screen that appears is the now-familiar Retrieve Spec, identical in form and function to the ones you filled out when doing database searches in Q&A File. Here you can control which records should be used when printing copies of the letter. As usual, if you press F10 at this point, you place no restrictions, and a letter will be produced for every person listed in the database.

Figure 4.6 shows you how to fill out this screen for printing your letters. In this case, you do not need to generate a letter for the Director of Personnel, Jennifer Raye (who wrote the letter and set up the meeting), or the President of the company, Edward Chang (who generated the plan). To exclude them and include all of the other employees, you enter

/Raye;Chang

in the Last Name field. If you remember, the forward slash means *not* and the semicolon means *or*, so that the condition can be translated as "use all of the records except those in which the last name is Raye or Chang."

Once you have entered this, press F8 to fill out a Sort Spec for the mail-merge operation as shown in Figure 4.7. Filling out a Sort Spec for the mail merge allows you to control the order in which the letters are printed. This is a very important function in mail merge. It is used most often when you are preparing form letters that need to be ordered by zipcode for the post office. In such a case, you would sort the database by zipcode field when printing both the letters and their corresponding mailing labels as you will do later in this chapter.

You will print your letters in the most common sort order for this database, first by department and then by employee. To do this, fill out the Sort Spec as it is shown in Figure 4.7 and then press F10 to perform the merge. You then receive the flashing message "Preparing for merge print . . .", during which you see all the forms that will be used in merge-printing quickly displayed in succession on your screen.

After Q&A finishes this operation, you receive the message box shown in Figure 4.8 on your screen. It informs you that your letter will be merged with 18 records from the database and asks you to confirm this by pressing Return to print or Esc to cancel the operation. Before going any further, you should make sure that your printer is turned on and that you have enough paper to print a few of these sample letters.

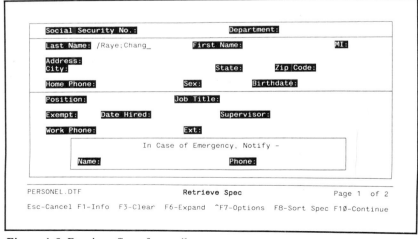

*Figure 4.6:* Retrieve Spec for mail merge

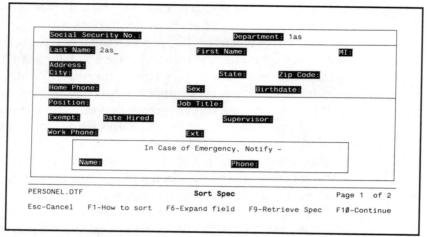

*Figure 4.7:* Merge-print Sort Spec

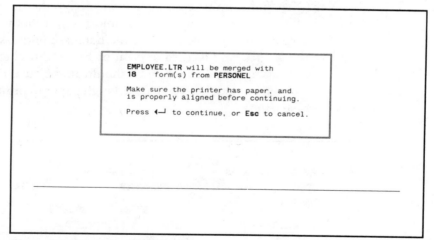

*Figure 4.8:* Final merge-print message

Because you have 20 records in the entire personnel database and
your Retrieve Spec excluded two of them, you can be fairly sure from
the number 18 that you entered this condition correctly. Press
Return to go ahead with printing. When you are doing mail merge
for your own applications, if the number listed in this box does not

seem to reflect the restriction you set up in the Retrieve Spec, you should press Esc to cancel and check that you entered the condition correctly before carrying out the printing.

After you press Return, you will see the familiar print status box on your screen as the letters are printed. Allow the program to print at least two sample letters so that you can verify that the merge is working correctly and that the letters are being properly paged. When you have verified that this is the case, press Esc to abort the mail merge. There is no need to print out all 18 letters. The first letter printed should be to Jessica Freels in the Accounting department. Make sure that her name has been correctly merged into the places specified in your letter. Then press Esc twice to return to Q&A's Main Menu.

## OTHER MAIL-MERGE FORMAT OPTIONS

Q&A gives you other ways to format information supplied from data files into your documents. The first one allows you to have data that has been entered on two separate lines in the database to be placed on the same line in the document. To do this, you simply add the code **(T)** (for *Together*) between the end of the field name and the final asterisk. For instance, if your database form had two lines for entering data in the street address field but you wanted the entire address to be printed on one single line in the form letter, you would enter the data variable containing the field name as

\*Street Address (T)\*

in the appropriate place in the letter. Then any two-line addresses in records would be printed on a single line in the form letter.

Other format options allow you to control the alignment of the data merged into the document despite differences in the fields' lengths in the data file. These options are most useful when you are using mail merge to prepare standard letters or forms that contain columns in which you want to keep variable-length data either left- or right-aligned.

To keep your data left-justified in the document, you enter the code **(L)** and as many additional spaces as you want to separate the entries in this column from those in the next column. You place this code after the field name and any additional spaces added and before the final asterisk. To right-justify your data, you do the same, only using the code **(R)** in place of (L).

For example, if you ran a travel agency, you might use mail merge to send out form letters letting potential customers know about some special promotional tours. After a general description of your services and specials, your letter could include a table displaying the tours described along with their prices. The first column of this table would contain the name of the tour and the second its price. You would want tour names to be left-justified in the table and their prices to be right-justified. Tour names will be supplied from three separate fields in the database, each with different maximum lengths. Each corresponding tour price field should be right-justified in its column. To separate the two columns properly, include enough spaces in the data variables to accommodate the longest entry. Make sure that the number of spaces you enter between the asterisks is equal to at least the longest tour name in the database.

Assume that the longest tour name—Hawaiian Holiday—has 16 characters. All three of the data variables should therefore contain at least 17 characters between the asterisks. You would enter the complete table describing your tours as follows:

```
*Tour #1 (L)*    *Tour price #1 (R)*
*Tour #2 (L)*    *Tour price #2 (R)*
*Tour #3 (L)*    *Tour price #3 (R)*
```

In the resulting form letter, after the data has been merged from the six database fields, the printed table would appear formatted like this:

```
Hawaiian Holidays    490.00
Tahitian Cruise      1750.00
Mexican Getaway      595.00
```

You can use these formatting codes very effectively whenever you need to generate forms that call for columns of financial figures like monthly billing statements to your customers.

## *MERGE-PRINTING ENVELOPES FROM LETTERS*

There is another printing feature you should be aware of when you enter letters in Q&A. That is its ability to take the address from a letter and automatically print it on an envelope.

To do this, you use the Get option on the Write Menu if the letter has been previously saved. Then choose the Print option either by pressing F2 from the Type/Edit screen or by choosing **p** from the Write Menu and pressing Return. Change the Line spacing option from Single to Envelope and press F10. (You do not have to change the Type of paper feed option to manual, because Q&A knows that envelopes must be fed into the printer one at a time.)

After you press F10, Q&A will prompt you to put an envelope in your printer. If you are using an impact printer, be sure that you have set it up to use friction feed and that the envelope is lined up with its top edge just under the print head. If you are using the HP Laser Jet printer, be sure that you have fed the envelope in properly and that you have set the manual feed option.

Make sure the correct database is listed as the Name of Merge File and then press Return to have the addresses from the database printed on the envelopes. It is important to complete the Retrieve Spec and Sort Spec exactly as you did for the letter itself so that they can easily be matched one for one.

Q&A finds and identifies the address by looking for the lines beneath the letter's date. It therefore ignores the return address that usually precedes the date of the letter. The program assumes that the lines following the date and ending with a blank line contain the name and address of the person to whom the letter is addressed. Assuming that the name and address are contained in this area, Q&A then automatically prints them centered on the envelope. If you do not follow this standard setup for a business letter, Q&A will print the wrong lines on the envelope. The program positions the address 10 lines down from the envelope's top edge and indents it $3^{1}/_{2}$ inches from the left edge.

You can also use the Envelope print option, with a letter that contains the actual address to be printed on the envelope. This is very convenient when writing a letter to one individual rather than a mail merge to a database file.

# MAILING LABELS

In Chapter 3 you used the File module of Q&A to design a mailing label. You can also use the Mailing labels option on the Q&A Write menu to produce mailing labels. When you use this method, you have additional flexibility in setting up the mailing label form. For example, you can add text or punctuation, like a comma after the city, to enhance the actual printed label. Using this feature, you can also print labels which are merged from data in your Q&A File database.

On the Write Menu when you choose the Mailing labels option Q&A provides you with a list of pre-defined mailing label specs, a merge label template document, and a special mailing label print options screen which makes the printing of labels a simple step-by-step process.

## USING THE MAILING LABEL OPTION

We'll use the Mailing label feature in Q&A Write to produce a set of labels from your personnel database. To begin, press Esc to go back to the Write Menu, or choose Write if you are currently on the Q&A Main Menu.

1.  Type **m** for Mailing labels and press Return.

Q&A presents you with a list of pre-defined mailing label specs. You can use any of these label specs to print your labels or create your own spec, just as you do when using File/Print. Notice in Figure 4.9 that some of the labels have been predefined with a specific printer in mind. For example, labels with an HP at the end are designed for the HP LaserJet, while those with an HP II at the end are for the HP LaserJet Series II. The pin fed labels can be used with most dot-matrix printers which have a tractor feed attachment. For your personnel mailing labels you will use a pin fed label.

2.  Use the ↓ key to move down the list until you highlight the first pin fed mailing label, called Pin fed 2 ½" x ¹⁵/₁₆" - 3 up. Press Return.

You will now be on the familiar screen for Type/Edit of a Q&A Write document. The document has already been formatted to the

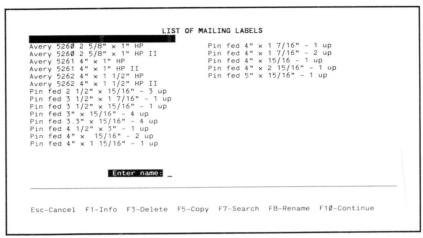

*Figure 4.9:* List of pre-defined mailing labels

size of a mailing label and it contains default merge field names. This template can be used along with the Identifier Spec to assign the actual field names, or you can edit the names now.

3. The only change that needs to be made for your personnel file is changing the *zip* field to its actual name of *Zip Code*. Press Alt-F7 and type in **personel** as your data file name. Then use the list of field names to select Zip Code. It will be automatically inserted onto the label. Use the Del key to erase the *zip* field. The label should then match the one shown in Figure 4.10.

If necessary, you can make modifications to the size of the label (similar to defining your page in a regular document) and change the number of characters per inch in which the text will be printed.

4. Press Ctrl-F6 for Define Page. Because Q&A has already made the proper page assignment for the mailing label, you do not need to change the height, width, or margins.

5. Press the Return key until Characters per inch is highlighted and use the → to change the number to 12. This will ensure that the text from your personnel data file fits easily on the label. The label definition should now look like the one shown in Figure 4.11.

```
*First name* *Last name*
*Address*
*City*, *State* *Zip Code* _
```

```
L[⊥⊥⊥T⊥⊥⊥⊥1⊥⊥⊥⊥T⊥⊥⊥⊥2⊥⊥⊥⊥T⊥⊥■⊥]⊥⊥⊥
Pin fed 2 1/                              0 %   Line 4 of Page 1 of 1

Esc-Exit   F2-Print   Ctrl F6-Def label   Alt F7-List fields   F10-Save & Print
```

*Figure 4.10:* Mailing label spec for PERSONEL.DTF

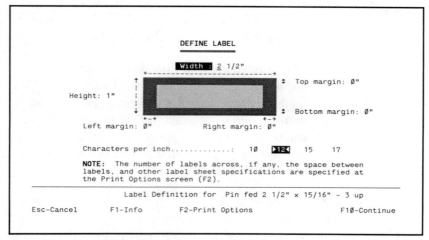

*Figure 4.11:* Label definition for personnel labels

6. Press F10 to advance to the Mailing Labels Print Options screen, and make sure that the criteria are the same as in Figure 4.12. Notice that you are printing to PtrA, three labels across the page, and that the data is being merged from your personnel database. Press F10 to print the labels.

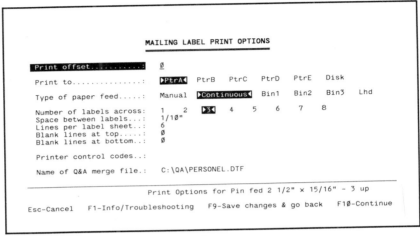

*Figure 4.12:* Mailing labels print option screen

7. Enter the same Retrieve Spec and Sort Spec that you did for your merge letter above. This will produce labels in the same order as your letter so that they can be easily collated.

It is also possible to use the mailing label option in Q&A Write without merging the information from a database. In that case you would substitute the merge fields with the actual text you want printed on the label, and no database would be specified on the Print Options screen.

## SPECIAL WORD PROCESSING EMBEDDED COMMANDS

Q&A Write includes several embedded commands which you did not learn in Chapter 2. These commands are similar to the *print* and *line spacing* commands in that they must be enclosed in a pair of asterisks (*) and entered on their own lines in the file. The embedded commands that you are about to learn allow you to join several documents together as one at print time, queue separate documents to be printed at the same time, and insert Lotus 1-2-3 spreadsheets and graphs into printed documents.

## CHAIN-PRINTING DOCUMENTS

There are two Q&A Write commands that allow you to chain-print documents; the *JOIN* and *QUEUE* commands.

The *JOIN* command can actually be used as another merge-printing function which allows you to chain together word processing documents saved in separate files and print them out as one long document. At times you may need to create a document that is too large to fit in your computer's memory. The way to do this is to save the document in individual files, stopping each one at a natural breaking point such as the beginning of a new section or chapter. To print these files out as one long document, you need to add an embedded code at the end of each file that tells Q&A the name of the file to be printed next. This embedded code must include the letter of the drive where the document file is located, if it is different from the default drive where Q&A usually looks for your data disks.

The complete embedded code is entered according to the pattern

```
*JOIN <drive:><filename>*
```

For example, if you have three document files named SECTION1, SECTION2, and SECTION3 which need to be printed as one, you would first edit the file called SECTION1 by entering the following embedded code on its last line:

```
*JOIN A:SECTION2*
```

(You only have to include the A: in this command if SECTION2 is found on a disk in drive A and drive A is not the default drive for data files. Also, JOIN can be abbreviated to J when using this embedded command.)

You would add a similar embedded code at the end of the document SECTION2, replacing the code *SECTION2* with *SECTION3*. If the three documents contain page numbers, you should also add a new beginning page number on the Define Page screens for both the SECTION2 and SECTION3 document files. Then all you have to do is give the command to print the first document, SECTION1. As soon as it has been printed, Q&A will automatically print the remaining two documents in the order specified by the embedded codes.

The *QUEUE* command is used to queue several documents to be printed at the same time. It differs from the *JOIN* command in that the documents are still printed separately. This embedded command merely indicates the order in which these print operations are to take place.

To use this command, you begin a new document in Write using Type/Edit and insert the *QUEUE* commands and document names that you wish to be printed. For example, the actual commands would be entered like this:

```
*QUEUE DOCUMENT1*
*QUEUE DOCUMENT2*
*QUEUE DOCUMENT3*
```

You can also have Q&A continue the pagination across the queued documents. To do this you would add ''P'' to the *QUEUE* command as shown below:

```
*QUEUEP DOCUMENT1*
*QUEUEP DOCUMENT2*
*QUEUEP DOCUMENT3*
```

If the first document is 10 pages and the second is 5 pages, the first page of the second document will be numbered 11 and the first page of the third document will be numbered 16.

## INCLUDING SPREADSHEETS AND GRAPHS

Sometimes documents need to include information which is stored in the form of a spreadsheet or graph in another software product. Q&A Write has two special commands enabling you to include a Lotus 1-2-3 spreadsheet or a graph at the time you print the document. These embedded commands are *SPREADSHEET* and *GRAPH*.

The *SPREADSHEET* command only works with a Lotus 1-2-3 worksheet. With it, you are able to specify the range of cells to be included. The command syntax is as follows:

*SPREADSHEET <worksheet name> <range name or cell range>*

Remember to include the drive and directory path as part of the <worksheet name> if the file is not located in the default directory you have set up for your Q&A Write document files. SPREAD-SHEET can be abbreviated to SS in this embedded command.

When using the *SPREADSHEET* command, you can restrict the data imported into your document to a specific range of cells in the Lotus 1-2-3 worksheet. If have used the Lotus 1-2-3 /Range Name command to assign a name to the group of cells you wish to import, you can enter this range name after the worksheet file name. You can also specify the range by their cell addresses. Use a hyphen (-) to separate the top left cell address from the bottom right cell address.

For instance, if you have created a schedule and given it the range name Yachts in a worksheet named YACHTS.WK1 saved in the C:\123 directory on your hard disk, you would enter the following *SPREADSHEET* embedded command:

*SPREADSHEET  C:\123\YACHTS.WK1  Yacht*

as shown in the same document in Figure 4.13. If you have not named the schedule, you can still import it by giving the addresses of the beginning and ending cells in the range as in

*SPREADSHEET  C:\123\YACHTS.WK1  B5-K10*

If you want the entire contents of the YACHTS.WK1 worksheet brought into your Q&A Write document, you enter

*SPREADSHEET  C:\123\YACHTS.WK1*

on its own line in the document.

Because the spreadsheet data is not shown in your document until you print it, you won't be able to tell by looking at the document on the Type/Edit screen whether your margins are sufficiently wide to accommodate the range of cells specified. (All you see is the line with the *SPREADSHEET* code.) If you know that you have specified a range of cells that is wider than your current margins, be sure to change them before printing the document.

The *GRAPH* command is used to include any .PIC file in your printed Q&A Write document and is used as shown below:

*GRAPH <filename>*

If you have created and saved a graph for this spreadsheet named VENDSALE.PIC in the directory C:\123\ACCOUNTS, you would enter

*GRAPH C:\123\YACHTS.PIC*

GRAPH in this embedded command can be abbreviated to G.

You can specify the density at which the graph is to be printed by using the code D for *double density* or Q for *quad density*. For example, to have a Lotus 1-2-3 bar graph showing the increase of yacht sales printed in double density at print time, you would enter

*GRAPH C:\123\YACHTS.PIC D*

as shown in the sample document in Figure 4.13. If you don't add a density code, Q&A uses single density. Also note that your printer must be capable of printing graphics for the *GRAPH* command to work properly. Figure 4.14 shows you how the sample document shown in Figure 4.13 appears when printed. There you can see the data brought in from the cell range Yacht as well as the bar graph created from it.

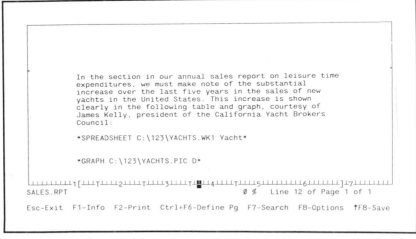

```
        In the section in our annual sales report on leisure time
        expenditures, we must make note of the substantial
        increase over the last five years in the sales of new
        yachts in the United States. This increase is shown
        clearly in the following table and graph, courtesy of
        James Kelly, president of the California Yacht Brokers
        Council:

        *SPREADSHEET C:\123\YACHTS.WK1 Yacht*


        *GRAPH C:\123\YACHTS.PIC D*
```
```
└┴┴┴┴┴┴┴┴┴1 [┴┴┴T┴┴┴2┴┴┴┴T┴┴┴3┴┴┴┴T┴█┴┴4┴┴┴T┴┴┴┴5┴┴┴┴┴┴┴6┴┴┴┴┴]┴7┴┴┴┴┴┴
SALES.RPT                                Ø %    Line 12 of Page 1 of 1

Esc-Exit   F1-Info   F2-Print   Ctrl+F6-Define Pg   F7-Search   F8-Options   ↑F8-Save
```

*Figure 4.13:* Sample document using the *SPREADSHEET* and *GRAPH* embedded commands

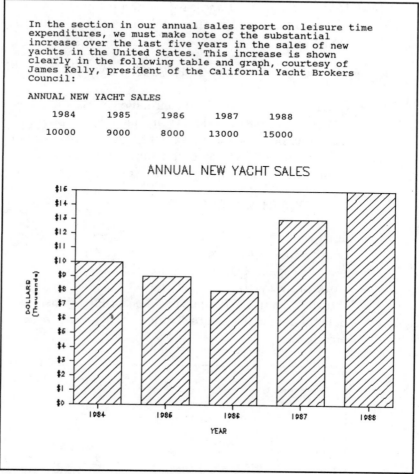

*Figure 4.14:* Printout of the sample document showing the data and graph imported from Lotus 1-2-3

# IMPORTING DOCUMENT FILES IN Q&A WRITE

When you are importing document files for use in Q&A Write, you will probably take them in as ASCII format files, unless the document was created in WordStar. This does not mean that you will always have to use the Import data option on the Utilities Menu;

many word processors provide their own utility for saving their document files as ASCII files. Some word processors, like WordPerfect and MultiMate, provide this translation as one of their menu options. Still other word processors create an ASCII file by allowing you to print the document to disk instead of to the printer. (You have already seen that Q&A itself uses this method.) Whenever possible, try to get a copy of the document file in ASCII form. This will save you the extra step of having to convert it yourself with the Import data option on the Utilities Menu.

ASCII document files will require some reformatting in Q&A Write. Remember, though, that when Q&A Write does not recognize a document file as one of its own, Q&A will display the Import Document menu shown in Figure 4.15. There you must indicate whether the document file format is ASCII, Special ASCII, Wordstar, or Lotus 1-2-3 or Symphony.

You can choose the Special ASCII option (2) on this menu to have it brought into Q&A Write with word wrap. This means that the text of the new document will be made to conform to the right margin setting without splitting up words that extend beyond the margin. After the document is imported, you are free to edit it just like any other Q&A document and later save your changes by typing Shift-F8 and giving it a new name.

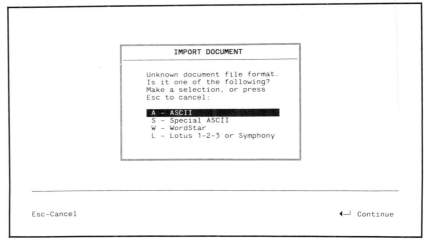

*Figure 4.15:* The Import Document Menu

If you want the ASCII document to retain all of the carriage returns and not be reformatted to conform to the margins of the Q&A Write document, then choose the ASCII option (1). You would use this option if you wanted to edit program listings in BASIC or dBASE, or DOS files like .BAT files, all of which require carriage returns at the end of each line. To retain this formatting in the edited files, you would save them in ASCII format by using the methods described in the next section rather than by using Q&A Write's Save command.

## EXPORTING Q&A WRITE DOCUMENTS

When you want to export a Q&A Write document to be used by another program, there are three methods from which you can choose. You can print a copy of it to disk using the Print to DISK option on the Print Menu, or you can use either the Standard or Document ASCII options on the Export Menu (see Figure 4.16). You will most often find it even easier to press Ctrl-F8 while editing the document—which will prompt you for an ASCII file name—because you can do this without having to exit the word processor.

Use the Print to DISK option on the Print menu (F2) when you want to save a file in ASCII file format used by the Macintosh computer. To do this, select the Macintosh ASCII format option from

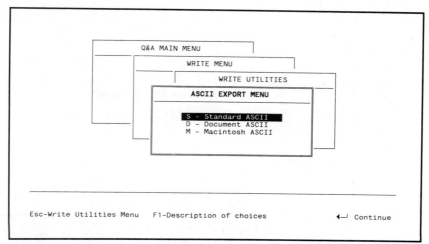

*Figure 4.16:* ASCII Export Menu

the menu that appears after you select the Print to DISK option, and press F10. Then enter the file name for the new ASCII file, and press Return to have it exported.

When you export a document for use with another program, Q&A will automatically remove any print enhancements (like boldface or underlining), headers, footers, and embedded printer commands. These special kinds of formats and graphics characters cannot be correctly translated into ASCII code. When you are finished using Q&A and have exited to the operating system, you can use the TYPE command to make sure that the ASCII document's contents are completely legible.

## SUMMARY

In this chapter, you have learned a number of important techniques that enable you to combine data stored in your Q&A database files and data stored in Lotus 1-2-3 spreadsheets with documents created with Q&A Write. In addition to learning how to integrate word processing with data processing in Q&A, you have also learned how to import and export your Q&A Write documents, using ASCII text files as the medium of exchange.

The techniques covered in this chapter include:

- preparing a standard document in Q&A Write that will merge data from a Q&A database file.

- Formatting the data merged from the database file in the standard file.

- Performing the merge operation that prints your form letters.

- Addressing and printing envelopes for the form letters created during the merge.

- Using Q&A's built-in Mailing Label feature to create mailing labels for the form letters created during the merge.

- Printing documents stored in separate files as one long document by inserting the *JOIN* embedded commands in a Q&A Write document.

- Establishing a print queue to batch-print a number of documents in the order you specify by inserting *QUEUE* embedded commands in a Q&A Write document.

- Inserting data from a Lotus 1-2-3 spreadsheet directly into a Q&A Write document.

- Inserting a Lotus 1-2-3 graph directly into a Q&A Write document.

- Importing a text file stored in ASCII format into a Q&A Write document.

- Exporting a Q&A Write document to the ASCII formats used by either IBM PC-compatible or Apple Macintosh computers.

In the chapter ahead, you will learn how to prepare and print reports using the data stored in your Q&A File databases. As you will see, Q&A Report gives you the perfect tool for organizing, formatting, and printing part or all of the information stored in your Q&A database files. You will find using Q&A Report very easy because you are already familiar with so many of its options.

5

# Q&A REPORT

# *Fast Track*

disk file by printing it to disk. If your report contains calculations such as subtotals and totals, you can print a summary report containing only these figures by changing the Totals only option to *Yes*.

**If your report is too wide**                                                    **240**

to fit the page width indicated, Q&A will alert you with a warning message before printing. To make adjustments, you can try to change the print pitch and margin settings or change the column width and column headings. Q&A can split very wide reports across pages, repeating the headers and footers on every page.

**Use the Define Page options**                                                   **245**

to change the page width, margin settings, or characters per inch. Here you can also define a header, a footer, or both for your report. These can contain such information as the report title, version number, and page number of the report. You can also use the @DATE($n$) or @TIME($n$) functions to date- or time-stamp your report when you print it.

**You can add derived columns**                                                   **248**

which calculate data that does not require actual fields in the database. To define a derived column, you assign a column heading, the formula that calculates the values for the column, and a column number as well as any letter codes. When creating the formula, you must preface the column numbers with the # symbol.

# CONTINUED

## GENERATING REPORTS WITH Q&A REPORT

Q&A Report makes it easy to generate all types of sophisticated printed reports from your databases. You do this by designing a Report Specification that is stored with a particular database. Once the Report Specification is defined, you may rerun the report as often as you need. Q&A Report also makes it easy to modify the report design later as your needs change, or to copy the basic format of one report and adapt it to another report. Each database file may have as many as 100 Report Specifications associated with it and used with it. The reports you create may include different fields from the database, or even the same fields arranged in a slightly different format.

Creating a Report Specification with Q&A Report is similar in many ways to creating a Print Specification with Q&A File. Where it differs significantly is in the amount and type of features you are offered. Each of these new features will be covered in detail with accompanying practice exercises using your sample personnel database. From these exercises you will get a good idea of the types of reports you can design for your own database files. As pointed out earlier, you use Q&A Report in preference to the Print option in Q&A File whenever you need to create more complicated reports— especially those that require calculations between fields, such as subtotals and totals of financial or numerical data.

## THE BASICS OF DESIGNING A REPORT

Although Q&A Report allows you to choose up to 50 fields to fit across the width of a printed page, even in compressed mode using 14-inch-wide paper you will have difficulty using more than 13 to 15 fields in a single report. Q&A always lets you know before printing if it is not possible to print all of the fields included in the report across the page, given the pitch and paper width specified.

Q&A Report gives you a great deal of control over the arrangement of these fields in the printed report. The data from each field called for in the report is printed down columns. You define the order of these columns across the page just as you define the order for printing fields in Print Specs in Q&A File. Normally, each column carries the field's name in the database as the column heading, though you can change this default and create headings of your own. The width of the columns and their spacing on the page are automatically determined by Q&A. If you need to, you can alter the width of a column by making it wider or narrower.

Within the report, you can have Q&A Report sort the data in any of these columns in either ascending or descending order. With currency and numeric fields, you can choose between a range of calculations that make it possible for you to print such things as subtotals, totals, item counts, averages, and the maximum and minimum values of the data in each column. You can also add derived columns in the report; these are based on calculations between numeric, currency, and date fields in the database but have no actual field of their own in the file. It is also possible to base the sorting of the data and calculations in other columns on what Q&A calls an *invisible* field—one that exists in the database but is not used in the printed report.

You can add a header and footer to be printed on every page of the report. Page numbers can be defined in a header or footer by using the same system you learned in the word processor. Q&A Report also allows you to use its @DATE($n$) and @TIME($n$) functions (where $n$ is a number representing one of the twenty different date formats or three difference time formats) in any headers and footers you define. If you remember, these functions supply the current date and time from the system. Used in a Report Specification, they ensure that each version of your report will always carry a current date and time stamp. The formatting of text in headers can be centered, left-justified, or right-justified, as you see fit.

Most of the time, page breaks in the report are handled automatically by Q&A Report. You can, however, specify a page break to occur at a particular field in the report. This is useful because it allows you to print a separate page for each key field in the report. With your personnel file, for instance, you could use this feature to design a report that has a separate page for each department, listing such information as the names of the employees, their supervisors, and the job titles for each.

## *COMPONENTS OF A REPORT*

Figure 5.1 shows you the major components of a Q&A report. It is the printout of a salary report that you will create later in this chapter as one of the practice exercises. Notice that the report contains both a header and footer and that the body of the report is made up of data from just four fields in the personnel database. The column headings in the report are the same as those you assigned to each field in the database itself. Q&A Report uses the field names as column headings unless you specify others. Later in this chapter you will learn how to override this default and add column headings of your own.

The body of the report includes subtotals of the salaries for each department as well as the salaries total for the entire company. Both the Department and Last Name columns are sorted in ascending order. This was done by adding the two-letter code *as* to each field in the Report Spec (just as you did when creating Print Specs in Chapter 4). You could just as well sort these columns in descending order. To do that, you would use the code **ds**, entering it in one field or the other or both fields in place of the **as** code.

This report is set up so that the salaries are subtotaled whenever the Department name changes in the first column. This is referred to as a *column break*. It occurs whenever you have Q&A sort a particular column in the report. Each time the program encounters a change in value in the sorted column, it automatically skips a line in the report before printing the next group in the column. If you have called for some type of calculation to be done, such as the subtotals in this report, it also adds a new line containing the label for the calculation and its results. In this case, it added the label *Total:* and summed all of the values up to the column break on a new line before skipping another line and printing the figures for the next department.

Because the Last Name column comes right before the Current Salary column and is also sorted, these salary subtotals would have been printed after each column break in the Last Name column (i.e., after each new last name) if a special code for suppressing these column breaks had not been entered in the Last Name field in the Report Specification. Q&A Report allows you to suppress column breaks in any sorted column by placing the code **cs** in the appropriate field. Without its use here, each different last name would have generated its own Total line. The only salaries that would have been

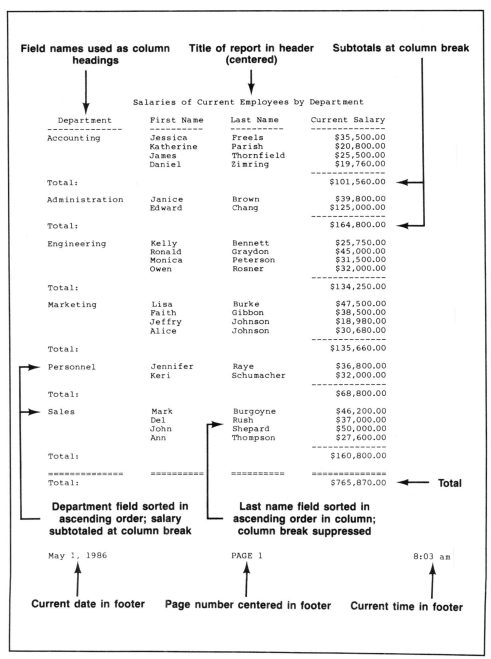

**Field names used as column headings**   **Title of report in header (centered)**   **Subtotals at column break**

```
                   Salaries of Current Employees by Department

    Department        First Name    Last Name     Current Salary
    --------------    ----------    ----------    ---------------
    Accounting        Jessica       Freels            $35,500.00
                      Katherine     Parish            $20,800.00
                      James         Thornfield        $25,500.00
                      Daniel        Zimring           $19,760.00
                                                  ---------------
    Total:                                           $101,560.00

    Administration    Janice        Brown             $39,800.00
                      Edward        Chang            $125,000.00
                                                  ---------------
    Total:                                           $164,800.00

    Engineering       Kelly         Bennett           $25,750.00
                      Ronald        Graydon           $45,000.00
                      Monica        Peterson          $31,500.00
                      Owen          Rosner            $32,000.00
                                                  ---------------
    Total:                                           $134,250.00

    Marketing         Lisa          Burke             $47,500.00
                      Faith         Gibbon            $38,500.00
                      Jeffry        Johnson           $18,980.00
                      Alice         Johnson           $30,680.00
                                                  ---------------
    Total:                                           $135,660.00

    Personnel         Jennifer      Raye              $36,800.00
                      Keri          Schumacher        $32,000.00
                                                  ---------------
    Total:                                            $68,800.00

    Sales             Mark          Burgoyne          $46,200.00
                      Del           Rush              $37,000.00
                      John          Shepard           $50,000.00
                      Ann           Thompson          $27,600.00
                                                  ---------------
    Total:                                           $160,800.00

    ==============    ==========    ==========    ===============
    Total:                                           $765,870.00
```

**Total**

**Department field sorted in ascending order; salary subtotaled at column break**   **Last name field sorted in ascending order in column; column break suppressed**

```
    May 1, 1986                     PAGE 1                      8:03 am
```

**Current date in footer**   **Page number centered in footer**   **Current time in footer**

*Figure 5.1:* Components of a Q&A report

summed together in this report would have been those of the two Johnsons, Alice and Jeffry, in the Marketing Department.

Notice that the name of each department appears only one time in the report. By default, the data in any sorted column is printed only once at the beginning of a column break. To override this and have Q&A Report repeatedly print the data in a sorted column before every subsequent entry, you must add another special code, **r** (for *Repeat*), in the Report Specification. It was necessary to add this code in the Last Name column so that the duplicate last name Johnson would be printed for both Alice and Jeffry Johnson. If this code had been entered in the Department field as well, Marketing would have been printed before each of the names of all four employees in this department rather than before the first one, Lisa Burke, alone.

Totaling the salaries of all of the employees in the database was called for by adding a Total code, **t**, in the Current Salary field. You can have totals done on currency and numeric fields in your database without using subtotals. Totals in columns are automatically placed at the very end of the report beneath a line of equal signs ( = = = = ).

Notice the header and the footer added to this report. The header contains the report title *Salaries of Current Employees by Department*. Q&A Report automatically centered it on the page because it was entered between a pair of exclamation points (!). You can also left- and right-justify information within the margins in a header or footer by ending or beginning the information with a single exclamation point. This effect can be seen in the report footer where the date and time are left- and right-justified and the page number is centered.

The date and time remain the current date and time because they were entered using the @DATE(*n*) and @TIME(*n*) functions. The date will be automatically updated when the same report is printed on another day. The time is so dynamic that it will be different whenever the report is reprinted, even on a second copy printed immediately after the first. The page number is supplied by Q&A through the use of the pound symbol (#) after the word *Page*. This works just as it does when you are setting up page numbers in word processing documents using Q&A Write.

## CODES USED IN REPORT SPECIFICATIONS

In addition to having Q&A Report do subtotals and totals, as was the case here, you can have it perform a number of other calculations in the columns of your reports. For instance, you could use this same report format and modify it to have it print the average salary of the employees, or even the highest salary in each department, where the subtotals of their salaries now are. All you have to do is enter a new letter code in the Current Salary field in the Report Specification. Table 5.1 gives you a complete list of the codes for all of the commands you can include in your reports, followed by an explanation of what each one does.

*Table 5.1:* Command codes for Q&A Report

| CODE | MEANING |
|------|---------|
| **AS** | Sort the column in ascending order (a to z or 0 to 9). Data in this column will be printed only once at column break. |
| **DS** | Sort the column in descending order (z to a or 9 to 0). Data in this column will be printed only once at column break. |
| **CS** | Cancel subcalculations and add a blank line at column breaks. Used with any sorted columns that should not show subcalculations after each line or that should not be separated by blank lines. |
| **R** | Repeat values in a sorted column until the column break. |
| **P** | Begin a new page of the report at each column break. |
| **DB** | Break and do subcalculations when day changes. |
| **MB** | Break and do subcalculations when month changes. |
| **YB** | Break and do subcalculations when year changes. |
| **ST** | Print the subtotal of the values in a sorted column at each column break. |
| **SA** | Print the average of the values in a sorted column at each column break. |
| **SC** | Count the number of items listed in a sorted column and print this number at each column break. |

*Table 5.1:* Command codes for Q&A Report (continued)

| CODE | MEANING |
|------|---------|
| **SMIN** | Print the minimum value of those listed in a sorted column at each column break. |
| **SMAX** | Print the maximum value of those listed in a sorted column at each column break. |
| **T** | Print the total of all of the values in this column at the end of the report. |
| **A** | Print the average of all of the values in this column at the end of the report. |
| **C** | Count the number of items in this column and print this number at the end of the report. |
| **MIN** | Print the minimum of all of the values in this column at the end of the report. |
| **MAX** | Print the maximum of all of the values in this column at the end of the report. |
| **I** | Don't print the values in this column as part of the report but do use them in sorting and/or doing calculations in the report. |
| **K** | Print a report based on the keywords in a keyword field in the database. This keyword field must be listed as the first column of the report as well as containing the K code. |

The use of any of these codes in the Report Specification is always optional. The only things you must define when creating a report are the fields to be included and the order in which they are to be arranged in columns. You do this by giving each field a number indicating its order in the report, just as you do when setting up a Print Spec in Q&A File. When assigning these numbers to fields, you do not have to start with 1 for the first field or use the next number in the sequence for subsequent fields. You can just as well start with another number and then skip by twos, fives, or tens when assigning the column order. In fact, doing so is a very good idea because it allows you to go back and add new fields to the report without being forced to renumber all of them.

When creating a report, you can use all of the records in your database, or you can restrict the records to be included. You do this by filling out a Retrieve Spec identical to those which you used when searching the database and creating Print Specs. To use all of the numbers, you simply press F10 at the Retrieve Spec. To restrict the records to be used, you enter a condition that must be matched, using the same symbols you use when searching your database.

## DESIGNING YOUR FIRST REPORT

Now that you have a basic understanding of how Q&A Report works and what it can do, it is time to get some experience setting up various types of reports using your sample personnel database file. If you are still at the Q&A File Menu from the previous exercise, just press Esc to back up to the Q&A's Main Menu. If you need to start up your computer and the Q&A program, do so now. Report is the second option on the Main Menu. To select it, type **r** and press Return (or type 2).

The Report Menu now on your screen contains four options, shown in Figure 5.2. The first option on this menu, Design/Redesign a report, is the one you want here. To access it, type **d**. You will then be prompted for the name of the database file to use. If you are using a data disk with more than just the personnel database on it, PERSONEL.DTF may not be listed as the default choice. If this is the case, press the space bar to delete the file name shown at the cursor, type **personel**, and press Return. (You can always get a complete listing of all of the database files stored on your data disk by blanking out the file name listed and then just pressing Return. If PERSONEL.DTF is listed, you simply move the cursor to it and press Return to select it.)

Once you give the name of the database to be used with your report, you must then give the report a unique name. It may contain up to 20 characters, including spaces and punctuation. You will call your first sample report **PERSONNEL BY DEPT-1** (the -1 stands for version 1 of the report). It will contain the names of all of the employees in the database, listed by department. You can type in the file

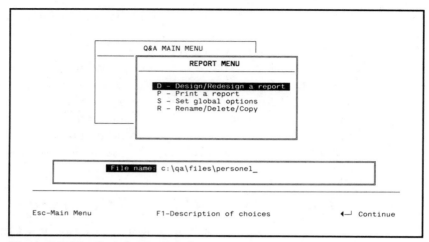

*Figure 5.2:* The Report Menu

name in all lowercase letters or with a combination of upper- and lowercase letters. Once you have typed in the name **Personnel By Dept-1**, press Return to continue.

The first screen that comes up after you define the report name is the now-familiar Retrieve Spec. If you wanted in some way to restrict the employees to be included in this report, you would enter the match condition in the appropriate field or fields of this form. You do not need to set up such a condition for this report, because it will use all 20 records in this database. To select all of the records, press F10 now.

### FILLING OUT THE COLUMN/SORT SPEC

Next, you are presented with a new screen entitled Column/Sort Spec for PERSONNEL BY DEPT-1 (shown in Figure 5.3). It is here that you define the fields to be included and their column order in the report. You also indicate which fields are to be sorted and in what order, as well as adding any necessary codes—such as those to suppress column breaks, repeat sorted entries, or perform any calculations in columns.

For this first report, you will use only four fields in the database: those of the Department, First Name, Last Name, and Job Title. You will want them to appear in columns in that order, so you must give them numbers in a consecutive order with the Department field

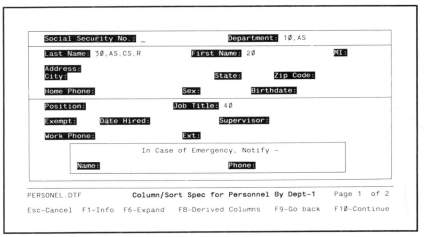

```
┌──────────────────────────────────────────────────────────────────────┐
│                                                                        │
│  ┌───────────────────────────────────────────────────────────────┐    │
│  │ Social Security No.: _              Department: 1Ø,AS          │    │
│  │                                                                 │    │
│  │ Last Name: 3Ø,AS,CS,R       First Name: 2Ø              MI:    │    │
│  │ Address:                                                        │    │
│  │ City:                        State:        Zip Code:            │    │
│  │                                                                 │    │
│  │ Home Phone:          Sex:           Birthdate:                  │    │
│  │                                                                 │    │
│  │ Position:            Job Title: 4Ø                              │    │
│  │                                                                 │    │
│  │ Exempt:     Date Hired:            Supervisor:                  │    │
│  │                                                                 │    │
│  │ Work Phone:              Ext:                                   │    │
│  │         ┌─────────────────────────────────────────────┐        │    │
│  │         │      In Case of Emergency, Notify -          │        │    │
│  │         │  Name:                    Phone:             │        │    │
│  │         └─────────────────────────────────────────────┘        │    │
│  └───────────────────────────────────────────────────────────────┘    │
│  ─────────────────────────────────────────────────────────────────    │
│  PERSONEL.DTF       Column/Sort Spec for Personnel By Dept-1   Page 1  of 2 │
│                                                                        │
│  Esc-Cancel  F1-Info  F6-Expand  F8-Derived Columns  F9-Go back  F1Ø-Continue │
│                                                                        │
└──────────────────────────────────────────────────────────────────────┘
```

*Figure 5.3:* Column/Sort Spec for the PERSONNEL BY DEPT-1 report

having the lowest value and the Job Title field the highest. Instead of assigning the number sequence 1, 2, 3, and 4 to these fields, use 10, 20, 30, and 40. That way, you can come back and add new fields between them when redesigning this report.

By the way, when assigning these numbers to your Column/Sort Spec, you do not have to try to give new numbers to fields that you may have already numbered in another Print or Report Specification used with the same database. Because each specification is stored under a separate name, you can use a similar numbering system in each.

You want the information in this report sorted in ascending order first by department and then by the employee's last name. This means that you must add the code **as** to both the Department and the Last Name fields after their numbers. Because you do not want a column break to occur at the Last Name field, you need to add the code **cs** to it. If you did not add it here, Q&A would skip a line between each employee listed in every department.

Remember that the Last Name field in your database contains two employees who have the same last name, Alice and Jeffry Johnson. Adding the **cs** code to the Last Name field will not only prevent blank lines between the names and job titles of each person in a single department, it will also suppress the printing of the second occurrence of Johnson. In order to print Johnson in the report both for Alice and Jeffry, you need to add the code **r** to this field. This is the repeat code; it overrides the suppression of repeated information at a column break. You will need to add this code to your own reports whenever the database contains duplicate data that you want to display in the report.

### FORMATTING COLUMNS AND SETTING HEADERS/ WIDTHS
Q&A give you full control over how your information in the columns prints out. You can enter formatting codes in the Column Spec to justify left, right, or center in the column, print with or without commas, format a date with any of the 20 options, control the number of decimal places, print all uppercase, and/or stop the wraparound feature. Table 5.2 shows the formatting codes for Report. For example, if you wanted the department field right-justified, you would enter

10,AS,F(JR)

*Table 5.2:* Formatting codes for Report

| CODE | MEANING |
|------|---------|
| JR | Justify right (done automatically to number and money fields) |
| JL | Justify left (done automatically to text) |
| JC | Justify center |
| U | Uppercase |
| C | Print numbers with commas |
| WC | Print money and number fields without commas |
| TR | Truncate values that are wider than column width |
| D$n$ | Date; $n$ is format number (1–20) |
| H$n$ | Time; $n$ is format number (1–3) |
| N$n$ | Number; $n$ is number of decimal places (1–7) |
| M | Treat value as money |
| T | Treat value as text |

To set a different header on your column or set the width you add **H(***n:newheader***)** where *n* is a number from 1 to 80 that will be your new width, followed by a colon, and *newheader* is the text of the new header. To continue with the department example above you might enter

10,AS,F(JR),H(15:All Departments)

to set the column width to 15 and the heading to *All Departments*.

Figure 5.3 shows you the completed Column/Sort Spec for this report. Press the Caps Lock key and move the cursor to each of the four fields, entering first their number and then their letter codes exactly as shown in this figure. When you have finished entering them and have checked them against the values shown in this figure, press F10 to continue.

## *PRINT OPTIONS FOR THE REPORT*

This will take you to the Print Options screen shown in Figure 5.4. As you can see, the options on this screen are very similar to those of the Print Options screen you used when defining Print Specifications in Q&A File. The first four options, in fact, are identical. Unlike the Print Options screen used when defining a Print Specification, this one does not allow you to print multiple copies of the report. Of course, there are no options for printing field labels and specifying the number of forms to be printed on a page, because neither of these are used in reports. In a report, the field labels are automatically used as the headings for each column in the report. You may also specify that the report body is to be printed to the left, right, or centered on the page.

***SUMMARY REPORTS***    The fifth option, Print totals only, is unique to the Report Print Options screen shown in Figure 5.4. It allows you to obtain a summary report showing only the subtotals and totals called for in the report. This is often useful when you want to get a quick summary of the financial or numerical data in a report.

You can use the page default values for printing this report, so there is no need to access the Define Page screen by pressing F8 now.

```
                         REPORT PRINT OPTIONS
                         _____

    ▶Print to..........:   ▶PtrA◀  PtrB   PtrC   PtrD   PtrE   DISK   SCREEN

     Type of paper feed........:   Manual  ▶Continuous◀  Bin1   Bin2   Bin3

     Printer offset............:   Ø

     Printer control codes.....:   _____

     Print totals only.........:   Yes  ▶No◀

     Justify report body.......:   ▶Left◀  Center   Right

   _____
    PERSONEL.DTF            Print Options for Personnel By Dept-1
    HP Laserjet II (Portrait) »» LPT1
    Esc-Cancel          F8-Define Page          F9-Go back          F1Ø-Continue
```

*Figure 5.4:* The Report Print Options screen for the PERSONNEL BY
DEPT-1 report

If the PtrA default for the Print to option is not correct for your
printer setup, change this value and then press F10 to save the report
definition. As soon as Q&A is finished saving your report to disk, you
will receive a message indicating that the report has been saved and
asking you if you want to print it now.

**PRINTING THE REPORT AFTER DEFINITION**   If you are
ready to print out this report now, press ← once to move the highlight
to Yes; then press Return. Just as before when printing forms in
Q&A File, you will see a boxed message indicating the program's
progress in scanning the forms in the database. Make sure that your
printer is turned on, and then press Return to obtain your printout.
You can always print a report at a later time by using the Print option
on the Report Menu.

**PRINTING THE REPORT TO THE SCREEN**   Figures 5.5 and
5.6 show you how the report would look if you had printed it to the
screen using the SCREEN option on the Report Print Options menu.
Notice in Figure 5.5 that column breaks occur only when the
department changes in the report. Look at the employees listed in the
Marketing Department in this figure. There, the last name Johnson is

```
        Department        First Name    Last Name         Job Title
        -------------     ----------    ----------    ---------------------------
        Accounting        Jessica       Freels        Senior Accountant II
                          Katherine     Parish        Clerk Typist IV
                          James         Thornfield    Bookkeeper I
                          Daniel        Zimring       Accounting Clerk I

        Administration    Janice        Brown         Administrative Assistant
                          Edward        Chang         President and CEO

        Engineering       Kelly         Bennett       Design/Drafter II
                          Ronald        Graydon       Head of Engineering
                          Monica        Peterson      Product Engineer I
                          Owen          Rosner        Design/Drafter III

        Marketing         Lisa          Burke         Vice President of Marketing
                          Faith         Gibbon        Director of Marketing
                          Jeffry        Johnson       Layout Artist II
                          Alice         Johnson       Clerk/Typist II

        Personnel         Jennifer      Raye          Director of Personnel

    PERSONEL.DTF

    Esc-Cancel   F2-Reprint    ( →←↑↓ )-Scroll    Shift F9-Redesign    F1Ø-Continue
```

*Figure 5.5:* First part of the personnel report printed to screen

```
        Department        First Name    Last Name         Job Title
        -------------     ----------    ----------    ---------------------------
                          Keri          Schumacher    Clerk/Typist III

        Sales             Mark          Burgoyne      East Coast Account Executive
                          Del           Rush          Western Account Executive
                          John          Shepard       Vice President of Sales
                          Ann           Thompson      Central Account Executive




    PERSONEL.DTF
    ****************************** END OF REPORT ********************************
    Esc-Cancel   F2-Reprint    ( →←↑↓ )-Scroll    Shift F9-Redesign    F1Ø-Continue
```

*Figure 5.6:* Last part of the personnel report printed to screen

repeated for both Alice and Jeffry. However, their names are not listed in alphabetical order. Jeffry comes before Alice in the printout.

If you had added the ascending sorting code, **as**, in the First Name field to rectify this situation, the last names would have been listed out of alphabetical order. Alice Johnson would have been listed first in the Marketing Department, followed by Faith Gibbon, Jeffry Johnson, and then Lisa Burke. The only effective way to order the employees alphabetically by both first and last names would be to redesign the report so that it is printed in last name, first name order by numbering the Last Name field so that it precedes the First Name field. Then you could have the First Name field sorted alphabetically (by adding the **as,cs** codes in this field) with no further disturbance to the report format. You must always pay attention to how the ordering of sorted columns in your reports will affect its final format.

At the bottom of this screen, Q&A indicates which cursor keys to use to navigate the on-screen report. Most of the time, it will not be possible for Q&A to display all of a report on one screen, 80 columns wide and 21 lines long. If the report contains too many columns to be displayed on the screen, you can press the → key to horizontally scroll hidden columns into view. You can press the → key as many times as you need to reach the end of the report. To get back to the first columns, you press the ← key a corresponding number of times.

To scroll down the screen vertically and bring new lines of information into view, press the PgDn key. It will show the next 21 lines of the report. You can keep pressing this key until you reach the end of the report. As you can see in Figure 5.6, Q&A boldly indicates the end of a report at the bottom of the screen by placing "END OF REPORT" between two strings of asterisks. Press F10 to return to the Report Menu.

## MODIFYING YOUR REPORT

You should now be back at the Report Menu. Next, you will modify the PERSONNEL BY DEPT-1 report you just created by adding the name of each employee's supervisor to the report. You will want the supervisor to appear in the second column of the report between the department and the employee's first name.

1. To redesign this report, choose the Design/Redesign a report option. Type **d** and press Return to select the PERSONEL.DTF file.

2. At the Name of Reports screen, choose PERSONNEL BY DEPT-1 by pressing the ↓ key once to highlight it. There is no need to type in the report name. Then press Return to select its use.

3. You will then be presented with the Retrieve Spec screen again. Press F10 to select all of the records, and the Column/ Sort Spec screen will come up. Figure 5.7 shows you the changes you must make to this screen. To have the Supervisor field printed between the Department and First Name fields, you must give it a number between 10 and 20. Enter the number **15** as the field number.

4. You want this field to be sorted in alphabetical order too, so enter a comma (,) and then the code **as** after this number.

5. While it would be perfectly all right to allow a blank line between the name of each supervisor and the group of employees he or she supervises, go ahead and suppress the blank line by typing another comma (,) and then **cs**.

Your entry in the Supervisor field should now match the one shown in Figure 5.7. If it does, press F10 to advance to the Print Options screen.

6. At the Report Print Options screen, change the first option from PtrA to SCREEN and then press F10 to save these modifications to this report.

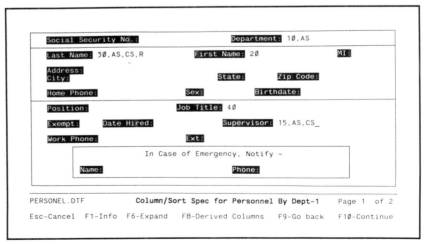

*Figure 5.7:* Adding a new column to the PERSONNEL BY DEPT-1 report

7.  Change the answer to *Yes* at the next prompt to print the report now, and press Return.

When Q&A finishes writing the first part of the report to the screen, it should look like the one shown in Figure 5.8.

## REPORTS TOO WIDE TO PRINT ON THE PAGE

As you can see from this screen preview, this modified report is now too wide for all of the columns to fit on the screen. This also is an indication that it is too wide to be printed properly on an 8½-inch-wide sheet of paper. If you had tried to print this report after saving it, you would have received the warning message shown in Figure 5.9. Q&A Report always warns you if your report will not fit on the page. As indicated in this figure, it then gives you the options of canceling the printing, truncating the right side of the report, returning to the report design to edit the Print option, or splitting the report across pages with Q&A repeating the headers and footers on every page.

When you first design a report and receive this warning message, it is better to use the Edit option and make some adjustments to the report. Even if you are not sure how to adjust the page to make it print properly, you can always just change the Print option to SCREEN and then reprint it. This allows you to preview the report

```
  Department          Supervisor        First Name    Last Name           Jo
--------------      ---------------    ----------    ---------      ----------
Accounting          Charlotte Dicke    Katherine     Parish         Clerk Typis
                    Janice Brown       Jessica       Freels         Senior Acco
                                       James         Thornfield     Bookkeeper
                                       Daniel        Zimring        Accounting

Administration                         Edward        Chang          President a
                    Edward Chang       Janice        Brown          Administrat

Engineering         Ron Graydon        Kelly         Bennett        Design/Draf
                                       Monica        Peterson       Product Eng
                                       Owen          Rosner         Design/Draf
                    Sally Zehm         Ronald        Graydon        Head of Eng

Marketing           Edward Chang       Lisa          Burke          Vice Presid
                    Janice Brown       Alice         Johnson        Clerk/Typis
                    Lisa Burke         Faith         Gibbon         Director of
                                       Jeffry        Johnson        Layout Arti

Personnel           Edward Chang       Jennifer      Raye           Director of
_____
PERSONEL.DTF

Esc-Cancel    F2-Reprint    { ←←↑↓ }-Scroll    Shift F9-Redesign    F10-Continue
```

***Figure 5.8:*** First half of modified personnel report printed to screen

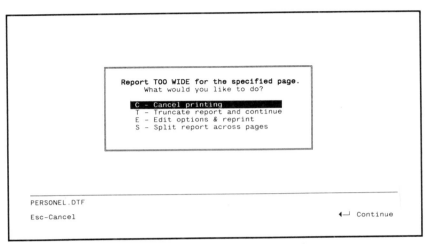

*Figure 5.9:* Q&A Report's too-wide warning message

on the screen as you are doing now. That way, you can get a good idea of the extent of the column overflow and how best to fix it.

To see the rest of the report on the screen, press → once. This will scroll the screen view to the right as shown in Figure 5.10. Notice that when Q&A scrolls a report horizontally, it overlaps most of the columns from one screen view to another. This is to help you keep your place in the report. If you wish to see the last part of the report now, press the PgDn key. To bring the first column of the report into view on your screen, press the ← key one time. Then press F10 to return to the Report Menu.

The easiest way to get this report to fit on an 8½- by 11-inch sheet of paper is to change the print pitch from 10 cpi to 15 cpi, called *compressed mode.* You can easily change it from the Design Page screen, accessed by pressing F8 at the Print Options menu. (If you are using an impact letter-quality printer, this will only work if you have a 15-pitch daisywheel or thimble to replace your 10-pitch element.)

## CHANGING THE PAGE PARAMETERS

1. To see how this is done, type **1** and press Return to select the personnel database.

2. Then select the report PERSONNEL BY DEPT-1 with the cursor, and press Return again at the Report Name screen.

```
     Supervisor          First Name    Last Name         Job Title
     ----------------    ----------    ----------        --------------------------
     Charlotte Dicke     Katherine     Parish            Clerk Typist IV
     Janice Brown        Jessica       Freels            Senior Accountant II
                         James         Thornfield        Bookkeeper I
                         Daniel        Zimring           Accounting Clerk I

                         Edward        Chang             President and CEO
     Edward Chang        Janice        Brown             Administrative Assistant

     Ron Graydon         Kelly         Bennett           Design/Drafter II
                         Monica        Peterson          Product Engineer I
                         Owen          Rosner            Design/Drafter III
     Sally Zehm          Ronald        Graydon           Head of Engineering

     Edward Chang        Lisa          Burke             Vice President of Marketing
     Janice Brown        Alice         Johnson           Clerk/Typist II
     Lisa Burke          Faith         Gibbon            Director of Marketing
                         Jeffry        Johnson           Layout Artist II

     Edward Chang        Jennifer      Raye              Director of Personnel

   PERSONEL.DTF

   Esc-Cancel   F2-Reprint    ( →←↑↓ )-Scroll     Shift F9-Redesign    F1Ø-Continue
```

*Figure 5.10:* Last half of modified personnel report printed to screen

3. Press F10 at both the Retrieve Spec and the Column/Sort Spec screens.

4. Now change the Print to option to the proper printer port on the Report Print Options screen, and then press F8 for Define Page. This screen is identical to the one you used when defining print specifications with Q&A File. From here you can control the page width and length as well as the left, right, top, and bottom margins. Below these options you set the characters per inch.

5. Move the cursor down to this line and then press the → key twice to highlight *15*. As you can see, you also use this screen to define any headers or footers you wish to add to your reports.

6. Press F10 to save the design; go ahead and answer all of the following prompts as you did earlier when you printed right after defining the report.

From your printout, you can see that at 15 cpi you could even fit a few more columns on an 8½-inch-wide page. At the end of this chapter you will learn about some other options for optimizing the number of columns you can use in a report.

## USING SUBTOTALS AND TOTALS IN A REPORT

For your next practice in designing reports, you will create the salary report shown in Figure 5.1 at the beginning of this chapter. This report contains subtotals and totals for the salaries listed by department. In creating this report, you will also learn how to add calculation codes to fields in your database that you want Q&A to calculate when generating the report. The most common need is for subtotals and totals, as shown in this example report, but the techniques covered here apply equally to calculating averages and minimum and maximum values in the fields.

1. At the Report Menu, type **d** and press Return to once again use the personnel database file for your report.

2. At the REPORT NAMES screen, give the new report the file name **salary by dept-1** and press Return.

3. At the Retrieve Spec screen, press F10 to use all of the records in the database.

4. Figure 5.11 shows you the Column/Sort Spec for this report. Again, you want to have the report listed by department in alphabetical order. Move the cursor to the Department field, type **10,as**, and press Return.

5. The Last Name field will again be the third column in the report sorted alphabetically with column breaks suppressed and repeating values displayed. To define it, type **30,as,cs,r** in this field and press Return to advance to the next field.

6. This is the First Name field that will be listed right before the last name. Type **20** as its number and press the PgDn key to access the second page of this form.

Figure 5.12 shows how this page looks. You want the values in the Current Salary field in the last column of this report. You also want subtotals displayed for each department. In addition, you want Q&A to sum up all of the salaries paid at the very end of the report. To get both of these displayed in the report, you must add both the **st** (subtotal) and **t** (total) codes in this field right after assigning a number to the field. Move the cursor to this field and type **40,st,t** there.

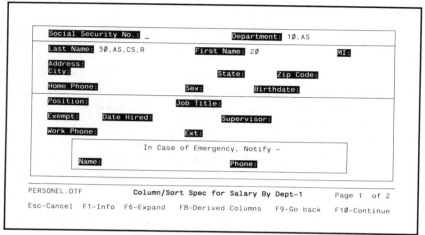

*Figure 5.11:* Column/Sort Spec for SALARY BY DEPT-1, Page 1

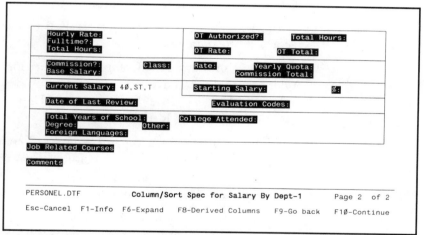

*Figure 5.12:* Column/Sort Spec for SALARY BY DEPT-1, Page 2

Note that this is not a sorted field, so you do not have to worry that any duplicate values in this column within a single department will be suppressed in the report. If you wanted to set up a salary report ordered by salaries in either ascending order (from lowest to highest paid) or descending order (highest to lowest paid), you would move this column to the second column right after the department and add the appropriate sorting code after the new number (between 10 and 20 in this example). If you didn't want the report to skip lines between each value in the salary column, you would then enter both **cs** and **r** as well as **st** and **t** in this field. This would not only suppress the column break but also would guard against unwanted suppression of identical salaries for different employees in the same department.

## OTHER CALCULATIONS
## IN A COLUMN/SORT SPEC

Having Q&A Report perform other calculations in columns of the report—like finding the average, the number of items (count), or the minimum and maximum values—works just as it does with subtotals and totals. For instance, if you wanted a count of the number of employees in each department, you would add the code **sc** after *as* in the Last Name field. If, further, you wanted the total count of the employees in the database printed at the end of the report, you would also add the code **c** there. Later, you will get experience with setting up a report that calculates averages as well as subtotals and totals for the sales department.

## ADDING HEADERS, FOOTERS, AND PAGE BREAKS TO A REPORT

After you have finished adding the field number, subtotal, and total codes to the Current Salary field, press F10 to advance to the Print Options screen. From here, press F8 to access the Define Page screen (shown in Figure 5.13). From here, you will adjust the top and bottom margin settings and add a header and footer to your report.

1. Press the ↓ key until the cursor is located after the Top Margin prompt. Change this to a one-inch margin by typing **6** over the 3, and press Return.

2. Then set the same one-inch margin for the bottom by typing **6** here.

3. You do not need to change the 10 characters per inch default to print this report, so press the ↓ key until the Title/Header

```
                          DEFINE PAGE
                          ──────────

         Page width.: 85          Page length..: 66

         Left margin: 5           Right margin.: 8Ø

         Top margin.: 6           Bottom margin: 6

         Characters per inch:  ▶1Ø◀  12   15   17
                        ──────── HEADER ────────
      1: !Salaries of Current Employees by Department!
      2:
      3:
                        ──────── FOOTER ────────
      1: @DATE(1)!PAGE #!@TIME_
      2:
      3:
      ──────────────────────────────────────────────
      PERSONEL.DTF          Define page for Salary By Dept-1

      Esc-Cancel          F9-Go Back to Print Options       F1Ø-Continue
```

*Figure 5.13:* Define Page screen for SALARY BY DEPT-1

prompt is highlighted and the cursor is located at the beginning of the line right below it.

## *FORMATTING TEXT IN THE HEADER AND FOOTER*

Headers and Footers appear on every page of the report. You can use up to three lines for the header and up to three lines for the footer. Notice in Figure 5.13 that the title of this report, Salaries of Current Employees by Department, is enclosed in a pair of exclamation points (!). These are used to instruct Q&A Report to center any text between them within the margins of the report. (This same technique can be used to center headers and footers in the Print Specifications you set up in Q&A File.) Type this title, including exclamation marks, as it appears in this figure and press Return.

Notice the use of the exclamation points in this footer. The page number will be centered because it is enclosed within a pair of exclamation points. At the same time, the time of printing (@TIME) will be right-justified because it is preceded by a single exclamation point. The date of printing—@DATE(1)—will remain left-justified as it was typed. The (1) after the @DATE specifies the format of the date. You have the same 20 different date formats that you have in File. Enter the footer here as it is shown in Figure 5.13.

If you had only the date and time of printing in the footer and still wanted them left- and right-justified respectively, you would have to terminate the @DATE(1) entry with an exclamation point of its own to keep it left-justified. It would appear as @DATE(1)!!@TIME on this line. This final exclamation point to keep text left-justified is required only when you want to format parts of the text of a footer differently on the line.

## DATE- AND TIME-STAMPING THE REPORT

Including the @DATE(*n*) and @TIME(*n*) functions in the footer causes the program to convert them to the system date and time at the very moment of printing. Each time the report is printed, the time will be different and, depending upon when you reprint it, the date may be different as well. This acts as a date and time stamp for the report.

## USING PAGE NUMBERS

You use the pound symbol (#) after Page in the footer to have the program automatically print the current page number of the report. You are familiar with this use of the pound symbol from your practice with the word processor. If you wanted to include the pound symbol as part of the page number (such as *Page #1*), you would have to enter two pound symbols in the footer (**Page ##**). Unfortunately, Q&A Report does not give you as much control over page numbers as does Q&A Write. You have no way here to specify a starting number other than 1 or to have the page number begin printing on a page other than the first page of the report.

## USING PAGE BREAKS

As mentioned earlier, Q&A Report automatically decides how to paginate your report if the amount of data in the columns is greater than will fit on the page length. You do not have the control here that you do in a word processing document. For example, you could not decide which departments should stay together on a page and which should go on a following page if you had so many records in your personnel database that this department list report would not all fit on a single page.

You can, however, add the Page code (p) to a field to designate that a new page is to be started at the occurrence of each column break. In our example, this would mean adding a **p** to the Department field. Q&A Report would then print the data for the Accounting department on page 1 of the report, the data for the Administration department on page 2, etc. The resulting report would then consist of six pages, one for each department in the database.

Because there are so few records in your personnel database that the entire report fits on one page, you will not add the page option as a part of the saved report. You can experiment with this command on your own.

Press F10 now to finish and save the design of your SALARY BY DEPT-1 report. If you wish, go ahead and print a copy of it before reading on. Compare it to the one shown in Figure 5.1. If yours does not match, choose the Design/Redesign option at the Report Menu and check both your Column/Sort Spec and Define Page screen against Figures 5.11, 5.12, and 5.13.

# USING DERIVED COLUMNS IN A REPORT

One of the most powerful features of Q&A Report is its ability to create new columns in the report that do not exist as fields in your database. The data in these columns is derived from mathematical calculations involving fields in your database. You can define up to sixteen of these derived columns in every report. This feature allows you to report on vital calculations without having to keep the data in calculated fields in the database, taking up precious storage space as part of the file. Derived columns exist nowhere except in formulas and specifications stored in the report file. Their data is calculated and only becomes real at the time you print out your report.

## MATHEMATICAL CALCULATIONS IN A DERIVED COLUMN

The mathematical calculations that you can have in derived columns include addition, subtraction, multiplication, and division.

You can also use subtotals and totals from other columns in these derived column calculations. In addition to these operations, you can use functions such as the @DATE, @TIME, @INT, @ROUND, @XLOOKUP, to name a few, in defining these calculations. The last function, @XLOOKUP, is explained in Chapter 8 with the XLOOKUP commands. Table 5.3 shows the symbols that are used to define these operations and explains their meaning in a formula.

*Table 5.3:* Symbols used with functions

| SYMBOL | FUNCTION | EXAMPLE | MEANING |
|---|---|---|---|
| + | Add | #3 + #4 | Add the value in column number 3 to that in column number 4. |
| − | Subtract | #3 − #4 | Subtract the value in column 4 from that in column 3. |
| * | Multiply | #3 * #4 | Multiply the value in column 3 by that in column 4. |
| / | Divide | #3/#4 | Divide the value in column 3 by that in column 4. |
| @DATE | Use current date | @DATE − #4 | Subtract the value in column 4 from today's date. The result is the number of days between the current date and the value in field 4. |
| @TIME | Use current time | @TIME + #3 | Add the value in column 3 to the current time. The result is the total number of minutes determined by adding the current time to the value in field 3. |

**Table 5.3:** Symbols used with functions (continued)

| SYMBOL | FUNCTION | EXAMPLE | MEANING |
|---|---|---|---|
| @INT(n) | Return the integer of value or calculation enclosed in the parentheses | @INT(#3/#4) | Return the whole-number part of the calculated result of dividing column 3 by column 4. |
| @ROUND(n,m) | Return the rounded value of n to the m decimal digits | @ROUND(#3,2) | Return the number in column 3, rounded to two decimal places. |
| @XLOOKUP (fn,pkf,xkf,lf) | Return the value of the lookup field from the filename, where the primary key field and external key field match | @XLOOKUP ("Personel", #1,"Social Security No.","Position") | Return the value in the field Position in the Personel database where the value in #1 of the current file matches the Social Security No. field in Personel. |

Notice in the table that, for example, when using the integer function you must enclose the value or calculation defined in a matched pair of parentheses. You can also use parentheses in formulas to alter the natural order of calculation. In this order, multiplication and division are done before addition or subtraction from left to right in the formula. You may often need to change this order to obtain the correct result. A good example of this would be if you wanted to subtract a date in a field of the database from the current date and express the result in years in the report. For example, if field number 5 contains this date, the formula would be (@DATE(n) − #5)/365. Because the result of the subtraction is the number of days, the result must be divided by 365 to display years in the report. If you failed to input the formula with parentheses, Q&A would divide the date in field #5 by 365 before obtaining the difference in days between today's date and that in field #5. This would result in errors throughout the column.

## *SUMMARY FUNCTIONS IN A DERIVED COLUMN*

Q&A can use the subtotals and totals from columns in calculation in derived columns. For example, if you wanted to list an employee's salary as a percentage of the department and as a percentage of the company, you would need to divide that salary by the department's total and the company's total. You will be using the subtotals and totals in derived columns in the next example report. Other summary functions include using grand totals or subtotals of total, average, count, minimum or maximum. Summary functions are used in derived columns only.

## *CREATING A REPORT WITH DERIVED COLUMNS*

To get experience defining derived columns in a report, you will now design a new salary report for exempt employees that shows both their starting and current salary and calculates the amount and percent of increase they received. This report will be ordered by department, just like the first two reports you have designed.

In fact, so much of the basic definition for this report is just like your SALARY BY DEPT-1 report that you can save time in designing it by copying the report using the Rename/Delete/Copy option on the Report Menu. You should now be at the Report Menu.

1. Choose this option by typing **r** and pressing Return (or by typing **4**).

2. Figure 5.14 shows you the Rename/Delete/Copy Menu. You want the Copy a report option, so type **c**.

3. Immediately, the "Copy from:" prompt appears and the cursor drops down to it. Enter **salary by dept-1** and press Return.

4. The "Copy to:" prompt appears next. You will name the new report SALARY INCREASE-1. Type it here as **salary increase-1** just as it is shown in Figure 5.14, and press Return.

5. After Q&A has finished copying the report and the "Working . . ." prompt disappears, press Esc to return to the Report Menu.

6. At this menu, choose the Design/Redesign option by typing **d**, and press Return to use your PERSONEL.DTF file.

7. At the REPORT NAMES screen, use the ↓ key to move the cursor to SALARY INCREASE-1, now shown on the directory below PERSONNEL BY DEPT-1 and SALARY BY DEPT-1 (Q&A keeps the directory of reports you have saved in alphabetical order).

## *DEFINING DERIVED COLUMNS IN YOUR REPORT*

You will want to use the Retrieve Spec to restrict the records used in this report. You want to use only those where the Exempt field is marked Y to indicate that the employee is salaried. Further, you do not want to include the records of the salespeople in the company in this report. Salespeople are paid on a base-plus-commission basis and therefore did not receive an entry for a starting salary.

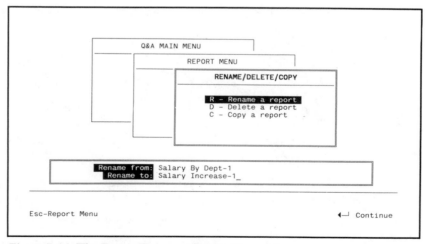

*Figure 5.14:* The Report Rename/Delete/Copy Menu

1. To fill out the Retrieve Spec so that Q&A uses only salaried employees who are not in sales, move the cursor first to the Exempt field on Page 1 of the form and enter **y** there.

2. Then press the PgDn key to advance to Page 2 of the form and move the cursor down to the Commission? field. Type **n** in this field and press F10 to go to the Column/Sort Spec.

Because you copied the report design from your SALARY BY DEPT-1 report, most of this screen is already filled in properly for you. All you have to do here is move the cursor to the Starting Salary field and give it a number and the codes to have it subtotaled and totaled. Figure 5.15 shows you how this field should be filled in.

3. Once the cursor is located in this field, type **35,st,t**. Because the Current Salary field is numbered 40, assigning 35 to this field causes it to be printed before the Current Salary column.

You now want to add two new derived fields that will be printed after the Current Salary column.

4. Look at the bottom of your screen (or at Figure 5.15) and see that the F8 key is given the function, Derived Columns, in

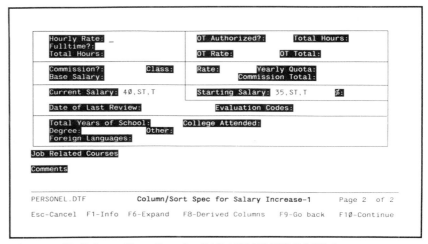

*Figure 5.15:* Column/Sort Spec for SALARY INCREASE-1

the Column/Sort Spec. Press F8 and you will see a new screen similar to the one shown in Figure 5.16, only not yet filled in.

There are three components to a derived column. The first is where you give the column a heading. Because a derived column has no corresponding field in the database, you must always enter a heading of your own after this prompt. The second is where you define the formula for the column. This formula can consist simply of an assigned value or, as is usually the case, a calculation between fields in the database using one or more of the mathematical operators or functions discussed above.

The third component of a derived column is called the Column Spec. This is where you give the derived column a number and specify any sorting or calculation codes that you want included in it. You must always give a derived column a number even if you do not need to use any other letter codes. This tells Q&A where to locate the column in relation to the other fields you are using in the report.

You may wonder how Q&A knows what field type to assign a derived column and how it is to be formatted. Basically, it looks at the field types and formats that are assigned to the fields involved with the formula you create; then it gives the derived column the same type and

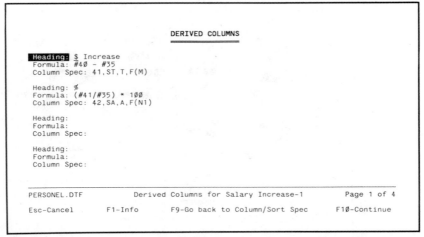

*Figure 5.16:* Defining the derived columns for the salary increase report

format. It assumes that you would want this new column to share the same field type and format that you assigned to the fields that are used in its calculation. However, if you are multiplying one type of field by a different type (i.e., money times a numeric), you can override the format Q&A gives the derived field. This is done by entering one of the following format codes in the Column Spec with the F( ), using D$n$, H$n$, M, N$n$, or T within the parentheses. The $n$ is to be replaced with a number representing the number of decimal places. For instance, F(N2) means "numeric with two decimal places."

Look at the first derived column in Figure 5.16.

5. Type in the heading **$ Increase** as shown there, and press Return.

The formula for the dollar increase is the Current Salary minus Starting Salary. In terms of column numbers, this translates into #40 - #35. Notice that when creating formulas in Q&A, you must precede the column number with the # symbol. While this is not required when assigning column numbers to fields, it is always required when defining formulas. You will find it is also the case when you begin programming the database in Chapter 8.

6. Go ahead and enter the formula **#40 - #35** for the dollar increase here just as it is shown; then press Return.

For the Column Spec, you will assign this new column the number 41. That way it will be placed immediately after the Current Salary column (40) in the report. You also want this data to be subtotaled and totaled in its column, so you will enter the codes **st** and **t** as well. Also set the format to money by adding **f(m)**.

7. Type **41,st,t,f(m)** and press Return.

You are now at the beginning of a new derived column definition. This column will show what percentage the increase of the employee's current salary represents over his or her starting salary.

8. Enter the heading for this field as % and press Return.

You will want to keep this field short because the figures in it will consist of only four digits at the most.

Notice that the formula to calculate this percentage requires the use of the figures in the first derived column. The formula is dollar increase divided by the starting salary. In column numbers, it translates to #41/#35. The result of this calculation will be a decimal number, and because percentages are expressed in relation to 100, the answer is multiplied by 100: (#41/#35) * 100. The use of the parentheses is not strictly required to obtain the correct result, though it does help to phrase the meaning of the formula more effectively.

In Figure 5.16, notice that the f(N1) format has been added to the Column Spec of this derived column. This is because Q&A will display the final result with seven decimal places in the column. Now the percentage will be shown with one decimal place.

    (#41/#35) * 100

If you make a mistake, don't worry; Q&A will alert you with an error message. It is very good about not accepting formulas and other types of entries that it cannot process.

The last thing to define for this second derived column is its column number and any calculations to be done within it. Assign it the next column number, 42. Use the subaverage and average codes in this field (you cannot sum percentages as you do regular figures). This will determine the average percent of increase for each department as well as the average for the whole company.

9. Type the entry for the Column Spec here as **42,sa,a,f(N1)**.

There are two more derived columns to show the subtotal and total summary functions of Q&A. Table 5.4 shows all of the summary functions that can be used in a derived column. These last two columns calculate the employee's current salary as a percentage of the department and as a percentage of the whole company.

10. Assign the third derived column the heading of %!of!**Dept** to stack the heading on three lines to keep the column width small.

Figure 5.19 shows you the fields and the codes that you will enter on this page. As you can see, you will need to number and code three of the fields here: the Yearly Quota, Base Salary, and Commission Total fields. Only two of these, Commission Total and Yearly Quota, will be printed in the report. The Base Salary field has been made invisible by the addition of the code letter *i*.

But the Base Salary field will be the first column of the report arranged in ascending order by the addition of the code **as**, thereby determining the order of all the subsequent data. You will assign it the number 5 so that it precedes even the Last Name field (number 10 on the previous page). Notice that the codes for the Yearly Quota and Commission Total both include not only totals but also the average for each column. You will have each of these two figures displayed in the printed report.

Go ahead and enter the numbers and code letters for each of these fields just as they are shown in Figure 5.19. When you have finished entering them, press F8 to define a derived column for this report.

Figure 5.20 shows how to fill this out. The heading for the column will be *Total Sales* because if each salesperson makes his or her yearly quota, this will represent the total sales for the company. Notice the formula defined for this column. Column #20 is the Yearly Quota, while column #25 is the number you will assign to this derived column. This shows you how to create a self-referencing formula. It

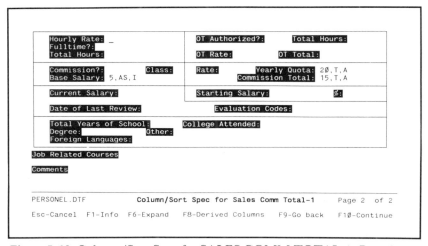

*Figure 5.19:* Column/Sort Spec for SALES COMM TOTAL-1, Page 2

```
                        DERIVED COLUMNS


        Heading: Total Sales
        Formula: #20 + #25
        Column Spec: 25

        Heading:
        Formula:
        Column Spec:

        Heading:
        Formula:
        Column Spec:

        Heading:
        Formula:
        Column Spec:


        PERSONEL.DTF         Derived Columns for Sales Comm Total-1      Page 1 of 4

        Esc-Cancel      F1-Info      F9-Go back to Column/Sort Spec      F10-Continue
```

***Figure 5.20:*** Derived column definition for SALES COMM TOTAL-1

takes each figure in the Yearly Quota column and adds it to the figure in the Sales Total column, in effect creating a running total.

Fill out the definition for this derived column as shown in Figure 5.20 and then press F10 to continue. At the Print Options screen, change the Print to option to SCREEN and press F10 again to save this report. Go ahead and print it when Q&A asks you if you want to print your report now. The report on your screen should match the report shown in Figure 5.21.

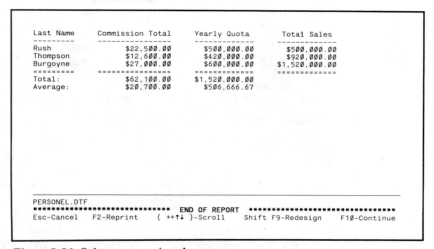

```
        Last Name     Commission Total     Yearly Quota      Total Sales
        ---------     ----------------     ------------      -----------
        Rush              $22,500.00        $500,000.00       $500,000.00
        Thompson          $12,600.00        $420,000.00       $920,000.00
        Burgoyne          $27,000.00        $600,000.00     $1,520,000.00
        =========     ================     ============      =============
        Total:            $62,100.00      $1,520,000.00
        Average:          $20,700.00        $506,666.67




        PERSONEL.DTF
        *******************************  END OF REPORT  *******************************
        Esc-Cancel    F2-Reprint    ( →←↑↓ )-Scroll    Shift F9-Redesign    F10-Continue
```

***Figure 5.21:*** Sales report printed to screen

The order of salespeople in this report is Rush, Thompson, and then Burgoyne. It was determined by the ascending order of your invisible Base Salary column where the figures for each are $14,500, $15,000, and $19,200. As you can see, the final figure in the Total Sales column matches that for the Yearly Quota, just as a running total should. If you wanted, you could easily expand such a report so that it also included the commission rate paid to each salesperson, though if you wanted to display their base salaries you would have to remove the *i* code from this field on the Column/Spec screen.

## KEYWORD REPORTS

There is a special type of report you should be aware of. It is called a *keyword report* because it is based on a *keyword field* in the database. When you design such a report, you must always make your keyword field the first column of the report. As with other columns in a report, you can add codes to have the column sorted, to suppress column breaks, and to repeat duplicate entries—just as you can in regular Q&A reports.

You can also limit the extent of the report of a keyword report by restricting the records it uses with the Retrieve Spec. Remember that when filling in a keyword field, separate entries must be separated by semicolons. If you used commas rather than semicolons to separate the entries in a keyword field, Q&A would see them as one entry. This would, of course, affect the records retrieved for such a report in unforeseen ways. If your keyword report does not contain the number or type of entries you expected, this is probably the cause. To rectify such a situation, use the Search/Update option on the File Menu and edit the necessary keyword fields before running your report again.

### DESIGNING A KEYWORD REPORT

For practice, you will design a keyword report that lists all the foreign languages known by the employees in the company. This report will be in alphabetical order of foreign language and will include the employee's first and last name and department.

1. To begin this report, type **1** at the Report Menu and press Return to use the personnel database.

2. When prompted for the report name, type **forlang by dept-1** and press Return.

You do not have to fill out the Retrieve Spec for this report because you want to include all of the foreign languages listed in the database. If you wanted to restrict the report to just certain languages, you would enter these in the Foreign Languages field. For instance, to generate a report that only lists French and Spanish, you would enter **French;Spanish** in the Foreign Languages field on the second page of this form. To restrict the report to those who know both French and Spanish, you would enter **&French;Spanish** there. Remember that the use of the ampersand creates an AND condition in a keyword field. Listing the match entries separated by semicolons alone means "this or that," the standard OR condition.

3. Press F10 to advance to the Column/Sort Spec. Figure 5.22 shows you how to fill this out for the first page of this form. The department column will be sorted in ascending order with the column break suppressed and duplicate entries printed.

4. Move the cursor to this field and enter **25,as,cs,r** there.

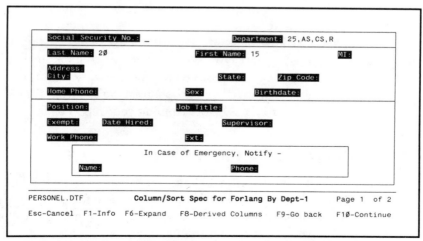

*Figure 5.22:* Column/Sort Spec for FORLANG BY DEPT-1, Page 1

5. Press Return and type **20** for the Last Name and, finally, **15** for the First Name. Then press the PgDn key to go to the second page of this form.

Figure 5.23 shows you how to fill it out. Notice that the Foreign Languages field has been given the lowest number so that it will appear as the first column of the report. This, plus the letter code K that follows, are essential for this type of report.

6. Move the cursor to this field and type **10,K**.

7. Press F10 to advance to the Print Options screen.

8. Press F10 to save the report (first change the Print to option to the proper printer, if necessary).

9. Answer **Yes** to the prompt to print the report now.

Your printed report should match the one shown in Figure 5.24. In addition to this keyword report, you could similarly design reports that listed the degrees held by the employees, their evaluation ratings, or even the job-related courses taken by them.

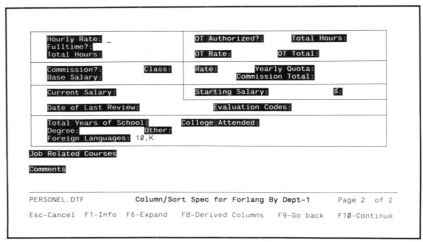

*Figure 5.23:* Column/Sort Spec for FORLANG BY DEPT-1, Page 2

```
Foreign Languages        First Name      Last Name      Department
-----------------        ----------      ---------      --------------
CHINESE                  John            Shepard        Sales

DUTCH                    Janice          Brown          Administration

FRENCH                   Edward          Chang          Administration
                         Kelly           Bennett        Engineering
                         Jeffry          Johnson        Marketing
                         Faith           Gibbon         Marketing
                         Jennifer        Raye           Personnel
                         Del             Rush           Sales

GERMAN                   James           Thornfield     Accounting
                         Edward          Chang          Administration
                         Janice          Brown          Administration
                         Owen            Rosner         Engineering
                         Ronald          Graydon        Engineering
                         Del             Rush           Sales
                         John            Shepard        Sales

ITALIAN                  Edward          Chang          Administration
                         Del             Rush           Sales

RUSSIAN                  John            Shepard        Sales

SPANISH                  Jessica         Freels         Accounting
                         Owen            Rosner         Engineering
                         Ronald          Graydon        Engineering
                         Alice           Johnson        Marketing
                         Lisa            Burke          Marketing
                         Del             Rush           Sales
                         Mark            Burgoyne       Sales

SWEDISH                  Monica          Peterson       Engineering
```

*Figure 5.24:* The foreign language report

# PRINTING THE REPORT

There are many times when the report you have designed contains too many columns to fit across a standard 8½-inch-wide sheet of paper. Q&A offers you a number of ways to alter your report so that it will print properly. You have already used the easiest method when you printed the modified **PERSONNEL BY DEPT-1** report using compressed type. In that case, you accommodated the column overflow by changing the characters per inch from 10 to 15 by using the Define Page options.

## CHANGING PAPER WIDTH AND MARGIN SETTINGS

This method will not, however, always work. Even after modifying the characters per inch, you may still find that Q&A gives you the warning message telling you that the report is too wide. If you have a printer with a carriage that will accommodate 14-inch-wide paper, you may find the best way around this is to change the margin settings for the report. To do this, you would redesign the report, accessing the Define Page options, and there change the Page width option from 85 to 140 for using 10 characters per inch.

The maximum page width in Report is 1000 characters. As in the word processor, you have the alternative of expressing the page width and length and the left and right margins in inches instead of the number of columns. You would enter **14"** (you must use the quote after the number) in place of 140. This works better because you do not have to make any further modifications if you should have to change the Characters per inch value as well. When changing the Page width, don't forget to change the right margin value also. If you forget, Q&A will still tell you that your report is too wide.

## CHANGING COLUMN WIDTHS AND HEADINGS

If you do not have a wide carriage printer or if you must produce the report on 8½-inch-wide paper, you will be forced to try some other way to fit your report. As mentioned earlier, Q&A Report gives you the option of setting new headings for your reports rather than using the field names from the database file. Choose the third option on the Report Menu, called Set Global Options, then the first option from the Global menu, Set Column Headings/Widths.

Using this option, it is possible not only to give your columns new headings but also to assign them new widths. This allows you control over Q&A's automatic setting of the column widths in a report. This is a global setting and will affect all of the reports for this database. If you want to set new headings and widths in just one report, you can add an **H(*n: newheading*)** in the column Sort Spec where *n* is the new width between 1 and 80, and *newheading* is the heading you want for this column.

This will allow you to modify the report so that it will fit on the page without requiring that you alter the basic design. Q&A bases its assignment of the column width on two factors: the width of the field name and the longest entry in that field.

If the width of the longest entry is longer than the field name, then changing the column width will cause the entry to wrap in that column. Most often, however, the field name is a lot longer than the longest entry in the field. For instance, in your sample database you assigned the field name Total Years of School to the field that contains, at most, a two-digit number. If you use this field in a report, Q&A Report will make the column at least 21 columns wide to accommodate the field name as a column heading, but you really only need two columns to print the values in the column. In such a case, you can use the Set new headings option to shorten the field name and greatly reduce the width of the column in the report. Doing this for all such fields in a report will make it possible to fit many more columns across the page.

Figure 5.25 shows how you could alter this and some of the other column headings on Page 2 of the form. Altering these would subsequently reduce the width of their columns in any reports in which they are used. Notice that the screen is called the Column Headings/ Width Spec. To get to this screen, you select the Set Column Headings/Widths option from the Report Global Options Menu. Once you select it, Q&A prompts you for the name of the database file to use with it. Be aware that any changes you make here to the column headings and column widths will affect all of the reports in which they appear. Because changes here globally affect all of the reports associated with the database, this is a separate option on the Report Menu rather than a choice within the Design/Redesign option. If you make a change to a heading that you do not want used in a particular report, you must return to this specification screen and modify it before running your report.

When using the Column Headings/Width Spec, you have two things that you can do in a field. You may first set the maximum column width by typing in the number of characters and then type in a new column heading. The column heading can be split to appear on several lines in the report. This is the meaning of the exclamation points separating parts of the new column headings entered in some of the fields in the figure.

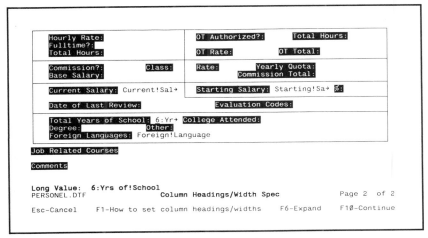

***Figure 5.25:*** Using the Set New Headings option

Look at the Long Value for the Total Years of School field shown in the figure. As is true when designing a database, you can enter any commands that will not fit within the field width by pressing F6, the Expand function. It places the cursor on a new line at the bottom of the screen after the prompt "Long Value:". Q&A always indicates the overflow condition and use of the long value by placing a → symbol at the end of the field. When the cursor is on the field, you can read the full entry on this line.

In this field, the column width was set to six characters by first entering a **6**. A colon is then used to separate the maximum column width from any new heading that is defined. In this case, a multiple-line heading is defined. The place to break the heading is indicated by the position of the exclamation point. The new heading will then consist of two lines. In a report, it would appear as follows:

**Yrs of
School**

The values in this column would then be right-justified within it. Even if the maximum width were not set to 6 here, making this change to the column heading would have the same effect. Instead of requiring a column about two inches wide in a report, the column will now be only slightly over half an inch wide.

Similar, though less dramatic, reductions will be brought about by the changes to the column headings in the Current Salary and Starting Salary fields in this specification. They are split into two line headings because their field names are both longer than values in their columns. No attempt has been made to set the maximum width because some of the reports in which they are used contain calculations like subtotals and totals, which can result in larger calculated numbers that require more space.

While this discussion has focused on how to narrow column widths, you can also use this specification to increase the size of columns or expand column headings. If you find that your field name is too abbreviated and therefore too cryptic for a formal printed report, you can use these methods just as well to develop headings to make your report read better.

At times, you will find that you need to do quite a bit of experimentation with the methods discussed above to get your report to print just right. In the most extreme cases, you may even have to eliminate some of the columns from your report to make it fit on the page. If that happens, try designing two reports that work together in telling your story. Don't forget that you can save yourself a lot of time and effort by first using the Rename/Delete/Copy option to copy the design of the report that you intend to split into two, before you make any changes.

## SUMMARY

You are now quite experienced at producing various types of reports with Q&A Report. Having reached this point in the book, you have gained knowledge and experience of all the basic functions of Q&A. The next step in mastery of this program is potentially the most exciting and certainly unique. In the next chapter, you will learn how to use Q&A's Intelligent Assistant module. Here you become the teacher instead of the student, because in order for the Intelligent Assistant to serve you, it must be taught some basic things about the database that you have designed. For your first experience with the Intelligent Assistant, you will use your sample personnel database, with which you are now quite familiar.

6

# THE INTELLIGENT ASSISTANT

*FastTrack*

**If the Intelligent Assistant does not understand**                    **312**

some part of your request, it will flag the term and ask you for clarification. You can reword the request or add to its vocabulary. Choosing to add to its vocabulary gives you limited access to the teaching lessons. You can also define synonyms that are saved with your database.

**If you use the Intelligent Assistant to create a report,**            **325**

you can print the report by pressing the F2 function key. This will take you to a Print Menu identical to the one you use in Q&A Report.

**To save a report,**                                                   **328**

you must use the Print to DISK option. It saves the file as an ASCII text file, which cannot be accessed through Q&A Report or the Intelligent Assistant. You can, however, modify the file and incorporate it into a document created with Q&A Write.

**When you are finished querying the database**                         **329**

with the Intelligent Assistant, always exit back to the Main Menu of Q&A before turning off the power to your computer. If you have a power interruption or if you do not exit through the menu system, you may not be able to access your database again. (Therefore, always keep a current backup copy of your entire database file.)

# INTRODUCING Q&A'S INTELLIGENT ASSISTANT

The most fascinating aspect of Q&A is undoubtedly its Intelligent Assistant (also known as the Assistant) module. It represents a first attempt in microcomputer software at allowing the user to query (locate and retrieve information from) a database by entering requests phrased entirely in conversational English sentences. This is most often referred to as a *natural language interface,* and it represents one of the major goals of computer research in the much-publicized area of artificial intelligence.

While many microcomputer database programs support English-like phrases and syntax when querying a database, there has not really been a true natural language interface offered before the introduction of Q&A. New users often find mastering an English-like query system as difficult as learning a bona fide programming language. The reason for this is simple: both have very formal and rigid structures.

For most people, the stumbling block to mastery of an English-like query system is not its formality but its rigidity. If a query written in such a system lacks so much as a comma, or misplaces some other required symbol, the program cannot process the request at all. In addition, it usually takes quite a bit of time and effort to become proficient with such a query system. And even after you have mastered it, if you do not use it continuously you will quickly forget many of its fine points and will be forced to take time to relearn them.

The Intelligent Assistant attempts to free you completely from the constraints of such a system by allowing you to express your requests to query your database in the most natural and intuitive way possible—in everyday, conversational English. By way of an example, compare the following simple query written in a popular English-like query language to its counterpart written for Q&A's Intelligent Assistant:

```
LIST NAME FOR CITY = 'CHICAGO'
Who lives in Chicago?
```

In the first request you have no latitude either in the words you use or in their order, whereas the English question for the Intelligent Assistant could be phrased in any of several ways. You could just as well ask, "Which of our employees lives in Chicago?" You can even set it up so that you can use all sorts of synonyms in a question. In this example, you might define synonyms such as "resides" or "dwells" for "lives" so that you could ask, "Who resides in Chicago?" and still have your request understood by Q&A.

However, a price is exacted for such flexibility and naturalness. While the Intelligent Assistant may appear to understand a request entered as an English sentence (because it gives the appropriate response), no real understanding takes place. The Intelligent Assistant takes each English query and painstakingly translates each word and phrase into a syntax and vocabulary that it can understand. The Intelligent Assistant needs time to successfully determine the meaning and respond appropriately. Once the Intelligent Assistant has finished translating, it always shows you its understanding of what you want it to do and asks you for approval to go ahead.

If you pose a really complex or somewhat ambiguous question, the Intelligent Assistant may have to stop and ask you to clarify certain terms more than once in order to process your request successfully. It may even mistranslate the query, forcing you to stop the Intelligent Assistant from processing the request and find another way to make it understand what you intended it to do.

The net result is that it can sometimes be more time-consuming to phrase your queries with the Intelligent Assistant than it would be to fill out a Retrieve Spec using Q&A File's Search/Update feature. Once the query has been translated and you give your approval, there is no difference in the amount of time it takes Q&A to process the request using either method.

As you will see, *ad hoc* (on the spot or at the moment) queries are usually easier to conceive and execute in English using the Intelligent Assistant despite the possible time delays or misunderstandings that can occur. You may find that you do not ask questions of certain kinds of databases, and will therefore not bother to use the Intelligent Assistant with them.

For example, if you keep a customer address file that is routinely used only to generate form letters and mailing labels, you would not really need to take the time to prepare it for use with the Intelligent Assistant. On the other hand, if you keep a customer profile database that includes vital information about your customers and their buying habits, and you use the information it contains in decision-making, you would definitely want to use this database with the Intelligent Assistant. In such a case, doing so is well worth the time required because it enables you to analyze data easily from various angles.

# PREPARING YOUR DATABASE FOR USE WITH THE ASSISTANT

The Intelligent Assistant has a built-in vocabulary of approximately 400 words. This makes it possible for the Assistant to answer many questions without you teaching it anything new. However, you must remember that the Intelligent Assistant is limited to the knowledge of your database. It learns the structure and contents— the field labels, types of data, and the content of each field—by looking at the database itself. The Intelligent Assistant builds a special type of index in which it stores the information necessary to answer your questions.

Each database you create and allow the Assistant to learn about has its own special index contained in the .IDX file associated with the .DTF file. Because the Assistant must scan the structure of your database (including the records that currently exist) in order to set up the index, it's a good idea to teach the Assistant before your database gets too large. After its first learning session, the Intelligent Assistant keeps track of new information on its own.

## REVIEWING THE INFORMATION IN YOUR DATABASE

To see how this works, you will now go through the procedure of having the Intelligent Assistant review the structure and data in your personnel file. If you need to, turn on your computer and start up Q&A. If you are still in the program, make sure you are at the Main Menu level. To enter the Assistant module, type **a** and press Return (or type **4**).

Figure 6.1 shows you the Assistant Menu that should now appear on your screen. There are only three options on this menu. The first, Get acquainted, offers a short tutorial explaining the potential uses of this module. It serves merely as an introduction to this part of Q&A.

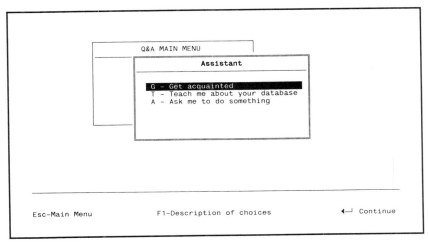

*Figure 6.1:* The Assistant Menu

The last two options are the command options on this menu. You will use the second, Teach me about your database, shortly to prepare your personnel database for use with the Intelligent Assistant. At present it is the third option, Ask me to do something, that you will use to rename the Intelligent Assistant.

1. Type **a**, and you will then be prompted for the name of a database file to use.

2. Type **personel** and press Return, or just press Return and move the highlight to its name on the next screen. If you use the pointing method, you must press Return again to select the file.

Once you select this database, Q&A will give you a message letting you know that before you can use the Intelligent Assistant, it must review the information in your database (shown in Figure 6.2). The time it takes to do this procedure varies, depending upon the complexity of the database form and the number of records that you have entered in the file.

3. The default response at this screen is Yes - Continue, so just press Return here.

To review the twenty records that you have in your personnel database will take Q&A about two mintues. This gives you an idea of

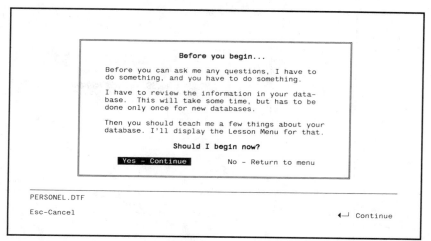

```
                    Before you begin...
      Before you can ask me any questions, I have to
      do something, and you have to do something.

      I have to review the information in your data-
      base.  This will take some time, but has to be
      done only once for new databases.

      Then you should teach me a few things about your
      database.  I'll display the Lesson Menu for that.

                    Should I begin now?
         Yes - Continue          No - Return to menu



 _____

  PERSONEL.DTF

  Esc-Cancel                                    ◄─┘ Continue
```

*Figure 6.2:* Preliminary Database Review Decision screen

how long the initial process would take with an actual working database containing hundreds or even thousands of records. As usual, Q&A keeps you informed of its progress through a percentage indicator that always lets you know how much of the database has been reviewed. It is part of the Please wait screen that has now appeared (shown in Figure 6.3).

Once Q&A has finished reviewing the structure and all of the records in your file, it automatically takes you to the Intelligent Assistant's Lesson Menu. This is the same menu that you see when you select the second option, Teach me about a database, from the Intelligent Assistant Menu.

4. You will return to this menu shortly and complete all of the lessons here, but for now exit by pressing Esc.

This takes you back to the Assistant Menu.

## RENAMING THE INTELLIGENT ASSISTANT

You can give the Intelligent Assistant a new name of your own choosing whenever you wish. Once you do so, you may refer to the Intelligent Assistant directly by that name, which "personalizes" the

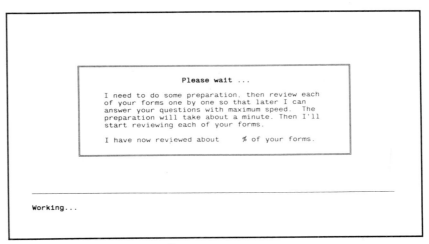

```
                    Please wait ...

     I need to do some preparation, then review each
     of your forms one by one so that later I can
     answer your questions with maximum speed.  The
     preparation will take about a minute. Then I'll
     start reviewing each of your forms.

     I have now reviewed about     % of your forms.
```

```
Working...
```

*Figure 6.3:* Review Status Indicator screen

interaction between you and the program. This name also replaces
all references to the Intelligent Assistant in Q&A's menu system.

1.  To rename the Intelligent Assistant, type **a** and press Return
    (or type **3**) to select again the Ask me to do something option
    from this menu.

This time, you receive a new screen (shown in Figure 6.4) that has
at the top a box for entering your questions and requests; it now contains the cursor. Below it is a larger box now containing explanatory
material and sample requests. As you can see, you may press F1, the
Help key, to get further suggestions on how to proceed. As you use
the Intelligent Assistant, you will become quite familiar with this
screen. The second box is also used to prompt you for more information when required, to give you the Intelligent Assistant's interpretation of what you want it to do, and to ask for your approval to proceed
once you have entered a request.

When you type in a request, the same editing functions are available as in the word processor. All you have to do is phrase the question or request as an English sentence, just as you would speak it. As
soon as you have your request phrased exactly the way you want it,
you press Return to signal to the Intelligent Assistant that you are
finished. It then analyzes the request word by word or phrase by

phrase, studying the structure and the vocabulary used. If the Intelligent Assistant does not understand the vocabulary, it will highlight the word or phrase in question and ask you for clarification. If it has no problem with translating your request, it will then show you how it has interpreted what you want and ask you for permission to go ahead and process the query.

Because you have not yet taught the Intelligent Assistant about the fields in your database and the vocabulary that you may use, your ability to query your personnel database is now quite limited. Nevertheless, you can go ahead and change the Intelligent Assistant's name and ask general questions of it without any further preparation.

Figure 6.4 shows you the text of the first request of the Intelligent Assistant. It is the command, "Change your name to Eli." The name Eli was chosen here as the acronym for English Language Interface. You may substitute whatever name you like in its place. Just be aware that in the rest of this chapter, *Eli* will appear wherever your own choice would otherwise be. (If you prefer a female persona for the Intelligent Assistant, a suggested acronym is *Mia*—for *My Intelligent Assistant* .)

You do not have to phrase the name-change command exactly as it shown in this example. The Intelligent Assistant would just as well understand "Your name is Eli" or "Name yourself Eli." To see how

```
┌──────────────────────────────────────────────────────────────┐
│ ┌────────────────────────────────────────────────────────┐   │
│ │Change your name to Eli._                                │   │
│ │                                                          │   │
│ └────────────────────────────────────────────────────────┘   │
│   ┌──────────────────────────────────────────────────────┐   │
│   │   Type your request in English in the box above, then │   │
│   │   press ◄─┘ .                                          │   │
│   │   Examples:                                            │   │
│   │   "List the average salary and average bonus from the  │   │
│   │    forms on which the sex is male and the department   │   │
│   │    is sales."                                          │   │
│   │   "Get the forms of the Administration employees,      │   │
│   │    sorted by city."                                    │   │
│   │            Press  ┌────┐  for more information.        │   │
│   │                   │ F1 │                               │   │
│   │                   └────┘                               │   │
│   └──────────────────────────────────────────────────────┘   │
│ ─────────────────────────────────────────────────────────    │
│ PERSONEL.DTF                                                  │
│                                                               │
│ Esc-Cancel   F1-How to ask   F6-See words   F8-Teach word  ◄─┘ Continue │
└──────────────────────────────────────────────────────────────┘
```

*Figure 6.4:* Changing the name of the Intelligent Assistant

the Intelligent Assistant processes a request, type in the following command, using either the name Eli or a new name of your own, and then press Return:

**Change your name to Eli.**

As soon as you press Return, notice that the Assistant converts the entire sentence to uppercase letters. This is always the case when the Intelligent Assistant processes a request. As a result, there is no way to make it case sensitive. This can be a problem when you request any changes that affect text fields in the database. They are always converted to all capital letters by the Intelligent Assistant. There is no way to prevent this from happening. Even text enclosed within quotation marks will be changed to uppercase text.

Watch as the Intelligent Assistant highlights each word of the request, jumping forward and backward as it translates the request into a form it can process. Because the creators of the Intelligent Assistant have already programmed it to understand this kind of request, it does not have to ask you for any clarification. Instead, once it has finished analyzing the entire request, it shows you its interpretation and asks for your approval to continue (Figure 6.5). Type **y** to have it change its name to ELI. Because you have not

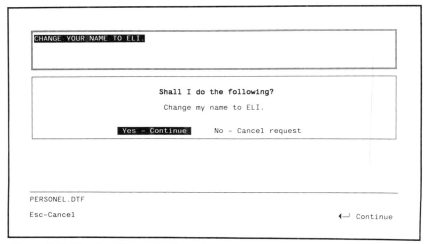

*Figure 6.5:* The Intelligent Assistant's interpretation

asked a question that calls for data retrieval, you will not receive an on-screen response to this request.

## ASKING GENERAL QUESTIONS OF THE INTELLIGENT ASSISTANT

Before you exit this part of the Intelligent Assistant and return to the Lessons Menu, experiment with asking ELI some general questions that do not pertain directly to the personnel database. Start by requesting the time of day:

**Eli, what time is it?**

As before, the Intelligent Assistant begins by converting the sentence to uppercase, and then analyzes each word within it. This time, it responds with the current time and date without asking for your approval to process the command. Besides requesting the date and time, you can also have the Intelligent Assistant perform mathematical calculations. Try this by entering the following:

**Eli, solve (45.5*233.75)/6.7**

As soon as you press Return, the Intelligent Assistant responds as before, only this time it stops and highlights the word *solve*, which it tells you is unknown to it (see Figure 6.6). You are now given four new options on how to proceed. You can edit the word, teach it the word, look at its vocabulary, or proceed without clarification. You do not want to use this last option if you feel that understanding the word is essential to the meaning of the request. Use this opportunity to take a look at the built-in vocabulary that the Intelligent Assistant currently has by typing s and pressing Return.

At this point, you see a new screen in which you can ask to see the built-in vocabulary, the vocabulary that you have assigned to the forms in your database, or the synonyms that you have assigned. Because you have neither taught the database nor had any reason to assign synonyms, choosing either of these options would not work. Type **b** and press Return here to see the words that ELI presently understands. Figures 6.7 and 6.8 show this vocabulary. At the first screen, press the PgDn key to see the rest of the words. Notice here that *solve* is not one of the terms that has been included in the list.

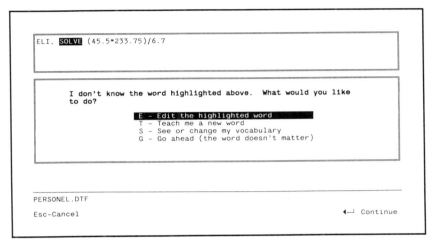

```
ELI, SOLVE (45.5*233.75)/6.7



       I don't know the word highlighted above.  What would you like
       to do?
                   E - Edit the highlighted word
                   T - Teach me a new word
                   S - See or change my vocabulary
                   G - Go ahead (the word doesn't matter)



PERSONEL.DTF

Esc-Cancel                                                ◀─┘ Continue
```

*Figure 6.6:* Highlighting an unknown word in the request

```
                            BUILT-IN VOCABULARY

  A             AT           COLUMN        DIVIDE       FEW          HELP          LARGE
  ABOUT         AUGUST       COMMENCING    DURING       FIELD        HER           LAST
  ABOVE         AVERAGE      CONCERN       EACH         FILE         HIGH          LATE
  ACCORDING     AWAY         CONSTRAINT    EARLY        FILL         HIM           LEAST
  ADD           BE           CONTAIN       EITHER       FIND         HIS           LESS
  AFTER         BEFORE       COUNT         EMPTY        FIRST        HOUR          LET
  AGAIN         BEGIN        CREATE        END          FOLLOWING    HOW           LIST
  ALL           BELOW        DATE          ENTER        FOR          I             LITTLE
  ALONG         BEST         DAY           ENTRY        FORM         IF            LOOK
  ALPHA         BETTER       DECEMBER      EQUAL        FOUND        IN            LOW
  ALPHABETICAL  BETWEEN      DECREASE      ERASE        FROM         INCLUDE       MAKE
  AN            BIG          DEFINE        EVERY        GET          INCLUSIVELY   MANY
  AND           BLANK        DEFINITION    EXCEED       GIVE         INCREASE      MARCH
  ANY           BOTTOM       DELETE        EXCLUDE      GOOD         IT            MATCH
  ANYONE        BUT          DESCENDING    EXCLUSIVELY  GREAT        JANUARY       MAXIMUM
  APRIL         BY           DETAIL        F            HALF         JULY          MEAN
  AS            CALCULATE    DIFFERENCE    FALSE        HAVE         JUNE          MINIMUM
  ASCENDING     CHANGE       DISPLAY       FEBRUARY     HE           KNOW          MINUS

PERSONEL.DTF

Esc-Cancel               PgDn-View More Definitions
```

*Figure 6.7:* The Intelligent Assistant's built-in vocabulary, Page 1

Press the PgUp key and notice that the verb *calculate* has been included.

You can easily reword this request to one that ELI understands by changing the verb from *solve* to *calculate*:

1.  Press Esc twice to return to the first screen; then type **e** and press Return to edit the word.

```
MINUTE        ONLY         REDUCE        SOME          THEN        VS        YES
MONTH         OR           REMOVE        SORT          THERE       WANT      YOU
MORE          ORDER        REPLACE       START         THESE       WE        YOUR
MOST          OUT          REPORT        STILL         THEY        WHAT      Z
MUCH          OVER         RESET         SUBAVERAGE    THIS        WHEN
MULTIPLY      PERCENT      RESTRICTION   SUBTOTAL      THOSE       WHERE
MUST          PLUS         RETRIEVE      SUBTRACT      THROUGH     WHETHER
N             POOR         REVERSE       SUCCEEDING    TIME        WHICH
NAME          POSITIVE     RUN           SUM           TO          WHO
NEGATIVE      PRECEDING    SAME          SUMMARY       TODAY       WHOM
NEITHER       PRESENT      SEARCH        SYNONYM       TOP         WHOSE
NEXT          PREVIOUS     SEE           T             TOTAL       WITH
NO            PRINT        SELECT        TABLE         TRUE        WITHIN
NOVEMBER      PRODUCT      SEPTEMBER     TAKE          TWICE       WITHOUT
NUMBER        QUOTIENT     SEQUENCE      TELL          UNDER       WNEC
OCTOBER       RAISE        SET           THAN          UP          WNIC
OF            RANK         SHE           THAT          US          WNRC
OK            RATIO        SHOW          THE           USE         WORSE
ON            RECENT       SINCE         THEIR         VALUE       Y
ONE           RECORD       SMALL         THEM          VIEW        YEAR
          . . ; : % * + - / ( ) = /= < > <> <= >=

PERSONEL.DTF

Esc-Cancel                    PgUp-View More Definitions
```

*Figure 6.8:* The Intelligent Assistant's built-in vocabulary, Page 2

2. Press Ins to get into insert mode.

3. Type **calculate** and press the space bar.

4. Then press F4 to delete the word *solve*, and press Return to have ELI process the revised request.

This time ELI correctly interprets the request by asking for approval to evaluate the mathematical expression that you entered. Press Return to have it go ahead and calculate the answer.

Figure 6.9 shows you how the final answer is presented to you. The Intelligent Assistant treats the request for calculated data just as it does a request for retrieving specific data from a database. It responds by creating an on-screen report. While using ELI this way is not the fastest way to perform calculations, you should remember that it is possible for ELI to do these kinds of math problems if necessary.

Press Esc now to tell ELI that you are finished reviewing the report. After it has cleared the screen, press Esc to return to the Assistant Menu. Notice, however, that this is now listed as the ELI Menu. Press Esc again to get back to the Main Menu. Here, E - ELI is listed as the fourth option in place of A - Assistant. Every place that carried the name Assistant now shows ELI.

```
┌─────────────────────────────────────────────────────────────────────┐
│  ┌──────────────────────────────────────────────────────────────┐   │
│  │Eli, calculate (45.5*233.75)/6.7                                │   │
│  │                                                                │   │
│  │                                                                │   │
│  └──────────────────────────────────────────────────────────────┘   │
│  ((45.5*233.75)/6.7)                                                  │
│  ─────────────────                                                    │
│        1,587.4067164                                                  │
│                                                                       │
│                                                                       │
│                                                                       │
│                                                                       │
│                                                                       │
│  ─────────────────────────────────────────────────────────────────  │
│  PERSONEL.DTF                                                         │
│  ****************************** END OF REPORT ********************************** │
│  Esc-Cancel     F2-Reprint      { → ← ↓ ↑ PgUp PgDn }-Scroll      F1Ø-Continue │
└─────────────────────────────────────────────────────────────────────┘
```

*Figure 6.9:* The calculated result in report form

# TEACHING THE INTELLIGENT ASSISTANT ABOUT YOUR DATABASE

To be able to use English queries when requesting information from your sample database with ELI (or the Intelligent Assistant), you must next go through a series of steps in which you instruct it about the English words and phrases you plan to use when asking it questions. To make this process simple, there are eight lessons divided into two sections—Basic Lessons and Advanced Lessons. You should complete the Basic Lessons for each database file you want to query by using the Intelligent Assistant. For ELI to understand more complex questions, you may choose to complete the Advanced Lessons—although this is not mandatory. While you may find that you are continually refining the Intelligent Assistant by adding to or modifying its vocabulary, it never again will require the time and energy that it did at the outset.

## LESSON 1: ADDING TERMS THAT CHARACTERIZE THE DATABASE

At the Main Menu, select the Intelligent Assistant module by typing **e** (now referred to as ELI on this menu) and pressing Return.

Then select the Teach me about your database option by typing **t** and pressing Return again. Figure 6.10 shows you this menu and the five options on it. The lessons that make up the first four choices are arranged in a sequential order. In order to teach ELI everything necessary about your personnel database, you will now complete all four lessons in order.

Begin the first lesson, What this database is about, by typing **1** and pressing Return (you can simply press Return if the first lesson is highlighted). The screen that now appears asks you to enter any words or phrases that would naturally complete the sentence "Each form contains information about a particular _____." (see Figure 6.11).

Here, you want to enter all general terms that characterize the content or theme of the database. It is appropriate to add any terms that you are likely to use when referring to the subject matter of the database, especially those that do not show up as field names in the database itself. For instance, although your sample database is mainly concerned with personnel commonly referred to as "employees," the word *employee* is not used within the database.

Figure 6.11 shows you how to fill out this screen. Notice that for most of the synonyms chosen, only the singular form is input. The Intelligent Assistant can understand regular plural forms (those that end in "s") without any problem. It cannot, however, supply irregular plural forms

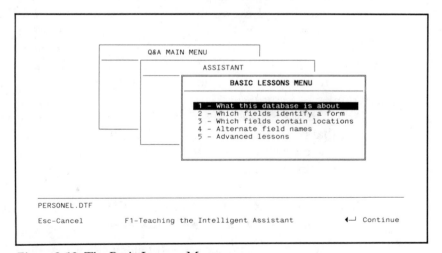

**Figure 6.10:** The Basic Lessons Menu

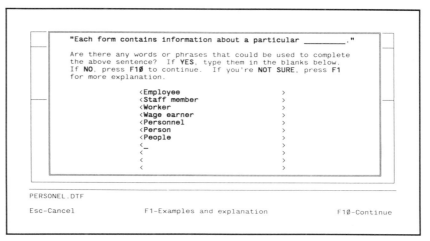

```
"Each form contains information about a particular _____."

Are there any words or phrases that could be used to complete
the above sentence?  If YES, type them in the blanks below.
If NO, press F1Ø to continue.  If you're NOT SURE, press F1
for more explanation.
                    <Employee                   >
                    <Staff member               >
                    <Worker                      >
                    <Wage earner                 >
                    <Personnel                   >
                    <Person                      >
                    <People                      >
                    <_                           >
                    <                            >
                    <                            >
                    <                            >
```

```
PERSONEL.DTF

Esc-Cancel              F1-Examples and explanation          F1Ø-Continue
```

***Figure 6.11:*** Supplying terms that characterize the content of the database

from the singular alone (such as *women* as the plural of *woman*). In such cases, you will have to enter both forms in separate blanks of the form. This is also true when supplying verb forms as well as adjectives and nouns in other lessons. Remember, though, that you never have to worry about the case you use when entering these forms because the Intelligent Assistant converts all entries to uppercase before analyzing the request.

Go ahead and enter the seven nouns shown in Figure 6.11 in this form. After you enter **employee** on the first line, you can press Return to move to the next line. If you make a typing mistake, use the Backspace key to delete any unwanted characters. You can insert new characters after pressing the Ins key to turn on insert mode. You can also use the up and down arrow keys to move between lines on this form.

If the subject of the database you have created is not readily described in single terms, you may also add simple phrases in these blanks, such as "potential clients". You cannot, however, add any descriptive phrases longer than will fit in the brackets. Each line must contain a self-contained description. You do not have to fill out this screen if you cannot think of general terms or phrases that you will be using when phrasing your database queries.

Once you have finished entering these terms, press F10 to save them. You will then be returned to the Lesson Menu. Press Return to go on to complete the next lesson.

## *LESSON 2: DESIGNATING WHICH FIELDS TO USE IN REPORTS*

Figure 6.12 shows you the first screen associated with this lesson. You are asked to designate which fields should always be included in on-screen reports resulting from your queries. In your personnel database, you almost always want at least the employees' last names and their departments displayed in these reports.

To designate the order in which they are to be shown in the report, you merely number them sequentially as you did when completing the Sort/Column Spec in Q&A Report. In this case, enter **1** in the Department field and **2** in the Last Name field of this screen. You move between fields in this and subsequent forms just as you do when filling out a Retrieve or Sort Spec. Press Return or the Tab key to move to the next field. You can also use the up and down arrow keys to move to different lines on the form. Press F10 when you are finished.

When you choose fields that identify a form and that will be later used in on-screen reports, the documentation suggests that you not use more than three fields. In some databases you will find it impossible to single out just a few fields that you always want included. In such a case, do not bother to fill out this screen. Later you will learn how to suppress identifying fields in reports that do not require them.

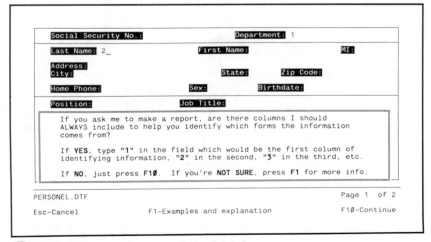

*Figure 6.12:* Designating identifying fields for reports

## *LESSON 3: DESIGNATING WHICH FIELDS CONTAIN LOCATIONS*

From the Lesson Menu, press Return. You should see the screen shown in Figure 6.13. In this lesson, you tell the Intelligent Assistant which fields in the database refer to locations. Giving this information allows you to formulate questions in your sample database that ask where an employee is located. The location can refer either to the department or to the home address of the person in question. Again, you designate the order in which you want the fields to appear in the resulting report by giving each location field a number.

Fill out this screen as shown in Figure 6.13. Number each of the fields that hold components of the home address so that they appear in their usual order of street, city, state, and zip code in any reports. Any time you ask where a particular employee is, you will receive his or her complete home address.

When you fill out this screen for your own database files, be sure that you do not include any fields other than those that refer to locations. If you inadvertently include fields that refer to people or other non-place names, the Intelligent Assistant will produce very strange reports whenever you ask a question inquiring where a person is.

Once you have numbered the four location fields in this screen, press F10 to save them and return to the Lesson Menu.

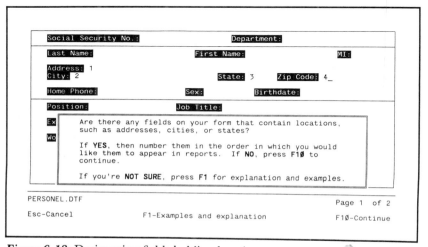

*Figure 6.13:* Designating fields holding locations

## *LESSON 4: DESIGNATING ALTERNATE FIELD NAMES*

The last lesson you must complete is Lesson 4. In it, you designate all of the alternate terms you want to use for all of the other fields in the database, just as you did for the fields containing people's names.

Press Return to begin this lesson. Q&A begins with the very first field, that of Social Security No. This field is highlighted at present, as shown in Figure 6.14. The actual field name is automatically supplied as the first alternate term. If you do not change it, it will be used as the column heading for reports as well as when the Intelligent Assistant needs to refer to it.

You must keep in mind when filling out these forms that the Intelligent Assistant will not allow you to use the same term for more than one field. If you try to assign a term that you already used in describing another field, the Intelligent Assistant will give you the error message

**Sorry. This word/phrase is already used. It must be unique.**

The only way around this is to add an additional modifier to the term. Intelligent Assistant will not object to the same term being used in a different phrase.

Sometimes this restriction can be frustrating when you wish to use the same term in two ways that carry very distinct meanings in English

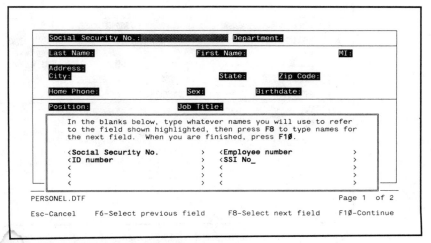

*Figure 6.14:* Designating alternate field names

usage but not in the Intelligent Assistant. For example, in your database you use the field name Class to refer to the classification of a salesperson (which, in turn, determines the commission). You might also want to use this term when asking what class a particular employee has taken from the Job Related Courses field. Because you cannot use the same term to describe the two fields, you would have to decide to which field it was better assigned. In this case, you might decide to use *classification* when referring to a salesperson's commission class, and *class* when referring to a course that an employee has taken. You must use terms consistently in your queries in order to avoid confusing the Intelligent Assistant.

When you designate alternate terms to use with the Intelligent Assistant, you use the F8 function key to tell the program that you have finished entering all of your alternate terms and to proceed to the next field. If you need to revise or review the entries in a previous field, press F6. Otherwise, use the up and down arrows as before to move between the blank lines. Not all of your fields will require that alternate terms be used. As before, if you later find that you need to refine these lists, you can return to the lesson and make any necessary changes.

Table 6.1 shows all of the alternate terms that you should assign to each field in your personnel database. Go ahead and fill out the list as given for each of the fields. If the first alternate term listed is not the same as the field name, you should change the field name supplied by Intelligent Assistant to a new term by typing the word shown over it. This new term will then be used as the column heading in any on-screen reports. For example, Q&A automatically supplied the field Name with *name* as its column heading. While it is descriptive enough in the context of the database screen form that contains the heading *In Case of Emergency, Notify* - above it, this word does not serve as a sufficiently descriptive column heading for reports. Replace *name* with the new list of alternate terms.

Because the first term will appear in the report as entered, each word begins with a capital letter. Subsequent entries are presented all in lowercase because the Intelligent Assistant will later automatically convert them to all uppercase letters regardless of how you input them. When you have finished entering terms for one field, press F8 to go on to the next one until you have entered them all.

*Table 6.1:* Alternate field names for the personnel database

| FIELD NAME | ALTERNATE TERMS | |
|---|---|---|
| Social Security No. | <Social Security No. | > |
| | <employee number | > |
| | <id number | > |
| | <ssi no | > |
| Department | <Department | > |
| | <dept | > |
| Last Name | <Last Name | > |
| | <surname | > |
| First Name | <First Name | > |
| | <given name | > |
| MI | <Initial | > |
| | <middle initial | > |
| Address | <Street | > |
| | <street address | > |
| City | <City | > |
| | <town | > |
| | <municipality | > |
| State | <State | > |
| Zip | <Zip Code | > |
| | <zip | > |
| Home Phone | <Home Phone | > |
| | <home number | > |
| | <home telephone number | > |
| Sex | <Sex | > |
| | <gender | > |
| Date of Birth | <Date of Birth | > |
| | <birthday | > |
| Position | <Position | > |
| | <job | > |
| | <function | > |
| Job Title | <Job Title | > |
| | <title | > |

*Table 6.1:* Alternate field names for the personnel database (continued)

| FIELD NAME | ALTERNATE TERMS | |
|---|---|---|
| Exempt | <Exempt | > |
| | <not eligible for overtime | > |
| Date Hired | <Date Hired | > |
| | <start date | > |
| | <anniversary date | > |
| Supervisor | <Supervisor | > |
| | <manager | > |
| | <boss | > |
| | <superior | > |
| Work Phone | <Work Phone | > |
| | <business phone | > |
| | <telephone number at work | > |
| | <work number | > |
| Ext | <Ext | > |
| | <extension | > |
| Name | <Emergency Contact | > |
| | <contact name | > |
| | <person to notify | > |
| | <personal reference | > |
| Phone | <Phone | > |
| | <emergency contact phone | > |
| | <emergency contact number | > |
| Hourly Rate | <Hourly Rate | > |
| | <hourly wage | > |
| OT Authorized? | <OT Authorized | > |
| | <allowed to work overtime | > |
| | <authorized for overtime | > |
| Total Hours | <Overtime Hours | > |
| | <overtime | > |
| | <ot | > |
| Fulltime? | <Full-Time | > |
| | <40 hours a week | > |

*Table 6.1:* Alternate field names for the personnel database (continued)

| FIELD NAME | ALTERNATE TERMS | |
|---|---|---|
| Total Hours | <Total Hours | > |
| | <yearly hours | > |
| | <hours a year | > |
| OT Rate | <OT Rate | > |
| | <overtime rate | > |
| | <overtime wage | > |
| | <rate of overtime pay | > |
| | <ot hourly rate | > |
| OT Total | <OT Cost | > |
| | <cost of overtime | > |
| Commission? | <Commission? | > |
| | <on commission | > |
| Class | <Classification | > |
| | <sales classification | > |
| | <commission classification | > |
| Rate | <Rate | > |
| | <commission rate | > |
| Yearly Quota | <Yearly Quota | > |
| | <quota | > |
| Base Salary | <Base Salary | > |
| | <base | > |
| Commission Total | <Commission | > |
| Current Salary | <Current Salary | > |
| | <salary | > |
| | <earnings | > |
| Starting Salary | <Starting Salary | > |
| | <beginning salary | > |
| % | <% | > |
| | <salary increase | > |
| Date of Last Review | <Last Reviewed | > |
| | <date of last review | > |
| | <evaluation date | > |
| | <last evaluated | > |

*Table 6.1:* Alternate field names for the personnel database (continued)

| FIELD NAME | ALTERNATE TERMS | |
|---|---|---|
| Evaluation Codes | <Evaluation Codes | > |
| | <evaluation scores | > |
| | <results of last review | > |
| | <scores | > |
| Total Years of School | <Years of School | > |
| | <time in school | > |
| | <years of education | > |
| | <education | > |
| College Attended | <College | > |
| | <university | > |
| | <school | > |
| Degree | <Degree | > |
| Other | <Other Training | > |
| | <certificate | > |
| | <award | > |
| | <training | > |
| Foreign Languages | <Foreign Languages | > |
| | <language | > |
| Job Related Courses | <Job Related Courses | > |
| | <classes | > |
| | <courses | > |
| Comments | <Comments | > |
| | <summary | > |
| | <remark | > |
| | <notes | > |
| | <observation | > |
| | <criticism | > |

When you assign alternate terms referring to specific fields in your database, be sure and add any abbreviations that you might want to use. For instance, when you filled in alternates for many of the overtime fields in this database, you entered the abbreviation *OT* as well as spelling out the word *overtime*. Many of the terms in this list were specifically chosen to be used as a verb or with a verb, just as you would do naturally in English. For example, the College Attended field was shortened to College in the first entry. This is because the verb *attend* will later be assigned to this field when completing Lesson 4, "Advanced Vocabulary: verbs", on the Advanced Lessons Menu. This makes it possible to ask, "What college (university, school) did she attend?"—which is much more natural than having to ask, "What is her college attended?"

Also, using the word *total* as part of the alternate term was avoided as much as possible. This was done to allow you to ask the Intelligent Assistant to give a total of these fields without confusion about what *total* refers to. *Total* is a built-in vocabulary word that signifies calculating the sum of the values in a particular field for many records. If you ask the Intelligent Assistant to create a report that gives you the total of overtime hours for all non-exempt employees, it will then be able to do so. If you had to phrase this request as "Total the total overtime hours for all non-exempt employees," the Intelligent Assistant could do it, but the possible ambiguity might well make it difficult to process the request the first time through.

Press F10 to save all of these alternate terms. This returns you to the Lesson Menu again. Now type **5** to choose Advanced Lessons, and press Return.

## TEACHING THE ASSISTANT USING ADVANCED LESSONS

You will now see the Advanced Lessons Menu as shown in Figure 6.15. There are four advanced lessons which can be used to further enhance the Intelligent Assistant's knowledge of your database. These lessons include teaching the Assistant about which fields refer to people's names, units of measure, adjectives, and vocabulary. To round out the Intelligent Assistant's information regarding the personnel file, continue now with these four lessons.

### ADVANCED LESSON 1: DESIGNATING WHICH FIELDS CONTAIN PEOPLE'S NAMES

Since the first lesson is already highlighted, press Return to select "What fields contain people's names." Figure 6.16 shows you the

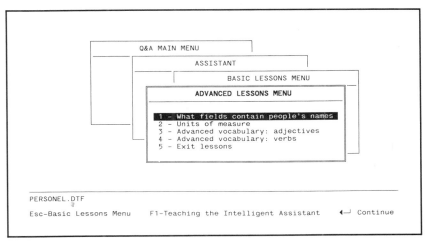

*Figure 6.15:* The Advanced Lessons Menu

```
┌─────────────────────────────────────────────────────────────────────┐
│  Social Security No.: _              Department:                      │
│                                                                       │
│  Last Name:              First Name:                  MI:             │
│                                                                       │
│  Address:                                                             │
│  City:                        State:        Zip Code:                 │
│                                                                       │
│  Home Phone:            Sex:            Birthdate:                     │
│                                                                       │
│  Position:              Job Title:                                    │
│  ┌──────────────────────────────────────────────────────────────┐    │
│  │                                                                │    │
│  │  Are there any fields that contain a person's name?           │    │
│  │                                                                │    │
│  │  If YES, then press F1 so that I can tell you what I need to know. │
│  │                                                                │    │
│  │  If NO, then just press F10 to continue to the next lesson.    │    │
│  │                                                                │    │
│  └──────────────────────────────────────────────────────────────┘    │
│                                                                       │
│  PERSONEL.DTF                                           Page 1 of 2   │
│                                                                       │
│  Esc-Cancel            F1-Examples and explanation      F10-Continue  │
└─────────────────────────────────────────────────────────────────────┘
```

*Figure 6.16:* Designating fields that contain names of people

screen that now appears. Here you are asked if there are any fields in
your database that contain a person's name. This screen informs you
that if there are, you should press F1 to get more information about
how to fill in these fields. Press F1 to see this information screen
(shown in Figure 6.17).

As you can see, this screen informs you that you must give a number
to each of the fields containing people's names and also tell whether the

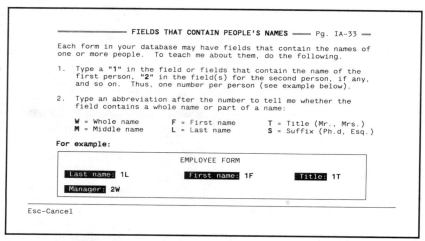

*Figure 6.17:* Advanced Lesson 1 Help screen

field contains the complete name or just a part of it. In the personnel database, there are three different people referred to: the employee, his or her supervisor, and the person to contact in an emergency. Each employee's name is contained in three separate fields. The first contains the last name, the second the first name, and the third the middle initial.

To tell the Intelligent Assistant that all three of these fields hold parts of the same name, you must use letter codes as shown on this Help screen. In this case, enter **1L** in the Last Name field, **1F** in the First Name field, and **1M** in the middle initial field. The use of the same number lets the Intelligent Assistant know that all of these fields belong to the same person.

Notice that you can also designate that a field contain the person's title—like Mr., Mrs., or Ms—by adding the code letter T after the number. You can add titles or degrees—like Esq., III, Ph.D.—at the end of a name by using the code letter S. This is very useful in mailing list files that must contain all of the possible components of each name in separate fields. Using these codes with the same number designation allows you to have the entire name displayed in on-screen reports generated with the Intelligent Assistant, while still retaining each part of the name in individual fields for use in mail-merge applications with the word processor.

Press Esc to return to the form and fill out the codes for the three name fields as shown in Figure 6.18. When you have finished, press the ↓ key to get down to the second half of the first page of this form.

You must tell the Intelligent Assistant that both the Supervisor and Name fields also contain people's names in this database. Both of these fields contain the full name, so you use the code letter W (*Whole name*) in each. Move the cursor first to the Supervisor field and type **2W**; then move down to the Name field and type **3W** there, as shown in Figure 6.19.

There are no other fields that have people's names—so, after you have finished making these entries, press F10 to continue. Once you do, the Intelligent Assistant will give you a message telling you to wait while it performs a new operation consisting of several steps. This is the last major processing delay involved in preparing the database for use with the Intelligent Assistant. Intelligent Assistant uses the information you just supplied about the fields containing people's names and compares it to the records in the database file as it continues to build the Intelligent Assistant index for this database. As usual, you are informed of the program's progress, this time with an indicator that says, "Now doing step ___ of ___." This operation will take a couple of minutes to complete, even with only 20 records in the file.

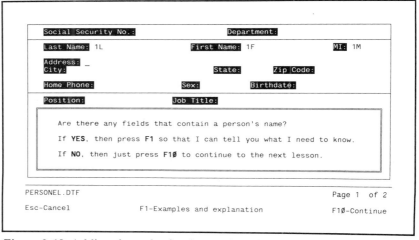

*Figure 6.18:* Adding the codes for the employee's name

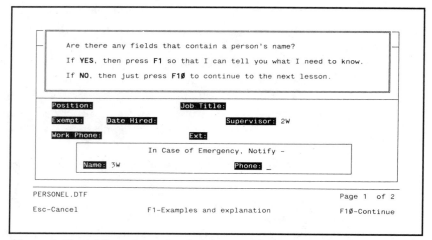

```
┌─────────────────────────────────────────────────────────────────────┐
│                                                                       │
│  ┌──────────────────────────────────────────────────────────────┐    │
│ ─┤   Are there any fields that contain a person's name?           ├─  │
│  │                                                                │    │
│  │   If YES, then press F1 so that I can tell you what I need to know.│
│  │                                                                │    │
│  │   If NO, then just press F10 to continue to the next lesson.   │    │
│  └──────────────────────────────────────────────────────────────┘    │
│                                                                       │
│   ┌──────────────────────────────────────────────────────────────┐   │
│   │ Position:               Job Title:                            │   │
│   │ Exempt:    Date Hired:              Supervisor: 2W            │   │
│   │ Work Phone:              Ext:                                 │   │
│   │            ┌───────── In Case of Emergency, Notify ─┐         │   │
│   │            │ Name: 3W                   Phone: _    │         │   │
│   │            └────────────────────────────────────────┘         │   │
│   └──────────────────────────────────────────────────────────────┘   │
│   PERSONEL.DTF                                         Page 1  of 2    │
│   Esc-Cancel              F1-Examples and explanation      F10-Continue│
│                                                                       │
└─────────────────────────────────────────────────────────────────────┘
```

*Figure 6.19:* Adding the codes for the supervisor and emergency contact names

Once the Intelligent Assistant is finished, a new screen will appear like the one shown in Figure 6.20. All of the fields that constitute the first name are highlighted with a new box prompting you for terms that you will use when referring to these fields (i.e., this person's name) in your queries. As you can see, the form consists of bracketed blanks just like those you filled out previously. Because this person's name is split into three separate components, you need to give the Intelligent Assistant an idea of any collective terms you plan to use which will apply to all of these fields.

In this case, you will most often refer to a person as an *employee* in your queries. Enter **employee** as the first term. Whatever you enter in the first blank will appear as the column heading in any reports that include the employee's name. The Intelligent Assistant will also display this first term when asking for confirmation of its interpretation of a query that it thinks should include the employee's name. Go on and enter the other alternate terms shown in Figure 6.20 and then press F10 to continue.

Next, you are asked to do the same for the second person referred to in the database (shown in Figure 6.21). This is the Supervisor field that you designated as containing the whole name. As you can see, Q&A automatically supplies the field names Supervisor, Manager,

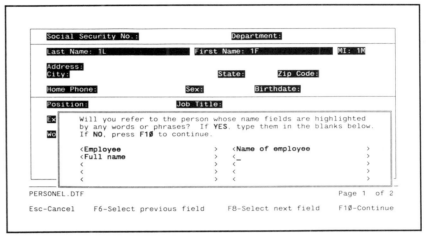

*Figure 6.20:* Adding terms referring to the first name in the database

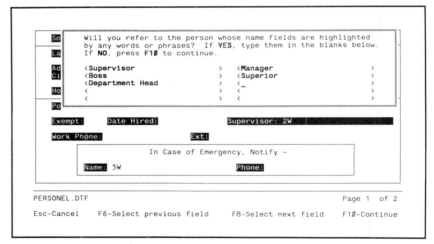

*Figure 6.21:* Adding terms referring to the second name in the database

Boss and Superior which you assigned as alternate field names during the Basic Lesson 4. Go on and add the other alternate term, **Department Head**, as listed in Figure 6.21. Adding such alternates allows you more flexibility when you ask about an employee's supervisor. You can then refer to the supervisor as the person's boss, manager, or superior without having the Intelligent Assistant stop and ask for clarification. You can always add other alternatives to this list later by accessing the lesson again. You can access the lesson either from the Lesson menu or from the See or change my vocabulary option that appears when the Intelligent Assistant requires clarification. Once you have entered these terms, press F10 again.

The next screen appears now. You are asked to do the same thing for the third person identified in the personnel database. This is the Name field that contains the name of the person to contact in an emergency. Notice that, as the alternate terms you assigned to the field during the Alternate Field Names lesson appear again here, your work has already been done for you. Press F10 to accept these assignments and you will return to the Advanced Lessons Menu.

## ADVANCED LESSON 2: SPECIFYING UNITS OF MEASURE

Choose Lesson 2 and press Return for the next lesson. Figure 6.22 shows you the screen that now appears. In this lesson you are asked to assign units of measure to all numeric fields (other than currency fields, which are automatically measured in dollars or pounds, depending upon how you designed the form). As you can see here, all of the numeric fields visible in this screen now contain number symbols. You designate the unit of measure for each by pressing F8 to advance to the next field, just as before.

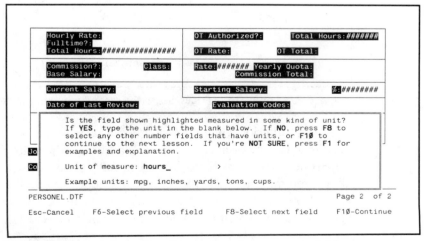

*Figure 6.22:* Assigning units of measurement to numeric fields

In your sample database, there are only three types of measure that you need to assign to the numeric fields now displayed—hours, years, and percent. The two Total Hours fields require hours, while the Total Years of School field naturally requires measurement in years. The Rate and % fields are both measured in percent. Go ahead and enter these three units as required.

Notice from the examples shown in the instruction box on the screen (and in Figure 6.22) that you can assign a wide variety of units. In your databases, you may have occasions that call for other types of measurement such as ounces, feet, square feet, liters, meters, degrees, radians, etc. You are not restricted to a particular type of unit or system of measurement (e.g., English versus metric) when you make these designations. The purpose here is to assign appropriate units so that the Intelligent Assistant will understand to which fields you are referring when you ask questions like "How many hours of authorized overtime does Katherine have?" or "Which employees have had a salary increase of 20 percent or better?"

Once you finish assigning the hours, years, and percent units to the numeric fields on this second page of the form, press F10 again to save them and go on to Lesson 3.

## ADVANCED LESSON 3: ASSIGNING ADJECTIVES TO DESIGNATE HIGH AND LOW VALUES

Press Return at the Lesson Menu to do the lesson on assigning the comparative adjectives you might want to use. In Lesson 3, you assign opposite pairs of adjectives to particular numeric and currency fields where you want to be able to ask questions about their high and low values. In many cases the Intelligent Assistant will need you to define the words you are using to refer to the high value (e.g., *huge*) and the low value (e.g., *tiny*). It can figure out words that are formed regularly, such as *old, older, oldest*. In addition, it already knows the more common irregular adjectives like *big, small, good* (with its irregular comparative *better* and its superlative *best*), *great, little, few* (*less, least*), *many, more*, and *much*. You must, however, teach it other adjectives that would be natural to use when asking about specific fields in the database. If the adjectives in question have irregular forms like *bad, worse, worst*, you must include all of them in your assignment.

Figure 6.23 shows you the screen that appears for your personnel database. Notice that in addition to all of the numeric fields that were highlighted in the previous lesson, all of your currency fields are now included. You can add comparisons involving descriptive adjectives like *expensive* and *cheap* to the currency fields.

The instruction box on this screen allows you to enter an adjective for both the high and low value. You typically place one adjective in the blank for the high value and one of its opposites in the blank for the low. You do not, however, have to enter an opposite or even fill out the low value. If you only intend to use a regular adjective (such as *tall*) in your queries, then you only have to enter it in the high-value blank. Any adjectives you assign are specifically related to the field in which you enter them. If you want to use the same adjectives when referring to other fields in the database, you must enter them in all of the other fields where they will be used as well.

Figure 6.24 shows you the Help screen associated with this lesson (accessed by pressing F1). You can see some examples like *old*, *young*, *heavy*, and *light*. Note that this screen indicates that you do not have to enter these adjectives in their comparative forms like *older* and *younger* or *oldest* and *youngest*. The Intelligent Assistant will understand these uses as long as their forms are regular (formed with *-er* and *-est* or with *more* and *most*).

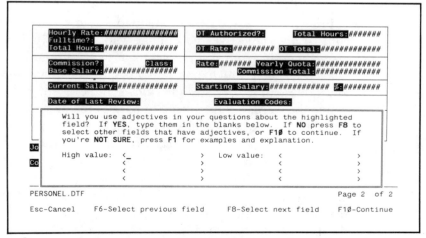

*Figure 6.23:* Adding adjectives with high and low values to fields

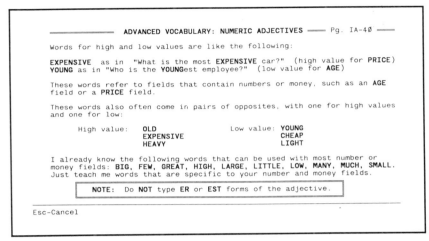

```
──────── ADVANCED VOCABULARY: NUMERIC ADJECTIVES ──── Pg. IA-4Ø ────

Words for high and low values are like the following:

EXPENSIVE  as in  "What is the most EXPENSIVE car?"  (high value for PRICE)
YOUNG  as in "Who is the YOUNGest employee?"  (low value for AGE)

These words refer to fields that contain numbers or money, such as an AGE
field or a PRICE field.

These words also often come in pairs of opposites, with one for high values
and one for low:

         High value:   OLD              Low value: YOUNG
                       EXPENSIVE                    CHEAP
                       HEAVY                        LIGHT

I already know the following words that can be used with most number or
money fields: BIG, FEW, GREAT, HIGH, LARGE, LITTLE, LOW, MANY, MUCH, SMALL.
Just teach me words that are specific to your number and money fields.
     ┌──────────────────────────────────────────────────────────┐
     │ NOTE:  Do NOT type ER or EST forms of the adjective.       │
     └──────────────────────────────────────────────────────────┘


Esc-Cancel
```

*Figure 6.24:* Advanced Lesson 3 Help screen

Most of the time, the adjectives already included in the Intelligent Assistant's vocabulary will be sufficient for all of your queries. If you do not add any special adjectives here but find yourself naturally using some that are not understood by the Intelligent Assistant, you can return to this lesson later to add them. For now, you do not need to add any special adjectives in your personnel database, so press Esc to return to the Lesson Menu.

## ADVANCED LESSON 4: DESIGNATING VERBS TO USE WHEN REFERRING TO FIELDS

Type **4** and press Return to start Lesson 4, which involves designating verbs that you will use when referring to certain fields in the database. This is the very last type of vocabulary that you need to define before using the Intelligent Assistant with your database. The screen that comes up when you access this lesson is familiar. It begins by highlighting the first field of the database. Blanks are provided within an accompanying instruction box in which you enter any particular verbs that you would like to associate with this field. As usual, you can press F1 to get a Help screen that explains the procedure with examples. Figure 6.25 shows you this screen.

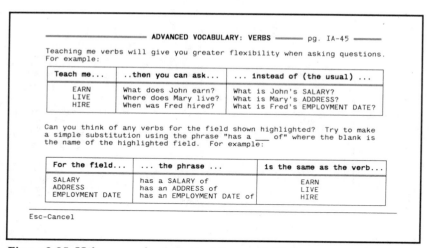

*Figure 6.25:* Help screen for Advanced Lesson 4: Verbs

As you can see here, by assigning verbs you can avoid using forms of the verb *to be* or having to begin your questions with *what*. You can have more flexibility in the way you state your queries, thereby approximating more closely the way you naturally converse about subjects. This Help screen gives an example that can help you think up possible verbs. Merely substitute the field name into the phrase "has a(n) __ of " and then think of a verb form that expresses the meaning of the phrase. For instance, in your sample database you could do this with the Current Salary field. The resulting phrase would then be "has a current salary of." Appropriate verb choices could be *receive* or *pay* (in the form "is paid"). Designating verbs to be used with fields is a lot like the process of assigning alternate field names which you learned in Basic Lesson 4. You cannot assign the same verb to different fields in the database, and you must include any irregular forms if you plan to use them.

The restriction of not being able to reuse words can be quite frustrating when designating verbs. One example in your sample database is the problem of which field should be assigned the verb *live*. It is very natural to want to ask both "In what city does so-and-so live?" and "In what state does so-and-so live?" But because City and State are separate fields in your database, you may not assign *live* to both of them. This restricts you to asking simply, "Where does so-and-so live?" The Intelligent Assistant will then give the city if you have assigned *live* to the City field, or the state if you have assigned *live* to the State field. The only way around this is to assign different verbs: for example, you could assign the verbs *reside* to the City field and *live* to the State field. This would allow you to ask "Where does so-and-so reside?" to find out the city, and "Where does so-and-so live?" to find out the state. You must, however, remember which verb is assigned to which field in order to get the type of response you are looking for.

The second restriction, the necessity of adding all the irregular forms of a verb when asking about a particular field, refers to those verbs that do not form their past tenses by adding *-ed* or *-en* to the verb stem—as with a verb like *grow*, which uses the irregular past tense forms *grew* and *grown*. For instance, if you assigned this verb to the % field and gave only the form *grow*, the Intelligent Assistant would not understand the question "How much has Ann Thompson's salary grown?"

Table 6.2 shows you alternate verbs to assign to some of the fields in your personnel database. As you can see, not all of the fields will have such verbs assigned to them. As before, you can always return to this lesson later to add any verbs that you find yourself using when asking about a particular field. Go ahead and fill in the verbs for those fields included in the table. As before, press F8 to advance to the next field and F6 to go back to the previous one.

*Table 6.2:* Verbs for particular fields of the personnel database

| FIELD NAME | VERBS | |
|---|---|---|
| Last Name | < call | > |
| City | < reside | > |
| State | < live | > |
| Home Phone | < telephone | > |
| | < reach | > |
| Date of Birth | < born | > |
| Position | < place | > |
| | < put | > |
| Job Title | < classify | > |

*Table 6.2:* Verbs for particular fields of the personnel database (continued)

| FIELD NAME | VERBS | |
|---|---|---|
| Date Hired | <hired | > |
| Supervisor | <supervise | > |
| | <oversee | > |
| Work Phone | <get in touch with | > |
| Name | <notify | > |
| Total Hours | <authorize | > |
| | <allow to work | > |
| | <work | > |
| OT Total | <charge | > |
| Yearly Quota | <sell | > |
| Base Salary | <get | > |
| | <got | > |
| | <gotten | > |
| Current Salary | <pay | > |
| | <paid | > |
| | <receive | > |
| Starting Salary | <start at | > |
| | <begin at | > |
| | <begun at | > |
| % | <raise | > |
| | <risen | > |
| | <grow | > |
| | <grown | > |
| Date of Last Review | <occur | > |
| | <take place | > |
| | <happen | > |
| Evaluation Codes | <critique | > |
| Total Years of School | <educate | > |

*Table 6.2:* Verbs for particular fields of the personnel database (continued)

| FIELD NAME | VERBS | |
|---|---|---|
| College Attended | <attend<br><go to<br><gone to<br><went to | ><br>><br>><br>> |
| Degree | <earn | > |
| Foreign Languages | <speak<br><know | ><br>> |
| Job Related Courses | <take | > |

When you have finished entering these verbs, press F10 to save them and you will be taken back to the Lessons Menu. You have now completed all of the lessons on this menu and are ready to go on and practice using English queries to obtain information from your personnel database. Type **5** to exit Lessons, press Return, and you will be back at the Assistant (ELI) Menu. You now have a good idea of what is involved in teaching the Intelligent Assistant about your databases. Each time you create a new database file that you want to use with it, you will have to go through the steps you just completed for the personnel file. It is now time to find out if it was worth the effort by testing how well ELI understands your English requests.

## ASKING BASIC QUESTIONS OF THE INTELLIGENT ASSISTANT

From the ELI menu, type **a** and press Return to select the Ask me to do something option. You are now presented with the same screen that you used when you changed the name of the Intelligent Assistant to ELI. Here you will enter your requests and questions in complete sentences. To cut down on the amount of typing, you are free to use abbreviations that the Intelligent Assistant already knows. Once you have asked a question about a specific employee or group within the database, you can ask follow-up questions by using pronouns such as *his*, *hers*, *their*, *he*, *she*, or *they*, as long as you are still referring to the same antecedent.

To see how this works, ask a simple question referring to Del Rush. Type it as shown below and then press Return. (If you make a mistake, the same editing functions that you used in the word processor are available.)

**Where is Del Rush?**

The Intelligent Assistant (ELI) performs as before, first converting your query to all uppercase letters and then analyzing each word and phrase. This process is displayed on your screen by the highlighting that jumps from word to word. Finally, when ELI has finished translating, the entire question remains highlighted.

ELI then shows you its interpretation of the question, which is contained in the box right below the one in which you entered your question (shown in Figure 6.26). Notice that not all of the interpretations will fit on one screen. Press the PgDn key to see the last line of the interpretation and then press PgUp to return. In this case, it has interpreted the word *where* as referring to all fields that you designated as containing locations. It therefore prepared to display a report including the street, city, state, and zipcode for Del Rush. These are

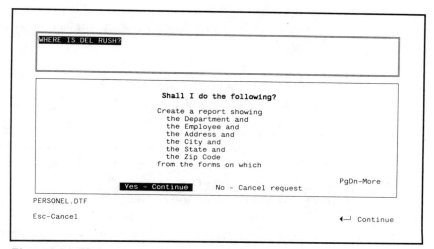

*Figure 6.26:* First query and interpretation

all the fields that you defined as containing locations in the personnel database.

Because you designated both the Department and Employee fields as identifying fields, they are automatically included as part of this report. If you did not want them to appear in the report, you would have to have added the phrase, "with no identification columns" to the question. This phrase can always be abbreviated to *wnic*.

Remember that when you completed Lesson 2, you designated the Last Name, First Name, and MI fields as belonging to one person referred to first as *employee* in the alternate terms. From now on, ELI will always refer to these fields by the name *employee*. In reports including the employee, it will therefore display the last name, first name, and middle initial of the person in question in the exact order these fields appear in the database.

Go ahead and press Return to confirm this interpretation and have ELI produce the report. When you do, the confirmation box disappears and is replaced by the familiar message box that keeps you informed of the program's progress in scanning the forms in your database. Once ELI has finished going through the entire database, this box disappears and the report containing one line with Del Rush's department, full name, and complete address is then displayed (shown in Figure 6.27).

```
┌─────────────────────────────────────────────────────────────────────┐
│ ┌───────────────────────────────────────────────────────────────┐   │
│ │Where is Del Rush?                                               │   │
│ │                                                                 │   │
│ └───────────────────────────────────────────────────────────────┘   │
│                                                                       │
│  Department    Employee         Street          City    State   Zip  │
│  ----------    ----------    ---------------     ----    -----   ---- │
│  Sales         Rush Del B.   1567 Kings Road West Niles  IL      6163 │
│                                                                       │
│                                                                       │
│                                                                       │
│                                                                       │
│                                                                       │
│  PERSONEL.DTF                                                         │
│  ****************************  END OF REPORT  ********************************│
│  Esc-Cancel     F2-Reprint     ( → ← ↓ ↑ PgUp PgDn )-Scroll    F10-Continue │
└─────────────────────────────────────────────────────────────────────┘
```

*Figure 6.27:* First report

As when printing reports to the screen in Q&A Report, you can use the → and ← keys to scroll the display right and left. You can use the PgUp and PgDn keys to scroll the screen up and down in reports longer than a single screen. The F10 function key will also act like the PgDn key here. Press the → key once to see the complete zipcode, which is not yet entirely visible. Notice that at the bottom of the screen the same end-of-report message is displayed as in your earlier reports printed to screen.

When you are finished viewing a report, you press Esc to erase the report and query box so that you can enter another query. Press this key now and enter a follow-up question about Del Rush. Because you have already identified him by name in the previous query, you need not reenter his name. Now ask to see his salary by entering the following question and then pressing Return:

**What is his salary?**

When it has finished translating, ELI correctly interprets this question as referring to the employee named Del Rush. It now asks for the go-ahead to produce a report showing his department, full name, and salary. Press Return to have ELI produce this report; press Esc when you have finished viewing it.

## ENTERING ANOTHER QUERY

For your next question, you will find out how many of the employees have an exempt status in the database. This question incorporates within it a request that must use the statistical COUNT function. In an English-like query system, this kind of query would have to be phrased something like COUNT FOR EXEMPT = 'Y'. All you have to enter in the query box for the Intelligent Assistant is

**How many employees are exempt?**

After you press Return and ELI has finished analyzing this request, it asks for confirmation on producing a report showing the departments, employees (full names), and the number of values in which the Exempt field is Y (shown in Figure 6.28). This is exactly what you asked for, so press Return to produce the report. Because

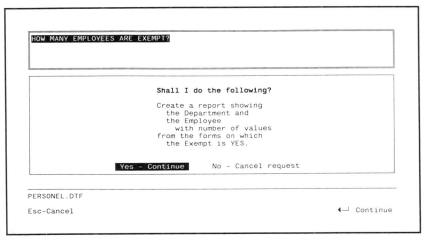

*Figure 6.28:* Interpretation of "how many" query

the report is longer than will fit on a single screen, press F10 to see the end of it. Notice that the count of 16 is displayed on this last line.

For your next query, find out which employees are in the Engineering department. Try it by entering the question stated in the following way; then press Return:

### Who is in the Engineering dept?

You do not have to spell out the word *department* because you already defined *dept* as an alternate term for this field. This time, ELI stops its translation at the word *in* and asks for clarification (Figure 6.29). It wants to know whether this refers to the State field in the database (it knows IN as the abbreviation for Indiana) or to one of its built-in vocabulary words. Type **2** and press Return to let ELI know that you mean *in* as it is defined in the vocabulary list. Be aware that using the preposition *in* in any of your queries will cause the program to stop and ask for this type of clarification. ELI is then able to interpret the rest of the query without any further need of your help.

ELI thinks you want a report showing not only the names of the employees but also those of the supervisors and emergency contacts in which the department is Engineering. This is because it has been programmed to interpret *who* as referring to all of the fields containing people's names in your database. Questions that begin "who is"

```
┌──────────────────────────────────────────────────────────────────┐
│  ┌────────────────────────────────────────────────────────────┐  │
│  │ WHO IS ▐IN▌ THE ENGINEERING DEPT?                            │  │
│  │                                                              │  │
│  │                                                              │  │
│  └────────────────────────────────────────────────────────────┘  │
│  ┌────────────────────────────────────────────────────────────┐  │
│  │                                                              │  │
│  │            Which of the following do you mean?               │  │
│  │                                                              │  │
│  │        1 - IN, a value in the field State                    │  │
│  │        2 - IN, a word in my built-in vocabulary              │  │
│  │        L - Look for another interpretation                   │  │
│  │                  ▐ Selection: ▌ _                            │  │
│  │                                                              │  │
│  └────────────────────────────────────────────────────────────┘  │
│                                                                    │
│                                                                    │
│  ───────────────────────────────────────────────────────────     │
│  PERSONEL.DTF                                                      │
│                                                                    │
│  Esc-Cancel    F1-How to ask    F6-See words    F8-Teach word   ◄─┘ Continue │
└──────────────────────────────────────────────────────────────────┘
```

*Figure 6.29:* Clarification of the use of "in" in the query

or "who are" are always taken to refer to all of the people fields, and they are automatically included in the resulting report.

To rectify this, press the → key to highlight the No - Cancel request response; then press Return. The cursor now returns to your question, which still remains on the screen. Change its wording to

### Which of the employees are in the Engineering dept?

To do this, press F4 twice to delete the words *Who* and *is* and then press Ins to change to insert mode. Then type **Which of the employees are** and press Return.

This time, ELI correctly interprets the question and asks for confirmation to produce a report showing only the department and employees for those records in which the department is Engineering. Press Return to have ELI produce this report; then press Esc when you have finished looking it over.

## DEFINING SYNONYMS

At times you will undoubtedly use terms unknown to the Intelligent Assistant which will require further definition. Most of the time, you can take care of these situations either by editing your query and using an alternate term that you have defined or by defining a new synonym. To see how this works, enter the following question and then press Return:

**Which salesperson has the highest quota?**

Because you have not defined the term *salesperson*, the Intelligent Assistant stops and asks you for clarification. Figure 6.30 shows you this screen. Instead of editing the word, this time type **t** and press Return to teach the meaning of *salesperson*.

Figure 6.31 shows you the next screen that appears. Here you can assign *salesperson* as a subject of the database, assign it as an alternate term for a specific field, define it as a synonym for something else, or define it as a verb referring to a specific field. The last option, Other, simply tells you that you can only teach the word here in one of the four ways mentioned before. To teach *salesperson* in any other way, you have to exit to the Intelligent Assistant and use the Teach me about your database option.

You want to define *salesperson* as a synonym, so type **s** and press Return. Once you do so, you are presented with a new screen as shown in Figure 6.32. There you enter the term you want to define in the blank on the left side. In this case, type **salesperson**. Then press Return and the cursor will move to the blank on the right side. There you will define *salesperson* as anyone in the Sales department who is

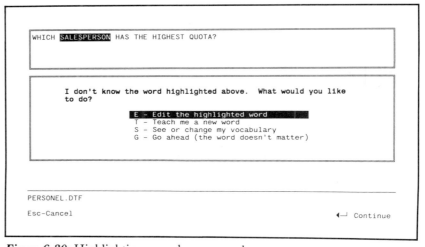

*Figure 6.30:* Highlighting an unknown word

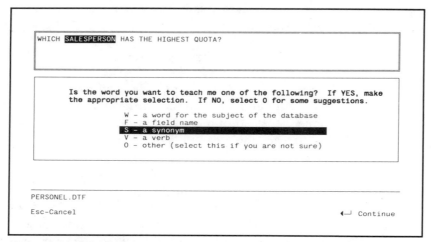

```
WHICH SALESPERSON HAS THE HIGHEST QUOTA?



     Is the word you want to teach me one of the following?  If YES, make
     the appropriate selection.  If NO, select O for some suggestions.

               W - a word for the subject of the database
               F - a field name
               S - a synonym
               V - a verb
               O - other (select this if you are not sure)



   PERSONEL.DTF

   Esc-Cancel                                              ◄─┘ Continue
```

*Figure 6.31:* Selecting the synonym option

```
WHICH SALESPERSON HAS THE HIGHEST QUOTA?


   Type the synonym you want to teach me in the first column and the word or
   phrase it stands for in the second.  (Ex:   New York   -  NY )
      SALESPERSON                           POSITION = SALES AND COMMISSION? = Y




   PERSONEL.DTF

   Esc-Cancel      F3-Delete synonym                        F1Ø-Continue
```

*Figure 6.32:* Defining the synonym

also on commission. You enter both conditions to exclude anyone like
the Vice President of Sales, who, even though he is in the Sales
department, receives a salary rather than base-plus-commission like
his salespeople.

You enter this definition much as you would fill out a Retrieve
Spec in Q&A File. The big difference is that you must also include
the name of the field. Enter the definition as **position = sales and**

**commission?** = **y** and press F10. This saves the synonym and returns you to your query.

Notice that your new synonym has replaced the original term *salesperson* in your query. ELI now analyzes the entire query using this new definition for *salesperson*. When it comes to the term *sales*, it asks whether you meant where the position is Sales or the department is Sales. Even though this distinction is unimportant in this case, type **1** and press Return to tell ELI to use *sales* as the position just as you originally requested. When it finishes analyzing this request, you can go ahead and confirm its understanding of the request by pressing Return. You will then see that the salesperson with the highest quota is Mark Burgoyne with a quota of $600,000. Press Esc to clear this report and the query box before going on.

## RETRIEVING RECORDS THROUGH THE ASSISTANT

In addition to pulling out specific information contained within records of the database, you can use the Intelligent Assistant to retrieve entire records. This provides an alternative to having to fill out a Retrieve Spec in the Q&A File module. Just as with the Retrieve Spec, you can ask for records for a specific employee or for a group that meets the criteria you have set up. The only difference is that you have more flexibility because you can include OR conditions in your searches.

To see how this is done, you will first retrieve and examine the record of Jessica Freels. Enter the following request and terminate your entry by pressing the Return key:

**Show me Jessica Freels' record.**

The Intelligent Assistant understands that *record* is a synonym for *form*, and responds by asking confirmation for retrieving the form in which the employee is Jessica Freels. Press Return to have it process your request and pull up her record. If you needed to, you could make any changes that were required in this record. Using the Intelligent Assistant in this way works just like using the Search/Update option on the Q&A File Menu.

Now enter a second request, this time asking for the group of records in which the last name ends in the letter *b*. Enter it as follows and press Return:

**Show me the records for the employees whose last names begin with "b".**

(You enclose the letter *b* in quotation marks so that it will be interpreted literally.)

When ELI shows its interpretation of this request, notice that in addition to understanding correctly that you want all of the records where the last name begins with "b," it thinks you want them sorted alphabetically by employee. This is the way the Intelligent Assistant interprets the phrase "for the employees." You can also get it to sort in a particular order by using the preposition *by* as in "by employee," or by adding the more explicit phrase "sorted by employee." If you want these records to be ordered by department instead of by employee, you could modify the request to something like

**Show me the records where the last name begins with "b" sorted by department.**

The Intelligent Assistant assumes an ascending sort order unless you tell it otherwise. To have it sort in descending order, you would amend this phrase to read "by decreasing department."

Press F10 to have it process the request. When the first record is displayed, notice that at the bottom of the screen Q&A tells you that this is Form 1 of 4. This tells you that four records have been located which meet your criteria. Press F10 to advance to the next record. When you have displayed the fourth record, press Esc to return to the Intelligent Assistant.

For your next practice query, you will retrieve the records in which the hourly rate is greater than $9.50 an hour, and you will have them sorted by department. This time, instead of typing the entire request, press Shift-F7 to have your previous request returned to the query box. Move the cursor to the word *for* in the line, and press F4 until you have deleted the rest of the words to the right. Then type in the rest of this new request. The edited line should appear as follows when you are finished:

**Show me the records where the hourly rate is greater than $9.50 by dept.**

Press Return to process this request. ELI then asks for confirmation to retrieve all those forms in which the hourly rate is greater than $9.50 sorted alphabetically by department. Press Return to view these records and then press Esc when you have viewed them all.

## UPDATING RECORDS

Having the Intelligent Assistant retrieve records and then update them manually is not the only way to make changes in the database. You can also type in a direct request to have the Intelligent Assistant make the changes for you. You may find, however, that using the Intelligent Assistant in this way involves slightly more work than making the modifications yourself. This is because you must be more careful in your phrasing of the request and make it as explicit as possible.

If the Intelligent Assistant does not fully understand what you want, you will receive a warning message telling you that it thinks you want to make some change to the database but is confused about some part of the request. This message also urges you to make certain that the Intelligent Assistant's interpretation is correct before you give your approval to make the changes. Always heed this advice, especially if you have requested updating that affects more than one record.

You will not want to use this method to make changes to text fields in your database unless you specifically want all of the updates to be in all uppercase letters. Remember what happened when you changed the name of the program from the Intelligent Assistant to ELI? Though you entered the name as Eli, it was converted to ELI once the change was made. The same would happen to any updates you make involving text, and there is no way around this. If uppercase is not acceptable, make such changes manually after retrieving the record as outlined above.

To see how this can work when you need to make changes to fields that do not contain text, you will now enter a request to change the salary and review date for Owen Rossner. You will tell ELI which fields to change and what changes to make. All of the new data will be enclosed in quotes. ELI already knows the meaning of the verb *change*, which will be repeated before each field name. If you do not repeat this verb each time, ELI will understand only that you want to change the first field mentioned. Enter this request as

> Change current salary to 35500 and change date of last review to 9/12/86 for Owen Rossner.

After you have pressed Return to process this, ELI will stop at the number 12. Type **2** and press Return to indicate to the Intelligent Assistant that 12 represents a number. ELI also stops and highlights Owen's last name, Rossner, telling you that it is an unknown term. Because there is only one Owen in the database, it is safe to type **g** and press Return to have ELI ignore this word. Go ahead and press Return to confirm its interpretation of this request. Once the program has finished scanning the forms, you receive a new warning message telling you the number of forms that will be updated, which is 1 in this case (see Figure 6.33). ELI asks you if you want to confirm each update individually and tells you to press Esc if you want to cancel this operation without making any updates. Choosing the default of updating each form individually allows you to make sure that the correct form has been retrieved before any changes are actually made.

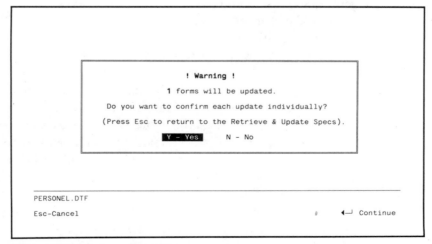

*Figure 6.33:* Update warning message

Press Return to select the Yes option and see how this works. Owen Rossner's record is then displayed. Notice that at the bottom of the screen, you are informed that pressing Shift-F10 will update this form. You could also press Esc to cancel the operation or F10 to continue to the next record and view the next record to be updated. In this case, press Shift-F10 to make the changes. Once this has been done, press Esc to return to the Intelligent Assistant.

Now check that the record has been properly updated by entering

**Show me Owen's record.**

Once you have given the go-ahead and his record is displayed on your screen, press PgDn to view the second page of this form. As you can see, it has been updated properly. Both of these entries have been automatically formatted as the fields call for. This is why you entered the salary without the dollar sign or commas. Now press Esc to return to the Intelligent Assistant.

This method of updating nontextual fields can also include formulas that calculate new results in the fields specified. For instance, if you wanted to give an across-the-board 10% raise to everyone in the Engineering department, you could do it by entering the request "Multiply all of the current salaries by 1.10 where the department is Engineering" in the query box.

## AD HOC QUERIES

The Intelligent Assistant lends itself very naturally to the development of ad hoc queries into the data and relationships in your database. In fact, because of its English-language interface, it encourages you to ask the types of questions that you otherwise might avoid if you had to figure out how to phrase them in a more rigid query system. Often, you will find that the answer to one question leads you to ask another. Because the Intelligent Assistant allows follow-up questioning, this process becomes very easy.

You will now practice making a series of ad hoc queries for data in your personnel database. You may find yourself using a very similar process when you query your own databases for information.

You will begin by finding out if any of the employees were born between 1962 and 1970. Ask this by entering

**Were any employees born between January 1, 1962 and January 1, 1970?**

Go ahead and confirm ELI's interpretation of this query. Figure 6.34 shows you the report that is then created. As you can see, four employees meet this condition. Press Esc and enter this follow-up question:

**What are their salaries and education wnrc?**

The code *wnrc* means "with no restriction columns." In this query, its use suppresses the Date of Birth column from the report. This is the criterion, or restriction, that controls whose salary and years of schooling are included. Figure 6.35 shows you the resulting report that is produced from this query. Notice that it still includes the Department and Employee columns. These could have been suppressed by adding the code *wnic* that was mentioned earlier. It suppresses the identifying columns (*department* and *employee* for this database) from the report. As you will see shortly, you can use another code, *wnec*, which stands for "with no extra columns," to suppress both the identifying and restriction columns from a report.

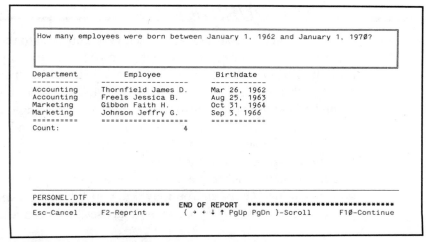

*Figure 6.34:* Employees born between 1/1/62 and 1/1/70

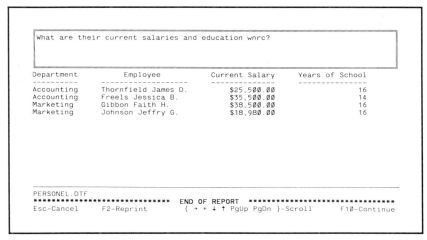

```
┌─────────────────────────────────────────────────────────────────────┐
│What are their current salaries and education wnrc?                    │
│                                                                       │
│                                                                       │
│                                                                       │
│                                                                       │
│ Department        Employee          Current Salary    Years of School │
│ ----------        --------          --------------    --------------- │
│ Accounting    Thornfield James D.     $25,500.00                   16 │
│ Accounting    Freels Jessica B.       $35,500.00                   14 │
│ Marketing     Gibbon Faith H.         $38,500.00                   16 │
│ Marketing     Johnson Jeffry G.       $18,980.00                   16 │
│                                                                       │
│                                                                       │
│                                                                       │
│                                                                       │
│                                                                       │
│ ─────────────────────────────────────────────────────────────────── │
│ PERSONEL.DTF                                                          │
│ ****************************** END OF REPORT ************************* │
│ Esc-Cancel     F2-Reprint      ( → ← ↓ ↑ PgUp PgDn )-Scroll   F10-Continue │
└─────────────────────────────────────────────────────────────────────┘
```

***Figure 6.35:*** Salaries and years of school for employees born between 1/1/62 and 1/1/70

In that case, only the fields you specifically name in the query will appear as columns in the resulting report.

For your next query, you will find out what colleges these people attended and find out if they earned any degrees. Press Esc to exit the current report; then enter

**What colleges did they attend and degrees did they earn wnrc?**

Figure 6.36 shows you the report you should get from this query. Again, it includes the identifying columns as well as those you specifically asked to see.

For your last follow-up question, you will tell ELI exactly what fields to include. The column order will be determined by their order in the query. Press Esc to clear the college and degree report; then type in the following:

**List their full names, any foreign languages they know, and their business phones and extensions wnec.**

ELI will stop at the word *know* to ask you if it refers to a field in the database or represents a word in its built-in vocabulary. Type **1** and press Return to let ELI know that this word is associated with a field in the database. Remember that you entered *know* as a verb to be used when asking about the Foreign Languages field.

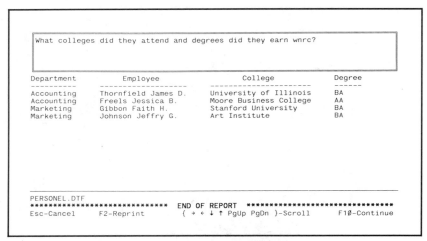

```
┌──────────────────────────────────────────────────────────────────────┐
│  ┌──────────────────────────────────────────────────────────────┐     │
│  │ What colleges did they attend and degrees did they earn wnrc?  │     │
│  │                                                                │     │
│  └──────────────────────────────────────────────────────────────┘     │
│  Department       Employee              College             Degree     │
│  ----------       --------              -------             ------     │
│  Accounting       Thornfield James D.   University of Illinois  BA      │
│  Accounting       Freels Jessica B.     Moore Business College  AA      │
│  Marketing        Gibbon Faith H.       Stanford University     BA      │
│  Marketing        Johnson Jeffry G.     Art Institute           BA      │
│                                                                        │
│                                                                        │
│                                                                        │
│  ──────────────────────────────────────────────────────────────────   │
│  PERSONEL.DTF                                                          │
│  **************************** END OF REPORT *************************** │
│  Esc-Cancel    F2-Reprint      { → ← ↓ ↑ PgUp PgDn }-Scroll  F10-Continue│
└──────────────────────────────────────────────────────────────────────┘
```

*Figure 6.36:* Colleges and degrees for employees born between 1/1/62 and 1/1/70

Figure 6.37 shows you the resulting report. Because you added the code *wnec* to this request, you had to explicitly tell ELI to list the full name as well as the other fields you wanted to see. If you had not done so, there would be no names associated with the languages and phone numbers. If one of these fields (Foreign Languages, Work Phone, or Ext) had been blank, that person's record would have been left out of the report. You should be aware of this aspect of the *wnec* code: it not only suppresses identifying and restriction columns but also suppresses any records containing blank fields as well.

You could now continue this line of questioning or even go off in a new direction. It all depends upon what conclusions you have been able to draw from the information you have gathered, and what new questions these may have brought to mind. You have already seen that the younger employees in the company are making relatively low salaries, but all have some sort of degree and even speak a foreign language.

You might want to go on and query for more information about this group in other areas. For instance, you could follow up by determining how long they have been with the company, what their starting salaries were, and even ask what types of job-related courses they have taken since coming on board. This exercise should give you a good idea of how easy it is to formulate such questions and use them to explore new relationships that might not have been obvious before.

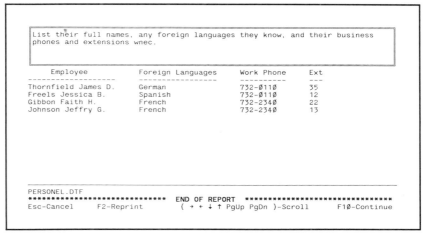

```
List their full names, any foreign languages they know, and their business
phones and extensions wnec.


      Employee            Foreign Languages      Work Phone    Ext
  -------------------    ------------------      ----------    ---
  Thornfield James D.    German                  732-0110      35
  Freels Jessica B.      Spanish                 732-0110      12
  Gibbon Faith H.        French                  732-2340      22
  Johnson Jeffry G.      French                  732-2340      13
```

PERSONEL.DTF
```
******************************* END OF REPORT *********************************
Esc-Cancel     F2-Reprint      ( → ← ↓ ↑ PgUp PgDn )-Scroll     F10-Continue
```

*Figure 6.37:* Foreign languages spoken and work phone numbers

## CREATING REPORTS

You can use the Intelligent Assistant to create reports almost identical to those generated in Q&A Report. The biggest difference is that the Intelligent Assistant does not understand the codes that suppress column breaks, so you are more limited in the sorting of your columns. Also, the only way to save a report from the Intelligent Assistant is to print it to disk from the Print Menu.

When you want to print any report created with the Intelligent Assistant, you press F2. This takes you to the same Print Menu you used in Q&A Report. To save the report in a disk file, you simply set the Print to option to Disk. To get a printed copy of the report, you set this option to the appropriate printer port (usually LPT1 or COM1). The Intelligent Assistant will also understand that you want to print a report created and saved in Q&A Report if you tell it to "run report" followed by the name of the report. It will then take you to this Print Menu, where you can make any necessary adjustments.

To practice generating reports with the Intelligent Assistant, you will begin by entering a request to see the departments and salaries arranged alphabetically by the names of the employees. Enter this as follows:

**What are the departments and salaries of the employees?**

Figure 6.38 shows you the first part of the report that is generated as a result of the request. Notice that ELI interpreted the phrase "of the employees" as meaning to sort the report alphabetically by employee. It has also automatically placed this sorted column first in the report.

To change the report so that it is sorted first by department and then by employee, all you have to do is reword the request. Press Esc to clear the report and the query box; then type the following:

**Show the salaries sorted by department and employee.**

Figure 6.39 shows you the first part of the report that ELI now produces. Notice that now both the department and employee names are sorted in ascending order. Next, you will create a new report that shows the totals for the salaries in each department. Press Esc to clear the report and query and enter this request:

**Show the total salaries by department.**

You can see in Figure 6.40 how the first part of this report should look once you give the go-ahead to ELI's interpretation. Because you included the word *total* before *salaries*, the result is a summary report sorted by department. The salaries within each are subtotaled at each column break with no other columns displayed because none were called for.

```
┌─────────────────────────────────────────────────────────────────┐
│ ┌───────────────────────────────────────────────────────────┐   │
│ │ What are the departments and salaries of the employees?    │   │
│ │                                                            │   │
│ │                                                            │   │
│ └───────────────────────────────────────────────────────────┘   │
│                                                                  │
│      Employee          Department      Current Salary            │
│   ------------------  ---------------  --------------            │
│   Bennett Kelly T.    Engineering         $25,750.00             │
│                                                                  │
│   Brown Janice F.     Administration      $39,800.00             │
│                                                                  │
│   Burgoyne Mark T.    Sales               $46,200.00             │
│                                                                  │
│   Burke Lisa A.       Marketing           $47,500.00             │
│                                                                  │
│   Chang Edward A.     Administration     $125,000.00             │
│                                                                  │
│   Freels Jessica B.   Accounting          $35,500.00             │
│                                                                  │
│   Gibbon Faith H.     Marketing           $38,500.00             │
│ ─────────────────────────────────────────────────────────────── │
│   PERSONEL.DTF                                                   │
│                                                                  │
│   Esc-Cancel    F2-Reprint    ( → ← ↓ ↑ PgUp PgDn )-Scroll    F10-Continue │
└─────────────────────────────────────────────────────────────────┘
```

*Figure 6.38:* Report sorted by employee

```
┌─────────────────────────────────────────────────────────────────────┐
│  ┌──────────────────────────────────────────────────────────────┐    │
│  │ Show the salaries sorted by department and employee.          │    │
│  │                                                                │    │
│  │                                                                │    │
│  └──────────────────────────────────────────────────────────────┘    │
│       Department            Employee           Current Salary         │
│       ---------------       ------------------   ---------------       │
│       Accounting            Freels Jessica B.        $35,500.00        │
│                                                                        │
│                             Parish Katherine A.      $20,800.00        │
│                                                                        │
│                             Thornfield James D.      $25,500.00        │
│                                                                        │
│                             Zimring Daniel J.        $19,760.00        │
│                                                                        │
│       Administration        Brown Janice F.          $39,800.00        │
│                                                                        │
│                             Chang Edward A.         $125,000.00        │
│                                                                        │
│       Engineering           Bennett Kelly T.         $25,750.00        │
│       PERSONEL.DTF                                                     │
│                                                                        │
│    Esc-Cancel     F2-Reprint      { → ← ↓ ↑ PgUp PgDn }-Scroll     F10-Continue │
└─────────────────────────────────────────────────────────────────────┘
```

*Figure 6.39:* Report sorted by department and employee

```
┌─────────────────────────────────────────────────────────────────────┐
│  ┌──────────────────────────────────────────────────────────────┐    │
│  │ Show the total salaries by department.                        │    │
│  │                                                                │    │
│  │                                                                │    │
│  └──────────────────────────────────────────────────────────────┘    │
│       Department            Current Salary                            │
│       ---------------       ---------------                           │
│       Accounting                                                      │
│                             ---------------                           │
│       Total:                    $101,560.00                           │
│       Administration                                                  │
│                             ---------------                           │
│       Total:                    $164,800.00                           │
│       Engineering                                                     │
│                             ---------------                           │
│       Total:                    $137,750.00                           │
│       Marketing                                                       │
│       PERSONEL.DTF                                                     │
│                                                                        │
│    Esc-Cancel     F2-Reprint      { → ← ↓ ↑ PgUp PgDn }-Scroll     F10-Continue │
└─────────────────────────────────────────────────────────────────────┘
```

*Figure 6.40:* Summary report

To make this report more complete, you would tell ELI to also list the employees and their salaries. You cannot, however, ask ELI to sort the employees alphabetically within each department, because there is no way to stop it from printing subtotals at each column break in the employee column (i.e., after each different last name).

1. Press Esc to clear this report and then press Shift-F7 to restore the previous query.

2.  Press End to move the cursor to the end of the line. Delete the period and amend the request so that it reads as follows:

    **Show the total salaries by department listing employee and current salary.**

The first part of the report that is generated from this request should match the one shown in Figure 6.41. You could now go on and further refine the report either by adding more calculations or more columns. Remember, you can always call for the averages, maximums, and minimums for each department to be included in the report, just as you did for the total here.

3.  Now press F2, marked as the Reprint key on the bottom of this screen.

4.  Change the "print to" prompt to the appropriate printer port, and press F10 to obtain a hard copy.

5.  When the report has been printed, press Shift-F7 to restore the query; then press Return to have the Intelligent Assistant analyze it.

6.  Give the commands to produce the report again, but this time press F2, change the Print to option to DISK, and press F10.

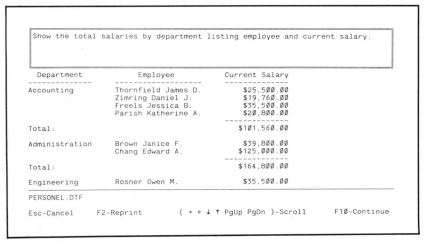

*Figure 6.41:* Final report with subtotals

7. When prompted for a file name, type **salary.rpt** and press Return. Q&A will then save your report under this name in an ASCII text file. To make any further editing changes to this report, you would access this file from Q&A Write, using its Get option, and make changes with the word processor.

8. Now press Esc to return to the Intelligent Assistant Menu (ELI Menu), and then press Esc once more to return to the Q&A Main Menu.

## *USING THE ASSISTANT WITHOUT TEACHING IT FIRST*

You can also query your database with the Intelligent Assistant without going through any of the teaching steps on either the Basic or Advanced Lesson Menus. This is useful if you are dealing with a database that you feel does not warrant taking all the time required for the eight teaching steps, but which does require querying in a way more suited to the Intelligent Assistant than to the Retrieve Spec in Q&A File. To use the Intelligent Assistant this way, you must still go through the very first preparation step in which it creates an index by analyzing the fields and data contained in the file. However, after that step you can use the Ask me to do something option without any further preparation.

As you can imagine, querying a database which has not been taught all of the alternate names, adjectives, and verbs that are a part of the teaching lessons greatly changes the way you phrase requests. In place of conversational English sentences, you will find yourself using an English-like query system. Although the system the Intelligent Assistant uses is not as rigid as the systems of some other database managers (since you can always use the Intelligent Assistant's built-in vocabulary, shown in Figures 6.7 and 6.8), it is similar to other database managers in its use of formal patterns.

To produce a report with columns made up of particular fields including all of the records in a database, you simply list the field names in the order you want them to appear. For example, to produce a report listing the departments, employees, and current salaries, you would enter

**Department, Last Name, First Name, Initial, Current Salary**

Notice that you must list all of the fields you want to have displayed by their field names (there are no identifying columns defined), and you can no longer refer to the Last Name, First Name, and Initial fields as the collective noun *employee*.

To produce this report sorted alphabetically by department, you have only to change the query slightly:

**Last Name, First Name, Initial, and Current Salary by Department**

To the Intelligent Assistant, the wording "by Department" still means to sort in ascending order. To sort a column or columns in descending order, you use the phrase "by descending" followed by the field name. Remember, though, that you cannot use abbreviations or other alternate terms when referring to the field name. You could not now, for example, shorten this phrase to "by dept" as you could do previously.

To produce a report including criteria for retrieving records, you add a "where" clause to the query. For instance, to look up the names and salaries of only the employees in the Engineering department, you would enter

**Last Name, First Name, Initial, Current Salary where Department is "Engineering"**

You can also set up criteria using the other relational operators, or specifying a range between which the values must fall. To find the employees born between January 1, 1962 and January 1, 1970, you would enter

**Last Name, First Name where Date of Birth is between January 1, 1962 and January 1, 1970**

Notice that the phrasing is very similar to the query you entered earlier, only this time you are required to use the proper field name,

Date of Birth. When setting up such criteria, you can also use formulas or the built-in statistical functions like average, maximum, and minimum. For example, entering the following query

> Department, Last Name, Starting Salary, Current Salary where Current Salary = maximum Current Salary

would produce a report showing the department, last name, starting and current salary for the employee whose salary is the highest in the company.

The following is an example of a query that includes a formula calculation:

> Department, Last Name, Current Salary where Current Salary – Starting Salary > = 10000

This report would include the department, last name, and current salary for all employees whose salaries have increased $10,000 or more.

You can also set up criteria for text and keyword fields in which certain characters must be matched. You can include the beginning or ending characters, or specify a particular string to be contained within an entry. An example of this kind of criterion is:

> Department, Last Name, Supervisor where Supervisor begins with "j"

This would produce a report showing the department, employee's last name, and the name of the supervisor for all records in which the supervisor's name begins with the letter *j*.

Another example of criteria using character strings is:

> Last Name, First Name, Department, Position where Last Name = "Johnson" and First Name ends in "y"

This condition limits the search to those records in which the last name is Johnson and the first name ends in the letter *y*. In this case, it would eliminate the record of Alice Johnson and retrieve the data only for Jeffry Johnson because of the second restriction.

In addition to setting up AND conditions as above, you can also specify OR conditions. As stated earlier, this is one of the features of using the Intelligent Assistant to query the database that is not always available when using Q&A File. An example of an OR condition in a query is:

> Last Name, First Name, Address, City, State, Zip Code where Department = "Administration" OR Department = "Personnel"

In this case, the report will give you the names and addresses for employees listed either in the Administration or Personnel departments.

You can also set up OR conditions that include different fields in the database, which is not possible when using the Retrieve Spec in Q&A File. An example of this is:

> First Name, Last Name, Position where Date of Last Review is on or later than January 15, 1986 or Date Hired is before December 12, 1979

To include totals and subtotals or other statistics in your reports, you add the appropriate term after the field name. If you also specify that a particular column should be sorted, a report will be produced showing subtotals, subaverages, and so forth at the column breaks. To produce a report including the total number of values, you would enter a query like this:

> Last Name with Count, Department, and Position where Department = "Marketing"

This would produce a report showing the last name, department, and position for all of the employees in the Marketing department. The report would also show the number of employees in this department.

To produce a report with subtotals and subaverages, you would enter a query like this:

> Last Name, First Name, Current Salary with total and average by department

This would produce a report showing the department, last name, first name, and current salary. The report would be arranged alphabetically by department name, with subtotals and subaverages for the salaries in each, and would include the grand total and average for all departments in the company.

You can also use the Intelligent Assistant to update data in the database. You simply give the new value after the field name and then state any criteria that apply. For instance, to update Owen Rossner's salary and date of last review, you would enter

> Current Salary = 35500 and Date of Last Review = 9/12/86
> where Last Name = "Rossner" and First Name = "Owen"

Upon confirmation of the Intelligent Assistant's interpretation of this request, you would follow the same steps that you did earlier. Whenever you use the Intelligent Assistant to update forms, you must tell it whether to do this on a case-by-case basis or globally without prior approval.

At times, when you are using the Intelligent Assistant without having done the teaching lessons, you may still want to define synonyms. You can do this directly, without having to use the menu system that appears when the Intelligent Assistant encounters an unknown term.

As an example of defining a new synonym, the following shows how you would define the synonym for *salesperson* without using the menu system:

> Define "salesperson" as "Position = Sales and Commission? = Y"

To view the definition of this synonym, you would enter

> Synonym "salesperson"

To delete this synonym, you would enter

> Delete synonym "salesperson"

You can also use these techniques to define, view, or delete groups of synonyms. To define more than one synonym, you enter the command **define synonyms**; you then see a screen on which you can enter as many synonyms as you want. To view all of the synonyms you have defined to date, you enter the command **synonym definitions** or simply **synonyms**. To delete more than one synonym, you give the command **delete synonyms** and then choose the synonyms for deletion from the list that appears. These techniques for defining, viewing, and deleting synonyms are also available to you when you use the Intelligent Assistant with a database for which you have already completed all of the teaching lessons.

As you can see from the previous examples, querying a database in the Intelligent Assistant when it has not been "taught" demands more attention to the form and detail of your request. Because of its built-in vocabulary, the system is not nearly as formal and un-English-like as you may have expected; nevertheless, you will have to spend time to think out your requests and make them fit the required patterns. Remember that you cannot use alternate terms or abbreviations to describe fields in the database. These will only be understood if they are referred to by their field names exactly as they are in the database itself. Also, you must translate your questions and sentences into a different syntax. For instance, all questions that ask "which employees" would have to be translated into Last Name, First Name. Where earlier you could ask, "Which employees reside in Chicago?" you would now have to enter

**Last Name, First Name where City = "Chicago"**

This is almost identical to the original example of an English-like query given at the introduction of the Intelligent Assistant.

Now that you know what is involved in using each system, you can decide which best suits your needs and your level of understanding. Table 6.3 gives you a summary of the types of commands and syntax that you can use when querying a database that has not been taught.

*Table 6.3:* Syntax and commands of queries in the Intelligent Assistant (using formal patterns)

| COMMAND AND SYNTAX | DESCRIPTION |
| --- | --- |
| **To retrieve entire records:** | |
| RECORDS | Entering **RECORDS** (or **FORMS**) alone is the same as pressing F10 with a blank Retrieve Spec in Q&A File. It retrieves all of the records in your database for viewing or updating. |

*Table 6.3:* Syntax and commands of queries in the Intelligent Assistant (using formal patterns) (continued)

| COMMAND AND SYNTAX | DESCRIPTION |
|---|---|
| **To retrieve entire records: (continued)** | |
| RECORDS WHERE <*condition*> | Restricts retrieval to only those records that meet the condition specified. |
| **To retrieve fields:** | |
| <*Fieldname*> | Creates a report containing columns with only the field names specified. With no condition, all records are used in creating the report. Series of field names are separated by commas or the word *and*. |
| <*Fieldname*> WHERE <*condition*> | Creates a report using only the data from records that meet the stated condition. |
| **To sort:** | |
| BY <*Fieldname*> | Sorts the column in ascending order. |
| BY DECREASING <*Fieldname*> | Sorts the column in descending order. |
| **To use statistical functions:** | |
| <*Fieldname*> WITH TOTAL | Totals the values in the column. You can also use AVERAGE, MAXIMUM, MINIMUM, and COUNT in this way. |

*Table 6.3:* Syntax and commands of queries in the Intelligent Assistant (using formal patterns) (continued)

| COMMAND AND SYNTAX | DESCRIPTION |
|---|---|
| **To use statistical functions: (continued)** | |
| *<Fieldname>* WITH TOTAL BY *<Fieldname>* | Subtotals the values in the column at each column break. You can also use AVERAGE, MAXIMUM, MINIMUM, and COUNT in this way. |
| **To add new records:** | |
| CREATE NEW FORM | Takes you to a blank form of the database. The record entered here becomes the very last record of the database. |
| CREATE NEW FORM WHERE *<condition>* | Adds a new record and enters data in fields as specified in the condition. |
| **To update existing records:** | |
| *<Fieldname>* = *<value>* | Changes the data in the field to the new value stated. Without a condition, it globally updates all fields in the database. |
| *<Fieldname>* = *<value>* WHERE *<condition>* | Changes the data in the field to the new value stated for those records that meet the stated condition. |

***Table 6.3:*** Syntax and commands of queries in the Intelligent Assistant (using formal patterns) (continued)

| COMMAND AND SYNTAX | DESCRIPTION |
|---|---|
| **To specify AND and OR conditions:** | |
| *<condition1>* AND *<condition2>* | Both conditions must be met for the record or fields specified to be retrieved. |
| *<condition1>* OR *<condition2>* | If either of the conditions is met, the record or fields specified will be retrieved. |
| **To set up a *<condition>*:** | |
| *<Fieldname>* = *<value>* * | Value in the field must be an exact match to the value. You can also use *is* or *equals* in place of =. |
| *<Fieldname>* > *<value>* | Value in the field must be greater than the value specified. You can use *is greater than* or *is after* in place of >. |
| *<Fieldname>* < *<value>* | Value in the field must be less than the value specified. You can use *is less than* or *is before* in place of <. |
| *<Fieldname>* > = *<value>* | Value must be greater than or equal to specified value. You can use *is greater than or equal to* or *is on or later than* in place of > =. |
| *<Fieldname>* < = *<value>* | Value must be less than or equal to specified value. You can use *is less than or equal to* or *is on or before* in place of > =. |

*Table 6.3:* Syntax and commands of queries in the Intelligent Assistant (using formal patterns) (continued)

| COMMAND AND SYNTAX | DESCRIPTION |
|---|---|
| **To set up a <*condition*>: (continued)** | |
| <*Fieldname*> / = <*value*> | Value must not be equal to the specified value. You can use *is not* or *is not equal to* in place of / = . |
| <*Fieldname*> IS BETWEEN <*value1*> AND <*value2*> | Value must fall between the first value and second value specified. |
| <*Fieldname*> BEGINS WITH <*string*>** | Entry in the field must begin with the character or characters specified in the string. |
| <*Fieldname*> ENDS WITH <*string*> | Entry in the field must end with the character or characters specified in the string. |
| <*Fieldname*> CONTAINS <*string*> | Entry in the field must contain within it the character or characters specified in the string. |
| <*Fieldname*> IS BLANK | There must be no entry in the field. |
| <*Fieldname*> INCLUDES <*strings*> | Used with keyword fields only. Entries in fields must match those specified in the strings. |

* Values can include numbers, dates, or text, but not all values are allowed with all types of fields. Text cannot be given as values for numeric, currency, or date fields.

** Strings are characters enclosed in a pair of quotation marks.

## SUMMARY

You have seen and experienced the power of the natural language interface Q&A provides when you query your database. As you now realize, in order to use this language interface fully you must go through a number of preparatory steps. However, the ability to receive answers to questions phrased in simple, conversational English outweighs the inconvenience of having to go through the Teaching lessons. Remember, you only have to complete these lessons once for each database that you create.

In the next chapter, you will be introduced to another versatile feature of Q&A—creating macros. Macros not only save you keystrokes but also allow you to tailor commands to suit your own ways of working with Q&A. You will learn how to create and save your macros in files, and learn how they can help you customize your use of Q&A Write and File.

C H A P T E R

7

MACROS

*FastTrack*

**To create a macro,**

press Shift-F2 and select the Define Macro option. When
prompted for the macro identifier, press the key combination
you wish to use to execute the macro. Then enter all of the commands and text you wish to save in your macro. Turn off the
macro recorder by pressing Shift-F2 again.

**To execute a macro,**

press the key combination that you used as the macro identifier.
Q&A will always warn you when you are about to assign one of
its key combinations to a macro. If you use a macro identifier
that you have already assigned to another macro, you will
receive the same warning. To go ahead and redefine the Q&A
command or a previously defined macro, type y in response to
the redefine message.

**To insert a pause in your macro**

which allows you to enter variable information, press Alt-F2
during its definition and type in a sample variable. Then, press
Alt-F2 to exit the pause and continue to define the macro keystrokes that are to be played back after the pause. When you
execute the macro, you will receive a message indicating that
the macro has paused and instructing you to press ← to continue execution. If you need to press the Return key as part of
the variable during the pause, press Alt-F2 instead of ←.

**To nest a macro within another,**

press the macro identifier keystrokes at the place where you
want the nested macro to be executed. You can nest up to five
levels of macros.

**When you finish recording the keystrokes in a macro,**     *359*

you are prompted to save the macro in the QAMACRO.ASC file. This file is automatically loaded each time you start Q&A. Any macros saved in this file are always available. To save the macro that you just created in this file, press Return. To save it in another file, type in the file name and press Return. If you don't want to save the macro in a file, press Esc (you can still save it and the others you define during the work session by pressing Shift-F2 and selecting the Save Macros option on the Macro Menu).

**To edit the commands and text recorded in a macro,**     *367*

select the Get option (g ⏎ or 4) on the Q&A Write menu. Then choose the ASCII without word wrap option (2) from the Import Document menu that appears and enter the name of the macro file.

**When editing the contents of the macro,**     *367*

you must enter each key according to its code, enclosed in angle brackets, as for instance <capsf6> for Shift-F6. If you are entering a new macro, be sure to separate it from others in the file with Returns and asterisks (*), and enter <begdef> at its beginning and <enddef> at its end.

**To save a macro that you have edited in Q&A Write,**     *370*

press the Esc key, select the Export option (e ⏎ or 8), and press Return.

**To add a macro as an alternate program**                              *372*

available on the Main menu, select the Utilities option (**u** ⏎ or
5), then choose Set global defaults (**s** ⏎ or 5), and press the
PgDn key. On the Alternate Programs line, enter the macro
key combination as **Alt-*n*** where *n* is a capital letter A through Z.
On the Menu selection line, enter up to 11 characters that
describe the macro. The first letter of the the menu selection
will be the menu choice letter. Press F10 to continue.

**To add an external program as an alternate program**          *373*

available on the Main menu, select the Utilities option (**u** ⏎ or
5), then choose Set global defaults (**s** ⏎ or 5), and press the
PgDn key. On the Alternate Programs line, enter the drive,
path, and startup command separated by backslashes (\). On
the Menu selection line, enter up to 11 characters that describe
the program. The first letter of the the menu selection will be
the menu choice letter. Press F10 to continue.

# ━━━ *WHAT IS A MACRO?* ━━━

A macro is a stored sequence of commands that allows you to keep a record of any keystrokes that you might want to replay when using the Q&A program. To define a macro, you assign the key combination (the macro name) that you will use to invoke the macro. You then go through the sequence of keystrokes that you wish to have recorded. With the macro recorder then turned on, every keystroke, whether it represents a keyboard character or a key associated with particular Q&A commands, is saved as part of the macro until you turn the macro recorder off. At this point your macro sequence is saved only in the memory of the computer. If you wish to reuse your macro in another session, you may also save it in a disk file along with any other macros that you have defined.

The uses of macros are varied, especially because these facilities for capturing and playing back keystrokes are available to you anywhere in the Q&A program. There are two widespread uses for macros. The first is to customize the program commands so that they are configured more closely to your own preferred way of working with the program. Most often, these preferences are based on methods that help you work more efficiently. As you will see as you create your first word processing macros, many of the examples given in this section are of this type. They are included primarily to give you ideas for customizing your use of the program. Many of them are designed to make it faster and easier to perform standard operations.

The second widespread use of macros is to automate repetitive procedures or the entry of standard text. These procedures may include just a few simple commands or a long, complex series. You can save simple phrases in macros, or even save long boilerplate paragraphs. Either way, having macros for these operations will save you time and energy as you work in Q&A. Macros that automate repetitive procedures might save and continue editing a document in Q&A Write, or perform a standard query of the data in your database. Macros that automate repetitive text entry might create a standard memo form ready to fill in, or might enter the name of your company anywhere in a document or data form. Of course, there is no reason at all not to combine command procedures and automatic text entry in the same macro. Indeed, you will often find situations calling for this.

If you have variable data to put into a macro, Q&A allows you to pause the macro during definition where the variable data would go. When the macro is played back, it will stop at the pause until the Return key is pressed. This allows new text or data to be entered from the keyboard before the macro continues.

## *USING Q&A'S MACRO RECORDER*

To create a macro, you first press Shift-F2 to access the Macro Menu shown in Figure 7.1. Notice from the figure that this menu has four options and that it was accessed from the Main Menu of Q&A. Selecting options from the Macro Menu works just like selecting options from any Q&A menu; move the highlight bar to the menu option and press Return or type its number (as **1** for Define Macro, **2** for Get Macros, and so on).

You use the first option, D - Define Macro, to create a new macro. The second, G - Get Macros, is used to call up and make available those macros contained in one of your macro files. The third, S - Save Macros, is used to save in a disk file any macro commands defined

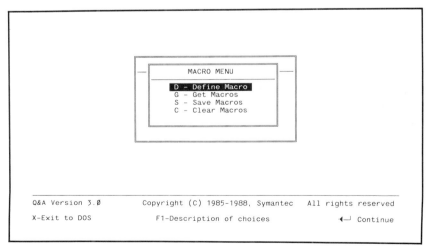

*Figure 7.1:* Macro Menu

during a session. You use the fourth, C - Clear Macros, to clear the memory of any macros that have either been created with the Define option or made resident with the Get option. If you use the Clear macros option after the Get option, the macros are deleted only from the computer's memory and are still on the disk file. To delete a macro file, you can either use one of Q&A's menu options to delete files (found on the DOS File Facilities menu or one of the Rename/Delete/Copy menus) or use the DOS DELETE or ERASE commands at the operating system level.

## NAMING MACROS

When you define a new macro, you are first asked to assign the key combination that you will use to invoke it. This is often thought of as the macro's name (or *macro identifier*), although in Q&A you input it by pressing the keys to start the macro rather than by entering a written description of it. Q&A allows you to name a macro by using a single letter key or function key prefaced by either the Shift, Ctrl, or Alt keys—such as Ctrl-B or Alt-F3.

As you know, many of these possible key combinations are already reserved by the program to carry out its own commands. Q&A will always remind you if your macro name is already used by the program in some way. You are still free to go ahead and redefine its function, although you should use caution in such circumstances. If you give a key combination a new function and do not redefine its old function under another macro name, you will have no way to use that command during the session. If you ever find that you have created such a situation and wish to enable the original command, all you have to do is use the C - Clear Macros option from the Macro Menu to get it back.

## CONTROL-KEY COMBINATIONS

In Q&A Write, you will also find that a number of Ctrl-letter key combinations are already defined for you. They emulate the way WordStar accomplishes some of its cursor movement and editing commands. Each of these combinations offers an alternative way of doing the same function in Q&A Write. Table 7.1 summarizes these key combinations, their commands, and the Q&A equivalents already taught to you. You may wish to reuse these as macro names if you are unfamiliar with WordStar or have become comfortable using their Q&A equivalents.

*Table 7.1:* WordStar Control-letter key sequences used by Q&A Write

| WORDSTAR COMMAND | FUNCTION | Q&A EQUIVALENT |
|---|---|---|
| **Cursor movement commands:** | | |
| Ctrl-A | Previous word | Ctrl-← |
| Ctrl-F | Next word | Ctrl-→ |
| Ctrl-S | Previous character | ← |
| Ctrl-D | Next character | → |
| Ctrl-E | Up one line | ↑ |
| Ctrl-X | Down one line | ↓ |
| Ctrl-R | First character of previous screen | PgUp |
| Ctrl-C | First character of next screen | PgDn |
| Ctrl-I | Tab | Tab |
| Ctrl-M | Return | ↵ |
| **Editing commands:** | | |
| Ctrl-G | Delete character at cursor | Del |
| Ctrl-T | Delete word at cursor | F4 |
| Ctrl-Y | Delete line at cursor | Shift-F4 |
| Ctrl-H | Backspace | ← |
| Ctrl-N | Insert line | Ins and ↵ |
| Ctrl-V | Insert mode (on and off toggle) | Ins |

Of these key combinations, the most useful from the point of view of a non-WordStar user is probably Ctrl-N, which inserts a blank line in the document. As you can see from the table, this command requires you to press Ins and Return in Q&A. You may want to use WordStar's method in preference to Q&A's, as it is a more efficient way of inserting lines.

When you name macros, be very prudent in your assignment of the Shift key with other keys. Q&A relies quite heavily on the Shift key in combination with the function keys, especially in Q&A Write. Usually, it is preferable to use the Ctrl and Alt keys when naming macros with the function keys. Even then, when using a function key as part of the macro name, be sure that you really wish to redefine its function before proceeding. You never want to use the Shift and a letter key as a macro name, because you will then not be able to capitalize that letter without using the Caps Lock key.

Most of the time, you will name your macros using the Ctrl and Alt keys in combination with one of the letter keys. As much as possible, choose a letter key that helps you remember its function. For instance, if you create a macro to center text in the word processor, Alt-C for *center* would be an excellent choice as its name.

## WORD PROCESSING MACROS

For your first practice in defining and using macros, you will create macros designed to be used in Q&A Write. You should start up your computer and Q&A. From the Main Menu choose the W - Write option, and from the Write Menu, the T - Type/Edit option. You will begin by defining a few simple macros that provide alternative ways of centering, boldfacing, and underlining text in a document.

### CENTERING TEXT

As you may remember, in Q&A Write the command to center text requires three keystrokes: pressing F8 to access the Options menu, typing **c** for *center*, and then pressing Return to invoke the command. You will now create a macro, Alt-C, that will do the same thing in two keystrokes. In the first line of this document, type

**This sentence will soon be centered.**

You will use this sentence to help you make sure that the keystrokes you define as part of this macro are working the way you intend them to. Later, you can use this same sentence to test out the macro.

Now, issue the command to turn on the macro recorder, and give the macro the name of Alt-C. It makes no difference whether you enter the letter keys in upper- or lowercase. Macro commands are not case-sensitive.

1.  Hold down one of the Shift keys and press F2 once. Then type **d** and press Return (or type **1**) to choose the D - Define option (Figure 7.2).

2.  Hold down the Alt key and type **c**. The macro menu disappears and you will see a flashing block at the bottom of the screen at the far right on the line with the function key assignments. This lets you know that the macro recorder is on and that any key you now press will be saved as part of the macro you are creating.

3.  Next, you issue the command to center the test sentence. Press F8, type **c**, and press Return. The test sentence is now centered.

4.  Finally, you turn off the macro recorder to complete the definition. Hold down one of the Shift keys and press F2. The block highlight disappears, letting you know that the macro recorder is turned off.

5.  You are then prompted to save the macro to a suggested file name, QAMACRO.ASC. This file is automatically loaded when you first start up Q&A so that your macros are in memory and ready to use. You can also use a different file name to keep, for example, your word processing macros separate from your file macros. For the following examples you will make separate macro files, so press the Esc key now.

Now, any time you press Alt-C (or Alt-c), the line of the text holding the cursor will be centered. To test out the macro, you have to first uncenter your test sentence. You might as well redefine this function too, while you're at it.

6. Press Shift-F2, type **d** and press Return (or type **1**). For the macro name, hold down the Ctrl key and type **c**.

7. Q&A now lets you know that this key combination is already in use (Figure 7.3). Ctrl-C is the WordStar equivalent of pressing PgDn. Type **y** to go ahead and redefine it.

8. Press F8, type **u**, and press Return.

9. Press Shift-F2 to complete the macro definition.

10. Save the macro by replacing the suggested file name QAMACRO.ASC with the name **WP.MAC**, and press Return.

Now test out your macro commands. Press Alt-C to recenter the test sentence and then press Ctrl-C to remove the centering command. In the sample macros which follow, this book will consistently use the Alt key with an appropriate mnemonic letter key to invoke a word processing command; it will use the Ctrl key with the same letter key to do its opposite.

## BOLDFACING AND UNDERLINING

The next word processing macros will begin the bold print and underlined print enhancements. Remember that all such enhancements are invoked by pressing Shift-F6 and typing the appropriate

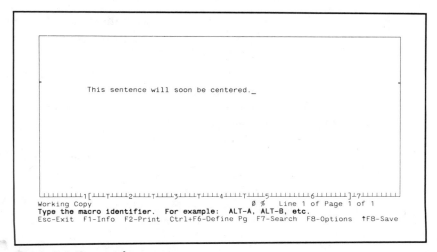

*Figure 7.2:* Prompt for macro name

```
                            This sentence will soon be centered._




  └┴┴┴┴┴┴┴┴1[┴┴┴┬┴┴┴┴2┴┴┴┴┬┴┴┴┴3┴┴┴┴┬┴┴┴┴4┴┴┴┬┴┴┴5┴┴┴┴┴┴■┴6┴┴┴┴┴┴]┴7┴┴┴┴┴┴┴
  Working Copy                                    Ø %   Line 1 of Page 1 of 1
  That key is already defined.  Do you want to redefine it? (Y/N):
  Esc-Exit  F1-Info  F2-Print  Ctrl+F6-Define Pg  F7-Search  F8-Options  ↑F8-Save
```

*Figure 7.3:* Prompt to redefine macro name

first letter of the enhancement's name. Then you use the cursor keys to highlight the text to be affected, and press F10 to complete the command. You will not try to include this last part of the command as part of the macro, because it would severely limit the macro's usefulness. If you included the keystrokes to highlight a word to be boldfaced or underlined, you could use this macro only to accomplish one or the other.

You will start by creating a macro to begin boldfacing the text. Press Home to take the cursor to the beginning of your test sentence, and then take the following steps:

1. Press Shift-F2 and then type **d** and press Return (or type **1**) to begin a new macro.

2. Press Alt and type **b** as the macro name or identifier.

3. Press Shift-F6 and type **b** as the macro keystroke.

4. Press Shift-F2 to end the macro definition.

5. Press Return to save the macro in the file WP.MAC.

Now press Esc and don't bother to highlight the text to be boldfaced. Instead, press Alt-B to begin this command. Then press End to highlight the entire sentence and press F10 to complete this command.

Next, define a macro that will do the same for underlining:

1. Press Shift-F2 and then type **d** and press Return (or type **1**) to begin a new macro.

2. Press Alt and type **u** as the macro identifier.

3. Press Shift-F6 and type **u** as the macro keystroke.

4. Press Shift-F2 to end the macro definition.

5. Press Return to save the macro in the file WP.MAC.

Press Esc to abort this command. Now press Alt-U and then press End to highlight to the end of the sentence and F10 to complete the command. Your test sentence is now boldfaced and underlined.

## TURNING RIGHT JUSTIFICATION ON AND OFF

For your next practice in creating macros, you will define macros to enter embedded printing commands that turn right justification on and off. First, you will create a macro called Alt-J to turn justification on. Press End and Return to move the cursor to the next line below your test sentence, and take the following steps:

1. Press Shift-F2 and then type **d** and press Return (or type **1**) to begin a new macro.

2. Press Alt and type **j** as the macro identifier.

3. Press Ins; then type **\*JUSTIFY YES\*** and press Return. Then press Ins.

4. Press Shift-F2 to end the macro definition.

5. Press Return to save the macro in the file WP.MAC.

In this macro, you included commands and text to be automatically entered. The Ins command was included so that you can place the cursor at the beginning of a line that already contains text without the embedded command typing over and destroying existing text. Of course, it will not work as intended if you use this macro when you are already in insert mode.

Now go ahead and define a macro that will turn off right justification:

1.  Press Shift-F2 and then type **d** and press Return (or type **1**) to define a new macro.

2.  Press Ctrl and type **j** as the macro identifier.

3.  Press Ins; then type **\*JUSTIFY NO\*** and press Return. Then press Ins again.

4.  Press Shift-F2 to end the macro definition.

5.  Press Return to save the macro in the file WP.MAC.

## SINGLE AND DOUBLE SPACING

To change between single and double spacing within a document, you enter the embedded codes **\*Ls 1\*** and **\*Ls 2\***. For this example you will use the macro pause feature to allow you type in the **1** or **2** to set the spacing to single or double spacing while the macro keystrokes are being played back.

You will call this macro Alt-L for *linespacing*. When you are defining the macro, you will press Alt-F2 at the place where the macro should pause for input. The cursor will change to a blinking box to indicate pause mode is active. You then type variable data and press Alt-F2 where the macro should start recording keystokes again.

1.  Press Shift-F2 and then type **d** and press Return (or type **1**) to define this macro.

2.  Press Alt and type **L** for the macro identifier.

3.  Press Ins, type **\*Ls**, press Alt-F2, **1**, press Alt-F2, **\***, press Return, and then press Ins again.

4.  Press Shift-F2 to end the macro definition.

5.  Press Return to save the macro in the file WP.MAC.

When this macro is played back, it will pause after the *\*Ls* so that you can type the *1* or *2* to set the line spacing. When you press Return, the macro will continue with the closing * and turn the insert mode off. If you need to press Return as part of the variable information while the macro is still paused, press Alt-F2 instead; it will act like Return but will not end the pause.

Now, test out your justification and line spacing macros in your blank document. Make sure that each creates a new line, that you have made no typing errors in the embedded commands, and that you have placed asterisks both before and after the body of the embedded command.

When you use the Alt-L macro, notice the message at the bottom of the screen indicating that the macro has paused and that you are to press ◄┘ to continue the keystroke playback. The first time you test this macro, type **2** as the variable during the pause before you press Return. Then type a line or two of text and try Alt-L again. This time, type **1** during the pause. You can now use Alt-L to go in and out of single and double spacing without having to remember the embedded commands.

The same is true of the Alt-J and Ctrl-J macros for turning right justification on and off. Now that you have learned how to use the macro pause to enter variable data, you could go back and redefine Alt-J so that you could enter **y** or **n** (or **Yes** or **No**) during a macro pause; that way you could use one macro to go in and out of justification in your documents.

## CHANGING MARGINS

Other kinds of macros are quite useful to have when word processing. This next one changes the right margin and page width settings from their default values of 68 and 80 to new values of 75 and 85. You will name this macro Alt-R (for *alternate ruler*). Create this macro as follows:

1. Press Shift-F2 and then type **d** and press Return (or type **1**).

2. Press Alt and type **r**.

3. Press Ctrl-F6 and press Return.

4. Type **75** for the right margin and press Return three times.

5. Type **85** for the page width and press F10.

6. Press Shift-F2 to stop recording.

7. Press Return to save the macro in WP.MAC.

This macro can be used whenever you begin a new document that requires left and right margins one inch wide, giving you a line length of six and a half inches. If you wanted to, you could also create a variation on this macro that changes the pitch and sets new tabs.

## *ADDING HEADERS AND FOOTERS*

In your next word processing macro, you will set up a procedure that automatically adds a footer containing the centered page number to your document. This can then become a standard macro command to use whenever you need page numbers centered at the bottom of the page. (You could also create a similar macro to define a standard header that your company uses.) Define this macro under the name Alt-F as follows:

1. Press Shift-F2 and then type **d** and press Return (or type **1**).

2. Press Alt and type **f**.

3. Press F8, type **f**, and press Return.

4. Press Return to add a blank line.

5. Type **Page #**.

6. Press F8, type **c**, and then press Return and F10.

7. Press Shift-F2.

8. Press Return to save the macro in WP.MAC.

Notice that even though you had already defined a macro, Alt-C, to center a line, the instructions had you define this command by pressing F8 and typing **c**. In this macro you alternatively could have typed Alt-C to call the other macro. This is called "embedding a macro within a macro." You may embed (or nest) macros five levels deep. Executing the Alt-C macro within the Alt-F would be an example of one level.

## *INSERTING PAGE BREAKS*

Another useful macro to have is one that will insert a user-defined page break. This command is given by pressing F8 and typing **n**. Create a macro called Alt-N (for *new page*) that makes this procedure a little easier to enter.

1. Press Shift-F2 and then type **d** and press Return (or type **1**).

2. Press Alt and type **n**.

3. Press F8, type **n**, and press Return.

4. Press Shift-F2.

5. Press Return to save the macro in WP.MAC.

Although this macro does not save keystrokes, it is easier to use (especially for touch typists) than Q&A Write's method. You are now on the second page of your practice document (because of the user-defined page break you entered when creating this last macro).

Here, you will enter one final word processing macro that builds a memo template. You can build similar macros that will automatically enter standard mailing addresses or boilerplate paragraphs into a document. This macro, which you will call Alt-M, is designed to cut down on typing and ensure accurate entry. Create the memo template macro from the following steps:

1. Press Shift-F2 and then type **d** and press Return (or type **1**).

2. Press Alt and type **m**.

3. Press F8, type **s**, and press Return.

4. Move the cursor to column 20, type **t**, and press F10.

5. Press the Caps Lock and type **MEMORANDUM**.

6. Press F8, type **c**, and press Return.

7. Press Return twice and type **TO:**.

8. Press Return twice and type **FROM:**.

9. Press Return twice and type **DATE:**.

10. Press Return twice, type **SUBJECT:**, and press Return twice again.

11. Press the ↑ key eight times, press Tab twice, and press Caps Lock.

12. Press Shift-F2.

13. Press Return to save the macro in the WP.MAC file.

This macro is designed to place the cursor at the beginning of the template where new text must be entered. It provides a new tab setting to make the alignment of the text in the memo header easier. Notice, however, that text entry must be done after the macro has finished adding all of the standardized text.

### TESTING YOUR MACROS

Now abandon this test document by pressing Esc. At the Write Menu, type **c** and press Return. Type **y** and press Return. Now test out your macro commands in the following sequence:

1. Press Alt-R to change the margins.

2. Press Alt-M to enter the memo template.

3. Move the cursor up to the first line containing MEMORAN-DUM and press Alt-B to begin boldfacing this title. Press End and F10.

4. Press Alt-F to enter the page number at the bottom of the page.

5. Save this under the file name MEMO1 by pressing Shift-F8, typing **memo1**, and pressing Return again.

### SAVING MACROS

If you don't save your macros in a file as you define them, you will want to save them before you end your work session in Q&A. To do this, press Shift-F2 and type **s** to use the Save macros option. You will see a new box that replaces the Macro Menu. This is where you enter the file name under which you want to save these macros.

Q&A suggests the file name, QAMACRO.ASC, after the prompt "Macro Filename:". This file is automatically loaded into memory every time you start up Q&A. You would save here any macros that you want to be available each time you use Q&A. Any macros stored in this file are available for use in any Q&A module.

Instead of saving your word processing macros under this file name, you save them in the file WP.MAC. Giving the file name the .MAC extension helps you identify it as a special macro file on any directory listing. After you type in your macro file name, remember to press Return to save it. To use these macros during a subsequent session in Q&A Write, all you have to do is press Shift-F2, type **g**, and press Return, then enter WP.MAC as the file to use, and press Return again. All of the macros you have just created will then be available for use as you create new documents or edit old ones.

## FILE AND REPORT MACROS

Press Esc twice now to get back to the Q&A Main Menu. You will continue your practice with creating macros by defining some for use in Q&A File. The macros that you create for Q&A File and Q&A Report will differ somewhat from those for Q&A Write. Instead of creating macros that redefine keys for invoking commmands, you will concentrate on macros that automate repetitive procedures. These can include such tasks as constructing complex database queries or running routine reports, or tasks that involve file management operations.

### AUTOMATED BATCH PROCESSING MACRO

Your first macro in Q&A File will perform a very useful batch processing operation. Before defining the macro, you will copy the structure of the personnel database into a new file that acts as a temporary repository for all new employee records. All data entry of new personnel records will be done in this temporary database rather than in the personnel database itself. The macro will then automatically copy all of the records entered in this temporary file into the main personnel database. After doing that, it will delete all of the records in the temporary personnel file so that it is purged of old records and is ready for new data entry.

The reason for creating such a macro is to cut down on the delayed response that you experience when you add new records into a large database. Your sample personnel database is still too small for you to have noted any such delays, even after having prepared it for use with the Intelligent Assistant. Nevertheless, in truly large database files containing many thousands of records (like customer files), such delays become noticeable.

This happens because with such large files you will have to use speed-up searches (see the section "Indexing Databases to Speed Up Retrieval" in Chapter 8) on almost all of the fields you wish to search when retrieving data. If you did not, you would have delays when searching the database for specific records. The procedure normally creates index files that must be updated whenever a new record is added to the database. If, on top of that, you have prepared the database for use with the Intelligent Assistant, the delay in adding a single new record becomes all the greater.

This kind of batch processing technique is the only way around delays when entering new records. While it is not called for in your personnel database, going through the steps here will teach you how to create this kind of macro when your own database files truly call for it.

First, you must copy the structure of the personnel database to a new file that will be called PERTEMP. To do this, you will use a new File command, Copy. At the Main Menu, choose the File option by typing **f** and pressing Return. Then follow the steps outlined below:

1. Type **c** to access the Copy option. When prompted for the name of the database to copy, type **personel** and press Return (see Figure 7.4).

2. At the Copy Menu, type **d** to copy only the design (structure). At the "Copy to:" prompt, type the new file name **pertemp** and press Return.

You will then receive a message asking you to please wait while the form design is copied. You are also informed that this procedure may take several minutes.

You now have an identical copy of your personnel database without any data in it. Figures 7.5 and 7.6 show you a new record that you need to add to the personnel database. Instead of entering it in your PERSONEL.DTF file, you will enter it in the new temporary database, PERTEMP.DTF.

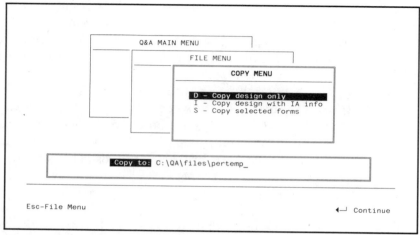

*Figure 7.4:* Copy Menu

3. Press Esc to return to the File menu and type **a** to select the Add data option.

4. Type **pertemp** over the suggested PERSONEL.DTF for the database to use and press Return.

5. Now enter Charlotte Dicke's record as it appears in Figure 7.5 and 7.6. When you are finished, press Shift-F10 to save it and return to the File Menu. You will use this record to test out the batch processing macro you are about to create.

In creating this macro, you will use the Copy option again, only this time you will use the Copy selected forms option, which copies actual data from one data file to another. This macro will be named Alt-B for *batch process*. Because it will be saved in a different macro file, there is no problem with reusing this name (remember, Alt-B in the word processing macro file starts boldfacing of text).

Follow carefully the steps outlined below to define this macro. Make sure that you enter the database file names correctly. If you mix them up, you can end up deleting all of the data in your personnel database, so make sure you have a current backup file of this database before testing out the macro.

1. Press Shift-F2 and then type **d** and press Return (or type **1**) to begin recording the new macro.

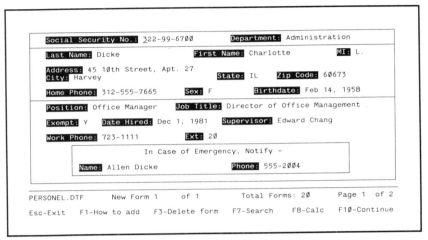

*Figure 7.5:* Charlotte Dicke's record, Page 1

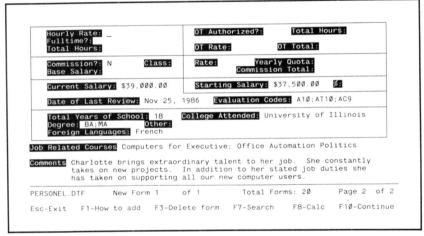

*Figure 7.6:* Charlotte Dicke's record, Page 2

2. Press Alt-B as the macro identifier.

3. Type **c**, type **pertemp**, and press Return.

4. Type **s**, type **personel**, and press Return.

5. At the Retrieve Spec, press F10 (to retrieve all of the records).

6. At the Merge Spec, press F10 (to use all of the fields).

7. Once the copying is complete, type **r**, type **pertemp**, and press Return.

8. At the Retrieve Spec, press F10 (to delete all of the records in this database).

9. Type **y** and press Return to verify that you want to make these deletions.

10. When the program is finished deleting the records and you are back at the File Menu, press Shift-F2 to end the macro definition.

11. Save the macro by typing in the name **file.mac** and pressing Return.

Now test out the macro by pressing Alt-B. If you have any problem during its execution, press Esc to abort it. Then go back and redefine the macro according to the steps listed above. If all goes well, Charlotte Dicke's record will be added to your personnel database. To verify that everything worked, use the Search/Update option to view this record. Retrieve it by entering Dicke in the Last Name field in the Retrieve Spec. After viewing the record, press Esc to return to the File Menu.

Next, choose the Add data option using the PERTEMP.DTF file. Verify that the file is now empty of data by checking the status indicator at the bottom of the screen. It should read "Form 1 of 1". Go ahead and enter the record shown in Figures 7.7 and 7.8 for Sally Zehm. When you have finished entering the record, press Shift-F10 to save it. You will use it to test the sorting macro in the next section.

## SORTING MACRO

The next macro that you create for Q&A File will automate a common sort for the personnel database, that which orders the records first by department and then alphabetically by employee. You can easily create such sorting macros based on the most common routine sorts that you need to do for your own database files. Make sure you are at the File Menu, and then take the following steps to create this sorting macro. It will be called Alt-1 because it is the most common sort for this database.

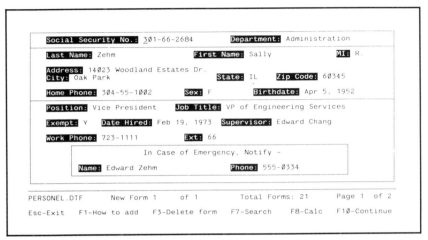

*Figure 7.7:* Sally Zehm's record, Page 1

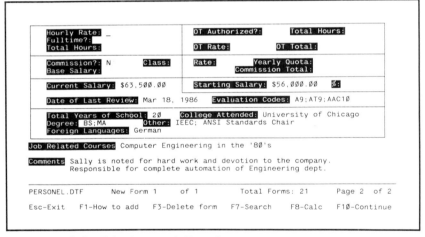

*Figure 7.8:* Sally Zehm's record, Page 2

1. Press Shift-F2 and then type **d** and press Return (or type **1**) to begin creating this macro.

2. Press Alt-1 as the macro identifier.

3. Type **s**; then type **personel** and press Return.

4. Press F8 (to access the Sort Spec).

5. Press Return and type **1as** in the Department field.

6. Press Return and type **2as** in the Last Name field.

7. Press Return and type **3as** in the First Name field.

8. Press F9 (to return to the Retrieve Spec) and press F10 (to use all of the records).

9. Press Shift-F2 to turn off the macro recorder.

10. Press Return to save the macro in FILE.MAC.

Press Esc to return to the File Menu. There, press Alt-B to add Sally Zehm's new record to the personnel database. When execution has finished, press Alt-1 to test out your new sorting macro. Once the database has been resorted, press F6 to get a table view. You should see Sally's name listed as the last employee in the Administration department. Press Esc to return to the File Menu.

## PHONE LIST PRINTING MACRO

As a last example of the type of macro you can create for the File and Report modules, you will define a macro that will automatically print your phone list report (Print Spec). Printing an updated version of a company's telephone list is a very repetitive task. Macros like this one can be created to automate the printing of all kinds of routinely run reports.

At the File Menu, take the following steps to create this macro, called Alt-T for *telephone list*:

1. Press Shift-F2 and then type **d** and press Return (or type **1**).

2. Press Alt-T for the macro identifier.

3. Type **p**; then type **personel** and press Return.

4. Type **p**; then type **phonelst** and press Return.

5. Make sure that your printer is turned on. Press Return to choose the No default at the prompt ''Do you wish to make any temporary changes?''

6. When the printing is finished, press Esc to return to the File Menu.

7. Press Shift-F2 to turn off the macro recorder.

8. Press Return to save the macro in FILE.MAC.

## *EDITING A MACRO FILE*

Earlier it was mentioned that it is possible to edit a macro file. To see how this works, press Esc to return to the Main Menu and choose the Write option. At the Write Menu, choose Get and give the file name as **wp.mac**. (Remember that macros are saved in the same directory as Q&A, so if your database and document files are stored elsewhere, you must enter the complete path name.) Figure 7.9 shows you the Import Document Menu that then appears. Macro files are not stored in the same format as Q&A Write document files. They are stored in ASCII format.

As you can see on this menu, there are two options for importing ASCII files into Q&A Write. You can choose either to import such a file with word wrap (Special ASCII) or without word wrap (ASCII). Choose ASCII to import a macro file, as it is much like a program listing. You need not be concerned with formatting because word wrap has no function in this type of file.

### *VIEWING MACRO FILES*

Type **a** and press Return to import this file. The first screen of this file is shown in Figure 7.10. Each of the word processing macros that you defined is separated from the others by asterisks which appear in

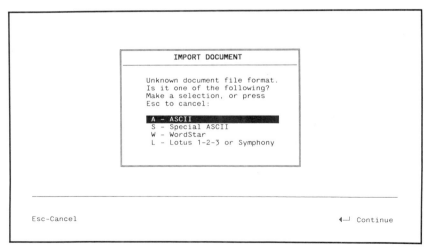

*Figure 7.9:* The Import Document Menu

```
        <begdef><altc><f8>c<enter><enddef>
        *
        <begdef><ctrlc><f8>u<enter><enddef>
        *
        <begdef><altb><capsf6>b<enddef>
        *
        <begdef><altu><capsf6>u<enddef>
        *
        <begdef><altj><ins><enter>*justify<sp>yes*<enter><ins><ent
        er><enddef>
        *
        <begdef><ctrlent><ins><enter>*justify<sp>no*<enter><ins><e
        nter><enddef>
        *
        <begdef><alt1><ins><enter>*ls<sp><altf2>*<enter><ins><endd
        ef>
        *
        <begdef><altr><ctrlf6><enter>75<enter><enter><enter>85<f10
        ><enddef>
        *
WP.MAC                              0 %    Line 1 of Page 1 of 1

Esc-Exit  F1-Info  F2-Print  Ctrl+F6-Define Pg  F7-Search  F8-Options  ↑F8-Save
```

*Figure 7.10:* Contents of the word processing macro file

the first column of otherwise blank lines. Notice that the macro
recorder has written coded forms for each of the keys that you pressed
during the macro's definition. Every key code is enclosed in a pair of
angular brackets; only the individual letters and text (including
punctuation) are not so enclosed.

The first macro listed in the file is your macro to center a line of text
by pressing Alt-C. It appears as

<begdef> <altc> <f8>c <enter> <enddef>

in the first line of the document. The first code, <begdef> (for *begin
definition*), is the way Q&A coded your pressing of Shift-F2 to turn on
the macro recorder. At the prompt to give the macro a name, you
pressed Alt and typed **c**. This was coded as <altc>, pretty much as it
appeared in the instructions for defining the macro. Pressing the
function key F8 to access the word processing Options menu was
coded verbatim as <f8>. The only difference between the way it
appears here and the way it appears in the text is that this book uses
the uppercase letter so that it more closely matches the key's appearance on your keyboard. In coding function keys, Q&A does not use
any capital letters.

The next key you pressed was the letter **c** to choose the Center
option from the Options menu. This is not a special function key, so

it is not enclosed in brackets. To complete the centering command, you then pressed the Return key. It is coded as <enter> in the macro. Finally, you turned off the macro recorder by pressing the key sequence Shift-F2 a second time. This has been coded as <enddef> (for *end definition*).

Read through the rest of the macro codes visible on this screen. Most of the codes are very close to the way they have been shown in this book. There are, however, notable exceptions. Look at the macro in the third line. There you pressed Shift-F6 to access the print enhancements. It is represented by <capsf6> in the macro. The Shift key is referred to as *caps* in macro files.

Also notice the way the name of the macro appears in the sixth macro, Ctrl-J, which turns off right justification. In the macro file, it is written as <ctrlent> (for *Control-Enter*). This is one of the few exceptions to showing letters verbatim in macros. This code describes the function of the key sequence. It serves as an alternate for pressing the Ctrl and the Return keys. This means that you can just as well execute this macro by pressing Ctrl-Return as by pressing Ctrl-J. It also means that you disabled the original function of Ctrl-Return when you defined the new macro definition for Ctrl-J. (Note that because of this kind of dual assignment, you should never give a macro the name Ctrl-M. Its key code is <enter>, which means that the macro defined under this name would be played any time you pressed Return in the document!)

## DEFINING NEW MACROS

You can not only view macro definitions in a file, you can also edit them or add new ones. For instance, if you wanted to change the name of the Ctrl-J macro, you could do so by changing the <ctrlent> to some other valid key code. (Your Q&A documentation contains a listing of all possible key codes in its section on Macros.) If all you want to do is rename a macro without modifying its function, editing the macro file saves you from having to redefine all of the keystrokes as would be required with the macro recorder.

Also, this method allows you to avoid actually performing each command in order to define it. You must, of course, be sure that you have included all of the necessary steps as you code them and enter them in the file. If you are not careful or if you are unsure of what you are doing, you could end up with some very surprising results when you test the macro.

***SAVE-AND-EDIT MACRO***    There is a kind of macro that must be defined by editing the macro file rather than using the macro recorder. This is a macro that exits you not only from a particular Q&A module to the Main Menu but also from Q&A Main Menu to the DOS operating system. Q&A's macro recorder can follow your keystrokes up to and including when you type the final **x** (for *eXit*) and press Return, but there is then no way to turn off the recorder and save the macro as soon as the command has erased Q&A from the computer's memory. The only way around this is to define such a macro in the macro file, where you can write out the final Shift-F2 to turn off the recorder and save the macro as part of the file.

To practice entering such a macro, you will create a macro that saves your document and then exits the Q&A program. This macro can then be used to shut down the program quickly when you are editing a document that has already been saved under a file name.

To create this macro, press PgDn and move the cursor to the first column in the line directly below the last line of the Memo macro, Alt-M. Type an asterisk (*) there and press Return. Now enter the key codes on this new line exactly as they appear below. You will name this new macro Alt-X.

<begdef><altx><capsf8><enter><esc><esc>x<enddef>

After you have finished entering this line, your macro should look just like the one in Figure 7.11.

The <capsf8> and <enter> codes save any edits made under the name previously given to the document. The two <esc> codes then take you back to the Main Menu, where you type **x** to return to DOS.

To save this macro file, you cannot use the regular Shift-F8 or Esc and Save option as you do to save regular document files. If you do, you will not be able to successfully open the WP.MAC file again. Instead, press Esc, type **e** (for *Export*), and press Return. Type **y** and press Return again to save the file under the same name.

```
<begdef><alt1><ins><enter>*1s<sp><altf2>*<enter><ins><endd
ef>
*
<begdef><altr><ctrlf6><enter>75<enter><enter><enter>85<f10
><enddef>
*
<begdef><altf><f8>f<enter><enter>Page<sp>#<f8>c<enter><f10
><enddef>
*
<begdef><altn><f8>n<enter><enddef>
*
<begdef><altm><f8>s<enter><rgt><rgt><rgt><rgt><rgt><r
gt><rgt>t<f10>
MEMORANDUM<f8>C<enter><enter><enter>TO:<enter><enter>FROM:
<enter><enter>
DATE:<enter><enter>SUBJECT:<enter><enter><up><up><up><up><
up><up><up>
<tab><tab><enddef>
*
<begdef><altx><capsf8><enter><esc><esc>x<enter><enddef>
```

```
WP.MAC                          Ø %   Line 34 of Page 1 of 1
Esc-Exit  F1-Info  F2-Print  Ctrl+F6-Define Pg  F7-Search  F8-Options  ↑F8-Save
```

*Figure 7.11:* Word processing macro file with new macro

**SAFE-EXIT MACRO**    You should also create a similar macro for
exiting from data entry in Q&A File. This is important because you
never want to quit a database file (if possible) without exiting through
the menu system. Exiting through a menu automatically closes the
database. If you do power down the system without first closing
the database file, you will not be able to reopen the file. (If this should
happen, all is not necessarily lost. If you do not have a backup copy of
your current database, you can run Recover Database from the
Main Menu Utilities.)

To create this macro, Get your FILE.MAC file and add these
codes on the last line (separated by an asterisk):

&lt;begdef&gt;&lt;altx&gt;&lt;capsf10&gt;&lt;esc&gt;x&lt;enddef&gt;

Save this file again, using Ctrl-F8 option to save this document as
an ASCII file. Once you have done this, test out the word processing
exit macro by using Get to open your MEMO1 document. Then
press Shift-F2 and type **g**. Enter the file name as **wp.mac** and press
Return. Once the file is loaded, press Alt-X.

If your macro file contains a typo or was not saved with Ctrl-F8,
you will receive an error message telling you that there is an illegal

macro definition and giving you its position in the file. If this happens, press Esc and reopen WP.MAC. Check your last macro for any errors and then save it again using Ctrl-F8. If all went well, you will now be at the operating system prompt, A> or C>.

# SETTING ALTERNATE PROGRAMS

You can install up to six different alternate DOS programs or Q&A macros on the Main Menu if you are using Q&A on a hard disk system. This lets you start your macros as a menu choice, so you do not need to remember the key combination or macro name. There are three things to remember when using a macro as an alternate program.

- The macro's key combination must be Alt followed by a letter from A to Z.

- The macro must be designed to start from the Main Menu.

- Macros used as alternate programs must be stored in QAMACRO.ASC (the Q&A startup macro file).

## INSTALLING MACROS AS ALTERNATE PROGRAMS

To install an alternate program, choose Utilities from the Main Menu, then choose Set global defaults (s and Return, or 5). Press PgDn to display the bottom portion of the screen (Figure 7.12). On the Alternate program 1 line, enter the macro key combination as **Alt-*n*** where *n* is a capital letter A through Z.

On the Menu selection line, enter up to 11 characters that describe the macro. The first letter of the menu selection will be the menu choice letter. You should avoid using menu selection descriptions that start with the letters that are already on the Main Menu (F, R, W, A, U, and X).

After you have installed your macros as alternate programs, press F-10 to continue. Then you can go back to the Main Menu and test the macros.

```
                          ALTERNATE PROGRAMS
                          ═══════════════════

            You can install up to six alternate programs for the Main Menu.
            You can then execute those programs by selecting them at that menu.
            When you exit from these programs, you will return automatically
            to the Main Menu.
                        ▌Alternate program 1:▐ _
                         Menu selection.....:
                         Alternate program 2:
                         Menu selection.....:
                         Alternate program 3:
                         Menu selection.....:
                         Alternate program 4:
                         Menu selection.....:
                         Alternate program 5:
                         Menu selection.....:
                         Alternate program 6:
                         Menu selection.....:
            ──────────────────────────────────────────────────────────────

     Esc-Cancel            PgUp-Set default directories         F1Ø-Continue
```

*Figure 7.12:* The Alternate Programs Menu

### INSTALLING DOS
### PROGRAMS AS ALTERNATE PROGRAMS

You may also install other DOS programs as alternate programs. By installing another program on the Main Menu, you can easily exit Q&A and load the other program with a keystroke or two. When you exit the other DOS program Q&A will automatically load again.

To install another program on the Main Menu on the alternate program line, type the drive, path, and the command used in DOS to start the program. Separate each component with a backslash (\). For example, if you have Lotus 1-2-3 on the hard disk in a subdirectory called 123, the alternate program line would be **C:\123\Lotus** (or **C:\123\123**, if you use *123* as the startup command instead of *Lotus*). On the Menu Selection line, type **Lotus 1-2-3**. On the Main Menu you will see ''L - Lotus 1-2-3'' as a new menu option at the top of a second column (Figure 7.13). To use your Lotus program, type **L** and press Return, or type **7**. When you exit from Lotus 1-2-3, Q&A will automatically be restarted. (You will see the message ''reloading Q&A'' at the bottom of the screen.)

## SUMMARY

Macros are very easy to create and use in Q&A. As you have seen, they can help by reducing typing, customizing keyboard commands,

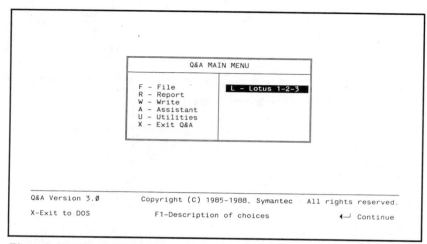

*Figure 7.13:* The Q&A Main Menu after adding Lotus 1-2-3 as a menu option

or by automating routine operations. They are available in every Q&A module and can even span different modules. Q&A's macro recorder captures keystrokes, which can later be played back by pressing the key sequence assigned as the macro name. During the playback, macros can pause for input from the keyboard.

Q&A also allows you to edit macro files that are stored as ASCII files. This allows you to change macros already defined or to add new macro definitions to the file. Any such modifications to your macro files must be saved in ASCII format using Q&A Write's Export option or Ctrl-F8 while in the document.

Up to six Macros can also be placed on Q&A's Main Menu. This makes using the macro a menu choice; therefore, remembering the key combination or macro name is not necessary. A menu selection description can take up to 11 characters, so you can better describe what the macro will do when it is played back. Other DOS programs can also be placed on the Main Menu so that you can easily change to another program and back to Q&A.

In the chapters ahead, you will go on to learn about other advanced features and techniques available to you in Q&A. Chief among these is the XLookup function, which allows you to retrieve data stored in another Q&A database. You will also work with techniques for further automating and controlling database file input by using the Customize File Menu. Finally, you will learn how you can import and export data between Q&A and other popular software programs, including other word processors, spreadsheets, and database management programs.

CHAPTER

8

# ADVANCED
# DATABASE
# APPLICATIONS

# *Fast Track*

which the calculations are to be performed, and/or the cursor movements that are to take place after the data is input in the appropriate fields in the Program form.

**To create a lookup table**                                                397

that supplies the values to be entered in particular fields, select the Edit lookup table option from the Customize Menu. Fill out the table by entering the values (either text or numbers) in the KEY column that are to match those entered in a particular field of the form. Then, enter the values in the numbered columns that are to be returned when a match occurs. In the form, enter the LOOKUP statement following the form LOOKUP(*key*,*column*, *field#* ) where *key* is the item you want looked up in the table, *column* is the number of the column in the table you want returned, and *field#* is the number of the field in the form where this value is to be entered.

**To perform a lookup in an external database file,**                       399

enter the @XLOOKUP function in the field where you want the information copied to. Enter the @XLOOKUP function according to the following form @XLOOKUP(*fn*,*pfk*,*xkf*,*lf* ) where *fn* is the name of the file from which the function returns its data, *pfk* is the ID number of the field in the primary file (called the primary key field) that has an equivalent in the external file, *xkf* is the name of the field in the external file that matches that of the primary key field, and *lf* is the name of the field in the external file whose values you want returned.

# CONTINUED

**To import**                                                              **442**

pfs:File, IBM Filing Assistant, Lotus 1-2-3, DIF, dBASE II or
dBASE III, or ASCII files into Q&A, select the Import Data
option on the Utilities Menu and then select the appropriate
option.

**To export**                                                              **450**

Q&A database files to ASCII, DIF, or dBASE files, select the
Export Data option on the Utilities Menu and then select
the appropriate option.

## OVERVIEW

In this chapter, you will explore the more advanced features of Q&A File and learn techniques for increasing the power of your database application. You will begin by looking again at Q&A's File module, this time with an eye toward the many ways in which you can customize the database design. You will learn valuable techniques that give you more control over data that can be entered in fields, allow you to add your own user Help messages, and even add programming statements that perform calculations, navigate the data entry form, and use lookup commands to speed up data entry. As usual, you will apply all of these techniques to your sample personnel database.

Finally, you will learn how to share data between Q&A and other popular software programs. Data transfer is a two-way street. At times you will want to take in data prepared by other application software programs for use in Q&A. This data could come from other database managers such as pfs:File or dBASE III Plus. Q&A makes importing foreign files extremely easy, as it provides for direct transfer of pfs:File, IBM Filing Assistant, dBase II/III, Lotus 1-2-3 files and Symphony files.

At other times you may need to transfer your Q&A data for use with other software programs. This can involve sending out data stored in a Q&A database file for use with a spreadsheet program, or more rarely, for use with another database management system. As you will learn, Q&A provides a facility for creating ASCII files as well as DIF and dBase II/II formats for such export operations.

## CUSTOMIZING THE DATABASE

Q&A offers you many options for customizing your database. To see what options are available, choose File from the Main Menu and then Design file from the File Menu. There are three options on the Design Menu, as shown in Figure 8.1. Choose the last, Customize a file. When you select this option, you must designate the name of the file to be used. Either type in **personel**, or press Return and select it from the List Manager by using the cursor to point to it and then pressing Return again. Figure 8.2 shows the Customize Menu with its nine options, which will then appear on your screen.

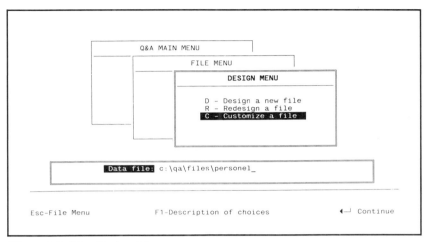

*Figure 8.1:* The Design Menu

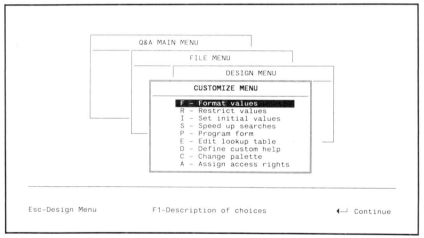

*Figure 8.2:* The Customize Menu

You became familiar with the eighth option on this menu, Change palette, in Chapter 3 when you designed your sample database. As you remember, you used this option to change the way the field names and data entry blanks were displayed on the screen. You will not need to use the Change palette option in making the refinements planned for the personnel database.

The first option, Format values, allows you to redefine the data types and display formats for the fields in your database. You use it to make changes to the display format codes that you assigned when designing the database. This option presents the same screens and works the same way as does assigning new data types and formats to all of the fields during the initial creation of a database. You became familiar with this procedure when you first designed and later modified the form for your personnel database. For now, you do not need to make any changes to the format display of the fields in your database.

## CONTROLLING DATA INPUT

The second option, Restrict values, allows you to define a range of valid entries for fields in the form. You will begin the process of customizing the personnel database by using this option to alert you, or any other data entry operator, to any invalid or unusual entries that have been entered in a particular field. When an entry outside the specified range is attempted, the message "Warning! Value not in specified range. Please verify before continuing" will be displayed. Q&A only warns that your input is not in a valid range; it does not prevent you from going ahead and entering it anyway.

Usually, when you define valid ranges for data entry, you also use the Define custom help option to add your own Help messages. These can be accessed immediately after receiving Q&A's warning message. This technique is especially recommended for situations in which many people with differing degrees of familiarity with the database will be updating it. Your own help message, specific to the data entry in the field, will replace the general online help messages available to the data entry operator. In these messages, you can include the range of valid entries and guide the operator in finding his or her error. Later, you will learn how easy it is to add these help messages by adding them to all of the fields where you restrict the range of valid entries in the exercise ahead.

Now type **r** and press Return (or type **2**) to access the Restrict values option. A screen containing the first page of a blank form for the personnel database then appears. Figure 8.3 shows you the two fields on this page that require restrictions placed on the data entry. The first is in the Department field.

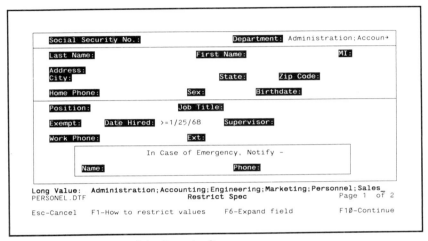

*Figure 8.3:* First page of the Restrict Spec

As you can see in this figure, the valid values listed there extend beyond the length of the Department field. Remember that when filling out any of these definition screens, you are not restricted to the width of the field blank. Any time you need to enter a formula, codes, or values that will not fit in the space allotted for proper data entry, you can extend the entry line by pressing F6. Q&A then places the cursor at the beginning of the first line at the bottom of the screen, following the prompt "Long value". This is what Q&A calls any entry that will not fit within the limits of a field blank. You can enter up to 69 characters. The use of a long value in a field is marked by the addition of a → following any characters that will fit inside its blank. Any time you place the cursor on such a field, the entire long value appears on this line, as shown in Figure 8.3. When you customize a database, you will probably need to use long values much more than you did when you originally designed it.

When you restrict a range of values in a field, you can use all of the same codes that you use when you fill out a Retrieve Spec using the Search/Update option in Q&A File, except for the MAX and MIN functions. (If you need to refresh your memory on how to enter these codes and their meanings, refer back to the table in Chapter 3 in the section "Retrieving Forms from a Database.")

Look again at Figure 8.3. Notice that the long value for the Department field contains the names of the six departments in this company. They are separated by semicolons that mean OR in the sense that you can enter either Administration or Accounting or Engineering or Marketing or Personnel or Sales. Chances are that you will not enter a fictitious department, but you might make a typing error when entering one of these six. You restrict the values to guard against such errors going undetected. If you do not have the department name spelled consistently in all records, your queries and reports will be inaccurate.

To enter the restriction values, move the cursor to this field and press F6. Then enter the names of the six fields as they are shown in Figure 8.3. Before you press Return, check for typing errors.

The second restriction is in the Date Hired field. Remember that Q&A already automatically questions impossible date entries like 12/36/87. It cannot, however, know to question a date that is impossible in other contexts. In this case, any hire date before January 25, 1968 is considered impossible because that was the date on which the company was founded. Again, you are entering a restriction here primarily to guard against typos, especially those that might occur when entering the year. Move the cursor down to the Date Hired field and enter

>= 1/25/68

This means that the date must be greater than (later than) or equal to (the same as) the founding date. After you have entered the restriction, press the PgDn key to enter the valid ranges for the fields on the second page of the form. These are shown in Figure 8.4.

The first restriction range on this page is in the Hourly Rate field. If you remember, this field carries a currency (Money) data type. The range of permissible values is between $5.00 and $20.00 an hour; it is entered as **5..20** (in a Money field, the dollar sign and two places after the decimal point will automatically be entered). You place restriction values in this and all of the other currency fields on the page to guard against costly typos. Later, you will add custom help messages to these fields which let the data entry operator not only know the lower and upper dollar limit specified here but also understand that it is unnecessary to enter anything more than numbers. This is because all formatting, including dollar signs, commas, and decimal points, is handled by Q&A itself.

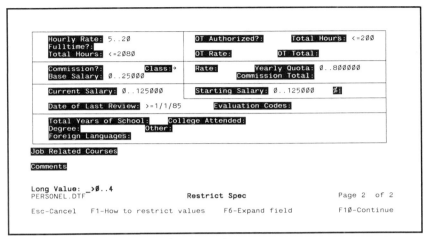

*Figure 8.4:* Second page of the Restrict Spec

In addition to the currency fields on this page, upper limits have been set for the Total Hours fields. The first contains the total overtime hours authorized. These are not to exceed 200 except in very rare instances. The second is the total number of hours that a nonexempt employee works a year. This is not to exceed 2,080, which is equivalent to full time. Anything beyond that must be counted as overtime and paid at the overtime rate.

Look at the value range that has been defined for the Class field in Figure 8.4. This field contains the classification for salespeople which determines their commission rate. Because this classification consists of a single digit, the field blank is too small to contain the restriction statement. The full entry is shown as a long value at the bottom of the screen. It restricts the valid entries to numbers between 1 and 4. Later you will add a new fourth-level classification when you set up a lookup table that automatically enters the proper commission rate into the Rate field. Because of this, you need to guard against data entry errors occurring here.

The last restriction value in your sample database is in the Date of Last Review field. All employees should have had their last review at least by the beginning of 1985. If this is not the case, the Personnel department will want to look into the situation. You will later attach a help message to this field which will ask the data entry operator to flag such an entry and alert Personnel.

Go ahead and enter all of these restriction values as shown in Figure 8.4. You will only have to use the Expand field command to enter a long value when specifying the range for the Class field. When you have finished, press F10 to save these restrictions and return to the Customize Menu.

## SETTING INITIAL VALUES

The third option on the Customize Menu allows you to set initial values that will appear in any new records added to the database. Setting initial values for fields saves time during data entry if you find that certain fields tend to require a fairly constant input value. Perhaps the most useful initial value is the current date. You set it by using the @DATE function that you are already familiar with. You can also use the @TIME function to display the current time in the data entry form. If your database contains a field that requires the date that the record was entered, you can use the @DATE function as the initial value. As soon as you save the record, the date and time will be frozen. They will not be dynamically updated when you go back to update the record later.

Any initial value can be overridden by the data entry operator by simply entering the correct value over it. If, for instance, you use the @DATE function in an invoicing database to set the order date to the current date, but that date is not appropriate for the invoices that you have to add, you merely replace the display of the current date with the earlier one marked on your paper invoice.

To see how you set up initial values in the database, type **i** and press Return (or type **3**) to access the Initial Values Spec shown in Figure 8.5. There you see that the @DATE function has been added to the Date Hired field. The assumption here is that you have added all of the existing employees to the personnel database and that any subsequent records will be for newly hired employees. Most often, their records will be added to the database on the day they come on board. Go ahead and enter the @DATE function in this field as shown. Be aware that the date that was current when the accompanying figures were prepared will no longer match the date you see displayed when you are using this book.

```
    Social Security No.:                    Department:

    Last Name:                    First Name:              MI:
    Address:
    City:                              State:      Zip Code:

    Home Phone:           Sex:             Birthdate:

    Position:                  Job Title:

    Exempt:        Date Hired: @DATE_        Supervisor:

    Work Phone:                  Ext:

                      In Case of Emergency, Notify -

              Name:                        Phone:


  PERSONEL.DTF                Initial Values Spec        Page 1  of 2

  Esc-Cancel  F1-How to set initial values     F3-Clear Spec     F10-Continue
```

*Figure 8.5:* The Initial Values Spec

There are no other fields in the personnel database that really justify setting initial values. This is one example of a diversified application that profits little from extensive use of initial values. However, you need to be aware of this option and how it works. You will find many good uses for it when you create databases for your own applications.

For example, the Q&A function, @NUMBER is often used in the Initial Values Spec to automatically number a field. Invoicing, purchase order and customer tracking applications are just a few that benefit from this feature. To use the @NUMBER function you simply type @NUMBER in the field you want numbered on the Initial Value Spec. When you choose Add Data from the File Menu and the first form to be filled in appears, the number 1 will already be assigned to the numbering field. As you add data the field will automatically be incremented by 1. If you want the number to increment by a large value you simply change the function to @NUMBER($n$), where $n$ equals the number by which you want the value to be incremented.

Q&A also provides a facility to reset the numbering function to a starting value other than 1. To do this you choose Add Data from the File Menu and when you get to the first form, press Ctrl-F8. A box will appear on the screen as shown in Figure 8.6. Type in the number that the function should currently hold. For example, if you want the next record to be numbered 1000, you would reset @NUMBER to 999, so the next record will receive the value 1000.

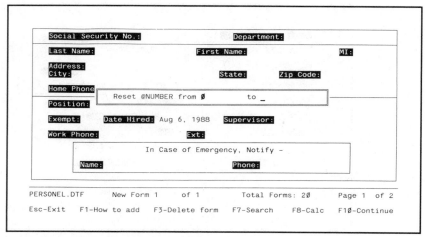

***Figure 8.6:*** Resetting the @NUMBER function

Since there is not an appropriate field on your personnel form for numbering, after you enter the @DATE function in the Date Hired field you should press F10 to save it and return to the Customize Menu.

## CREATING INDEXES TO SPEED UP DATA RETRIEVAL

The fourth option, Speed up searches, is a very important one when you are working with a large database containing from hundreds to thousands of records. When searching for specific information in a large database, you may find yourself waiting up to several minutes for the program to locate your data. How long this takes depends upon where the record you want is located in the database. If it was entered early in the database and is therefore located near the beginning, you may not have a long delay. If, on the other hand, your record was entered fairly late in the building of the database and is therefore located near the end, you will experience a delay that you may find intolerable.

It is important to realize that Q&A is no slower in sequentially reading a thousand records than any other microcomputer database program. The relatively long response time is due to limitations of the computer hardware more than the Q&A program. The way to cut down on this response time is to create indexes for each of the fields that you habitually use in doing searches in the database. This is what the Speed up searches option does. For every field you mark with an *s* (for *Speed up*), Q&A creates its version of an index file.

These indexes give the program a much faster way to locate specific records when you use either the Search/Update option in Q&A File or English queries in the Intelligent Assistant. Normally, Q&A File only keeps track of the order in which records are entered. When you initially add records to a database, you may be able to enter them according to some kind of order or you may not. In your personnel database, you entered records grouped primarily by department, though even they were not in strict alphabetical order. Regardless of how well organized the records are when they are initially entered, there will come a time in updating the database when you must enter new records that cannot conform to this original order. For example, new employees will be hired in departments whose original records are all located in the first part of the database.

Normally, sorting the database takes care of this by physically reordering the records. However, such is not the case with Q&A. As you have seen, each time you search the database you must reenter the Sort Spec (which is the reason for creating the sorting macro command in Chapter 7). The records always remain in the order that they were entered in the database.

But even when sorting changes the physical order, you still need to be able to create indexes. Sorting by department and last name may help you quickly locate a particular employee if you search for him by name, but it will not help if you search for him by his current salary. By creating an index for each of these fields, Q&A can keep tabs on their location in the database without having to alter the way in which the records were entered. You can assign up to 115 fields in a database as speedy fields (in other words, you can create up to 115 indexes). Doing so will speed up Q&A during queries that use these fields.

Unfortunately, it will also increase the time it takes for Q&A to add new records to the database. This issue was first raised when you created the batch processing macro in the last chapter. Each time you add a new record to the database, Q&A updates all of the indexes for all of the fields that you have designated as speedy fields.

The way around this data entry delay is to create a batch processing macro similar to the one you defined in Chapter 7. When you use this procedure with your own database files, be sure to copy the design of the database after you have finalized it by using all of the customizing options you need except the Speed up searches option. Do this before you teach the Intelligent Assistant about the database (this is a step you did not take when you created your practice macro for updating the personnel database). That way, you will not experience delays due to index files when you add new records to the temporary data entry file. You will know to anticipate delays as part of the batch processing that automatically copies the new records to the permanent file (containing all of the speedy fields and the Assistant information).

Figures 8.7 and 8.8 show you all of the fields to be marked as speedy fields in your sample database. All you have to do is enter an **s** in each field, as shown in these figures. These fields were chosen as speedy fields because they are the most likely to be used in defining search criteria or in phrasing English queries. With the addition of seven indexes to your personnel database, you may notice a slight delay when you later add new records to the file.

Unfortunately, you will not be able to perceive a corresponding decrease in retrieval time when you search, because your sample database still contains only a handful of records. If this company had 500 employees (and if you had the patience to enter all these records in an application that does not relate directly to your own situation!) you would notice the improvement.

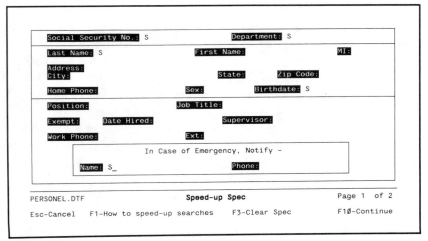

*Figure 8.7:* Speedy fields for Page 1 of the database form

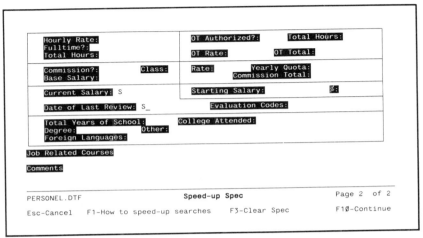

*Figure 8.8:* Speedy fields for Page 2 of the database form

Go ahead and add an **s** to each field as shown in Figures 8.7 and 8.8. When you are finished, press F10. Q&A will give you a message informing you that you must wait while it creates all of these new indexes and goes through each existing record in the personnel database, marking the position of the data in each speedy field in its corresponding index. When it has finished, you will be returned to the Customize Menu.

If you find later that you need to designate other fields as speedy fields, you can use this option again and enter an **s** in each field. To remove a speedy field, you simply use this same option again and delete the *s* from the field or fields you no longer need indexed.

## *AUTOMATING DATA ENTRY*

The next option on the Customize Menu is called Program form. If Symantec's use of the term *programming* makes you a little uneasy, understand that much of what this entails is no harder than, and in fact very similar to, entering definitions for derived columns as you did in Chapter 5 when you learned how to create report forms. Don't worry if you are completely unfamiliar with programming (and want to stay that way). You do not have to have a background in BASIC or COBOL or a database development language to master these very versatile techniques for automating data entry in your forms.

Essentially, you can automate data entry in four different ways:

- By adding formulas that calculate the values to be entered in particular fields

- By setting up conditions under which different calculations will be performed or cursor movements will be made to fields

- By creating lookup tables from which values will be entered into fields

- By programming the form to look up information contained in another Q&A database

You will get a chance to try the first three methods as you automate the data entry in your personnel database form. Then you'll create a new database to implement an external lookup to your personnel file.

***ASSIGNING FIELD NUMBERS***    All of these methods require that you number the fields involved, much as you did when specifying which fields to include in a report form in Q&A Report. The difference is that all numbers assigned to fields are always prefaced by the number symbol (#). The order of the numbers does not have to correspond to the order in which you want the calculations, conditions, or cursor movements to be performed during data entry. As you will see in the following exercises, you often number the fields consecutively according to the order in which they are laid out—but this is not a requirement.

***CALCULATIONS***    As mentioned before when you defined the formulas for the derived columns in your sample reports, you must be mindful of the natural order that Q&A follows when evaluating and solving formulas. Multiplication and division are performed before addition and subtraction from left to right in a formula. If you need to change this order, you enclose the part of the formula that you want evaluated first. For instance, consider the following formula:

#10/#15 + #20

It calls for the value entered in field number 10 to be divided by that in field number 15 before this result is added to that in field number 20. If instead you wanted the value in field 10 to be divided by the result of adding the value in field 15 to that in 20, you would add parentheses to indicate this. The formula would then be entered as

#10/(#15 + #20)

***CONDITIONS*** In addition to the mathematical operators denoting addition, subtraction, multiplication, and division, your formulas can include relational and logical operators. Relational operators are those that compare two values to each other, like #10 = #20 or #30 > #40. Relational operators are often used in conditional statements introduced by an IF . . . THEN clause. Consider the following statement:

IF #30 > #20 THEN #40 = #20

This means "If the value in field 30 is found to be more than that of field 20, then make the value of field 40 the same as that in field 20." In an IF . . . THEN clause, if the condition in the IF statement is found to be true, the condition contained in the THEN clause is performed. You can amend such conditional statements by adding a second condition that will be performed if the IF statement is found to be false. You do this with an IF . . . THEN . . . ELSE statement (ELSE can be translated as "otherwise"). Consider the new meaning of the IF . . . THEN example shown above when it is amended with an ELSE clause as follows:

IF #30 > #20 THEN #40 = #20 ELSE #40 = #30

This means "If the value in field 30 is found to be greater than that in field 20, then make the value in field 40 equal to that of field 20; otherwise (if it is not found to be greater than 20) make the value in field 40 equal to that of field 30."

Logical operators (sometimes referred to as Boolean operators) are used in conditional statements when you need to join two conditions into a single statement. There are three logical operators: AND, OR, and NOT. Logical operators can be added to IF . . . THEN or IF . . . THEN . . . ELSE clauses. For instance, you could enter this condition:

IF #30 > #20 AND #10 = #20 THEN #40 = #20

In this statement, both conditions following the IF clause must be true in order for the value in field 40 to be made equal to that of field 20. If you replaced AND with OR in the statement, the change to the value of field 40 would be made if either condition following the IF clause were true. When you use NOT, you reverse the condition. Consider the meaning of this conditional statement:

IF NOT #30 > #20 THEN #40 = #20

It means the same thing as this condition:

IF #30 < = #20 THEN #40 = #20

(Later, when you automate your data entry form, you will come upon a situation in which you cannot simply reverse the condition and thereby avoid the use of the logical operator NOT.)

You can have multiple statements following an IF clause or an ELSE by using the special words BEGIN and END. For example:

IF #30 > #20 THEN BEGIN #1 = 3;  #4 = 0;  #5 = "N" END

This means that if the value in field 30 is greater than that in field 20, then Q&A will input 3 in field 1, 0 in field 4, and N in field 5. The BEGIN and END commands indicate that Q&A is to perform all three substitutions in the order they are entered whenever the condition field "30 is greater than 20" is true.

***CURSOR MOVEMENTS***    In addition to setting up conditions in which you change the values in fields or perform a particular calculation, you can specify cursor moves to particular fields in the form as the results of conditions. This allows you to effectively control which parts of the form are filled out under what conditions and in what order. You will be adding a lot of these cursor moves as results of conditions that you are going to define for the personnel form. These conditions will speed up entering each new record to the database and save you a great deal of time in the long run. Table 8.1 summarizes the cursor moves that you can specify and the commands you use when defining them.

**THE BUILT-IN LOOKUP TABLE** In addition to setting up formulas to be calculated or cursor jumps to be performed, you can also create lookup tables containing set values you want to enter in fields. You create the lookup table by using the Edit lookup table option on the Customize Menu. Figure 8.9 shows you the lookup table that you will create for the personnel database.

As you can see in this figure, the lookup table is organized in columns and rows. The first column in the table contains the heading Key, followed by column numbers 1 to 4. The Key column contains values that are matched against those contained in particular fields in the database. The numbered columns contain the values that will be returned and entered into other fields when a match to the corresponding key value is made.

*Table 8.1:* Summary of cursor-movement commands

| COMMAND | CURSOR MOVEMENT |
|---------|-----------------|
| GOTO # | Takes the cursor to the field specified by the number following the number symbol. For instance, GOTO #30 will take the cursor to the field designated as #30. |
| CNEXT | Takes the cursor to the next field in the form. |
| CPREV | Takes the cursor to the previous field in the form. |
| CHOME | Takes the cursor to the first field in the form. |
| CEND | Takes the cursor to the last field in the form. |
| PgDn | Takes the cursor to the first field on the next page of the form. |
| PgUp | Takes the cursor to the first field on the previous page of the form. |

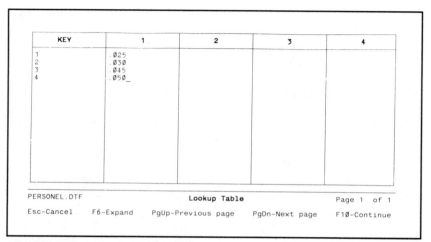

|  | KEY | 1 | 2 | 3 | 4 |
|---|---|---|---|---|---|
| 1 | | .025 | | | |
| 2 | | .030 | | | |
| 3 | | .045 | | | |
| 4 | | .050_ | | | |

PERSONEL.DTF                    Lookup Table                  Page 1  of 1

Esc-Cancel      F6-Expand     PgUp-Previous page    PgDn-Next page    F10-Continue

*Figure 8.9:* Commission rate lookup table

To make this clearer, consider the purpose of the lookup table shown in Figure 8.9. The Key column contains the four classifications for salespeople in the company. Column 1 contains the corresponding commission rate for each classification. This means that you can have the program look up the classification in the Class field that you enter in this table and then have it automatically enter the appropriate commission rate in the Rate field in the database.

To do this, you enter a formula using Q&A's special LOOKUP statement. In the LOOKUP statement for this table, you specify first the number of the Class field, then *1* for the number of the column containing the commission rates, and finally, the number of the Rate field where you want the value to be entered.

When you set up other LOOKUP statements for your own database files, you will always use this pattern:

1. First, specify the number of the field whose value Q&A is to use when locating matches in the Key column.

2. Then specify the number of the column in the table that contains the values you want Q&A to enter.

3. Finally, specify the number of the field where Q&A is to enter this value.

When you use the LOOKUP statement, you must place all three of these items in parentheses separated by commas, as shown below. This is the LOOKUP formula you will later enter in your form; it uses the lookup table shown in Figure 8.9:

LOOKUP(#110,1,#120)

The lookup table used by this formula is quite small. It consists of only four entries and uses only one column. You can create much larger and more sophisticated tables. The values in the Key column do not have to be numerical. You can also set up lookup tables with text in the Key column.

One very useful application for such a lookup table is to set up a shipping rate table. In it, you enter the abbreviations for the states into the Key column and the corresponding shipping rates in the numbered columns. You then use the LOOKUP statement to enter the correct shipping charge into its own field in an invoicing form. You can have it get the abbreviation of the state to be looked up from the State field in the Ship to address.

When you enter different tables in the Lookup Table form shown in Figure 8.9, you do not separate them from each other except by using unique key values in the Key column. Only the values entered in the Key column must be unique; there can be duplicate values in any of the four numbered columns. There are 64,000 bytes of information allowed in this Lookup Table form, which gives you plenty of room to create all kinds of lookup tables to be used in a particular database.

Go ahead and create this lookup table for your personnel database. Type **e** and press Return (or type **6**). A blank Lookup Table form will appear on your screen. Enter the values as shown in Figure 8.9. You can use the cursor arrow keys to move from column to column and from row to row in this form. Once you have finished adding these values, press F10 to save the table and return to the Customize Menu.

***EXTERNAL LOOKUP COMMANDS*** In Q&A you can look up information in the built-in Lookup Table (an *internal lookup*), or you can look up information in another Q&A database. This is called an *external lookup*, and the command used to perform this operation is written as XLOOKUP (as opposed to the LOOKUP statement described above). In all, there are eight Lookup commands available, as summarized in Table 8.2.

*Table 8.2:* Lookup commands in Q&A

|  | **STATEMENTS** | **FUNCTIONS** |
|---|---|---|
| Using built-in Lookup Table | LOOKUP<br>LOOKUPR | @LOOKUP<br>@LOOKUPR |
| Using another Q&A Database | XLOOKUP<br>XLOOKUPR | @XLOOKUP<br>@XLOOKUPR |

The Lookup commands fall into two categories: statements and functions. In general, they are referred to as a group of commands, but the way in which you enter a specific command makes it either a function or a statement. The difference between a statement and a function is the way the resulting value is placed in a field. A statement contains a parameter that tells Q&A into which field to place the retrieved value. A function, on the other hand, is already placed in the field where the value is to be entered.

In the XLOOKUP statement

```
#30:XLOOKUP("PERSONEL",#1,"SOCIAL SECURITY NO.",
"FIRST NAME",#2)
```

the last parameter, ``#2'', tells Q&A to place the value retrieved from the First Name field into field #2 on the current form. In the @XLOOKUP function

```
#30 = @XLOOKUP("PERSONEL",#1,"SOCIAL SECURITY NO.",
"FIRST NAME")
```

the value which is retrieved, the First Name, is already assigned (set equal to) the field #30.

The parameters (or arguments) that you enter as part of an XLOOKUP statement or function are the same as illustrated by the following @XLOOKUP function below:

```
@XLOOKUP(fn,pfk,xkf,lf )
```

where *fn* is the name of the file from which the function returns its data, *pfk* is the ID number of the field in the primary file (called the primary key field) that has an equivalent in the external file, *xkf* is name of the field in the external file that matches that of the primary key field, and *lf* is the name of the field in the external file whose values you want returned.

In the example above, the external file (that is, the one you want the data looked up in and returned from) is your personnel database designated by ''PERSONEL'' (note that the name of the database file must be enclosed in quotes when in the @XLOOKUP function, although you don't have to add the .DTF extension).

In the primary file (that is, the database to receive the data that is to be looked up), the Social Security field is given the field ID number #1, therefore #1 is entered as the next argument in the function that identifies the primary key field in the primary file. When this field is referred to in the external file, it is entered by name (enclosed in quotation marks) as ''SOCIAL SECURITY NO.''

Note that although these fields are referred to in different ways in the @XLOOKUP function (first by field number and then by field name), they represent a common field that occurs in both files. You *can't* use the XLOOKUP statement or function unless you set up the two database files whose information is to be related so that they both have a common field. It is by this common field that information from the external file can be brought into the primary file without having to reenter it. (Technically, the field common to the two files is called a *primary key* in the primary file and a *foreign key* in the external file.)

In the earlier @XLOOKUP example, the information to be copied from the external database (the personnel file) into the database that contains this function is the employee's last name. For this reason, the *lf* argument is entered as ''LAST NAME'' (notice that this field name must also be enclosed in quotation marks in the function). In essence, what happens when this @XLOOKUP function is executed is that Q&A looks up the social security number of the first form in the PERSONEL.DTF file and automatically enters the correct last name in the file that contains this function without your having to type it in.

Later on in this chapter, you will have ample opportunity to practice using the @XLOOKUP function when you create a new database for tracking the attendance of the employees in your personnel database.

***DETERMINING STATEMENT EXECUTION*** There is only one more thing that you have to keep in mind when using these procedures to automate data entry into your forms. That is when Q&A is to carry out the instructions that you have entered in a particular field. You have two choices: you can have the program execute the instructions contained in the field as soon as the cursor enters the field, or have the program execute them as the cursor leaves the field. You use the less-than symbol (<) to designate the former (coming into) and the greater-than symbol (>) to designate the latter (going out of).

Each calculation, condition, or cursor movement statement that you enter into a field must be prefaced with one of these two symbols. Q&A will not allow you to enter any of these statements without one or the other. Generally, you use the greater-than symbol when you want Q&A to allow you to enter data in a field before a calculation takes place or before the cursor jumps to a different field. You usually use the less-than symbol when you want Q&A to perform a calculation in the field the cursor is entering. In such a case, because the formula has already been defined, you want the result to be entered in the cell as soon as the cursor enters the field. Normally, you will also include a cursor-movement command after such a calculation, so that the cursor will move to the next field to be entered. You can string together separate statements in a single field as long as they are separated by semicolons. When to use each command will become much clearer as you define the statements to automate data entry in your sample database.

## *AUTOMATING YOUR PERSONNEL FORM*

To begin, select the Program form option by typing **p** and pressing Return (or by typing **5**) from the Customize Menu. A blank Program Spec form similar to the one shown in Figure 8.10 will appear on your screen. Before you begin entering the actual statements that will automate the data entry of the personnel form, you need to have a clear understanding of how data is presently entered manually and how you can streamline it.

Look at Page 1 of the form in Figure 8.10. Currently, data entry begins with the Social Security number in the first field and moves left to right across, then down each line, including every field on the

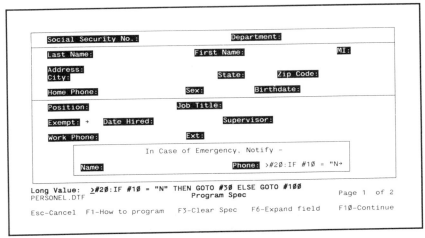

```
┌──────────────────────────────────────────────────────────────────┐
│  ┌──────────────────────────────────────────────────────────┐     │
│  │ Social Security No.:            Department:               │     │
│  │                                                           │     │
│  │ Last Name:            First Name:              MI:        │     │
│  │ Address:                                                  │     │
│  │ City:                      State:     Zip Code:           │     │
│  │                                                           │     │
│  │ Home Phone:        Sex:       Birthdate:                  │     │
│  │                                                           │     │
│  │ Position:          Job Title:                             │     │
│  │                                                           │     │
│  │ Exempt: →   Date Hired:          Supervisor:              │     │
│  │                                                           │     │
│  │ Work Phone:          Ext:                                 │     │
│  └───────────────────────────────────────────────────────┐  │     │
│          In Case of Emergency, Notify -                   │        │
│     ┌───────┐                     ┌────────┐                       │
│     │ Name: │                     │ Phone: │ >#20:IF #10 = "N→     │
│     └───────┘                     └────────┘                       │
│  ─────────────────────────────────────────────────────────────    │
│  Long Value:  >#20:IF #10 = "N" THEN GOTO #30 ELSE GOTO #100       │
│  PERSONEL.DTF                 Program Spec          Page 1  of 2   │
│                                                                    │
│  Esc-Cancel  F1-How to program   F3-Clear Spec  F6-Expand field  F10-Continue │
└──────────────────────────────────────────────────────────────────┘
```

*Figure 8.10:* Page 1 of the Program Spec

page. There is not much that can or should be automated here. Each field should be filled in, and the flow progresses very naturally (assuming that the form has been designed just like the paper form that supplies the data).

Now look at Page 2 of the form (Figure 8.11). Never are all of these fields to be filled in for a particular employee. He or she cannot have both exempt and nonexempt status. There are three groups of fields separated by boxes at the top of this page of the form. The first is for hourly, nonexempt employees. The second is for salespeople who are exempt and commissioned. The third is for exempt employees who are not in sales, though most of its fields apply to every person in the company (they all have a salary and receive performance reviews). The rest of the fields on this page are like those on the first page: they pertain to every employee despite the category (exempt or nonexempt) the employee falls into.

If the employee is nonexempt, all of the first group of fields that apply are to be filled out (starting with Hourly Rate and ending with OT Total), but the second group of fields (starting with Commission? and ending with Commission Total) are skipped entirely. All the rest of the fields that pertain to the employee in question are then to be filled in, more or less in their field order in the form.

If the employee is exempt, none of the first group of fields applies, and these fields are to be skipped. Data entry on the second page then

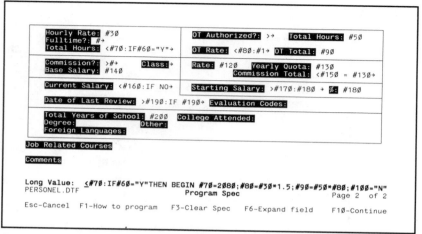

*Figure 8.11:* Page 2 of the Program Spec

begins with the Commission? field. If the employee does not receive a commission (that is, if the employee is not a salesperson), then the second group of fields do not apply, and the data entry operator can skip to the Current Salary field and continue on to all the rest of the fields that apply.

If the employee receives a commission, then all of the fields in the second group should be filled in. Data entry then starts in the third group with the Current Salary field. For a salesperson, the entry in this field does not represent a true salary figure. It is, in fact, an estimate of his or her earning potential recorded in this field for budgeting purposes. It will be actualized only if that salesperson makes quota every month for the entire year. Because of this, the starting salary and percent of increase fields are not filled in. Data entry then goes from the Current Salary field to the Date of Last Review field and continues on, including all of the remaining fields that apply.

The natural flow of data entry on this page (from left to right down each line) is not well suited to the various conditions under which certain fields are to be skipped. As you may have guessed, you will shortly automate this flow to save the data entry operator a great deal of time and energy.

Beyond streamlining the flow of data entry, you can also have Q&A calculate the data to be entered in many of the fields on this page. There is no need to rely on manual calculation. Nonexempt employees' salaries are based on their hourly rate times the total hours they work. If they are authorized for overtime, the total amount is based on their overtime rate times the total number of hours authorized. In fact, the overtime rate is calculated as one-and-a-half times the hourly rate (assuming that only time-and-a-half is paid, not double time).

For salespeople, their classification determines the commission rate. As indicated in the discussion of lookup tables, this can be automatically calculated by using the LOOKUP function. Once their commission rate has been determined, their commission can be totaled by multiplying the rate times the yearly quota figure. The current salary (the budget estimate, in this case) is calculated simply by adding the base salary figure to the commission total.

For nonexempt employees and for exempt employees who are not in sales, the percent of salary increase is determined by dividing the difference between their current and starting salaries by the current salary and multiplying the result by 100. In addition to streamlining the flow of data entry, you can easily have Q&A calculate all of these formulas as the form is being filled out.

Now you are ready to begin adding the necessary statements to accomplish these goals. Each step will be explained as you enter it. If you find yourself confused about what a particular statement does or why it is included, just go ahead and carefully enter it as indicated anyway. How everything fits and works together is probably best seen at the end when you test it out by seeing the effect on adding new records to the personnel database. Then, once you have seen how it works (and that it works!), you can return to this section and review any of the steps that are still a little unclear to you.

To begin, move the cursor to the Exempt field. This field must be expanded to hold three characters and must also be numbered—not because it will contain a condition or calculation, but because it will be referred to in a following statement. You will number your fields by 10s, so use the F6 key to expand the Exempt field, and enter

#10

After entering this field number (or any of the subsequent statements), you need to press Return to enter it in the field. If, as you go along, you notice that you have made a mistake in entering a previous field, move the cursor back to this field and edit it as you would any other Q&A form.

When the data entry operator finishes entering the phone number in the very last field on this page, you will want to direct the cursor to one of two areas on the second page. If the Exempt status in field #10 is Yes, the cursor should jump to the Commission? field. If it is No, then the cursor should go to the Hourly Rate field at the top of the second page. From Figure 8.10 you can see that the conditional statement to accomplish this will not fit entirely in the Phone field, so you will have to expand it to a long value by pressing F6. The Phone field will be #20.

Because this statement contains more than just the field number, you must begin it either with < (perform the statement as soon as the cursor enters the field) or > (perform it as soon as the cursor leaves the field). If you have Q&A perform the cursor jump as the cursor enters the Phone field, the data entry operator will never have a chance to enter the telephone number in it, so you must preface the field number with >.

When you are adding a calculation or conditional statement in a field, you separate the field number you are assigning that field from the text of the statement itself by using a colon.

Now enter the following into the Phone field:

>#20:IF #10 = "N" THEN GOTO #30 ELSE GOTO #100

(The GOTO statements refer to the numbers of the Hourly Rate and Commission? fields, respectively.) This means "Upon leaving this field (#20), evaluate the contents of the Exempt field (#10). If that field contains N (for No), take the cursor to the Hourly Rate field (#30); otherwise (meaning if it contains Yes) take the cursor to the Commission? field (#100)." Notice that you enclosed the N in a pair of quotation marks to tell Q&A that it represents the literal contents of this field and to avoid any possibility of the program's misunderstanding what it is to evaluate.

After pressing Return to enter this statement, press PgDn to move the cursor to the Hourly Rate field. Because this is the very first field of the second page, you did not really have to use the GOTO #30 statement. You could just as well have used CNEXT or PgDn in its place.

The hourly rate must be entered manually, so all that it requires is that you give it a field number (#30):

#30

The next field is OT Authorized?, which is also a logical field. Here you want Q&A to evaluate the entry that is made manually. If it contains No, then the Total Hours field doesn't need to be filled in, and the data entry operator should go directly to the Fulltime? field. Enter it as follows:

>#40:IF #40 = "N" THEN GOTO #60 ELSE CNEXT

This statement refers to its own entry. Upon leaving the field (after Y or N has been entered there), it evaluates its own contents. If No was entered, it skips to the Fulltime? field (#60). Otherwise, if Yes has been entered, data entry proceeds to the next field where the total hours are entered.

Total hours is a manual entry, so you need only give it a field number:

#50

The same is true of the Fulltime? field. The data entry operator must make a manual entry of Y or N here. All you have to enter here is the next field number:

#60

The next field, Total Hours, contains a multiple statement that is the most complex that you will enter. In fact, it is so long that it takes up the entire Long value line and you cannot add spaces between its parts to enhance its legibility (see the Long value prompt in Figure 8.11). When you have such a long statement, you cannot always successfully compress it as much as is done here. If it contains built-in functions like @DATE and @TIME, these must contain a trailing space after their entry. Otherwise Q&A cannot recognize them and will give you an error message when you try to enter them in the field. (Q&A will not allow you to enter a statement which it cannot process. It forces you to debug it before continuing.)

If your statement will not fit on the Long value line even with all unnecessary spaces removed, you will have to place it elsewhere in a longer field. We have two such fields on this page, those of the Job Related Courses and Comments. The limit to long value characters per field is 240. However, it is possible to produce conditions so long and complex that Q&A cannot handle them.

The statement in the Total Hours field is made up of five separate calculations. It totally automates the data entry for its own field and the OT Rate, OT Total, and Commission? fields. First, it evaluates the contents of the Fulltime? field. If it is Yes, then the number of hours entered into this field is 2080. It then calculates the overtime rate by multiplying the contents of the Hourly Rate field by 1.5. It also calculates the OT Total by multiplying the newly calculated OT Rate by the number entered in the Total Hours field. Finally, it enters N in the Commission? field and jumps the cursor to the Current Salary field. It does all of this as the cursor enters the field.

Enter this statement as follows (you do not need to enter spaces between the statements; the semicolon marks them):

```
<#70:IF #60 = "Y" THEN BEGIN #70 = 2080; #80 = #30*1.5;
#90 = #50*#80; #100 = "N" END; GOTO#160
```

This is an example of multiple statements that are performed based on one condition. All of these calculations and the cursor jump are accomplished only if the Fulltime? field contains Y. This means "If the Fulltime? field contains Yes, then Total Hours (#70) are 2080, so make the overtime rate (#80) equal to one-and-a-half times the hourly rate (#30), the overtime total amount (#90) equal to total hours (#50) allotted times the overtime rate (#80), and the entry in the Commission? field (#100) equal to No, and then move the cursor to the Current Salary field (#160)."

But what happens if the employee is not full time—that is, if an N is entered in the Fulltime? field? You can answer this by entering the following statement in the OT Rate field:

```
<#80:#100 = "N";GOTO #160
```

As soon as the cursor advances to this field after the number of hours has been entered manually and Return has been pressed, N is entered into the Commission? field and the cursor jumps to the Current Salary field just as it does when you enter a record for a full-time nonexempt employee. The only difference is that when Fulltime? is No, the data entry operator must be given a chance to manually enter the appropriate number of hours in the Total Hours field.

The next field, OT Total, only requires a field number, so enter it as

#90

Next, you need to enter the field number for the Commission? field (# 100). You also need to expand the field and set up a condition here that will evaluate the contents of the field after data entry. This is because if the Exempt field contains Y, then the cursor jumps right to this field. If the data entry operator is entering a record for an employee who is not in sales, there is no need to go through the rest of the fields that pertain only to salespeople. To take advantage of this, enter

>#100:IF #100 = "N" THEN GOTO #160

In the Class field, you enter the LOOKUP statement that will use the lookup table you created earlier. You have already seen this statement out of context. Now enter it as part of the entire condition in the Class field as follows:

>#110:LOOKUP(#110,1,#120);GOTO #130

This statement means "Upon leaving the field (that is, after the classification has been entered), evaluate the contents of the Class field (#110). Use the lookup table attached to this database and match this entry against those in the Key column. Once you have found a match, look in the first column of the table and return the value listed there to the Rate field (#120). After doing that, jump the cursor to the Yearly Quota field (#130)."

The next three fields—Rate, Yearly Quota, and Base Salary— only require field numbers. Enter them as

| | |
|---|---|
| Rate | #120 |
| Yearly Quota | #130 |
| Base Salary | #140 |

Next, you will want Q&A to calculate the commission total in the Commission Total field as soon as the cursor enters this field. It is equal to the Rate (#120) times the Yearly Quota (#130). While you're at it, you can have the program calculate and enter the sum of the Base Salary (#140) plus the Commission Total (#150) in the Current Salary field (#160). Because you do not have to fill out the Starting Salary and % fields for a salesperson, the cursor can then advance right to the Date of Last Review field (#190). Enter all three of these statements in the Commission Total field as follows:

<#150 = #130 * #120;#160 = #140 + #150;GOTO #190

Notice that the first statement for calculating the total commission is a little different from the others you have entered so far. Instead of following the field number with a colon to separate it from the formulas that come after, you can tell Q&A its field number and how to derive it in one statement. Notice also that the GOTO # statement is listed last. If you entered it before either of the two formulas, Q&A would advance straight to the Date of Last Review field without having had a chance to do the necessary calculating first.

The Current Salary field must be filled in manually if the employee is exempt and is not a salesperson. If the employee is a salesperson, this field will be automatically calculated by the formula in the previous statement.

What if the employee is nonexempt? You can get Q&A to calculate the salary by multiplying the hourly rate by the total number of hours (#30 * #70). To do this, you will have to have Q&A refer to the contents of the Hourly Rate field. If is empty, then the employee is exempt and the salary must be entered manually. If not, then the program will perform the necessary calculation. To set this up, you will use the NOT logical operator in the following condition:

<#160:IF NOT #30 = " " THEN #160 = #30 * #70

The logic of this NOT condition may be a little hard to follow. This means "If the Hourly Rate field (#30) is not empty (is NOT equal to a blank character denoted by a literal space), then the value of the Current Salary (#160) is equal to the product of the Hourly Rate (#30) times the Total Hours (#70)." You had to use the NOT condition because there simply is no other way to test this field for no entry. You cannot supply a literal between the quotes that would satisfy all the possible hourly rates which could be entered in this field.

The Starting Salary field must be entered manually. Once this has been done, you can have Q&A calculate the percentage of increase and move to the Date of Last Review field. Enter the formula as:

>#170:#180 = (#160 − #170)/#160 * 100;GOTO #190

Notice the use of parentheses to alter the natural order of calculation. The difference between the current and starting salaries must divided by the current salary. The only way to accomplish this is to add the parentheses around the subtraction. The result is multiplied by 100 because it is a percentage.

The % field requires only that you give its field number:

#180

Now, enter the last statement into the Date of Last Review field. It will evaluate the contents of this field. If the field is empty, meaning that the employee was hired so recently that he or she has not yet been reviewed, there is no need to advance to the Evaluation Codes field because it too will be blank. Enter this as:

>#190:IF #190 = " " THEN GOTO #200

Finally, finish your Program Spec by giving the Total Years of School field a number:

#200

All of the remaining fields must be filled in manually as they apply to each employee. Save the form now by pressing F10.

## *ADDING CUSTOM HELP MESSAGES*

Before leaving the Customize Menu to test out your automated form entry, you should now define help messages to guide the data entry operator when he or she tries to enter a value outside the restriction ranges you set up earlier. To do this, type **d** and press Return (or type **7**). Figure 8.12 shows you the Help Spec that then appears on your screen.

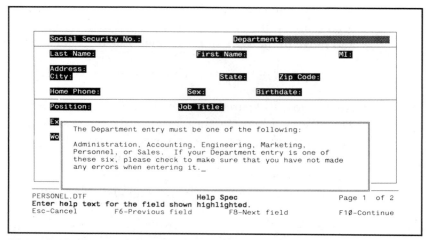

*Figure 8.12:* Help message for the Department field

The first custom help message that you should add is for the Department field. Press F8 to move the cursor highlight to this field and enter the message as it is shown in this figure. Your custom help messages can consist of six lines of text. The same editing features are available here as when filling out any specification form, and word wrap is in effect. Notice that the help message for this field not only states all of the permissible entries but also instructs the data entry operator to check for possible data entry errors. It is unlikely that he or she would try to enter a completely new department. Of course, if the company creates a new department, then the Restriction Spec and Help Spec will have to be modified.

After entering this message, press Return and then press F8 until you are in the Date Hired field. There, enter the following help message:

> The Date Hired must be a date later than or equal to Jan 25, 1968. Please check and retry your entry.

Then press Return and F8 until you advance the cursor highlight to the Hourly Rate field on the second page of the form. Enter this message there:

> The Hourly Rate must be a figure between 5 and 20. You need only enter numbers here like 9.5 for $9.50 or 12 for $12.00 an hour. Please check and retry your entry.

The next restricted field is the Total Hours field. Enter the following help message there:

> Total Hours cannot exceed 2080. For half-time employees, use the figure 1040. Please check and retry your entry.

In the Class field, enter this help message:

> The Classification for salespeople must be a whole number between 1 and 4. Please check and retry your entry.

Now go on and enter similar help messages in the rest of the currency fields. The first part of the message should tell the operator the permissible range of values. The following table gives you the range for each field:

| | |
|---|---|
| Yearly Quota | 0 and 800000 |
| Base Salary | 0 and 25000 |
| Current Salary | 0 and 125000 |
| Starting Salary | 0 and 125000 |

The last field that requires a help message is the Date of Last Review field. Remember that here you restricted the value to January 1, 1985 or earlier. If someone in the company has not had an evaluation since then, the Personnel department will want to find out why. Enter this last message to tell the data entry operator how to handle this situation:

> The Date of Last Review should be no earlier than Jan 1, 1985. If this is not the case, please make a special note and inform the Director of Personnel. Otherwise, check the date entered and retry your entry.

Press F10 to save your Help Spec and return to the Customize Menu. Before returning to the File Menu to add some test records, you will want to change the formatting of the % field. When you originally designed the personnel form, you formatted this field with three decimal places. You should use the first option on this menu to reset this value to two decimal places. Type **f** and press Return (or type **1**).

At the Format Spec, press Return until the cursor is located in the % field. Once there, change the format code from N4 to N2 and press F10 twice to save this change. When you are back at the Customize Menu, press Esc to Return to the File Menu. Notice that this marks an exception to the way Q&A usually works when you press Esc. Instead of taking you from the Customize Menu to the Design Menu, Q&A bypasses this menu entirely when it goes directly to the File Menu.

## *TESTING YOUR AUTOMATED DATA ENTRY FORM*

You have made many improvements that you will want to test out by adding sample records to the database. Choose the Add data option from the File Menu. Once you are in a blank form, enter the Social Security number as **455-02-7754** and press Return. In the Department field, make a deliberate mistake to test out your data restriction and see how the custom help message works. Type **Sale** and press Return in this field.

Figure 8.13 shows you the error message that you should receive. As you can see, it does not refer you to online help. It only asks you to verify your entry. It is your responsibility to instruct your data entry operators to press F1 for help whenever they are unsure how to proceed in a field.

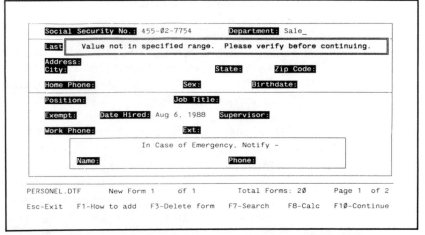

*Figure 8.13:* Error message returned for entry out of restricted range

Press F1 to get help. Figure 8.14 shows you how your custom help message for this field should look on your screen. In place of the standard help screen associated with the Add data option, your custom screen is accessed. If you had not added your own help message, Q&A's standard message would have been displayed. Press Esc, as you are instructed at the bottom of the help message box, and add an **s** to your entry.

Figure 8.15 shows you the rest of the first page of this new record for Mary Rose, a new salesperson. Notice that your form now displays the current date in the Date Hired field. Go ahead and change it to the date shown in this figure when you enter all of the data on this first page.

When you press Return to enter the emergency contact telephone number in the Phone field, the cursor should jump to the Commission? field. Figure 8.16 shows the data for the second page. Enter **y** in this field and press Return. In the Class field, enter **4** and press Return. When you do, the rate .0500 should be automatically entered in the Rate field and the cursor should jump to the Yearly Quota. Enter the figure **750000** here and press Return.

Make another deliberate error in the Base Salary field. Try entering a base of **30000** here. When you receive the error message, press F1 and check your help screen. Then press Esc, correct the entry so

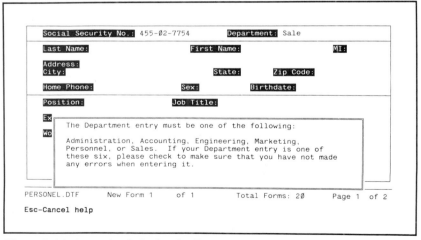

*Figure 8.14:* Accessing help for the Department field

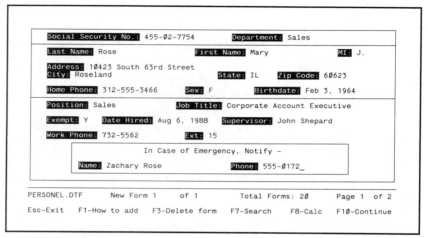

*Figure 8.15:* Page 1 of first test record

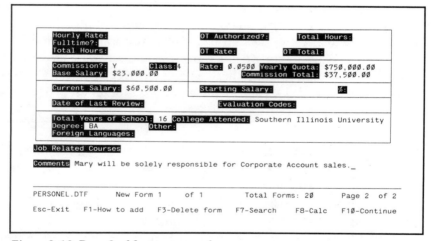

*Figure 8.16:* Page 2 of first test record

that it reads **23000**, and press Return. When you do, the Commission Total and Current Salary fields are automatically filled in and the cursor is advanced to the Date of Last Review field. Press Return here, because Mary Rose is a new employee. The cursor should jump to the Total Years of School field.

If your form did not behave as it should, press Esc, type **y**, and press Return, to abandon this record without saving it. Then return to the Customize Menu and use the Program form option. Check your formulas carefully against those listed previously. If your cursor behaved correctly but the formulas didn't work, check your calculations. If your cursor movements were erratic, check the field numbers you entered in the GOTO statements. Once you have tracked down and taken care of any errors, press F10 to save the Program Spec again. Then try to add this record again. Once all is working as it should, press F10 to save this form. Notice that it takes longer for the form to be saved to disk. This is the result of adding all of those speedy fields to the personnel database.

Now add a second test record, that of Thomas Mahler, a nonexempt employee. Figure 8.17 shows you how to enter the fields on the first page of his form. Once you have entered the number for the Phone field at the end of this page, the cursor should advance to the Hourly Rate field. Enter the first four fields of his form as shown in Figure 8.18. As soon as you type **y** and press Return for the Fulltime? field, Total Hours, OT Rate, OT Total, Commission?, and Current Salary are immediately filled in. When you enter the Starting Salary (in this case the same as the Current Salary), the % field is filled in and the cursor should advance to the Date of Last Review field. Press Return here, enter **12** for Total Years of School, and press Shift-F10 to save this form and return to the File Menu.

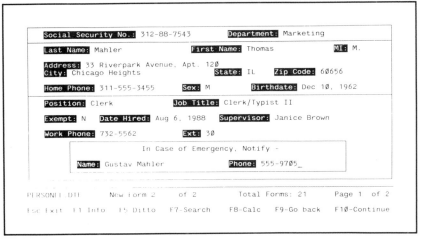

*Figure 8.17:* Page 1 of second test record

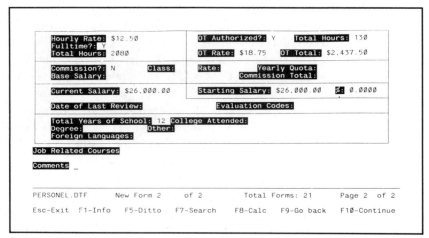

*Figure 8.18:* Page 2 of second test record

You should also add a record for your own employees to test out various conditions. Add a record for an exempt employee who is not in sales, a nonexempt employee who is not full time, and so forth. In this way you can be sure that the automated data entry form is working exactly as planned. You will have to do this same kind of testing when you automate your own database forms.

Be aware that Q&A has two modes, automatic and manual, for calculating formulas in fields. In automatic mode, the calculation is performed as the cursor leaves the field. You can change it to manual mode by pressing Shift-F8 and typing **m** (for *manual* ) when you begin updating or adding new forms to your database. In manual mode, calculations are only made when you press F8. You can do this right before leaving the updated form. You will probably prefer this method if you find that data entry is appreciably slowed because of recalculating each formula as you go from field to field. The program remains in the calculation mode you set until you change it again. To change the mode back to automatic, you press Shift-F8 and type **a**.

Any records that you have already entered manually in your database must be updated. For instance, in the personnel database, the percentage of salary increase will still remain blank for all of those records in which it applies. To update them, you must access each one individually. In automatic mode, you must then pass the cursor through this field. In manual mode, you merely press F8.

## USING THE XLOOKUP COMMANDS

The programming you have done thus far has been performed using a single file, your personnel database. However, in most applications, including personnel departments, you often need to have more than one database. Each database usually references a particular subject or activity. The personnel file you have created, for example, is the master file containing one record for each employee. Yet as the employees continue to work for your company they will sign up for benefit programs, take time off, participate in projects, etc. Each of these things is another type of record to maintain.

Sometimes, even though the activity requires a new type of record, much of the information—like the name and department—will be duplicated from your master personnel file. In Q&A, by using the XLOOKUP commands, you can easily retrieve this data and not have to re-enter it. To see how these commands work, you will create a new database called ATTEND.DTF. This database will be used by the department managers to record each employee's attendance. Specifically the database will track vacation, sick, personal time, etc. Each record will cover a particular pay period and track the amount of time absent. The accounting department can then reference this database to adjust the payroll correctly.

***DESIGNING A NEW FORM***   To create this file, choose File from the Main Menu. Select Design, then select Design a new file. When you see the blank screen, continue by designing the form exactly as is shown in Figure 8.19.

Notice that Date, Leave Code, Description, and # of Hours are column headers, not actual fields. The fields (where the data will be stored) are marked by the series of colons below each header. Q&A does not require a field label in order to design a valid holding place for the information you wish to enter. For this example you will create six fields below each column header by entering colons as shown in Figure 8.19. In practice, this may not be enough for tracking an entire pay period for a given employee, but this number can always be increased.

On the Format Spec screen, change each of the date fields to **D** (for Date) and each of the # of Hours fields to **N1** (for numeric with one decimal place). Change the Exempt format to **YU** (for logical field and uppercase) and add **U** (uppercase) to the T (text field) designation for the MI field, for all of the fields under the heading Leave

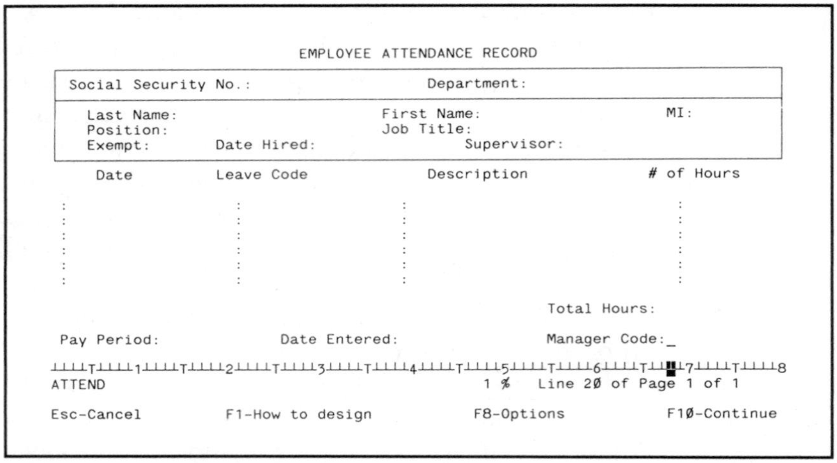

*Figure 8.19:* Form design for ATTEND database

Code, and for the Manager Code field. Press F10 to save these changes, and F10 again on the Global Format Options screen. You now have a complete form design for the attendance database.

***PROGRAMMING THE @XLOOKUP FUNCTION*** The next step in preparing your database is to program the form using the customize features. You will use the @XLOOKUP function to retrieve the employee's Department, Last Name, First Name, MI, Position, Job Title, Exempt, Date Hired and Supervisor. This will do two things to automate your attendance record database—speed up data entry and guarantee correct information (since it will be coming directly from the master record).

Choose Design on the File Menu and then select the Customize a file option. When you reach the Customize File Menu, press **p** for Program form. Make sure the database you have selected is the ATTEND data file. On the Program Spec, you will assign field ID numbers to each field to be used in a programming statement or calculation. Begin by numbering Social Security No., #1, and entering the @XLOOKUP functions into the appropriate fields as follows:

Department: <#5:#5 = @XLOOKUP("PERSONEL",#1,"SOCIAL SECURITY NO.","DEPARTMENT");GOTO #10

Last Name: <#10:#10 = @XLOOKUP("PERSONEL",#1,
"SOCIAL SECURITY NO.","LAST NAME");GOTO #20

First Name: <#20:#20 = @XLOOKUP("PERSONEL",#1,
"SOCIAL SECURITY NO.","FIRST NAME");GOTO #30

MI: <#30:#30 = @XLOOKUP("PERSONEL",#1,"SOCIAL
SECURITY     NO.","MI");GOTO #40

Position: <#40:#40 = @XLOOKUP("PERSONEL",#1,"SOCIAL
SECURITY NO.","POSITION");GOTO #50

Job Title: <#50:#50 = @XLOOKUP("PERSONEL",#1,"SOCIAL
SECURITY NO.","JOB TITLE");GOTO #60

Exempt: <#60:#60 = @XLOOKUP("PERSONEL",#1,"SOCIAL
SECURITY NO.","EXEMPT");GOTO #70

Date Hired: <#70:#70 = @XLOOKUP("PERSONEL",#1,
"SOCIAL SECURITY NO.","DATE HIRED");GOTO #80

Supervisor: <#80:#80 = @XLOOKUP("PERSONEL",#1,
"SOCIAL SECURITY NO.","SUPERVISOR");GOTO #90

None of the programming statements will fit into the space available for each field, so you must press F6 to display the "Long value:" prompt at the bottom of the screen. There, you can easily type in the entire statement for each field.

Before saving the Program Spec, let's take a moment to evaluate the first of these statements using the @XLOOKUP function and to understand how Q&A will interpret it. Move the cursor to your completed Department field and look at the Long value display at the bottom of the screen as shown in Figure 8.20.

Let's examine each part of this program statement. The execution symbol, <, tells Q&A to execute the statement when the cursor enters the field. The field ID number, #5:, is a unique number, which references the field within a formula. The assignment, #5 =, sets the field equal to whatever function or formula follows.

The @XLOOKUP function is next. Notice that it requires four pieces of information (or arguments), each of which are separated

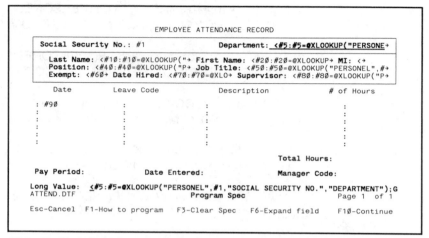

```
                         EMPLOYEE ATTENDANCE RECORD

    ┌──────────────────────────────────────────────────────────────────────┐
    │ Social Security No.: #1              Department: <#5:#5=@XLOOKUP("PERSONE→│
    ├──────────────────────────────────────────────────────────────────────┤
    │ Last Name: <#10:#10=@XLOOKUP("→ First Name: <#20:#20=@XLOOKUP→ MI: <→   │
    │ Position: <#40:#40=@XLOOKUP("P→ Job Title: <#50:#50=@XLOOKUP("PERSONEL",#→│
    │ Exempt: <#60→ Date Hired: <#70:#70=@XLO→ Supervisor: <#80:#80=@XLOOKUP("P→│
    └──────────────────────────────────────────────────────────────────────┘

        Date         Leave Code        Description          # of Hours

    : #90             :                 :                    :
    :                 :                 :                    :
    :                 :                 :                    :
    :                 :                 :                    :
    :                 :                 :                    :

                                               Total Hours:

    Pay Period:           Date Entered:          Manager Code:

    Long Value:  <#5:#5=@XLOOKUP("PERSONEL",#1,"SOCIAL SECURITY NO.","DEPARTMENT");G
    ATTEND.DTF                      Program Spec                   Page 1  of 1

    Esc-Cancel  F1-How to program   F3-Clear Spec   F6-Expand field    F10-Continue
```

*Figure 8.20:* Long Value display of Department field

from one another by commas, and all of which are enclosed in parentheses. Notice too, that there are no spaces between @XLOOKUP and its arguments. The first argument of the @XLOOKUP function, "PERSONEL", gives the name of the external file in quotes from which the function retrieves its data. The second argument of the @XLOOKUP function, #1, identifies the primary key field or ID# of the field in the current file which has a matching field in the external file. The third argument of the @XLOOKUP function, "SOCIAL SECURITY NO.", is the external key field or name of the field in the external file which matches the primary key field. The fourth argument of the @XLOOKUP function, "DEPART-MENT", is the lookup field or the name of the field in the external field whose values you are retrieving. Immediately following the @XLOOKUP function is the GOTO #10 command. This cursor navigation statement tells Q&A to advance to field #10 in the primary file.

The entire programming statement can be translated as follows: "Upon entering field #5 (department), execute the statement and assign the value that is returned by the function @XLOOKUP to the field itself (department). In the function @XLOOKUP—look in the database named PERSONEL—take the value that is in field # 1 of the current form and match it to the Social Security No. field in the PERSONEL database. When a match is found, retrieve the value from the Department field on that record. Then, advance to the field numbered 10 on the current form.''

After you complete the Program Spec for the above fields, press F10 to save it to disk. You will now be back on the Customize File Menu. Before you leave this menu, you need to select the Speed up searches option and make a slight change to the designation of the speedy field, Social Security No. Because this represents the key field in the PER-SONEL database that will be used to relate its data with that of the ATTEND database, you must mark it as a unique speedy field.

This prevents any duplicate Social Security numbers from being added to the index file arranged according to this number. This step is necessary because if there were two records with the same social security number, Q&A would not know which one to use when retrieving data from this database. When you mark the key field as **su**, if there are any records with duplicates in this field, only the first record will be added to the index.

1. Move the highlight bar to the Speed up searches option and press Return, or type **s** and press Return. The cursor will be located in the Social Security No. field under the *S* marking it as a speedy field.

2. Press the → once and type **u**. The designation for this field will now be SU (speedy unique).

3. Press F10 to save your change and return to the Customize Menu.

You must always designate the key field in the external file as unique, just as you did here. If you don't mark it as unique, Q&A will not be able to retrieve the information from the external database when you use the XLOOKUP statement or function.

It is often a good idea to stop and test your programming before spending the time to complete every field that will eventually need a program statement or function. This way you can easily ''debug'' your work without too much confusion. Go ahead and test the @XLOOKUP functions in your attendance database now.

***TESTING THE @XLOOKUP FUNCTION*** If you are still at the Customize Menu, press Esc to return to the File Menu. Choose Add data and type in ATTEND for the data file name. The first form to be completed will appear on the screen and the cursor should be in the Social Security No. field.

In order to test the programming you have completed to perform @XLOOKUP, you will need to enter some sample records and make sure that the data being retrieved from your personnel database is correct. You will also need to make sure that the right information is placed in the appropriate fields on the form.

1. Type **360-31-5633** into the Social Security No. field and press Return.

If your programming is correct, the information (name, address, etc.) for Jessica Freels should automatically be placed into the form and your cursor should end up in the first Date field, as shown in Figure 8.21. If your cursor is not in the Date field, or the information was not retrieved, check to see if there is an error message at the bottom of the screen. One simple mistake is incorrectly typing the key value that is necessary to match the record in the external database. Try typing an incorrect Social Security number and notice the message displayed at the bottom of the screen by Q&A.

2. Press F3 to delete the record for Jessica Freels. Type **y** for *Yes* to confirm the deletion, and your cursor will return to the beginning of the form. Now type in the number **111-11-1111** and press Return.

You should see the message ''The lookup file does not have the key value: 111-11-1111'' as shown in Figure 8.22. Whenever you receive this type of message, check to make sure you have correctly typed the key value.

3. Type **672-01-9942** over the incorrect number and press Return. The information for Ronald Graydon should be filled into each field on the form. Press Esc and type **y** to exit without saving the form.

You can enter data into the attendance database later, after you have completed all of the necessary programming for the entire record.

```
                         EMPLOYEE ATTENDANCE RECORD
 Social Security No.: 360-31-5633        Department: Accounting

   Last Name: Freels                    First Name: Jessica           MI: B.
   Position: Accountant                 Job Title: Senior Accountant II
   Exempt: Y       Date Hired: Jun 1, 1985     Supervisor: Janice Brown
     Date          Leave Code              Description              # of Hours
 :____________   :                      :                          :
 :               :                      :                          :
 :               :                      :                          :
 :               :                      :                          :
 :               :                      :                          :

                                                    Total Hours:

 Pay Period:                Date Entered: Aug 6, 1988   Manager Code:

 ATTEND.DTF         New Form 1     of 1         Total Forms: 0        Page 1  of 1
 Esc-Exit    F1-How to add    F3-Delete form    F7-Search     F8-Calc    F10-Continue
```

*Figure 8.21:* @XLOOKUP of Jessica Freels information

```
                         EMPLOYEE ATTENDANCE RECORD
 Social Security No.: 111 11-1111        Department:

   Last Name:                           First Name:                   MI:
   Position:                            Job Title:
   Exempt:         Date Hired:                 Supervisor:
     Date          Leave Code              Description              # of Hours
 :____________   :                      :                          :
 :               :                      :                          :
 :               :                      :                          :
 :               :                      :                          :
 :               :                      :                          :

                                                    Total Hours:

 Pay Period:                Date Entered: Aug 6, 1988   Manager Code:

 ATTEND.DTF         New Form 1     of 1         Total Forms: 0        Page 1  of 1
 The lookup file does not have the key value: 111-11-1111
 Esc-Exit    F1-How to add    F3-Delete form    F7-Search     F8-Calc    F10-Continue
```

*Figure 8.22:* Error message during an external lookup

***EDITING THE LOOKUP TABLE*** In order to easily enter the attendance activity that has occurred for the employees, you can use the built-in Lookup Table to store the codes and corresponding descriptions for each type of personnel leave possible.

Remember that programming your database to use the Lookup Table is a two-step process. First you must edit the Lookup Table and fill the table with information. Then you must program the form so that Q&A knows how to access the table correctly.

Choose Design from the File Menu, and then choose Customize a file. Move the highlighted bar down until E - Edit Lookup Table is highlighted and press Return. Enter the following information into the Lookup Table for your attendance database:

| Key | Column 1 |
|-----|----------|
| A | Accident at Work |
| AH | Accident at Home |
| D | Disciplinary Leave |
| FD | Family Death |
| FI | Family Illness |
| H | Holiday |
| I | Illness |
| J | Jury Duty |
| X | Unknown Cause |
| L | Leave of Absence |
| LO | Layoff |
| P | Personal Reasons |
| V | Vacation |

If the description of the leave code is too large for the column, press F6 for Long Value and enter the entire description. Q&A will indicate that there is additional Long Value data by replacing the last visible character with a right arrow. Your completed Lookup Table should look like the one shown in Figure 8.23.

**COMPLETING THE PROGRAM SPEC**    The final step in programming the attendance database is to complete the Program Spec. You need to add the programming statements to perform the lookups from the built-in Lookup Table, and also the @SUM function to correctly total the number of hours for each pay period.

```
        KEY              1              2         3         4

     A            Accident at Wo→
     AH           Accident at Ho→
     D            Disciplinary L→
     FD           Family Death
     FI           Family Illness
     H            Holiday
     I            Illness
     J            Jury Duty
     X            Unknown Cause
     L            Leave of Absen→
     LO           Layoff
     P            Personal Reaso→
     V            Vacation



Long Value: Accident at Work
ATTEND.DTF                           Lookup Table              Page 1  of 1

Esc-Cancel     F6-Expand     PgUp-Previous page     PgDn-Next page     F1Ø-Continue
```

*Figure 8.23:* Lookup Table for the ATTEND database

To do this, choose P - Program form from the Customize Menu. You already have #90 entered as the field ID for the first date field. Complete the column of date fields by entering the following IF...THEN statements for each field:

```
: >#91:IF #91 = " " THEN GOTO #300
: >#92:IF #92 = " " THEN GOTO #300
: >#93:IF #93 = " " THEN GOTO #300
: >#94:IF #94 = " " THEN GOTO #300
: >#95:IF #95 = " " THEN GOTO #300
```

These statements test to see whether the date field is empty when the cursor leaves the field; if it is, the cursor is forwarded to field #300. In this case, field #300 will be the Pay Period field. After you finish entering each of the above statements, move the cursor to the Pay Period field and enter the field ID #300.

Next, you will program each Leave Code field to lookup the leave code in the Lookup Table and bring back the corresponding description, placing it in the Description field. Enter the following statements in the Leave Code column:

```
: >#100:LOOKUP(#100,1,#160);GOTO #220
: >#110:LOOKUP(#110,1,#170);GOTO #230
: >#120:LOOKUP(#120,1,#180);GOTO #240
```

```
: >#130:LOOKUP(#130,1,#190);GOTO #250
: >#140:LOOKUP(#140,1,#200);GOTO #260
: >#150:LOOKUP(#150,1,#210);GOTO #270
```

In order for these statements to perform properly, you still need to give each field that is being referenced its own field ID #. Number the description fields with the field ID #s 160, 170, 180, 190, 200, and 210 from top to bottom in the column. Then number the # of Hours fields with the field ID #s 220, 230, 240, 250, 260, and 270 from top to bottom.

Finally, place your cursor in the Total Hours field and enter the following @SUM function to automatically total each of the hours fields:

#280 = @SUM(#220..#270)

When you have completed all of the above programming and your cursor is positioned in the Total Hours field, your Program Spec should match that of Figure 8.24.

Press F10 to save the spec, and press Esc to return to the File Menu. Here select A - Add data and press return. When the form appears on the screen, press Shift-F8. Type **a** for *Automatic Calc*. This will set your attendance database to automatic calculation mode so that any programming such as the @SUM function in the Total Hours field will be performed whenever data is entered that changes

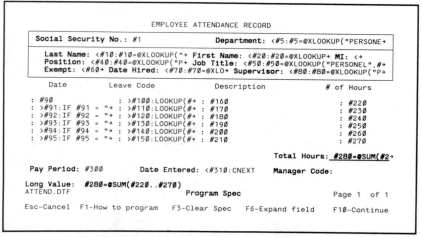

*Figure 8.24:* Completed Program Spec for the ATTEND database

the total. Manual calculation would require you to press the F8 calc key in order to perform the calculation. In the other programming statements you have entered, you used the cursor navigation symbols < and > to tell Q&A to execute the statements either upon entering or exiting the fields. Once a mode has been set for a database, it will remain set unless you change it again.

Now, you are ready to enter a complete record into the attendance database which will use all of the programming you have completed.

1. Type **521-30-7892** into the Social Security No. field and press Return. The information for James Thornfield should be filled into the Department, Last Name, First Name, Address, MI, Position, Job Title, Exempt, Date Hired, and Supervisor fields and your cursor should be sitting in the first Date field.

2. Type in the date of the first leave occurrence as **7-4-88** and press Return.

3. Now type in the appropriate Leave Code, which is **H**, and press Return. You will see the description field completed with the word ''Holiday'' and your cursor will advance to the # of Hours field.

4. Here, type **8** and press Return. Notice how Q&A reformatted the value to read 8.0 since you had previously defined it as a field type of N1.

Now your cursor is sitting in the next Date field, ready for the next Leave record to be entered. So far the total number of hours is 8.0 and it has already been calculated for you, since you have set the Attendance file to auto calc mode.

5. Now enter another leave record for James Thornfield. Complete the date as **7-12-88**, the leave code as **I**, and the number of hours as **6**. The Total Hours field should now read 14.0.

6. Since you are finished with James Thornfield's Leave information, press Return on the third Date field. The programming you entered moves the cursor to the Pay Period field instead of making you press Return through each field. Type **7-1 to 7-15** in the Pay Period field and press Enter.

7. Enter your initials in the Manager Code field, and press Shift
F10 to save the form.

You have now successfully programmed your database to use both
external and internal lookups, IF...THEN statements, and the @SUM
function.

***REPORTS USING @XLOOKUP***   It is often necessary to produce
a report that requires information which is stored in more than one
database. Q&A gives you the ability to do this by using the
@XLOOKUP function in the derived column of your report. This
allows you to display a column of data in the report for your database
which is actually stored in another file. This can be especially useful
when producing reports based on ad hoc requests. The individuals
making such requests do not know that certain information is stored
in another file. All they know is that for their purpose it is necessary to
see everything in one report.

The PERSONEL.DTF file and the ATTEND.DTF file are
examples of databases which store related information. You have
already used the @XLOOKUP function in the Program Spec for
the attendance database. Now, you need to produce a report showing
the total number of paid leave hours by department. The employee
salary needs to be included in the report from the PERSONEL.DTF
file so that the personnel department can correctly estimate the percentage of overhead.

Before creating the report, choose File from the Main Menu, then
select Add data and enter the data shown in Table 8.3. Remember
that your programming will be executed, automatically filling in
most of the information necessary. When you type in the Social Security No., Q&A will fill in several fields. Then you type in the Date
and the Leave Code, and Q&A will complete the description. After
you enter the # of Hours and have entered all the leave activity for
that employee, you simply enter the pay period and press F10 to save
the form.

Now, you are ready to create your report using two database files.

1. Choose Report from the Main Menu and then choose
Design/Redesign a report. Enter **attend** as the datafile name.

*Table 8.3:* Data for the ATTEND database

| SOCIAL SECURITY NO. | DATE | LEAVE CODE | # OF HOURS | PAY PERIOD |
|---|---|---|---|---|
| 306-31-5633 | 7-4-88 | H | 8 | 7-1 to 7-15 |
|  | 7-5-88 | V | 8 |  |
| 501-11-4523 | 7-1-88 | V | 8 | 7-1 to 7-15 |
|  | 7-4-88 | H | 8 |  |
| 456-71-0034 | 7-4-88 | H | 8 | 7-1 to 7-15 |
|  | 7-7-88 | I | 4 |  |
| 586-03-3187 | 7-4-88 | H | 8 | 7-1 to 7-15 |
|  | 7-11-88 | P | 5 |  |
| 606-33-0915 | 7-4-88 | H | 8 | 7-1 to 7-15 |
| 892-44-5591 | 7-4-88 | H | 8 | 7-1 to 7-15 |
| 225-88-3421 | 7-4-88 | H | 8 | 7-1 to 7-15 |
|  | 7-13-88 | J | 8 |  |
|  | 7-14-88 | J | 8 |  |
|  | 7-15-88 | J | 8 |  |
| 448-35-9622 | 7-4-88 | H | 8 | 7-1 to 7-15 |
| 901-77-3351 | 7-4-88 | H | 8 | 7-1 to 7-15 |
|  | 7-5-88 | X | 8 |  |

2. When Q&A prompts you for the name of the Report Spec, type **attendance report** and press Return.

3. The first screen will be the Retrieve Spec. Leave this screen blank so that your report will include all of the records in the Attend file. Press F10 to save the Retrieve Spec.

4. The next screen will be the Column/Sort Spec. Here, you will choose which fields to include in the report, as well as the sort order and calculations you want performed. For this report, you will be using the Social Security No. field and the key value for matching the corresponding record in the PERSONEL.DTF file. Because it's not necessary to actually

print the Social Security No. as a column in the report, type **1,i** into the field to designate the first field to be used in the report as an invisible column.

5. To use the Department field as the first column of your report and the primary sort, type **2,as** in the Department field.

6. Next, enter **3** in the Last Name field and **4** in the First Name field for the next two columns.

7. Move the cursor to the Total Hours field and enter **5,st,t** as the spec. This will subtotal the number of hours each time the department changes, and will also produce a grand total.

Your Column/Sort Spec should now look like the spec shown in Figure 8.25.

8. To complete the report, you need to add a Derived Column. The derived column will perform the @XLOOKUP function and create a salary column which retrieves the information from the PERSONEL.DTF file.

9. Press F8 from the Column/Sort Spec screen. Enter Salary as the heading for the column.

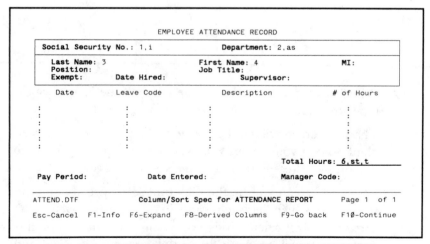

**Figure 8.25:** Column/Sort Spec for the ATTENDANCE REPORT

10. Enter the following statement as the formula for the derived column:

> @XLOOKUP("PERSONEL",#1,"SOCIAL SECURITY NO.","CURRENT SALARY")

11. Type the number **4** as the Column Spec for the derived column. This will position the salary information as the third printed column of the report.

Check the Derived Column screen to make sure it matches the screen shown in Figure 8.26. If so, press F10 to save the Column/ Sort spec and Derived Columns screen, and advance to the Print Options.

12. Change the Print To selection on the Print Options screen to highlight SCREEN, and press F10 to save the Report Spec.

13. Press **y** for *Yes* when asked if you wish to print the report now.

The report will print to your screen as shown in Figures 8.27 and 8.28. Notice how the salary information has been incorporated into the report as though it was actually stored within the attendance database. The data has been virtually joined to form a more useful and informative report.

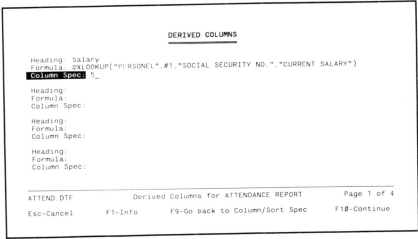

**Figure 8.26:** Derived Columns for ATTENDANCE REPORT

As you continue to use your Q&A databases, you will need to implement various maintenance procedures to preserve the integrity of your data and database files. Q&A File provides three commands for this: Copy, Remove, and Mass Update. You have already been introduced to the Copy command when preparing the batch processing macro in Chapter 7. With it, you can copy just the structure (design) of your database or you can copy the records in it. The Remove command allows you to delete records that are no longer needed, thus keeping the database as compact as possible. The Mass Update command allows you to make changes to many records in the database at one time, thus saving you from having to update each record individually.

## USING THE COPY COMMAND

The Copy Menu contains three options; D for Copy design only, I for Copy design with IA info, and S for Copy selected forms. You used the Copy design and Copy selected forms options when you created a temporary data entry file and then copied the records you added to it to the permanent personnel database. The standard procedure is first to copy the design of a database using Copy design and then to copy the data into it using Copy selected forms, just as you did with the personnel database.

| Department | Last Name | First Name | Salary | Total Hours |
|---|---|---|---|---|
| Accounting | Thornfield | James | 25500.00 | 14.0 |
| | Freels | Jessica | 35500.00 | 16.0 |
| Total: | | | | 30.0 |
| Administration | Brown | Janice | 39800.00 | 8.0 |
| Total: | | | | 8.0 |
| Engineering | Peterson | Monica | 31500.00 | 32.0 |
| | Bennett | Kelly | 25750.00 | 16.0 |
| Total: | | | | 48.0 |
| Marketing | Johnson | Jeffry | 18980.00 | 12.0 |
| | Burke | Lisa | 47500.00 | 13.0 |
| Total: | | | | 25.0 |

ATTEND.DTF

Esc-Cancel    F2-Reprint    ( →←↑↓ )-Scroll    Shift F9-Redesign    F10-Continue

*Figure 8.27:* First half of the ATTENDANCE REPORT

```
       Department        Last Name       First Name       Salary       Total Hours
       ---------------   -----------      -----------      --------     -----------
       Personnel         Raye             Jennifer         36800.00            16.0
                                                                        -----------
       Total:                                                                  16.0

       Sales             Rush             Del              37000.00             8.0
                         Thompson         Ann              27600.00             8.0
                                                                        -----------
       Total:                                                                  16.0

       ===============   ==========       ==========       ========    ===========
       Total:                                                                 143.0




   ATTEND.DTF
   ****************************** END OF REPORT *********************************
   Esc-Cancel    F2-Reprint   ( →←↑↓ )-Scroll    Shift F9-Redesign   F10-Continue
```

*Figure 8.28:* Second half of the ATTENDANCE REPORT

Creating a temporary data entry database is only one of the possible applications for the Copy command. You can also use it to save time in creating a second database that shares some of the same fields and data as one you have already set up. For instance, you might need to create other database files for the Personnel department. One might keep track of employee vacation time, as you have done with the attendance database, while another might keep track of benefit programs. Each of these new databases will contain some of the same fields as the personnel database, such as Social Security number, Name, and Department. Rather than reenter all of this information manually, you can use one of the Copy Design options and then the Copy selected forms option to have them entered automatically.

Unfortunately, you cannot simply direct Q&A to copy particular fields from one file to another. You must use the Retrieve Spec to restrict which records are copied, and a Merge Spec to correctly position the information in the right fields. To do this you must go through the following four-step process:

1. Copy the design to the new database file.

2. Redesign the form for the new database file, eliminating all unnecessary fields, modifying the layout of those fields that you want to retain, and adding new fields.

3. Copy all of the records to the new database, selecting which data you would like in the new fields. Data for fields that no longer exist will be discarded.

4. Manually enter the data for all of the new fields by using the Search/Update option.

To illustrate how this can work, you will create a new database file called BENEFITS.DTF using the Social Security No., Department, Last Name, MI, and First Name fields and the data already entered in them in your PERSONEL.DTF file.

To begin this operation, choose the Copy option from the File Menu and give PERSONEL as the file to copy from. Choose the Copy option from this menu and give BENEFITS as the file to copy to. Once the program has finished copying the design (it will take a few minutes) to your new BENEFITS.DTF, press Esc to return to the File Menu.

Next, choose the Design option on the File Menu. You will use the Redesign option on this menu. Be sure that you change the filename to BENEFITS when you are prompted for the database to use. Figure 8.29 shows you the arrangement of the five fields that you will

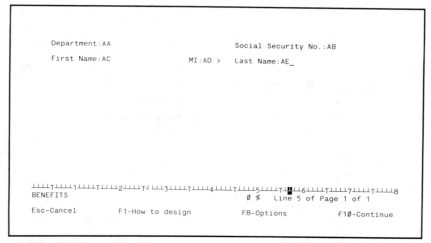

*Figure 8.29:* Modifying the design copied from the personnel database

keep in the new database. All of the rest will be deleted from this form. You can delete, one line at a time, all of the rows below those containing the Last Name, First Name, and MI fields by pressing Shift-F4. You should also delete the lines bordering the remaining fields. Just be careful that you do not delete the field names and their codes as well.

As you can see in Figure 8.29, you will change the arrangement of the five remaining fields for the new database. You can do this without having to retype the field names and codes if you use the Move function (Shift-F5). Once you have got the fields arranged as they are in this figure, press F10 to save the design. You will make no change to the field type or global format of this form, so you can press F10 at these screens also.

At the File Menu, choose the Copy option again. First, you will be prompted for the file that is the source of the copy. This is your PERSONEL.DTF file. Replace the suggested BENEFITS file with this file name and press Return. This time, use the Copy selected forms option on the Copy menu. Give the name of the file to copy to as BENEFITS and press Return again.

At the Retrieve Spec, press F8 because you want to sort the records in the personnel database before copying them to the new file. Fill in the Sort Spec as you normally would, sorting alphabetically by department, then by last name, and finally, by first name. Then return to the Retrieve Spec and press F10 to use all of the forms.

The Merge Spec will then be displayed on your screen. Figure 8.30 shows you how to fill it out. The numbers in the first five fields correspond to their new order in the benefits database. Because you have rearranged the order of the Department and Social Security Number fields as well as the order of the parts of the employee's name, you must give them these numbers. If you did not, Q&A would copy the department names into the Social Security Number field (and vice versa). Once you have placed these numbers in the Merge Spec, press F10 to have the records copied.

Because you have eliminated all but these five common fields, all the data in all the other fields is discarded during the copy. As the copy process takes place, you will see each record displayed in the personnel database and each new record that is created in the benefits database. When this has been completed, choose the Search/Update option from the File Menu, using BENEFITS as the file. You will then receive the error message shown in Figure 8.31, indicating that

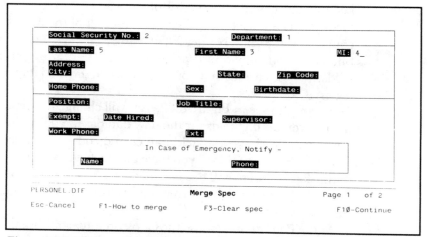

*Figure 8.30:* Filling out the Merge Spec for copying the records

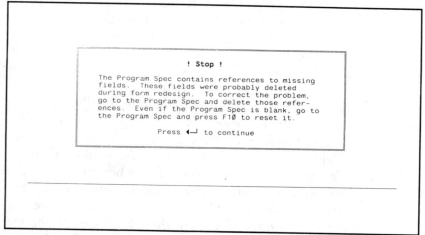

*Figure 8.31:* Program Spec warning message

the Program Spec (automatically copied to the benefits file as part of the Copy design option) refers to fields that are now missing.

To get into the benefits database, you must delete those references. Press Return as indicated in the message box and then choose the Design option from the File Menu. Then choose Customize a file from the Design Menu and select VACATION as the file. Then select Program form from the Customize File Menu. Once you are in the Program Spec, press F3 to clear it and then F10 to save it. You can now get into your new benefits database by using the Search/Update option on the File Menu. At the Retrieve Spec, press F10. You should see displayed the first record of your new database, that of Jessica Freels (shown in Figure 8.32).

At this point, you could go on and add all of the new fields specific to this benefits database using the Redesign option. Once you have designed the database as you want it, you would then use the Search/Update option to add all of the necessary data to these new fields.

## DELETING RECORDS IN THE DATABASE

You delete unneeded records from your database files by using the Remove option on the File Menu. As you have seen, you can purge a database of all records by pressing F10 at the Retrieve Spec that you fill out as part of the removal process. As is true with all applications for the Retrieve Spec, you can also enter specific criteria for finding the records you need to delete. Be aware that unlike some other database programs, in Q&A there is no way to undelete the records that you process with the Remove option. Once they are deleted, they are gone for good. To guard against a loss of data, always make a backup copy of the database before you use the Remove option.

Before actually doing the deletions, Q&A will display a message box indicating how many records meet your criteria for removal and

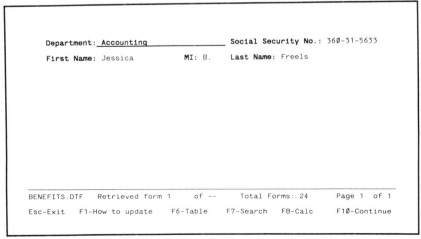

*Figure 8.32:* First record in the new BENEFITS database

asking for your confirmation to go ahead and actually delete them. You can cancel the entire operation from this screen if you wish. You can also continue but specify that you wish to preview each record before deletion. If you choose this option, you press F3 to delete the record displayed on your screen and F10 to retain it. While this process is much more time-consuming than having Q&A go ahead and perform a mass deletion, it may be well worth your time to go through the preview process, especially when you are still getting used to setting up search criteria.

## MAKING MASS UPDATES TO THE DATABASE

While using the Search/Update option to make changes to your database is fine when you only need to modify a few records, using the Mass Update option is much more efficient when you need to make global changes to the records. For instance, if you make a policy decision that affects the entire database, you will want it reflected in all of the records. This might be, for instance, a change in a benefit program whereby each employee will receive a dollar-for-dollar match on his or her contribution to the 401K plan. To change the contribution rate field in your benefits database, you would use the Mass Update option to change it in every form in the database.

Mass Update works a lot like the Copy and Remove options. You first select the records to be affected by filling out a Retrieve Spec. If you want to update all of the records in the database, you press F10. The next screen you see is called the Update Spec. There you specify the update to be made. It can be a new value (as in the contribution rate example) or a calculation (like an across-the-board raise of 5% for every employee). If you are using a calculation, you define it just as you would in the Program Spec. You give the field a number (prefaced by #) and then enter the formula indicating how the new value is to be calculated. In the case of the raise, you would give the Current Salary field a number (say #10) and then define the formula in this field as

$$\#10 = \#10 * 1.05$$

After saving the Retrieve and Update Specs with F10, you can preview the records to be affected, just as you can when deleting records with the Remove option. As when making mass deletions, you should make a backup copy of the entire database before making any wide-ranging changes to your database.

# USING Q&A WITH OTHER SOFTWARE

You will undoubtedly have occasion to use data files created by other software programs with Q&A. Most often, you will probably want to import data into Q&A File so as to avoid having to reenter the data. However, you may also find that you need to export your Q&A database so that it can be used in other application software. These kinds of functions are generally handled by the Import data and Export data options on the Utilities Menu (shown in Figure 8.33). You access this menu from the Main Menu, where it is the fifth option.

Q&A provides options that can directly import some of the various file formats favored by different application software programs. It will read pfs:File, IBM Filing Assistant, Lotus 1-2-3 or Symphony, DIF (used by spreadsheet programs like VisiCalc and SuperCalc), and dBase II/III file formats. If the file you wish to import into Q&A is not one of these, you can import it as either a standard or fixed ASCII file.

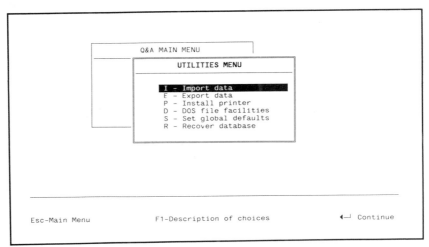

*Figure 8.33:* The Utilities Menu

The ASCII (American Standard Code for Information Interchange, pronounced *ASKey*) code provides a standard format for storing data that can be read by all microcomputer application programs. It provides a kind of universal translation medium through which different types of software can communicate. It is not used internally by software programs for saving their own data because it is not as compact as other storage formats. The way to tell if you have an ASCII file is to use the DOS TYPE command that prints the contents of a file on your screen. If you can read all of the text and data as though you had printed a Q&A file to the screen, then the file has been saved as an ASCII file.

Q&A offers two type of ASCII formats—standard and fixed. In the standard ASCII format, each data item is separated by some punctuation (usually a comma) and each record is separated by a carriage return. In addition, all text items (those that have spaces, like an address) are surrounded with quotation marks. This separation of fields and records makes this file a *delimited file*. Fixed ASCII, on the other hand, contains no delimitation. Each field starts at a fixed position or column in the file and therefore every record can be read by Q&A in exactly the same way. This format of ASCII is most often found on mainframe computers and can be important if the source for the data you wish to import has come from this kind of environment.

When you are exporting a Q&A data file to be used with some other software program, you have five choices for translating your file: you can save it as a DIF file (Data Interchange Format file, used by most major spreadsheet programs), standard or fixed ASCII (which can be used by all other types of programs), and dBASE II or III.

## IMPORTING DATA FILES IN Q&A FILE

Figure 8.34 shows you the options on the Import Menu attached to the Utilities Menu you looked at earlier. When you import data from pfs:File, IBM Filing Assistant, or dBASE II/III, you do not have to have an existing Q&A database file designed into which to copy their data. On the other hand, when you use any of the other three options—Lotus 1-2-3, DIF, or ASCII—you are required to have an existing database file ready; such imports act like a special Copy function that adds new records to the prepared database during the conversion.

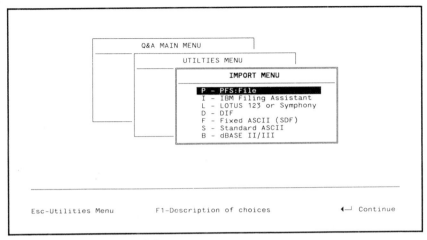

```
                    Q&A MAIN MENU
                       UTILITIES MENU
                            IMPORT MENU
                     P - PFS:File
                     I - IBM Filing Assistant
                     L - LOTUS 123 or Symphony
                     D - DIF
                     F - Fixed ASCII (SDF)
                     S - Standard ASCII
                     B - dBASE II/III



      ─────────────────────────────────────────────────────

      Esc-Utilities Menu      F1-Description of choices       ◄─┘ Continue
```

*Figure 8.34:* The Import Menu

***PFS:FILE AND IBM FILING ASSISTANT*** Because of the similarity between Q&A data files and those created by pfs:File and the IBM Filing Assistant, new Q&A databases can be created directly during the conversion. There is no need to first design a new database file unless you wish to. Once the conversion has taken place and all of the data has been copied over, you can modify the design of these new databases just as you would with any Q&A data file. Q&A will also convert any Report or Print Specifications that you have attached to the database.

Both these types of database files contain only Text type fields. Once you have converted the files to Q&A, you can modify them and add more specific field types like Date, Money, Numeric, and so forth. You can also format them as you do any other Q&A file: you can convert entries to uppercase, specify decimal places, and so on.

A pfs:File or IBM Filing Assistant file can present problems for Q&A during conversion if your files contain fields that consist of multiple-line entries or if your files contain attachment fields. Data in multiple-line fields will be truncated if the entry does not fit on a single line in the new Q&A database, and attachment fields will be completely discarded. To avoid this, you must redesign the entry form before the conversion so that the corresponding Q&A database fields contain sufficient space to accommodate the data. The following step-by-step procedure, showing how to import either of these two types of data files, tells you how to do this:

1. Choose the appropriate option from the Import Menu. Type either **p** for pfs:File or **i** for IBM Filing Assistant and press Return.

2. Enter the file name of the file to be imported into Q&A.

3. Enter a file name for your new Q&A database (it can be the same).

4. When Q&A displays the Format Spec, make any changes to the field type and its format and then press F10.

5. If the file you wish to convert contains multiple-line or attachment fields, press Esc when Q&A displays the Format Spec screen. Then choose the Redesign option from the Design Menu. Use the file name that you gave for the new Q&A database. Enlarge all of the multiple-line fields so that they contain enough lines to accommodate their counterparts in the other file, and terminate the last line of the field with >. For attachment fields, press PgDn to start a new page for the form. Place < in the upper left corner and > at the end of the last line on this page. Save your design; then go through the first four steps as outlined above and the next step below.

6. If during redesign you changed the order of any of the fields in the new Q&A database, use the Merge Spec screen that next appears to let Q&A know how to copy the data. Enter numbers in each field in the blank form corresponding to their position in the pfs or IBM Assistant file; then press F10. If you have not made any changes, press F10 at the Merge Spec screen without entering any numbers. Q&A will then copy all of the data into your new Q&A database.

*LOTUS 1-2-3*  When you import Lotus 1-2-3 files into Q&A databases, you must first create a new database that contains corresponding fields for every column of data in the Lotus worksheet. Each row in the worksheet will become a record in the new database. If the worksheet you wish to convert contains dates, numbers, or currency, you should assign these field types in the new Q&A file. You should also format these fields as you want them. Q&A will disregard any format that you have assigned in Lotus with the Range Format command, and all formulas will be converted to static values during conversion.

Once you have designed the Q&A database, use the Lotus 1-2-3 option on the Import Menu. You will be asked to designate the range containing the data to be copied. It can consist of the cell addresses or a range name. In either case, be sure that the range contains only data and does not include column headings (field names, if this is a Lotus database). If the worksheet contains only data, you may designate the entire worksheet as the range of cells. Your Lotus worksheet can carry the file extension .WKS or .WK1. Q&A will work with worksheets created with Lotus 1-2-3 Release 1A or Release 2.

Figure 8.35 shows you a small orders worksheet created as a Lotus database. A Q&A database was designed with one field for each of the eight columns shown here. The third column containing the order date was made a Date field and the last four fields were made Numeric fields in the new database. The other three fields were all designated as Text fields.

After giving the name of the Lotus worksheet file (ORDER-686.WKS) and the name of the Q&A database created for it (ORDERS.DTF), the Define Range screen shown in Figure 8.36

```
A1: [W13] 'Melodic Music Center Orders                          READY

              A          B        C        D      E    F        G       H
     1   Melodic Music Center Orders
     2       08-Aug-88
     3
     4   LNAME      FNAME    DATE      PART #  QTY    PRICE DISCOUNT ORDER AMT
     5   Holtzman   Andrew   08-Aug-88 FP110   13    10.50   6.00%    128.31
     6   Adams      Brian    09-Aug-88 SP115    1    19.95   0.00%     19.95
     7   Shorenstein William 09-Aug-88 HP124    3   199.95   2.00%    587.85
     8   Harrison   Sharon   11-Aug-88 FP120    1    22.50   0.00%     22.50
     9   Miafuni    Jessica  15-Aug-88 FP125    6 1,550.00   3.00% 9,021.00
    10   Riverra    Jose     15-Aug-88 FP110    2   500.00   0.00% 1,000.00
    11   Forrest    George   16-Aug-88 HP125    6    22.95   3.00%    133.57
    12   Jameson    Scott    17-Aug-88 HP126    1   150.00   0.00%    150.00
    13
    14
    15
    16
    17
    18
    19
    20
         01-Sep-88   03:45 PM
```

*Figure 8.35:* Lotus worksheet to be imported into Q&A

was displayed. (When telling Q&A which files to use, you do not have to enter either the .WKS or the .DTF extension as part of the file name.) As you can see in this figure, the range was given as A5 to H12. Notice in Figure 8.36 that this range includes only the data to be converted, not the field names or title of the worksheet.

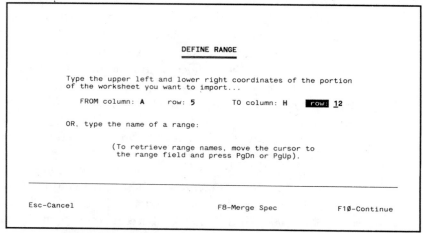

*Figure 8.36:* The Define Range menu

Because the order of the columns in the worksheet was modified when their corresponding fields were laid out in the new database, the Merge Spec was then used by pressing F8. Figure 8.37 shows you how it was filled out. In the Q&A database, the order date will appear first in the form. Because this is the third column in the Lotus database, the number 3 was entered here. The order of the first name was also reversed, so 2 was entered for the first name (in the second column in the worksheet) and 1 was entered for the last name. All of the other fields are in the same order as in the worksheet.

After the Merge Spec was filled out and F10 was pressed, Q&A copied all the data in the ORDER686 worksheet into the new ORDERS database. Figure 8.38 shows you the first record in the resulting database.

**DIF FILES**   Q&A will also read DIF files into its databases. This file format is used by spreadsheets like VisiCalc and SuperCalc. To save a VisiCalc spreadsheet in DIF format, you use the /S# command

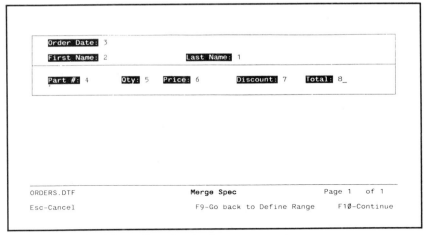

*Figure 8.37:* The Merge Spec for the Lotus conversion

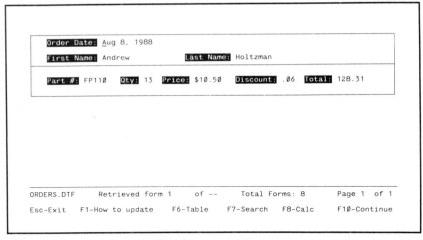

*Figure 8.38:* The first record in the new database

and the Save option. To save a SuperCalc spreadsheet in DIF format, you use the SuperData Interchange utility and its SuperCalc to SuperData Interchange option.

***STANDARD AND FIXED ASCII*** To import most software program files into Q&A, you can choose either Standard or Fixed ASCII as the format. This requires, of course, that the other software program can export to an ASCII file. Once you have created this file in either Standard ASCII (fields are delimited and records separated with carriage returns) or Fixed ASCII (fields are placed in a fixed position on each record and records are separated by a carriage return), you can easily import the file into Q&A.

You must create a Q&A database file containing corresponding fields for all of those fields in the database that you wish to convert. If the file is stored in the Standard ASCII format, Q&A will prompt you with the ASCII Options screen shown in Figure 8.39. Here you can specify whether or not the file contains quotes around strings of text (like an address field), and which field delimiter was used. The possible field delimiters include: Return, Semicolon, Comma, Space. The most common ASCII format produced uses quotes around text strings and the comma as the delimiter, and these are the default options in Q&A.

Each item is read into the fields in your Q&A database in the same order in which it appears on each line of the file. If you have rearranged your fields in the Q&A form so that this order must be modified, be sure and use the Merge Spec to let Q&A know where to put each data item.

To import a Fixed ASCII file into Q&A, you must use the Merge Spec to indicate the column number in which each data item begins, as well as its length. Q&A will prompt you automatically with the

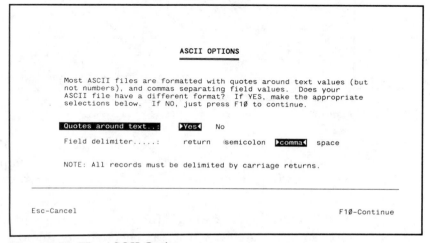

*Figure 8.39:* The ASCII Options menu

Merge Spec screen, as shown in Figure 8.40. In each field to which you want data to be imported, you type the column number and length of the value's location in the ASCII file. For example, if you wanted the Last Name imported and it began in column 10 and was 25 characters in length, you would type **10,25** in the Last Name field.

***DBASE II AND DBASE III*** Q&A will also create any dBASE II or dBASE III form design for you during an import of these database fields. If you want to design your own new Q&A database file format, you can, but this is not necessary.

When using the direct to Q&A procedure (letting Q&A create the design for you), you will be prompted with a Format Spec screen in which you can add the proper information type to each field—such as numeric, date, text, etc. Next you will receive the Merge Spec. Again, if you wish to eliminate some fields or change the order in which the fields are imported, you should complete the Merge Spec. Any dBASE II/III fields not referenced will be ignored, and any fields not filled in on the spec will remain empty.

Two limitations exist when you are importing dBASE II/III files. Q&A can import no more than 21 lines from a Memo field, and any numbers with more than seven decimal places will be truncated.

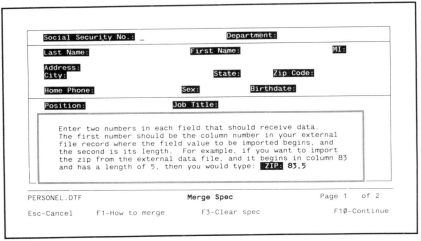

*Figure 8.40:* Fixed ASCII Import Merge Spec

## *EXPORTING DATA FILES FROM Q&A FILE*

When you need to send data from one of your Q&A databases to another software program, your file format choices are ASCII, DIF, or dBASE II/III. If you are exporting your file for use in a Lotus 1-2-3, VisiCalc, or SuperCalc worksheet, use the DIF option. You can then use the file translation utilities of those programs to convert the data contained in the resulting DIF file into a spreadsheet file. In Lotus, you use the DIF option from its Translate Menu. In VisiCalc, you use the /S# command and the Load option. In SuperCalc, you use the SuperData Interchange utility and its SuperData Interchange to SuperCalc option.

In all other cases, except for dBASE files, use one of the ASCII options on the Export Menu. During the translation process, you will see the ASCII Options Menu shown in Figure 8.39, just as you do when importing. Before choosing a format, you should check the documentation of the program that will use the file and see what format it prefers.

## *SUMMARY*

This chapter has introduced a variety of techniques that you can apply to your own work with Q&A. You saw the many ways in which you can refine your Q&A data entry forms to speed up data entry and to cut down on costly errors. You learned how to set up initial values, restrict ranges of permissible values, set up formulas that calculate values in fields, use lookup tables for data entry, and add your own help messages to guide the operator. In addition, you designed an application that used multiple files with the external lookup commands to give you control over data entry.

Then you learned techniques for maintaining your databases as they grow in size. You saw how Q&A's speedy fields (indexes) can help reduce delays in searching the database, and you looked at the trade-offs involved with their use. You examined ways to use the Copy function to eliminate redundant data entry and to reduce the work required to streamline the creation of new database files. After that, you examined routine maintenance operations, including methods of removing unnecessary records and making mass updates to the file.

Finally, you looked at techniques for using Q&A with other software programs. You learned how to share data between Q&A and other database or spreadsheet programs. You learned how to import data from these programs—eliminating the need for manual reentry—and how to export data to them so as to make better use of their specific capabilities. You will undoubtedly find all of these techniques and applications helpful as you continue using this versatile program to take care of your business needs.

9

# USING Q&A
## ON A
# NETWORK

# Fast Track

**To run Q&A Version 3.0 on a DOS network system,**                    **454**

you need to have a local area network that supports DOS 3.1 or higher with a minimum of 640K. To use Q&A from the network server, each user's computer must also have at least 484K of free memory.

**To set your network ID,**                    **455**

select the Utilities option from the Main Menu by typing **u** and pressing Return (or by typing **5**), and then choose the Set global defaults option by typing **s** and pressing Return (or by typing **5**). Use the ↓ to highlight the heading Network ID and type in your name and work phone number. Press F10 to exit this screen.

**To prevent a database on the network server from being shared**                    **457**

by other users on the network, select the Declare sharing mode option (**d** ↵ or **2**) on the Access Menu and select the Disallow option. To get to the Access Menu, select the File option from the Main Menu (**f** ↵ or **1**), then the Design File option (**d** ↵ or **1**), followed by the Customize a file option (**c** ↵ or **3**) and, finally, the Assign access rights option (**a** ↵ or **9**).

**To run Q&A on a network,**                    **457**

you need to purchase the Q&A Network Pack in addition to a copy of the regular Q&A software. Each Network Pack allows you to add three Q&A users.

**To set your personal path,**

type **QA -P<Drivename:Pathname>** at the DOS prompt where <Drivename:Pathname> is the drive and directory path used to store your files.

**To add a password to a database,**

select the File option from the Main Menu by typing **f** and pressing Return (or by typing **1**), and then choose the Design File option by typing **d** and pressing Return (or by typing **1**). Next, select the Customize a file option by typing **c** and pressing Return (or by typing **3**), and select the Assign access rights option by typing **a** and pressing Return (or by typing **9**). Press Return again to get to the Access Control Screen. Enter your user ID and your password. Then set your permissions and press Shift-F10 to return to the Access Menu.

**To change the password assigned to your database,**

select one of the File options and enter the name of the database file. When you are asked for your user ID and password, press F8. Then enter your user ID, the current password, and the new password you want to assign to the database file.

## ADVANTAGES OF USING Q&A ON A MULTI-USER SYSTEM

The primary advantage of using Q&A on a multi-user system like a Local Area Network (often referred to as a LAN) is that it enables several users to share the same database information. For instance, one person can be adding new records to a database, while another can be searching and updating information on an existing record, and yet another can be printing, all from the same file. A second important advantage of using Q&A on a multi-user system is that it allows several users to share the same software program (code). This means that although only one copy of the software is actually installed, more than one person at a time can access it. To run Q&A on a Local Area Network as a multi-user system requires the purchasing of another add-on product called the Network Pack, which changes the basic characteristic of the software from single-user to multi-user.

In this chapter we will discuss both of these advantages to using Q&A on a networked multi-user system. In addition, you will learn how to set your personal path—which specifies the location of your preference files (those that contain information on the default settings you have set up for Q&A)—and how to assign passwords to your database files which restrict access to them.

### SHARING A Q&A DATABASE

When you use Q&A on a network, more than one person can access a database at the same time. A network is made up of two or more computers that are physically cabled to each other and/or to a central processor or file server. A network also includes special software that keeps track of which computer is doing what and when. Q&A can run on any DOS-compatible network which uses PC-DOS or MS-DOS 3.1 or higher and does not itself require more than 140K of RAM. Note that total memory of the network server must be a minimum of 640K.

**RECORD-LOCKING**   When you share a Q&A database on a network, the first person to use a particular record has both read and write privileges. This means that he or she can view the data and can change it as well. The second user to retrieve the same record will only be able to view that form (read only). A message displayed at the bottom of the screen tells the second user that this form is being edited by someone else.

Certain functions in Q&A require that no one else use the database when they are in use. Such functions are called *locked file functions*. They usually affect the underlying structure of the database. Other functions do not lock the file but can be used by only one person at a time. For example, only one person at a time can Design/Redesign a report. A second person who wanted to design a report would have to wait until the first person was done.

Printing a report, in contrast, is a multi-user function. Several people can be printing reports at the same time. Table 9.1 shows a list of functions in Q&A and whether they are locked file, single-user, or multi-user functions.

With many users changing or adding information at the same time, you might wonder exactly which data is used if someone prints a report, performs a mail merge, etc., while updating is in progress. Before Q&A prints, it takes a snapshot look at the data; it prints out the forms the way they were at the moment the print job was started.

**SETTING THE NETWORK ID**   When you set a network ID, you are enabling Q&A to identify the current editor of the form for the next person trying to access that form. To set your network ID, choose Utilities from the Main Menu, then choose Set global defaults. At the bottom of the Set Default Directories screen you will see

Network ID....:  Network ID not set

To set your network ID, press the ↓ to move the highlight to Network ID.... and then type in your name.

The network ID that you enter here is not the same as your username (the name you use to log on to the network). Q&A's network ID simply informs other users that you are using the database. If you want, you can add your phone extension to your network ID. This will help other users contact you if they need the form you are editing.

*Table 9.1:* Locked file and Shared file functions.

| Functions that lock the file. (All other people must be out of the database.) | | |
|---|---|---|
| **IN FILE** | **IN IA** | **IN UTILITIES** |
| Redesign | Teach | Recover Database |
| Customize | Mass Update | DOS functions on DTF |
| Mass Update | | |
| Remove Forms | | |

| Functions used by one person at a time. (Other people can be using other functions.) | |
|---|---|
| **IN FILE** | **IN REPORT** |
| Design Print Spec | Design Report |
| Assign Passwords | |

| Functions that are multi-user. (Many people can use the same function at the same time.) | | |
|---|---|---|
| **IN FILE** | **IN REPORT** | **IN IA** |
| Search/update | Report Print | Search/update |
| Add Data | | Add Data |
| Form Printing | | Report Print |
| Copy Design | | |
| Copy Forms | | |

*Table 9.1:* Locked file and Shared file functions  (continued)

| IN WRITE | IN UTILITIES |
|----------|--------------|
| Mail Merge | Import Data<br>Export Data |

***DECLARE SHARING MODE***   Q&A will automatically check to see whether a database is stored on a network file server. If the database is on the server, Q&A will allow concurrent sharing. If the database is not on the server, Q&A will not allow sharing. Sometimes you may want to override this by storing a database on the server without allowing it to be shared. The Declare Sharing Mode lets you tell Q&A whether or not this database should be shared. Figure 9.1 shows the Access Menu from which you select Declare Sharing Mode. You can Allow sharing (multi-user), Disallow sharing (single-user), or choose Automatic (Q&A will decide).

## USING THE NETWORK PACK

To be able to put one copy of the software on the file server and have many users running Q&A, you must purchase another Symantec product from your computer dealer. This is called the Network Pack. The Network Pack allows you to add three more users to one copy of Q&A Version 3.0. The Network Pack does not work with older versions of Q&A or Q&A Write.

Using one copy of the software with the Network Pack saves you valuable space on the server's hard disk. It is also less costly than buying a separate copy of Q&A for each person on the network. When the Network Pack is installed, the Main Menu displays the current number of users out of the total number permitted under your license.

When the number of current users matches the number permitted under your license, no one else can get into Q&A. However, as soon as one user exits Q&A from the Main Menu, a new user may access the program. Note that if a user doesn't use the Exit option from the

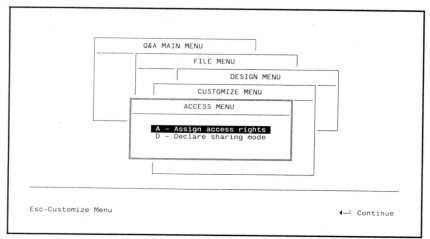

*Figure 9.1:* The Access Menu

Main Menu but rather reboots the computer or simply turns it off, his or her exit from Q&A will not be reflected in the current user count. For this reason, users of Q&A on a network should be instructed to exit properly from the program.

***INSTALLING Q&A ON A NETWORK***   To install Q&A on your network, you first need to copy all of the disks from your single-user version of the program into the Q&A network directory that you create. This procedure is no different from the installation procedure described in detail in Chapter 1.

After installing Q&A on the network directory, one person can use Q&A. To increase the number of users who can access the program, follow the steps outlined below:

1. Place the Network Upgrade Disk into drive A of the network server.

2. Type **A:** and press Return.

3. Type **adduser** and press Return.

4. When the program prompts you, enter the drive and path to the Q&A network directory. For example, if you copied

Q&A on the network drive E:, you would enter

**E:\QA**

and press Return. The program will then copy Q&A's serial number to the Network Upgrade Disk and the Network Upgrade Disk's serial number to the network copy. Put the Network Upgrade Disk in a safe place. You'll need it again only if you ever have to reinstall the Network Pack.

Note that after you have used the Network Upgrade Disk with the copy of Q&A Version 3.0 on the network, you can't use it with any other copy of Q&A (because of the exchange of serial numbers). Also, once you have followed this procedure to upgrade Q&A from single- to multi-user, you can no longer copy it or use it on one of the hard disks on the computers which are connected to the network.

***SETTING YOUR PERSONAL PATH*** Q&A contains files specified for a particular user—such as personal dictionaries, choice of printers, page defaults, editing options, and so forth. These files can be stored in your own subdirectory so that other people's files will not overwrite them. To do this you must establish a personal path for each user. After installing the Network Pack, you can set your personal path by starting Q&A with the following command:

**QA  -P<Drivename:Pathname>**

The -P command tells Q&A that what follows is a personal path. *Drivename* is the letter of the drive, and *Pathname* is the subdirectory used to store your files. Note that you must not add a space between -P and <Drivename:Pathname>.

This personal path can easily point to your own hard disk, thus freeing up network server disk space. For example, if you used a directory named QAGH on the C: drive of your computer, you would enter

**QA  -PC:\QAGH**

and press Return to start Q&A and set your personal path to C:\QAGH.

To make it easier for users to start Q&A on a network, the system adminstrator can create a startup batch file that is stored in a public directory. Typically, such a startup batch file would contain the following commands:

```
E:
CD\QA
QA %1 -PC:\
```

This sample batch file assumes that Q&A is stored in E:\QA on the network server. It makes drive E: current and the directory E:\QA the default. Then, it gives the Q&A startup command and pauses. The %1 variable allows the user to type a command indicating the location (that is, name) of his or her personal directory. In creating a similar startup batch file for your own system, you would substitute the correct drive letter and directory name. You can also add more than one variable, if you wish the user to be able to enter more than one command from DOS after starting Q&A.

***USING THE SHARE COMMAND***   Some networks require that you run the DOS SHARE command in order for the network to support the record-locking calls in Q&A. IBM PC-Net and Microsoft MS-Net both require the use of this command, while Novell and 3Com networks do not. You should check the manual for your particular network software to see if yours requires the use of SHARE.

## PASSWORDS

Q&A also allows you to set passwords to restrict access and privileges of individual databases. It's important to understand that passwords are not limited to use with networks. You can assign a password to any Q&A database whether or not it is being shared via network. However, data security is an important issue in a network environment, so a discussion of password protection is appropriate at this point.

A password can:

1.  Keep an unauthorized person out of the database completely.

2. Limit a user to reading the data only.

3. Allow reading (viewing) and writing (updating) of the data.

4. Establish the identity of the system administrator of the database.

It can also:

5. Allow/disallow a user to redesign reports.

6. Allow/disallow a user to redesign the form.

Q&A will automatically prompt you for your username and password the first time you access a database that is password-protected. Your username and password remain in memory until you exit Q&A.

## *SETTING PASSWORDS FOR PERSONNEL DATABASE*

Your sample database PERSONEL.DTF contains sensitive information about your employees. The following example will take you through password-protecting this database. As the system administrator, you will have access to the PERSONEL.DTF file. One other person, Director of Personnel Jennifer Raye, will be allowed access to this information.

To establish passwords for the personnel database, follow these steps:

1. Start Q&A, press the ↓ key to highlight the File option on the Main Menu, and press Return. Press Return again to choose Design file.

2. Use the ↓ to highlight Customize a file, and press Return. Type **personel** for the Datafile name and press Return.

3. Press the ↓ key until the last option, Assign access rights, is highlighted, and press Return. Press Return again to get to the Access Control screen.

Refer back to Figure 9.1 to see the Access Menu. Figure 9.2 shows

```
                          ACCESS CONTROL

                    User ID:  _
              Initial Password:  PASSWORD
    Make the selections below to indicate what rights this person has:
    Administrative rights?...:   ▶Yes◀   No
    Change form design?......:   ▶Yes◀   No
    Change report design?....:   ▶Yes◀   No
    Data access..............:   ▶Read & Write◀   Read only
    _____
    PERSONEL.DTF          Access Control Form 1      of 1
    Esc-Cancel   F3-Del  Ctrl F6-Add user   F9-Prev   F10-Next   Shift F10-Continue
```

*Figure 9.2:* Access Control Form

the Access Control screen. This is where you, as the system administrator, complete an access form for anyone who has the right to use
the database.

The User ID is the name you will use when entering this database.
This does not need to be the same name as your network ID or your
network username.

4.  Enter your name on the User ID line.

5.  Leave the password set to "password," all the rights to Yes,
    and data access to Read & Write.

If the first person entered does not have administrative rights, then
no one else's password can be entered. Figure 9.3 shows how your
form should look; your initial password will be "Password."

6.  After you enter your form, press F10 to continue to the next
    form.

The next person who can use the PERSONEL.DTF database is
Jennifer Raye.

7.  To keep typing to a minimum, enter **JRaye**, then set her ini-
    tial password to **JRaye** as well.

Figure 9.4 shows the form for JRaye. She will be able to read and write data and change or create new reports, but will not be able to change the design or have administrative rights.

Only two people will be allowed to use the Personnel database. Other databases may have hundreds of people who receive access with varying levels of protection. The limit to the number of usernames you can assign to a database is 1000. If access is needed by

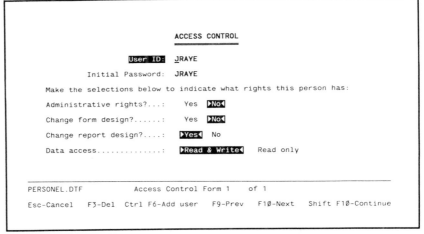

*Figure 9.3:* Your Access Control Form

*Figure 9.4:* Jennifer Raye's Access Control Form

more than 1000 people, you can assign a generic username and password (such as USER) and tell many people to type User as their name and password. (Remind them not to change the password, as others are using it also.)

8.  Press Shift-F10 to return to the Access Menu.

9.  Press Esc until you have returned to the Main Menu.

10. Select the Exit option by typing **x**.

11. Restart Q&A by typing **qa** at the DOS prompt.

12. Press the ↓ key to highlight the File option on the Main Menu, and press Return.

13. Select the Add data option by typing **a** and pressing Return.

14. When you are prompted for your user ID and password, type your name and press Return.

15. Type **password** for the password, and press Return.

Notice that when you enter your password, Q&A doesn't display the letters you type on the screen. That way, no one else can see your password as you enter it.

If you enter your password incorrectly, you will receive the error message

> **Not a valid user ID/password for this operation. Enter one or Esc to cancel.**

16. Press Esc to leave the first form.

17. Press Esc until you are at the Main Menu and then select the Exit option by typing **x**.

From now on, you must be able to enter your user ID and password or Jennifer Raye's user ID and password in order to have access to your PERSONEL.DTF file.

**CHANGING YOUR PASSWORD**   You can change your password whenever Q&A asks for your user ID and password by pressing F8 before you enter your user ID and the current password. When you press F8, the prompt will change and Q&A will then ask you to enter your user ID and your old password as well as the new password you want to use.

Be sure to remember your password. Only the system administrator can give you a new password if you forget. Q&A prompts you for your ID and password the first time you use a database that has passwords assigned. As long as you don't exit Q&A or turn off the computer, Q&A will remember who you are. If you want to leave your computer but don't want to exit Q&A, you can clear the current user ID from memory by pressing Shift-F6 at the Main Menu.

## *SUMMARY*

Sharing information in a multi-user environment gives you many advantages.

- All users can search, update, and print from the most current information.

- Disk storage can be saved by having only one copy of the database and/or Q&A on the network server.

- Each user's changes for the day can be saved in a single backup of the database (providing that you make backups nightly).

Additionally, using the Symantec Network Pack is less costly than buying separate copies of Q&A for each workstation. A Network Pack also saves disk space, as all workstations are accessing the same copy of the Q&A software. Each individual's setup files for macros, default directories, alternate programs, etc., can be stored in separate subdirectories—making it seem as though everyone has his or her own copy of the software.

Passwords can be assigned to any database, shared or not, to protect the design of the information. Passwords have several levels of protection including Read only, Read and Write, Change form design, and Change report design.

# APPENDIX A

# DATA FOR THE PERSONNEL DATABASE

The following contains all the data you need to input in your sample database called PERSONEL.DTF. It begins with the information for screen Page 1 of 1 in your database in order from Form 1 to Form 20. The field names are shown to help you keep your place. You enter only the data that follows each field tag.

Instructions on how to enter this data are given in Chapter 3 in the section "Adding Data to Forms." After you have finished adding the data for Page 1 of 1, Form 20, you can stop and return to the section in Chapter 3 called "Editing Data in Forms." You will also use this data to do the exercises on retrieving and sorting the database that follow next in the chapter.

In the section "Redesigning a Database" in Chapter 3, you will add some new fields in the database on a second screen page of the form called 2 of 2. The data you need to add to these fields is listed in this appendix immediately after the data for Page 1 of 1, Form 20. Input this information into your sample database as shown after each field tag for each form from Form 1 to 20. Instructions are given in Chapter 3 in the section "Adding Data to Your Redesigned Database." You will use this data in the exercises on printing forms in the database in Chapters 3, 5, and 6.

```
                        Data for Page 1 of 1
Form 1 of 20
Social Security No.: 521-30-7892        Department: Accounting
Last Name: Thornfield        First Name: James        MI: D.
Address: 345 South Birch Street
City: Riverdale                State: IL    Zip Code: 60635
Home Phone: 303-555-2345     Sex: M        Birthdate: Mar 26, 1962
Position: Bookkeeper        Job Title: Bookkeeper I
Exempt: y   Date Hired: Jan 5, 1984   Supervisor: Janice Brown
Work Phone: 732-0110        Ext: 35
In Case of Emergency, Notify -
Name: Brenda Thornfield          Phone: 555-2345
Form 2 of 20
Social Security No.: 202-56-9078        Department: Accounting
Last Name: Zimring            First Name: Daniel        MI: J.
Address: 67 Tower Street, Apt. 202
City: Elmgrove                State: IL    Zip Code: 61630
Home Phone: 303-555-4567     Sex: M        Birthdate: Apr 15, 1955
Position: Clerk            Job Title: Accounting Clerk I
Exempt: n   Date Hired: Feb 13, 1979  Supervisor: Janice Brown
Work Phone: 732-0110        Ext: 15
In Case of Emergency, Notify -
Name: Samuel Zimring            Phone: 555-0230
```

Data for the Personnel Database

```
Form 3 of 20

Social Security No.: 360-31-5633      Department: Accounting
Last Name: Freels            First Name: Jessica         MI: B.
Address: 7823 Chase Plaza, Apt. 345
City: Chicago                      State: IL     Zip Code: 60635
Home Phone: 303-555-1120     Sex: F        Birthdate: Aug 25, 1963
Position: Accountant      Job Title: Senior Accountant II
Exempt: y   Date Hired: Jun 1, 1985   Supervisor: Janice Brown
Work Phone: 732-0110      Ext: 12
In Case of Emergency, Notify -
Name: Roberta Stone              Phone: 555-1120


Form 4 of 20

Social Security No.: 567-21-3456      Department: Accounting
Last Name: Parish            First Name: Katherine       MI: A.
Address: 7890 South Marsh Avenue
City: Crestview                    State: IL     Zip Code: 62612
Home Phone: 313-555-0923     Sex: F        Birthdate: Jul 23, 1959
Position: Secretary       Job Title: Clerk Typist IV
Exempt: n   Date Hired: Nov 28, 1983   Supervisor: Charlotte Dicke
Work Phone: 732-0112      Ext: 16
In Case of Emergency, Notify -
Name: Maxfield Parish            Phone: 555-0923


Form 5 of 20

Social Security No.: 501-11-4523      Department: Engineering
Last Name: Bennett           First Name: Kelly           MI: T.
Address: 123467 North Main Street
City: Hillsdale                    State: IL     Zip Code: 62314
Home Phone: 312-555-1138     Sex: M        Birthdate: Mar 5, 1958
Position: Drafter         Job Title: Design/Drafter II
Exempt: y   Date Hired: Mar 31, 1984   Supervisor: Ron Graydon
Work Phone: 732-1555      Ext: 36
In Case of Emergency, Notify -
Name: Barry Bennett              Phone: 555-0366


Form 6 of 20

Social Security No.: 234-57-8908      Department: Engineering
Last Name: Rosner            First Name: Owen            MI: M.
Address: 7834 Middlefield Road
City: Richland                     State: IL     Zip Code: 60673
Home Phone: 302-555-4562     Sex: M        Birthdate: Aug 14, 1959
Position: Drafter         Job Title: Design/Drafter III
Exempt: y   Date Hired: Jan 16, 1985   Supervisor: Ron Graydon
Work Phone: 732-1555      Ext: 6
In Case of Emergency, Notify -
Name: Brian Walker              Phone: 555-4562


Form 7 of 20

Social Security No.: 225-88-3421      Department: Engineering
Last Name: Peterson          First Name: Monica          MI: L.
Address: 6782 First Street, Apt. 2
City: Wakefield                    State: IL     Zip Code: 60645
```

Data for the Personnel Database (continued)

```
Home Phone: 312-555-6501      Sex: F           Birthdate: Dec 5, 1961
Position: Engineer       Job Title: Product Engineer I
Exempt: y   Date Hired: Apr 12, 1981  Supervisor: Ron Graydon
Work Phone: 732-1555          Ext: 45
In Case of Emergency, Notify -
Name: Daniel Peterson         Phone: 555-3331


Form 8 of 20


Social Security No.: 672-01-9942       Department: Engineering
Last Name: Graydon            First Name: Ronald           MI: F.
Address: 670 Glen Way, Apt. 7010
City: Chicago                 State: IL    Zip Code: 60601
Home Phone: 303-555-2203      Sex: M          Birthdate: Sep 22, 1957
Position: Engineer       Job Title: Head of Engineering
Exempt: y   Date Hired: Oct 4, 1982   Supervisor: Sally Zehm
Work Phone: 732-1555          Ext: 1
In Case of Emergency, Notify -
Name: Lisa Graydon            Phone: 555-2203


Form 9 of 20


Security No.: 456-71-0034       Department: Marketing
Last Name: Johnson            First Name: Jeffry           MI: G.
Address: 73 North Cortland Street
City: Barrington              State: IL    Zip Code: 61655
Home Phone: 314-555-1135      Sex: M          Birthdate: Sep 3, 1966
Position: Artist         Job Title: Layout Artist II
Exempt: n   Date Hired: Apr 13, 1986  Supervisor: Lisa Burke
Work Phone: 732-2340          Ext: 13
In Case of Emergency, Notify -
Name: Linda Johnson           Phone: 555-0970


Form 10 of 20


Social Security No.: 781-15-0632       Department: Marketing
Last Name: Gibbon             First Name: Faith            MI: H.
Address: 5023 Gateway Court
City: Skokie                  State: IL    Zip Code: 61604
Home Phone: 305-555-4453      Sex: F          Birthdate: Oct 31, 1964
Position: Director       Job Title: Director of Marketing
Exempt: y   Date Hired: May 15, 1982  Supervisor: Lisa Burke
Work Phone: 732-2340          Ext: 22
In Case of Emergency, Notify -
Name: Brian Hall             Phone: 555-4453


Form 11 of 20


Social Security No.: 586-03-3187       Department: Marketing
Last Name: Burke              First Name: Lisa             MI: A.
Address: 10 Hollings Court, Apt. 21
City: Gary                    State: IN    Zip Code: 72104
Home Phone: 405-555-9972      Sex: F          Birthdate: Feb 28, 1959
Position: Vice President   Job Title: Vice President of Marketing
Exempt: y   Date Hired: Mar 26, 1980  Supervisor: Edward Chang
Work Phone: 732-2340          Ext: 1
In Case of Emergency, Notify -
Name: Collin Burke            Phone: 555-2145
```

Data for the Personnel Database (continued)

```
Form 12 of 20

Social Security No.: 985-41-112      Department: Sales
Last Name: Burgoyne      First Name: Mark           MI: T.
Address: 6044 Central Avenue, Apt. 42
City: Homewood               State: IL    Zip Code: 60670
Home Phone: 315-555-0048     Sex: M        Birthdate: Jan 20, 1961
Position: Sales        Job Title: East Coast Account Executive
Exempt: y    Date Hired: Jul 4, 1984   Supervisor: John Shepard
Work Phone: 732-5562      Ext: 70
In Case of Emergency, Notify -
Name: Ann Burgoyne              Phone: 555-0048


Form 13 of 20

Social Security No.: 606-33-0915     Department: Sales
Last Name: Thompson      First Name: Ann           MI: M.
Address: 7002 15th Street
City: Hillsdale              State: IL    Zip Code: 61683
Home Phone: 302-555-3377     Sex: F        Birthdate: Apr 26, 1960
Position: Sales        Job Title: Central Account Executive
Exempt: y    Date Hired: Oct 10, 1982  Supervisor: John Shepard
Work Phone: 732-5562      Ext: 21
In Case of Emergency, Notify -
Name: Neil Thompson            Phone: 555-0831


Form 14 of 20

Social Security No.: 892-44-5591     Department: Sales
Last Name: Rush      First Name: Del               MI: B.
Address: 1567 Kings Road West
City: Niles                  State: IL    Zip Code: 61633
Home Phone: 314-555-0528     Sex: M        Birthdate: Nov 2, 1958
Position: Sales        Job Title: Western Account Executive
Exempt: y    Date Hired: Jul 17, 1983  Supervisor: John Shepard
Work Phone: 732-5562      Ext: 44
In Case of Emergency, Notify -
Name: Victoria Stapelton       Phone: 555-5877


Form 15 of 20

Social Security No.: 453-02-2285     Department: Sales
Last Name: Shepard      First Name: John           MI: G.
Address: 90034 Deerfield Road
City: Olympia Fields         State: IL    Zip Code: 60355
Home Phone: 312-555-1122     Sex: M        Birthdate: Aug 27, 1952
Position: Vice President    Job Title: Vice President of Sales
Exempt: y   Date Hired: Sep 3, 1971   Supervisor: Edward Chang
Work Phone: 732-5562      Ext: 1
In Case of Emergency, Notify -
Name: Carolyn Meese            Phone: 555-3003


Form 16 of 20

Social Security No.: 553-04-0126     Department: Marketing
Last Name: Johnson      First Name: Alice          MI: M.
Address: 5789 Meadowfield Road
City: Glenpark               State: IL    Zip Code: 61655
```

Data for the Personnel Database (continued)

```
Home Phone: 302-555-0579      Sex: F         Birthdate: Mar 29, 1961
Position: Secretary          Job Title: Clerk/Typist II
Exempt: n   Date Hired: Sep 25, 1978  Supervisor: Janice Brown
Work Phone: 732-5562          Ext: 2
In Case of Emergency, Notify -
Name: George Johnson              Phone: 555-5744


Form 17 of 20

Social Security No.: 399-75-2205      Department: Personnel
Last Name: Schumacher         First Name: Keri          MI: A.
Address: 805 Lake Shore Drive, Apt. 5602
City: Chicago                 State: IL    Zip Code: 60601
Home Phone: 312-555-2210      Sex: F         Birthdate: May 12, 1957
Position: Secretary          Job Title: Clerk/Typist III
Exempt: y   Date Hired: Feb 19, 1982  Supervisor: Janice Brown
Work Phone: 732-4503          Ext: 16
In Case of Emergency, Notify -
Name: Jeff Schumacher             Phone: 555-6995


Form 18 of 20

Social Security No.: 901-77-3351      Department: Personnel
Last Name: Raye               First Name: Jennifer      MI: R.
Address: 7267 Apple Circle
City: Des Plaines                State: IL    Zip Code: 61605
Home Phone: 316-555-1087      Sex: F         Birthdate: Jun 2, 1950
Position: Director           Job Title: Director of Personnel
Exempt: y   Date Hired: Nov 1, 1978   Supervisor: Edward Chang
Work Phone: 732-4503          Ext: 1
In Case of Emergency, Notify -
Name: Harold Raye                 Phone: 555-1087


Form 19 of 20

Social Security No.: 448-35-9622      Department: Administration
Last Name: Brown              First Name: Janice        MI: F.
Address: 8903 River Street
City: Waukegan                   State: IL    Zip Code: 61635
Home Phone: 303-555-0037      Sex: F         Birthdate: Jan 26, 1961
Position: Supervisor         Job Title: Administrative Assistant
Exempt: y   Date Hired: May 14, 1973  Supervisor: Edward Chang
Work Phone: 732-1111          Ext: 4
In Case of Emergency, Notify -
Name: Carl Brown                  Phone: 555-2434


Form 20 of 20

Social Security No.: 589-11-3276      Department: Administration
Last Name: Chang              First Name: Edward        MI: A.
Address: 70345 Cedar Street
City: Highland Park              State: IL    Zip Code: 61632
Home Phone: 303-555-1304      Sex: M         Birthdate: Aug 12, 1947
Position: President          Job Title: President and CEO
Exempt: y   Date Hired: Jun 24, 1975  Supervisor:
Work Phone: 732-1111          Ext: 1
In Case of Emergency, Notify -
Name: Janet Fielding              Phone: 555-1304
```

Data for the Personnel Database (continued)

```
                        Data for Page 2 of 2

Form 1 of 20

Hourly Rate:                   OT Authorized?:       Total Hours:
Fulltime?:
Total Hours:                   OT Rate:       OT Total:
Commission?: N      Class:     Rate:       Yearly Quota:
Base Salary:                            Commission Total:
Current Salary: $25,500.00     Starting Salary: $23,500.00    %:
Date of Last Review: Jan 20, 1986    Evaluation Codes: A8,AT10,AC9
Total Years of School: 16    College Attended: University of Illinois
Degree: BA          Other:
Foreign Languages: German
Job Related Courses Management Training

Comments James is due for promotion to Bookkeeper II at next review

Form 2 of 20

Hourly Rate: $9.50            OT Authorized?: Y    Total Hours: 120
Fulltime?: Y
Total Hours: 2080             OT Rate: $14.25   OT Total: $1,710.00
Commission?: N      Class:    Rate:       Yearly Quota:
Base Salary:                           Commission Total:
Current Salary: $19,760.00    Starting Salary: $15,375.00    %:
Date of Last Review: Mar 3, 1986    Evaluation Codes: A9.5,AT8,AC7.5
Total Years of School: 13    College Attended: Rosehill JC
Degree:             Other:
Foreign Languages:
Job Related Courses

Comments Dan is a very hard worker and shows a lot of enthusiasm. Needs to
         increase his skills to upgrade position. Supervisor has indicated
         suggested course of study.

Form 3 of 20

Hourly Rate:                  OT Authorized?:       Total Hours:
Fulltime?:
Total Hours:                  OT Rate:       OT Total:
Commission?: N      Class:    Rate:       Yearly Quota:
Base Salary:                           Commission Total:
Current Salary: $35,500.00    Starting Salary: $26,000.00    %:
Date of Last Review: Dec 12, 1985    Evaluation Codes: A10,AT9,AC10
Total Years of School: 14    College Attended: Moore Business College
Degree: AA          Other:
Foreign Languages: Spanish
Job Related Courses Accounting for Managers

Comments Jessica is an ideal worker, accurate and fast. Always willing to
         do whatever it takes to get the job done.

Form 4 of 20

Hourly Rate: $10.00           OT Authorized?: Y    Total Hours: 75
Fulltime?: Y
Total Hours: 2080             OT Rate: $15.00   OT Total: $1,125.00
```

Data for the Personnel Database (continued)

```
Commission?: N       Class:       Rate:        Yearly Quota:
Base Salary:                                   Commission Total:
Current Salary: $20,800.00       Starting Salary: $17,500.00    %:
Date of Last Review: Jan 5, 1985       Evaluation Codes: A7.5,AT5,AC8
Total Years of School: 12   College Attended:
Degree:            Other:
Foreign Languages:
Job Related Courses

Comments Katherine received a substandard rating on attendance. She must
          make a better effort to be on the job more to get her next raise.

Form 5 of 20

Hourly Rate:                     OT Authorized?:       Total Hours:
Fulltime?:
Total Hours:                     OT Rate:         OT Total:
Commission?: N       Class:       Rate:        Yearly Quota:
Base Salary:                                   Commission Total:
Current Salary: $25,750.00       Starting Salary: $22,000.00    %:
Date of Last Review: Apr 3, 1985       Evaluation Codes: A9,AT10,AC7
Total Years of School: 16   College Attended: Winston JC
Degree: AS           Other: Certificate of Drafting
Foreign Languages: French
Job Related Courses Stress Analysis, Designer 1, Cost Estimation

Comments Kelly is quick to learn and very attentive to detail, though
          supervisor reports that he does not always work up to potential.

Form 6 of 20

Hourly Rate:                     OT Authorized?:       Total Hours:
Fulltime?:
Total Hours:                     OT Rate:         OT Total:
Commission?: N       Class:       Rate:        Yearly Quota:
Base Salary:                                   Commission Total:
Current Salary: $32,000.00       Starting Salary: $32,000.00    %:
Date of Last Review:                     Evaluation Codes:
Total Years of School: 16   College Attended: University of Chicago
Degree: BS           Other:
Foreign Languages: Spanish; German
Job Related Courses

Comments

Form 7 of 20

Hourly Rate:                     OT Authorized?:       Total Hours:
Fulltime?:
Total Hours:                     OT Rate:         OT Total:
Commission?: N       Class:       Rate:        Yearly Quota:
Base Salary:                                   Commission Total:
Current Salary: $31,500.00       Starting Salary: $20,500.00    %:
Date of Last Review: May 1, 1986       Evaluation Codes: A9.5,AT9,AC10
Total Years of School: 16   College Attended: Darnell College
Degree: BS           Other:
Foreign Languages: Swedish
Job Related Courses Drafting and Design I, Stress Analysis, Engineering
Math
```

Data for the Personnel Database (continued)

```
Comments Monica continues to progress in all areas. Promoted from
         Design/Drafter III to Junior Engineer 5/86

Form 8 of 20

Hourly Rate:                OT Authorized?:      Total Hours:
Fulltime?:
Total Hours:                OT Rate:        OT Total:
Commission?: N    Class:    Rate:       Yearly Quota:
Base Salary:                        Commission Total:
Current Salary: $45,000.00    Starting Salary: $38,500.00    %:
Date of Last Review: Nov 15, 1985   Evaluation Codes: A10,AT10,AC10
Total Years of School: 18   College Attended: De Paul University
Degree: BS, MA       Other:
Foreign Languages: German, Spanish
Job Related Courses

Comments As Head of Engineering, Ron has met all production schedules and
         quotas. Voted most valuable Employee of 1986.

Form 9 of 20

Hourly Rate: $18.25         OT Authorized?: N     Total Hours:
Fulltime?: N
Total Hours: 1040           OT Rate:        OT Total:
Commission?: N    Class:    Rate:       Yearly Quota:
Base Salary:                        Commission Total:
Current Salary: $18,980.00    Starting Salary: $18,980.00    %:
Date of Last Review:                Evaluation Codes:
Total Years of School: 16   College Attended: Art Institute
Degree: BA           Other:
Foreign Languages: French
Job Related Courses

Comments Fast and accurate. Due for step increase at next evaluation.

Form 10 of 20

Hourly Rate:                OT Authorized?:      Total Hours:
Fulltime?:
Total Hours:                OT Rate:        OT Total:
Commission?: N    Class:    Rate:       Yearly Quota:
Base Salary:                        Commission Total:
Current Salary: $38,500.00    Starting Salary: $30,000.00    %:
Date of Last Review: Jun 6, 1986    Evaluation Codes: A9,AT8.5,AC7
Total Years of School: 16   College Attended: Stanford University
Degree: BA           Other:
Foreign Languages: French
Job Related Courses Marketing in the '80's

Comments Faith is hard working but needs to work on being a team player.

Form 11 of 20

Hourly Rate:                OT Authorized?:      Total Hours:
Fulltime?:
Total Hours:                OT Rate:        OT Total:
```

Data for the Personnel Database (continued)

```
Commission?: N      Class:        Rate:          Yearly Quota:
Base Salary:                             Commission Total:
Current Salary: $47,500.00      Starting Salary: $34,000.00    %:
Date of Last Review: Apr 22, 1986   Evaluation Codes: A10,AT9,AC9
Total Years of School: 18   College Attended: University of Chicago
Degree: BA, MBA      Other:
Foreign Languages: Spanish
Job Related Courses Marketing in the '80's

Comments Model manager and employee. Has worked diligently with sales to
         increase communication.

Form 12 of 20

Hourly Rate:                OT Authorized?:      Total Hours:
Fulltime?:
Total Hours:                OT Rate:         OT Total:
Commission?: Y    Class: 3    Rate: .0450   Yearly Quota: $600,000.00
Base Salary: $19,200.00                 Commission Total: $27,000.00
Current Salary: $46,200.00      Starting Salary:            %:
Date of Last Review: Jul 20, 1986   Evaluation Codes: A8,AC10
Total Years of School: 14   College Attended: University of Iowa
Degree: BA         Other:
Foreign Languages: Spanish
Job Related Courses Selling in the '80's

Comments Mark is outstanding on presentation. He has improved his
         salesmanship and always meets his quota.

Form 13 of 20

Hourly Rate:                OT Authorized?:      Total Hours:
Fulltime?:
Total Hours:                OT Rate:         OT Total:
Commission?: Y      Class: 2    Rate: .0300   Yearly Quota: $420,000.00
Base Salary: $15,000.00                 Commission Total: $12,600.00
Current Salary: $27,600.00      Starting Salary:            %:
Date of Last Review: Oct 10, 1985   Evaluation Codes: A10,AC7
Total Years of School: 12   College Attended:
Degree:            Other:
Foreign Languages:
Job Related Courses Sales in the '80's, Going for the Close

Comments Good attitude and presentation. Still needs more experience in the
         field. Supervisor has to give her a lot of help.

Form 14 of 20

Hourly Rate:                OT Authorized?:      Total Hours:
Fulltime?:
Total Hours:                OT Rate:         OT Total:
Commission?: Y    Class: 3    Rate: .0450   Yearly Quota: $500,000.00
Base Salary: $14,500.00                 Commission Total: $22,500.00
Current Salary: $37,000.00      Starting Salary:            %:
Date of Last Review: Jul 17, 1986   Evaluation Codes: A8,AC9
Total Years of School: 16   College Attended: Illinois State University
Degree: BA         Other:
Foreign Languages: Spanish, German, French, Italian
```

Data for the Personnel Database (continued)

```
Job Related Courses Boosting Sales and Having Fun, Sales in the '80's

Comments Del is a real "go getter" and shows real promise. He was
         transferred to Sales from Marketing in 11/85. Has had some
         trouble in meeting his quotas.


Form 15 of 20

Hourly Rate:                    OT Authorized?:      Total Hours:
Fulltime?:
Total Hours:                    OT Rate:        OT Total:
Commission?:      Class:        Rate:        Yearly Quota:
Base Salary:                            Commission Total:
Current Salary: $50,000.00      Starting Salary: $42,000.00    %:
Date of Last Review: Sep 30, 1986   Evaluation Codes: A10,AT9,AC9.5
Total Years of School: 18   College Attended: University of Indiana
Degree: BA, MBA      Other:
Foreign Languages: German, Russian, Chinese
Job Related Courses

Comments John is considered one of the finest managers in the company. As
         VP of Sales, he has increased revenues by 35%.


Form 16 of 20

Hourly Rate: $14.75             OT Authorized?: Y    Total Hours: 100
Fulltime?: Y
Total Hours: 2080               OT Rate: $21.38   OT Total: $2,138.00
Commission?: N     Class:       Rate:        Yearly Quota:
Base Salary:                            Commission Total:
Current Salary: $30,680.00      Starting Salary: $17,800.00    %:
Date of Last Review: Jan 1, 1986    Evaluation Codes: A10,AT8.5,AC9.5
Total Years of School: 16   College Attended: UC Santa Cruz
Degree: BA          Other:
Foreign Languages: Spanish
Job Related Courses Administration for Administrative Assistants

Comments Alice is a phenomenon. She works harder than almost anyone in the
         company. Lately, her work has suffered from family problems.


Form 17 of 20

Hourly Rate:                    OT Authorized?:      Total Hours:
Fulltime?:
Total Hours:                    OT Rate:        OT Total:
Commission?: N     Class:       Rate:        Yearly Quota:
Base Salary:                            Commission Total:
Current Salary: $32,000.00      Starting Salary: $25,500.00    %:
Date of Last Review: Feb 28, 1986   Evaluation Codes: A7.5,AT9,AC9.5
Total Years of School: 14   College Attended: Elgin Junior College
Degree: AA          Other:
Foreign Languages:
Job Related Courses Introduction to IBM-PC, Q&A, WordStar 2000

Comments Keri shows great aptitude and enthusiasm for the computer. Since
         her introduction to word and data processing, her output has
         shown dramatic increase.
```

Data for the Personnel Database (continued)

```
Form 18 of 20

Hourly Rate:                    OT Authorized?:       Total Hours:
Fulltime?:
Total Hours:                    OT Rate:        OT Total:
Commission?: N     Class:       Rate:        Yearly Quota:
Base Salary:                        Commission Total:
Current Salary: $36,800.00      Starting Salary: $25,000.00   %:
Date of Last Review: Nov 1, 1986    Evaluation Codes: A10,AT9,AC8.5
Total Years of School: 16   College Attended: University of Illinois
Degree: BA       Other:
Foreign Languages: French
Job Related Courses Computers for Executives, Stress in the Workplace

Comments Jennifer does an outstanding job. Has instituted many new programs
         that have led to reduced stress and anxiety on the job. Great
         coordinator.

Form 19 of 20

Hourly Rate:                    OT Authorized?:       Total Hours:
Fulltime?:
Total Hours:                    OT Rate:        OT Total:
Commission?: N     Class:       Rate:        Yearly Quota:
Base Salary:                        Commission Total:
Current Salary: $39,800.00      Starting Salary: $25,000.00   %:
Date of Last Review: May 24, 1985   Evaluation Codes: A8,AT6,AC8
Total Years of School: 16   College Attended: Queens College
Degree: BA       Other:
Foreign Languages: German, Dutch
Job Related Courses Administration, Policies and Politics

Comments Janice does her work well but has some trouble getting along with
         other staff members. Needs to work at being a better team player.

Form 20 of 20

Hourly Rate:                    OT Authorized?:       Total Hours:
Fulltime?:
Total Hours:                    OT Rate:        OT Total:
Commission?: N     Class:       Rate:        Yearly Quota:
Base Salary:                        Commission Total:
Current Salary: $125,000.00     Starting Salary: $115,000.00   %:
Date of Last Review:                Evaluation Codes:
Total Years of School: 21   College Attended: University of Chicago
Degree: BA,MA,PHD    Other: MBA from Stanford University
Foreign Languages: French, German, Italian
Job Related Courses Computers for Executives, Increased Profits in the
'80's

Comments
```

Data for the Personnel Database (continued)

## WORD PROCESSING FUNCTIONS

### Function keys used alone:

| | |
|---|---|
| F1 | Get online help |
| F2 | Print document (same as choosing the Print option on the Write Menu) |
| F3 | Delete a block of text (by marking with cursor highlight) |
| F4 | Delete an entire word and trailing space if cursor is at the first letter; otherwise, delete from cursor position to word's end and leave trailing space |
| F5 | Copy a block of text within a document (by marking with cursor highlight) |
| F6 | Set a temporary indented left or right margin or clear temporary indent |
| F7 | Search-and-replace text in a document. Press PgDn for advanced search options |
| F8 | Access the Options Menu to add headers or footers, center or uncenter a line, set tabs on ruler, insert text from a separate document file, add a page break, or use the line drawing set (draw mode) |
| F9 | Scroll down document window |
| F10 | Confirm command selection and tell Q&A to carry it out |

### Function keys used with Shift:

| | |
|---|---|
| Shift-F1 | Spell-check the entire document |
| Shift-F2 | Define a macro sequence, record keystrokes or word processing commands, or save or load a new macro file |
| Shift-F4 | Delete the line containing the cursor |

| | |
|---|---|
| Shift-F5 | Move a block of text (by marking with cursor highlight) |
| Shift-F6 | Define print enhancements such as underlining, boldface, italics, and superscripts and subscripts, or return text to normal |
| Shift-F7 | Undo key to bring back just-deleted text before making further deletions or before copying or moving a block of text |
| Shift-F8 | Save document in memory (same as Save option on Write Menu) |
| Shift-F9 | Scroll up document window |

### Function keys used with Ctrl:

| | |
|---|---|
| Ctrl-F1 | Spell-check the word containing the cursor |
| Ctrl-F2 | Print only the block of text defined with the cursor highlight |
| Ctrl-F3 | Display document statistics |
| Ctrl-F4 | Delete from the cursor to the end of the line |
| Ctrl-F5 | Copy a block of text defined with the cursor highlight into a new document file |
| Ctrl-F6 | Define a page (same as Define a page option on Write Menu) |
| Ctrl-F7 | Go to a specified page or line |
| Ctrl-F8 | Export the document to ASCII text |
| Ctrl-F9 | Assign fonts to the current document |

### Function keys used with Alt:

| | |
|---|---|
| Alt-F5 | Move a block of text defined with cursor highlight into a new document file |
| Alt-F6 | Add a soft hyphen |

| Alt-F7 | List the field names of the associated merge data file |
| Alt-F8 | Print mailing labels |
| Alt-F9 | Calculate a row or column of numbers |

## *WORDSTAR CURSOR AND EDITING KEYS*

| Ctrl-A | To previous word—same as Ctrl-← |
| Ctrl-S | To previous character—same as ← |
| Ctrl-D | To next character—same as → |
| Ctrl-F | To next word—same as Ctrl-→ |
| Ctrl-E | Up one line—same as ↑ |
| Ctrl-X | Down one line—same as ↓ |
| Ctrl-R | To first character of previous screen—same as PgUp |
| Ctrl-C | To first character of next screen—same as PgDn |
| Ctrl-G | Delete character at cursor—same as Del |
| Ctrl-T | Delete word at cursor—same as F4 |
| Ctrl-Y | Delete line at cursor—same as Shift-F4 |
| Ctrl-N | Insert blank line—same as Ins-↵ |

## *Q&A FILE*

The following keys move the cursor and perform special functions in Q&A File.

## *CURSOR MOVEMENT IN THE FORM*

| ↑ | Up a line in the form |
| ↓ | Down a line in the form |

| | |
|---|---|
| → | One character to the right in a field |
| ← | One character to the left in a field |
| Ctrl-→ | One word to the right in a field |
| Ctrl-← | One word to the left in a field |
| Home | 1st time—first character of the current field |
| | 2nd time—first character of the first field of the current page |
| | 3rd time—first character of the form |
| Ctrl-Home | First form in the database |
| End | 1st time—last character of the current field |
| | 2nd time—first character of the last field of the current page |
| | 3rd time—first character of the last field of the form |
| Ctrl-End | Last form in the database |
| PgUp | To the previous page of the form |
| PgDn | To the next page of the form |
| Tab | To the beginning of the next field in the form |
| ← (Return) | To the beginning of the next field in the form—in multi-line fields, to the beginning of the following line |
| Shift-Tab | To the beginning of the previous field in the form |

## WHEN ADDING RECORDS

| | |
|---|---|
| F5 | Copy the value of the same field from the previous record |
| F10 | Save the current form and add a blank form for entry |

| | |
|---|---|
| Shift-F5 | Copy all the values from the previous record |
| Shift-F9 | Go to any customize spec (bypass menu) |
| Shift-F10 | Save the current form and return to the File Menu |
| Ctrl-F5 | Auto-type the current date |
| Alt-F5 | Auto-type the current time |

## WHEN SEARCHING AND SORTING THE DATABASE

| | |
|---|---|
| F6 | Expand the field to allow entry of search criteria longer than the field (the so-called Long value) |
| F8 | Go from Retrieve Spec to Sort Spec |
| F9 | Return to Retrieve Spec from Sort Spec |
| Shift-F7 | Restore the previous Retrieve Spec or Sort Spec |
| Ctrl-F7 | Display Search Options box for NOT and OR search specs |

## WHEN UPDATING THE DATABASE

| | |
|---|---|
| F6 | Go from a view of a single record to a table view containing the first few fields of 17 records at one time |
| F7 | Go directly to Retrieve Spec (bypass menu) |
| F8 | Calculate formulas (if in Manual mode) |
| F9 | Go to previous record |
| Shift-F8 | Set calculation to either Manual or Automatic mode |
| Shift-F9 | Go to any customize spec (bypass menu) |
| Ctrl-F6 | Switch to adding a new form (bypass menu) |
| Ctrl-F8 | Reset the @NUMBER function to a new starting number |

# Q&A REPORT

| | |
|---|---|
| F6 | Expand the field to allow entry of search criteria longer than the field (the so-called Long value) |
| F8 | Go to Derived Columns Spec from Column Spec or to Define Page Options from Print Options |
| F9 | Return to the previous spec |
| Shift-F7 | Restore previous Retrieve Spec or Sort Spec |

# INTELLIGENT ASSISTANT

The following keys move the cursor and perform special functions in Q&A's Intelligent Assistant.

## WHEN COMPLETING THE TEACHING LESSONS

| | |
|---|---|
| F6 | Back up to the previous field |
| F8 | Go to the next field |

## WHEN ASKING QUESTIONS

| | |
|---|---|
| F6 | See vocabulary, including built-in words, field labels, and synonyms |
| F8 | Teach the Assistant a new word |
| Shift-F7 | Restore the previous request |

# APPENDIX C

# USING Q&A'S
# LIST
# MANAGER

Q&A provides a utility called List Manager that allows you to
search for files or delete, rename, or copy them. You can access this
utility from any of Q&A's modules. Whenever you need to use a file
saved on one of your data disks, you can get a complete alphabetical
listing of the files the disk contains by pressing Return at the prompt
for the file name. If the prompt already contains a suggested file
name, press the space bar to clear it before you press Return. On a
hard disk, you can restrict this listing to a specified subdirectory by
typing in the full path name (see the section "Setting the Default
Drive and Directory" in Chapter 1). If you need to reset the current
directory, you can clear the suggested path name by using the Backspace key or by pressing Shift-F4 to erase the entire line.

If you use the List Manager from the DOS File Facilities or Write
Menu, you can also restrict the listing to a particular subset of file
names by using any of the DOS wildcard characters as shown in
Table C.1. When you are using the List Manager from the File,
Report, or Assistant menus, wildcard characters may only be used in
the part of the file name which precedes the mandatory extension
.DTF.

Figure C.1 shows you the directory of all the files on a subdirectory
of \QA called \FILES. In this figure, the heading reads "List of
Files" because this screen was accessed by using the List Manager in
Q&A Write (using the Get command and then pressing Return).
Because no DOS wildcards were used to restrict this listing, it shows
all the files—including database and macro files saved in the
subdirectory, not just document files created with Q&A Write. The
directory listing does not, however, include any print or report specifications that have been saved on the disk. These are not saved as a
separate DOS file. They are stored within the .DTF file and can only
be accessed from Q&A File. To rename, copy, or delete these files,
you must use the Rename/Copy/Delete menus associated with
either the Print Menu or the Report Menu.

At the bottom of the screen shown in Figure C.1 you can see the function key assignments for the List Manager. You press F3 to delete a file,
F5 to copy a file, F7 to search for a file, and F8 to rename a file. Any of
these functions affect only the file currently highlighted on the directory
listing. With the exception of searching for a file, all of these commands
work just as they do from the DOS operating system. Q&A just makes
them easier to use because it prompts you as you use them.

*Table C.1:* Using DOS * and ? wildcard characters to restrict the file list

| EXAMPLE | RESULT |
|---------|--------|
| *.DTF | Lists any file that has the file name extension .DTF. |
| PERSONEL.* | Lists any file named PERSONEL regardless of the extension given to it, such as PERSONEL.DTF, PERSONEL.LET, PERSONEL.MEM, etc. |
| WP*.* | Lists any file that begins with the two letters *wp*, regardless of how many characters follow or which file name extension is used. |
| *.* | Lists all files regardless of name. This produces the same listing as does pressing Return at the File name prompt. |
| * | Lists all files that do not have file name extensions given to them, regardless of name. |
| PER????.* | Lists all files that begin with the three letters *per* and have four characters following in the file name. (The question mark is a wildcard for any single character in the file name.) |

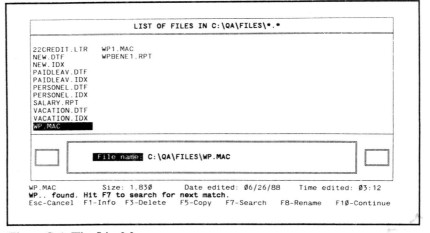

*Figure C.1:* The List Manager screen

When you use the F7-Search function to locate a file in a long directory listing, you can use Q&A wildcard characters rather than having to type in the complete file name. Table C.2 illustrates how you can use these wildcards.

To use the Search function, you type in the entire file name—or part of it, using the appropriate Q&A wildcards—and then press F7. (If you press Return instead of F7, you will receive an error message, "Character cannot be used in file name", and the cursor will be positioned on the faulty character.) In Figure C.1, the file name WP.MAC was located by typing only the letters **wp** followed by  .. and then pressing F7. As you can see in the message at the bottom of this screen, Q&A tells you when it has located a match and lets you know that you can press F7 to search again for the next occurrence. If WP.MAC turned out not to be the file you wanted, pressing F7 again would locate the next file beginning with the letters *wp*. In this case, Q&A would supply WP1.MAC as its next selection.

Note in Figure C.2 that the List Manager is arranged a little differently when you access it from the Utilities Menu. To get to this

*Table C.2:* Using Q&A wildcards with the List Manager Search function

| EXAMPLE | RESULT |
| --- | --- |
| V.. | Locates and highlights the first file in the directory listing whose name begins with the letter *v*. In Figure C.1 this would be the file named VACATION.DTF. |
| ..C | Locates and highlights the first file in the directory listing whose name ends in the letter *c*. In Figure C.1 this would be the file named WP.MAC. |
| ..NEL.. | Locates and highlights the first file whose name contains the three letters *nel* within it. In Figure C.1 this would be the file named PERSONEL.DTF. |
| ...RPT | Locates and highlights the first file with the extension .RPT (the third period is for the extension). In Figure C.1 this would be the file named SALARY.RPT. |

menu, you choose Utilities from the Main Menu and then select the DOS file facilities option. This leads you to the DOS File Facilities Menu shown in this figure. You choose the first option, List Files, by typing **L** and pressing Return or by typing **1**. Because Q&A provides you with the equivalents of the DOS commands DIR, RENAME, COPY, and DEL, you never have to use these commands at the operating system level.

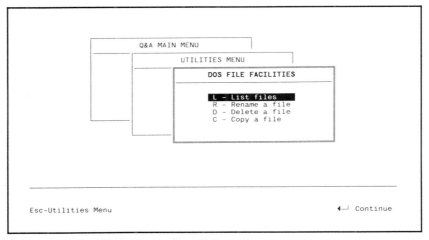

*Figure C.2:* The DOS File Facilities Menu

# APPENDIX D

# USING SPECIAL
# CHARACTERS
# IN Q&A

The following ASCII chart shows all of the ASCII decimal codes and characters for code 000 to 255. Codes higher than 127 are standardized only on the IBM PC and compatible computers. They can be used to add special screen characters such as foreign language, mathematical and scientific, and currency symbols, as well as graphics characters, to your Q&A documents. You can also use them when designing a form for your database files.

To use a particular character shown on this chart, hold down the Alt key and type in the decimal code number associated with it by using the numbers on the cursor/10-key numeric pad (you cannot use the number keys on the top line of the keyboard). As soon as you have typed in the three-digit number and released the Alt key, the symbol will appear on your screen. For instance, to add the Pound currency symbol (£) to a document or input screen form, you merely press Alt and type **156**. However, be aware that many printers cannot interpret these nonstandard ASCII codes and therefore cannot correctly print the desired symbols. If your printer is unable to print the line drawing symbols that you used in the exercises in Chapters 2 and 3, then it will also be unable to print the other screen characters shown in this chart.

| ASCII Value | Character | Control Character | ASCII Value | Character |
|---|---|---|---|---|
| 000 | (null) | NUL | 032 | (space) |
| 001 | ☺ | SOH | 033 | ! |
| 002 | ● | STX | 034 | '' |
| 003 | ♥ | ETX | 035 | # |
| 004 | ♦ | EOT | 036 | $ |
| 005 | ♣ | ENQ | 037 | % |
| 006 | ♠ | ACK | 038 | & |
| 007 | (beep) | BEL | 039 | ' |
| 008 | ▪ | BS | 040 | ( |
| 009 | (tab) | HT | 041 | ) |
| 010 | (line feed) | LF | 042 | * |
| 011 | (home) | VT | 043 | + |
| 012 | (form feed) | FF | 044 | , |
| 013 | (carriage return) | CR | 045 | - |
| 014 | ♫ | SO | 046 | . |
| 015 | ☼ | SI | 047 | / |
| 016 | ► | DLE | 048 | 0 |
| 017 | ◄ | DC1 | 049 | 1 |
| 018 | ↕ | DC2 | 050 | 2 |
| 019 | ‼ | DC3 | 051 | 3 |
| 020 | ¶ | DC4 | 052 | 4 |
| 021 | § | NAK | 053 | 5 |
| 022 | ▬ | SYN | 054 | 6 |
| 023 | ↨ | ETB | 055 | 7 |
| 024 | ↑ | CAN | 056 | 8 |
| 025 | ↓ | EM | 057 | 9 |
| 026 | → | SUB | 058 | : |
| 027 | ← | ESC | 059 | ; |
| 028 | (cursor right) | FS | 060 | < |
| 029 | (cursor left) | GS | 061 | = |
| 030 | (cursor up) | RS | 062 | > |
| 031 | (cursor down) | US | 063 | ? |

ASCII Character Codes

| ASCII Value | Character | ASCII Value | Character |
|---|---|---|---|
| 064 | @ | 096 | ` |
| 065 | A | 097 | a |
| 066 | B | 098 | b |
| 067 | C | 099 | c |
| 068 | D | 100 | d |
| 069 | E | 101 | e |
| 070 | F | 102 | f |
| 071 | G | 103 | g |
| 072 | H | 104 | h |
| 073 | I | 105 | i |
| 074 | J | 106 | j |
| 075 | K | 107 | k |
| 076 | L | 108 | l |
| 077 | M | 109 | m |
| 078 | N | 110 | n |
| 079 | O | 111 | o |
| 080 | P | 112 | p |
| 081 | Q | 113 | q |
| 082 | R | 114 | r |
| 083 | S | 115 | s |
| 084 | T | 116 | t |
| 085 | U | 117 | u |
| 086 | V | 118 | v |
| 087 | W | 119 | w |
| 088 | X | 120 | x |
| 089 | Y | 121 | y |
| 090 | Z | 122 | z |
| 091 | [ | 123 | ¦ |
| 092 | \ | 124 | ¦ |
| 093 | ] | 125 | } |
| 094 | ∧ | 126 | ~ |
| 095 | — | 127 | ⌂ |

ASCII Character Codes (continued)

| ASCII Value | Character | ASCII Value | Character |
|---|---|---|---|
| 128 | Ç | 160 | á |
| 129 | u | 161 | í |
| 130 | é | 162 | ó |
| 131 | â | 163 | ú |
| 132 | a | 164 | ñ |
| 133 | à | 165 | Ñ |
| 134 | å | 166 | ª |
| 135 | ç | 167 | º |
| 136 | ê | 168 | ¿ |
| 137 | ë | 169 | ⌐ |
| 138 | è | 170 | ¬ |
| 139 | ï | 171 | ½ |
| 140 | î | 172 | ¼ |
| 141 | ì | 173 | ¡ |
| 142 | Ä | 174 | « |
| 143 | Å | 175 | » |
| 144 | É | 176 | ░ |
| 145 | æ | 177 | ▒ |
| 146 | Æ | 178 | ▓ |
| 147 | ô | 179 | │ |
| 148 | ö | 180 | ┤ |
| 149 | ò | 181 | ╡ |
| 150 | û | 182 | ╢ |
| 151 | ù | 183 | ╖ |
| 152 | ÿ | 184 | ╕ |
| 153 | Ö | 185 | ╣ |
| 154 | Ü | 186 | ║ |
| 155 | ¢ | 187 | ╗ |
| 156 | £ | 188 | ╝ |
| 157 | ¥ | 189 | ╜ |
| 158 | Pt | 190 | ╛ |
| 159 | ƒ | 191 | ┐ |

ASCII Character Codes (continued)

| ASCII Value | Character | ASCII Value | Character |
|---|---|---|---|
| 192 | └ | 224 | α |
| 193 | ┴ | 225 | β |
| 194 | ┬ | 226 | Γ |
| 195 | ├ | 227 | π |
| 196 | — | 228 | Σ |
| 197 | + | 229 | σ |
| 198 | ╞ | 230 | μ |
| 199 | ╟ | 231 | τ |
| 200 | ╚ | 232 | Φ |
| 201 | ╔ | 233 | θ |
| 202 | ╩ | 234 | Ω |
| 203 | ╦ | 235 | δ |
| 204 | ╠ | 236 | ∞ |
| 205 | ═ | 237 | ∅ |
| 206 | ╬ | 238 | ∈ |
| 207 | ╧ | 239 | ∩ |
| 208 | ╨ | 240 | ≡ |
| 209 | ╤ | 241 | ± |
| 210 | ╥ | 242 | ≥ |
| 211 | ╙ | 243 | ≤ |
| 212 | ╘ | 244 | ⌠ |
| 213 | ╒ | 245 | ⌡ |
| 214 | ╓ | 246 | ÷ |
| 215 | ╫ | 247 | ≈ |
| 216 | ╪ | 248 | ° |
| 217 | ┘ | 249 | • |
| 218 | ┌ | 250 | · |
| 219 | █ | 251 | √ |
| 220 | ▄ | 252 | ⁿ |
| 221 | ▌ | 253 | ² |
| 222 | ▐ | 254 | ■ |
| 223 | ▀ | 255 | (blank 'FF') |

ASCII Character Codes (continued)

APPENDIX **E**

# Q&A'S
# BUILT-IN
# FUNCTIONS

# FUNCTIONS IN Q&A WRITE

There are two built-in functions that you can use in the documents you create in Q&A Write, @DATE(*n*) and @TIME(*n*). These functions can be used in the document's header or footer to date- or time-stamp the printout, or they can be used in the body of the text. However, you must enclose them in a pair of asterisks just like any other embedded command. For example, entering

    *@DATE(1)*

at the top of a letter or in your header will cause Q&A to insert the current date in the printout. The number placed in the parentheses tells Q&A how to format the date or time. There are twenty different date formats and three different time formats from which to choose.

The following list below summarizes how these two functions can be used.

@DATE(*n*)     Inserts current date in header, footer, or text. When you use this function, enclose it in a pair of asterisks. Substitute the number of the date format you wish to use (1–20) for the *n* in the parentheses.

@TIME(*n*)     Inserts current time in header, footer, or text. When you use this function, enclose it in a pair of asterisks. Substitute the number of the time format you wish to use (1–3) for the *n* in the parentheses.

## SEARCHING WITH BUILT-IN FUNCTIONS

When you use various text enhancements like bold or underlining, Q&A Write inserts codes into the document that are not visible on your editing screen. If you need to locate the occurrence of a text enhancement, a carriage return, or a forced page break (inserted with the New page option) in the text, you can do so by entering one of the following built-in functions as the search string. For example, to locate the next occurrence of underlining in the text, you press F7, enter @UL as the search string, and press F7 again. Q&A Write will locate the cursor at the beginning of the next section of text that is underlined.

Using these functions with the Search feature is very useful when your monitor cannot accurately display the text enhancement, such as when you are using a new font in the document. Search can also be used to replace text enhancements. For instance, if you have underlined a particular heading in your document and would rather use boldface type for it, you can change it by pressing F7, entering **@UL** as the search string, then entering **@BD** as the replacement string, and pressing F7 to perform the search-and-replace. When Q&A locates the correct heading, press F10 to have the underlining replaced with bold.

| | |
|---|---|
| @BD | Bold text |
| @CR | Carriage return (entered with the Return key) |
| @CT | Centered line |
| @F1 | Font 1 |
| @F2 | Font 2 |
| @F3 | Font 3 |
| @F4 | Font 4 |
| @F5 | Font 5 |
| @F6 | Font 6 |
| @F7 | Font 7 |
| @F8 | Font 8 |
| @IT | Italicized text |
| @NP | New page (forced page break) |
| @RG | Regular text |
| @SB | Subscripted text |
| @SP | Superscripted text |
| @UL | Underlined text |
| @XO | Strikeout text |

# FUNCTIONS IN Q&A FILE AND Q&A REPORT

Q&A includes many built-in programming functions which perform various calculations. These include financial functions such as @PMT, which calculates the payment required to amortize a loan; statistical functions such as @MAX, which returns the highest value in a list of fields; mathematical functions such as @ABS, which returns the absolute (or positive) value of any number in a particular field; and string functions such as @LEN, which returns the length of the entry in a particular field. Table E.1 summarizes these functions and gives you a brief description of how they are used. These functions are arranged alphabetically by category.

*Table E.1:* Q&A's Built-in Programming Functions

| Context Functions | |
|---|---|
| @ADD | Executes whatever command statement follows it only when the program is adding forms. Usually used in an IF statement. |
| @UPDATE | Executes whatever command statement follows it only when the program is updating forms. Usually used in an IF statement. |
| **Date/Time Functions** | |
| @DATE | Inserts the current date. |
| @TIME | Inserts the current time. |
| **Financial Functions** | |
| @CGR( $p,f,l$ ) | Calculates the compound growth rate where $p$ represents the principal, $f$ the future value, and $l$ the life of loan (i.e., term). |
| @FV( $p,i,l$ ) | Calculates the future value of an investment where $p$ represents the principal, $i$ the periodic interest rate, and $l$ the life of loan (i.e., term). |

*Table E.1:* Q&A's Built-in Programming Functions (continued)

| Financial Functions (continued) | |
|---|---|
| @PMT( *p,i,l* ) | Calculates the payment of a loan where *p* represents the principal, *i* the periodic interest rate, and *l* the life of loan (i.e., term). |
| @PV( *p,i,l* ) | Calculates the present value of an investment where *p* represents the principal, *i* the periodic interest rate, and *l* the life of loan (i.e., term). |

| Mathematical Functions | |
|---|---|
| @ABS(*n*) | Returns the absolute value of *n* where *n* is a number entered as a constant, by field identifier, or as an expression. |
| @AVG( *list* ) | Calculates the average of the numbers in the list, where *list* is the list of field identifiers that hold these numbers. |
| @INT(*n*) | Returns the integer portion of *n* where *n* is a number entered as a constant, by field identifier, or as an expression. |
| @MAX(*list* ) | Returns the highest number in the list, where *list* is the list of field identifiers that hold these numbers. |
| @MIN(*list* ) | Returns the lowest number in the list where *list* is the list of field identifiers that hold these numbers. |
| @NUM(*x*) | Returns the number in *x* where *x* is a text value entered as a constant, by field identifier, or as an expression. |
| @ROUND(*n,m*) | Rounds off *n* to the *m* decimal places where *n* and *m* are numbers entered as constants, by field identifiers, or as expressions. |

***Table E.1:*** Q&A's Built-in Programming Functions (continued)

| Mathematical Functions (continued) | |
|---|---|
| @SGN(*x*) | Returns the sign of *x* where *x* is a text value entered as a constant, by field identifier, or as an expression. |
| @SQRT(*n*) | Calculates the square root of *n* where *n* is a number entered as a constant, by field identifier, or as an expression. |
| @STD(*list*) | Calculates the standard deviations of a list where *list* is the list of field identifiers that hold these numbers. |
| @SUM(*list*) | Calculates the sum of the values in a list where *list* is the list of field identifiers that hold these values. |
| @VAR(*list*) | Calculates the variance in a list where *list* is the list of field identifiers that hold these numbers. |
| **Numbering Functions** | |
| @NUMBER | Returns a unique number that is always 1 greater than the number it returned the last time this function was used. This function is used to sequentially number a field or to ensure that a form has a unique number. |
| @NUMBER(*n*) | Returns a unique number that is always *n* greater than the number it returned the last time this function was used. Use a positive number for *n* when you want to increase the numbering by a particular increment. Use a negative number for *n* when you want to decrease the numbering by a particular increment. |

***Table E.1:*** Q&A's Built-in Programming Functions (continued)

| **Programming Commands** | |
| --- | --- |
| LOOKUP<br>(*key,column, field#* ) | Looks for the key in the lookup table you construct and returns the corresponding value to an assigned field number. The *key* represents the name of the item you want looked up. The *column* represents the column number in the lookup table that you want returned. The *field#* represents the field where you want this data to appear. |
| @LOOKUP<br>(*key,column*) | Looks for a key in the lookup table you construct and returns the corresponding value from one of the columns. The *key* represents the name of the item you want looked up. The *column* represents the column number in the lookup table that you want returned. |
| @XLOOKUP<br>( *fn,pkf,xkf,lf* ) | Looks for the key in a separate Q&A database file and returns the value from that file. The *fn* argument represents the name of the Q&A database file (enclosed in quotation marks) from which the data is to be retrieved. The *pkf* argument represents the primary key field, which is the ID number of the field in the primary file that has an equivalent field in the external file. The *xkf* argument represents the external field name (enclosed in quotation marks), which is the field in the external file that matches the value in the primary key field. The *lf* argument represents the lookup field (enclosed in quotation marks), which is the field in the external file whose values you are retrieving. |

*Table E.1:* Q&A's Built-in Programming Functions (continued)

| Text/String Functions | |
|---|---|
| @ASC(*x*) | Returns the ASCII decimal value of the first character of *x* where *x* is a text value entered as a constant, by field identifier, or as an expression. |
| @CHR(*n*) | Returns the ASCII character equivalent of *n* where *n* is a number entered as a constant, by field identifier, or as an expression. |
| @DEL(*x,n,m*) | Deletes *m* characters from *x* starting at position *n* where *x* is a text value and *n* and *m* are numbers entered as constants, as field identifiers, or as expressions. |
| @DITTO(*list*) | Returns values from the list of fields in previous forms where *list* is a list of field identifiers that hold these numbers. |
| @FILENAME | Returns the name of the current file. |
| @HELP(*n*) | Displays a user-defined help message for field *n* where *n* is a number entered as a constant, by field identifier, or as an expression. |
| @INSTR(*x,y*) | Returns the position (as an integer) of the first occurrence of *y* in *x* where *x* and *y* are text values entered as constants, by field identifiers, or as expressions. |
| @LEFT(*x,n*) | Returns *n* characters from *x* starting at the leftmost position in *x* where *x* is a text value and *n* is a number entered as a constant, by field identifier, or as an expression. |
| @LEN(*x*) | Returns the length of field *x* where *x* is a text value entered as a constant, by field identifier, or as an expression. |

*Table E.1:* Q&A's Built-in Programming Functions (continued)

| Text/String Functions (continued) | |
|---|---|
| @MID($x,n,m$) | Returns $m$ characters from $x$ starting at position $n$ where $x$ is a text value and $n$ or $m$ are numbers entered as constants, by field identifiers, or as expressions. |
| @MSG($x$) | Displays message $x$ on the message line where $x$ is a text value entered as a constant, by field identifier, or as an expression. |
| @RIGHT($x,n$) | Returns $n$ characters from $x$ starting at the rightmost position (and working left) in $x$ where $x$ is a text value and $n$ is a number entered as a constant, by field identifier, or as an expression. |
| @STR($n$) | Returns the text equivalent of $n$ where $n$ is a number entered as a constant, by field identifier, or as an expression. |
| @TEXT($n,x$) | Returns a text value consisting of $n$ characters of $x$ where $n$ is a number and $x$ is a text value entered as a constant, by field identifier, or as an expression. |
| @WIDTH($n$) | Returns the width of field $n$ where $n$ is a number entered as a constant, by field identifier, or as an expression. |

# APPENDIX F

# USING FONTS
# IN Q&A
# WRITE

IF YOUR PRINTER IS CAPABLE OF PRINTING DIFFERENT fonts—as are some dot matrix printers like those in the Epson FX or LQ series and all of the laser printers such as the HP LaserJet Series II and Apple LaserWriter—you can enhance the look of your Q&A Write documents. You apply fonts to the text of the document using the same process by which you apply boldfacing and underlining to text.

## HOW Q&A DEFINES A FONT

Q&A defines a font as a set of type all of one size and style. When referring to the set of type in a font, the term *typeface* is most often used. It describes the shapes given to each letter and character by the type designer. Of all the factors that differentiate one font from another, typeface is the most important.

There are two basic kinds of letterforms that a typeface design can use: *serif* and *sans serif*. Serifs are the little strokes added to the ends of a letter's major strokes—like the small horizontal strokes at the bottom of an *h* or those at the top of a *u*. They help make each letter that uses vertical strokes more distinctive. *Sans* means *without* in French. A sans serif type doesn't use any serifs. Its letterforms are not finished off with smaller strokes. To compare the visual impact of serif and sans serif type, look at Figure F.5. The Q&A Write report shown in this figure uses a sans serif typeface (called Helvetica) for all of its headings. The body text in each paragraph uses a serif typeface (called Times Roman).

If you are using a laser printer like one of the HP LaserJet series, you have a choice of many more fonts than if you are using an Epson dot matrix printer. However, both types of printers allow you to choose between fonts that are *monospaced* and those which are *proportionally spaced*. With a monospaced font such as 10 pitch Courier (one of the resident, or built-in, fonts in the HP LaserJet), each character takes up the same amount of horizontal space—in this case, $\frac{1}{10}$th of an inch. With a proportionally spaced font such as 10 point Times Roman (a nonresident font that can be loaded into the HP LaserJet either from cartridge or disk), characters vary in the amount of horizontal space they require in printing. For example, an uppercase *M* in this font requires nearly three times the space that it takes to print a lowercase *i*.

The sizes of monospaced fonts are described by the term *pitch*, which indicates the number of characters that fit in one line-inch. Pitch is a horizontal measurement. A 10 pitch font prints 10 characters per inch while a 12 pitch font prints 12 characters per inch. The sizes of proportionally spaced fonts are described by the term *point*. A point is a vertical measurement. A 10 point font has a measurement of 10 points from the top of an ascender (such as the stem of the letter *d*) to the bottom of a descender (such as the tail of the letter *g*).

Most typeset material, like the printing in this book, uses proportionally spaced fonts. If your printer supports this type of font, you can give your Q&A Write documents a typeset look. If you own a laser printer like the HP LaserJet Series II, you must purchase proportional fonts separately (since all of the fonts built into this printer are monospaced).

Three terms are usually used to describe the style of a font: *regular* (sometimes called *medium*), *bold*, and *italic*. Regular and bold describe the weight of the printed characters in the font, with regular representing the normal weight of the typeface while bold represents a heavier and therefore darker version of the same typeface. Italic type represents a version of the typeface wherein the letters are slanted to the right, mimicking the slant we give to our letters when writing by hand. It is possible for a particular font to combine two type styles. For example, you might purchase a font described as "bold italic." This would represent a heavier (darker) version of the typeface using italicized characters.

## FONTS AND YOUR PRINTER

Fonts can come from three sources: they can be built into the printer, they can be supplied from cartridges inserted in the printer, or they can come on disk and be loaded into the printer's memory. Fonts for HP LaserJet printers, for example, come in all three forms. A limited number of fonts are already resident in these printers. You can also purchase fonts for them directly from Hewlett-Packard or from your computer dealer on cartridge (there are about 26 different cartridges available at present) or on disk (the fonts come in a disk set that usually includes many different sizes and type styles for a couple of typefaces like Helvetica and Times Roman).

Fonts on disk are called *soft fonts* or *downloadable fonts*. Before you can print with them, you must use a utility that copies them from disk into the printer's memory. (This utility is supplied as one of the files in the disk set.) If you forget to load the fonts you want used in your Q&A Write document before you print the document, it will be printed in 10 pitch Courier (the default font for LaserJet printers).

While cartridge fonts are easier to install, they give you fewer font choices than soft font disk sets. They will also wear out so that eventually the print quality will suffer. Soft fonts are not subect to this type of wear and tear. Because they are not copy-protected, you can always make new copies from the master disks even if the working copies you are using have begun to fail.

If you are using a PostScript laser printer like the Apple LaserWriter, your printer doesn't use cartridge fonts; it will only accept soft fonts. However, PostScript printers have many more built-in fonts than do non-PostScript printers like the HP LaserJet models. Q&A supports all of the fonts built into PostScript printers.

## *INSTALLING CARTRIDGE FONTS*

If you are using an HP LaserJet, your printer can use the fonts supplied on cartridges. If you have an HP LaserJet Series II, your printer can accept up to two different cartridges. Before you try to print a Q&A Write document using the fonts on a cartridge, the cartridge must be seated in its slot at the front of the printer. To change cartridges, take the printer off-line by pressing the ON LINE button on the printer control panel. Remove the cartridge you don't want to use and replace it with the cartridge you do want to use. Then press the ON LINE button again. Make sure that the light above ON LINE is lit, meaning that the printer is online, before you try to print your document.

## *DOWNLOADING SOFT FONTS*

If you are using soft fonts, you must download them to the printer before you start Q&A and try to print a Q&A Write document with them. The soft font set you purchased includes a download utility; refer to the documentation that accompanied the disk set for specific instructions on how to use this utility. Normally, you must give the download command for each font that you plan to use. The fonts that you download to the memory of the printer remain there until you turn the power off.

This means that if during a work session you ever lose power to the printer and need to restart it, you will have to exit Q&A and download the fonts again before you can use them. The same downloading procedure must be followed each time you start a new work session with the printer and Q&A.

## *INSTALLING THE FONTS*
## *TO BE USED IN YOUR DOCUMENT*

You can use up to eight different fonts in a Q&A Write document. This represents just a few of the fonts included on a cartridge or in a soft font disk set. This means that you must choose fonts from the cartridge or the set you wish to use in printing. Once you have made your selections, use the Font Assignments screen to specify which fonts are to be assigned to each of the eight possible selections. Note that before you do this, you must make sure that the printer which uses these fonts has already been properly installed. (If you need help with this, refer to the section ''Installing Your Printer'' in Chapter 1 of this book.)

The procedure for assigning fonts to each of the eight possible Font options is outlined below.

1. Start Q&A Write and select the Type/Edit option if you are beginning a new document, or the Get option if you want to use the fonts in an existing document.

2. From the Type/Edit screen, press Ctrl-F9. This brings up the Font Assignments screen as shown in Figure F.1.

3. Press F6. This brings up the list of font description files as shown in Figure F.2.

4. Move the highlight bar to the appropriate .FNT file and press Return. This returns you to the Font Assignments screen.

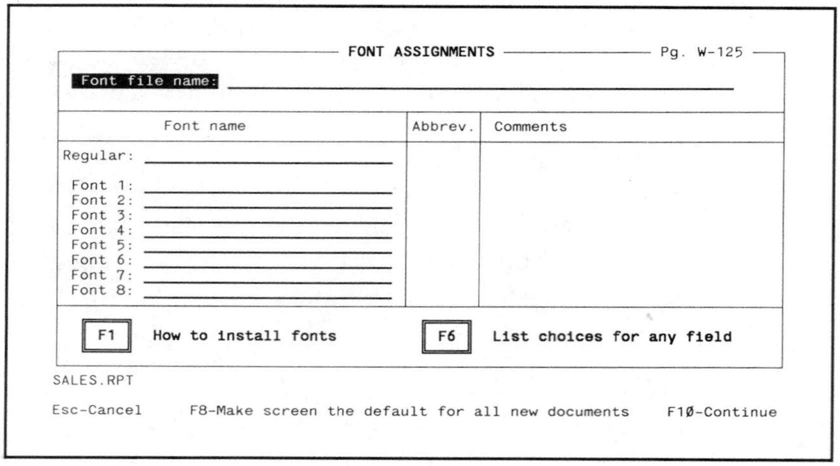

*Figure F.1:* The Font Assignments screen

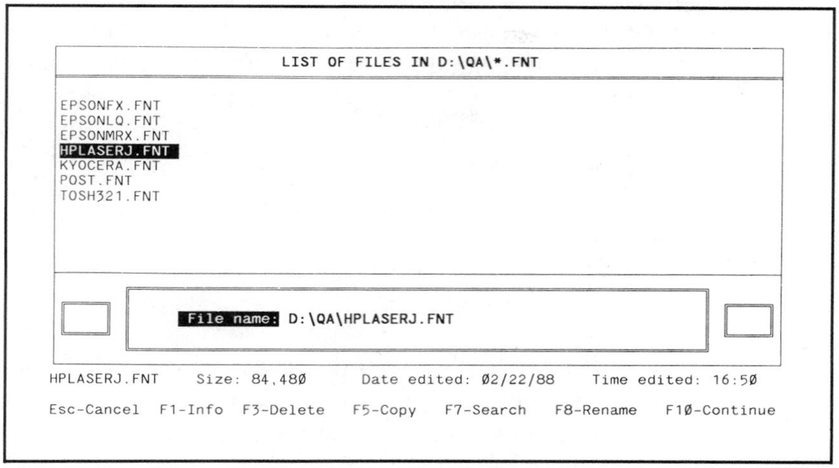

*Figure F.2:* The list of font description files

If you have an Epson printer, be sure that you select the correct .FNT file for your model. If you have an HP LaserJet or a printer that emulates it, select the HPLASERJ.FNT file. If you have a LaserWriter or any other type of PostScript laser printer (such as an AST TurboLaser or QMS PS-810), select the POST.FNT file. If your printer is not listed and neither emulates an HP LaserJet nor uses PostScript, refer to your Q&A documentation for information on how to create or modify a font description file.

5. Press the ↓ key to move the cursor to the line that contains the heading Regular. The Regular font is the default font that will be used to print the document unless you apply one of the other font selections to sections of the text. If you don't assign a font to Regular, Q&A will use the default resident font for your particular printer.

6. To assign a font to Regular, press F6. This brings up a list of available fonts for your printer similar to the one shown in Figure F.3.

7. Move the highlight bar to the name of the font you wish to assign to Regular. Press PgDn to scroll down the list or PgUp to scroll up.

8. Press F10 once you have highlighted the name of the font you want. This returns you to the Font Assignments screen, where you will see the name of the font you have chosen after the heading Regular.

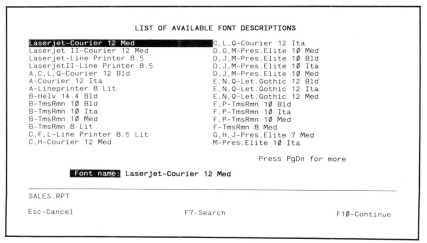

*Figure F.3:* The first part of the list of font descriptions for the HP LaserJet font description file

9. If you want this font to be the default not only for the document you are currently creating or editing but also for all new documents that you plan to create, press F8.

10. Install fonts for Font 1 through Font 8, using the same procedure outlined in steps 5 through 9.

11. When you have finished assigning all of the fonts you wish to use in this document, press F10 to return to the Type/Edit screen.

Figure F.4 shows you the Font Assignments screen after designating a Regular font and assigning fonts to Font 1 through Font 8. Notice that the Font name column indicates the name of the soft font set (AC in this case), the name of the font (TmsRmn for *Times Roman* and Helv for *Helvetica*), its point size, and its type style (Med for *medium* or *regular*, Bld for *bold*, and Ita for *Italic*). Because all of these fonts were designated as the new default fonts (for this and future documents), you see their abbreviations in the next column. If you don't designate any of your font selections as the new defaults, the Abbrev. column remains empty.

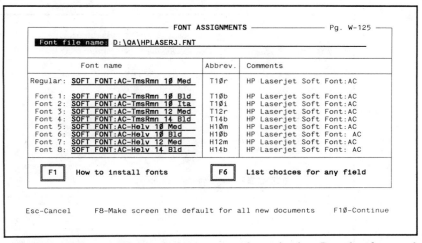

*Figure F.4:* The Font Assignments screen after selecting Regular font and assigning fonts to Font 1 through Font 8

When you select such a font for use in the document as described in the next section, you will see only Fon1 through Fon8 after the eight selection numbers on the Font Enhancement menu. If, however, you designate a font as the default, you will see its abbreviation as shown in the Abbrev. column after its font number (as in T10b for Font 1). To help you remember which font you have assigned to each number when you have not made them the defaults, you should obtain a printout of the completed Font Assignments screen by pressing Shift-PrtSc with your printer on. If you can't use Shift-PrtSc with your printer (Postscript printers do not support direct screen printing), you will need to write the assignments down before leaving this screen.

## *APPLYING THE FONTS TO TEXT IN YOUR DOCUMENT*

To use the fonts that you assign from the Font Assignments screen in the document you are creating and editing, you employ the same technique that you use to boldface or underline text. Place the cursor at the beginning of the text that you want to print in a new font, and press Shift-F6 to bring up the Enhancement menu. Select the Font option by typing **f**, and the Font Enhancement menu will appear. Select your desired font by typing its number (**1–8**). Then highlight all of the text that is to be printed in this font by using the cursor movement keys, and press F10.

Figure F.5 shows you a printout of the first page of a document printed in three fonts. The section headings and the text of the header are printed in 14 point Helvetica Bold, the body text is printed in 10 point Times Roman, and the footer is printed in 10 point Helvetica Italic. Because the Regular font for this document is 10 point Times Roman, only the section headings and the text of the header and footer had to be enhanced using the technique described above. To enhance the text of a header or footer, you only need to edit the header or footer and then apply the font enhancement as you would to any text in the document.

## The Transition to Word Processing

### History

It seems like only *yesterday* that the word processor replaced the electric typewriter in our office. While the transition from mechanical to electronic media was not without its ups and downs, there is not a single secretary or clerk in any of our departments who would willingly give up his or her computer and go back to the "good old days" of the typing pool!

At the close of this past fiscal year, we have in place a total of 25 personal computers dedicated primarily to word processing throughout our five departments. The benefits reported by our managers and supervisors as a result of this transition can be summarized as follows:

1.  Improved morale and decreased absenteeism among all secretaries and clerk typists.

2.  Increased document production. Average turn around time is now 2.5 hours a decrease of approximately 30% from last year's average.

3.  A significant improvement in the overall accuracy of the documents produced with fewer reedits required due to typing errors.

### The Departments and Personnel Affected

The five departments involved in this transition to word processing are: Personnel, Accounting, Marketing and Sales, Engineering, and Research and Development. Each department has assigned to it a different number of secretaries and clerk typists responsible for producing all required written documents. The total number affected is 27. Table 1 on the next page gives their breakdown by department .

### Background of the People

The word processing background of the personnel affected by this transition varied greatly. A questionnaire polling their experience and comfort level with computers and word processing was sent to all. A copy of this questionnaire is included in Appendix A of this report.

From this, it was determined that over 75% of our staff had no prior experience with computer technology or word processing. Of the other 25%, only 2 people had any extensive experience with either. Both of these are in the Research and Development department. Interestingly, all polled showed a great willingness to make the transition from secretary to word processing operator.

### Computers, Printers, and Software

The computers purchased numbered 25 and were all IBM PCs and XTs. All secretaries were equipped with their own IBM XT with a 10 MB hard disk and 640K RAM. The remaining 16 computers purchased for the clerk typists were IBM PCs with two disk drives and 512K RAM. These machines are shared among the 18 clerk typists.

The printers purchased are of two types: Epson FX/100 dot-matrix printers and IBM Quietwriter letter-quality printers. From a total of 25 printers, five are letter quality and 10 are dot matrix. Each department is equipped with its own letter-quality printer attached to the senior secretary's computer.

The software purchased consists of WordStar 2000 and Q&A, an integrated program offering a word processing, mail merge, and data file management. Five units of WordStar 2000 were purchased along with 20 units of Q&A.

*Page 1*

***Figure F.5:*** Printout of the first page of the sales report using three different fonts

# INDEX

DOS programs
  importing, 216
  installing as alternates, 372–373
DOS RENAME command, 493
DOS SHARE command, 460
DOS TYPE command, 442
dot-matrix printers, 68, 512
double density, 213
double spacing, 69–70, 97,
  355–356
downloadable fonts, 514
downloading soft fonts, 514–515
drawing lines and boxes, 90–93,
  127–130
drives, default, 20–22
DTF (data file) filename extension,
  122, 162, 276
DTF filename extension, 490

**E**
editing
  data in database forms,
    143–149
  documents, 28, 47–57, 74–93
  fields, 164
  macros, 367–370
either-or search criteria, 156–157
elite (12 cpi), 45, 60
embedded commands, 66–70,
  97–98, 209–214, 217, 354
END function, 396
End key, 50–52, 482, 486
envelopes, printing with
  merge-print, 205
Epson printers, 46, 68–69, 91,
  512, 516
equals sign ( = ), above column
  totals, 228
erasing, documents, 29
escape characters, 68–69
Escape key, 15, 22, 42, 45

exclamation point (!), 228, 246,
  268
exiting Q&A, 457–458
exporting
  documents, 216–217
  files, 441, 450
Export menu, 32–33
external lookups, 399–401

**F**
@F1, @F2, etc. functions, 503
F1, F2, etc. *See* function keys
fields
  adding, 164–167
  controlling order of printing of,
    173–174
  defined, 111
  defining in databases, 115–120,
    161–170
  defining in reports, 27,
    224–225, 237–238
  designating for use of the
    Intelligent Assistant, 288–296
  editing, 164
  formatting, 131–135
  handling empty in
    merge-printing, 199
  invisible, 225
  keyword, 230, 263–266
  naming in files, 112
  naming in merge-printing
    operations, 198
  numbering sequentially, 389,
    394, 506
  overflow of, 385
  restricting data ranges in,
    384–388
  retrieving, 335
  returning length/width of,
    508–509
  returning values from, 508

# Selections from The SYBEX Library

## *DATABASE MANAGEMENT*

### The ABC's of Paradox
**Charles Siegel**

300pp. Ref.573-5

Easy to understand and use, this introduction is written so that the computer novice can create, edit, and manage complex Paradox databases. This primer is filled with examples of the Paradox 3.0 menu structure.

### Mastering Paradox (Fourth Edition)
**Alan Simpson**

636pp. Ref. 612-X

Best selling author Alan Simpson simplifies all aspects of Paradox for the beginning to intermediate user. The book starts with database basics, covers multiple tables, graphics, custom applications with PAL, and the Personal Programmer. For Version 3.0.

### Quick Guide to dBASE: The Visual Approach
**David Kolodney**

382pp. Ref. 596-4

This illustrated tutorial provides the beginner with a working knowledge of all the basic functions of dBASE IV. Images of each successive dBASE screen tell how to create and modify a database, add, edit, sort and select records, and print custom labels and reports.

### The ABC's of dBASE IV
**Robert Cowart**

338pp. Ref. 531-X

This superb tutorial introduces beginners

to the concept of databases and practical dBASE IV applications featuring the new menu-driven interface, the new report writer, and Query by Example.

### Understanding dBASE IV (Special Edition)
**Alan Simpson**

880pp. Ref. 509-3

This Special Edition is the best introduction to dBASE IV, written by 1 million-reader-strong dBASE expert Alan Simpson. First it gives basic skills for creating and manipulating efficient databases. Then the author explains how to make reports, manage multiple databases, and build applications. Includes Fast Track speed notes.

### Mastering dBASE IV Programming
**Carl Townsend**

496pp. Ref. 540-9

This task-oriented book introduces structured dBASE IV programming and commands by setting up a general ledger system, an invoice system, and a quotation management system. The author carefully explores the unique character of dBASE IV based on his in-depth understanding of the program.

### dBASE IV User's Instant Reference SYBEX Prompter Series
**Alan Simpson**

349pp. Ref. 605-7, 4 ¾" × 8"

This handy pocket-sized reference book gives every new dBASE IV user fast and easy access to any dBASE command. Arranged alphabetically and by function, each entry includes a description, exact syntax, an example, and special tips from Alan Simpson.

## dBASE IV Programmer's Instant Reference
### SYBEX Prompter Series
**Alan Simpson**

544pp. Ref.538-7, 4 ¾" × 8"

This comprehensive reference to every dBASE command and function has everything for the dBASE programmer in a compact, pocket-sized book. Fast and easy access to adding data, sorting, performing calculations, managing multiple databases, memory variables and arrays, windows and menus, networking, and much more. Version 1.1.

## dBASE IV User's Desktop Companion
### SYBEX Ready Reference Series
**Alan Simpson**

950pp. Ref. 523-9

This easy-to-use reference provides an exhaustive resource guide to taking full advantage of the powerful non-programming features of the dBASE IV Control Center. This book discusses query by example, custom reports and data entry screens, macros, the application generator, and the dBASE command and programming language.

## dBASE IV Programmer's Reference Guide
### SYBEX Ready Reference Series
**Alan Simpson**

1000pp. Ref. 539-5

This exhaustive seven-part reference for dBASE IV users includes sections on getting started, using menu-driven dBASE, command-driven · dBASE, multiuser dBASE, programming in dBASE, common algorithms, and getting the most out of dBASE. Includes Simpson's tips on the best ways to use this completely redesigned and more powerful program.

## The ABC's of dBASE III PLUS
**Robert Cowart**

264pp. Ref. 379-1

The most efficient way to get beginners

up and running with dBASE. Every 'how' and 'why' of database management is demonstrated through tutorials and practical dBASE III PLUS applications.

## Understanding dBASE III PLUS
**Alan Simpson**

415pp. Ref. 349-X

A solid sourcebook of training and ongoing support. Everything from creating a first database to command file programming is presented in working examples, with tips and techniques you won't find anywhere else.

## Mastering dBASE III PLUS: A Structured Approach
**Carl Townsend**

342pp. Ref. 372-4

In-depth treatment of structured programming for custom dBASE solutions. An ideal study and reference guide for applications developers, new and experienced users with an interest in efficient programming.

## Also:
## Understanding dBASE III
**Alan Simpson**

300pp. Ref. 267-1

## Advanced Techniques in dBASE III PLUS
**Alan Simpson**

454pp. Ref. 369-4

A full course in database design and structured programming, with routines for inventory control, accounts receivable, system management, and integrated databases.

## Simpson's dBASE Tips and Tricks (For dBASE III PLUS)
**Alan Simpson**

420pp. Ref. 383-X

A unique library of techniques and programs shows how creative use of built-in features can solve all your needs—without expensive add-on products or external languages. Spreadsheet functions, graphics, and much more.

### dBASE III PLUS Programmer's Reference Guide
### SYBEX Ready Reference Series
**Alan Simpson**
1056pp. Ref. 508-5

Programmers will save untold hours and effort using this comprehensive, well-organized dBASE encyclopedia. Complete technical details on commands and functions, plus scores of often-needed algorithms.

### dBASE Instant Reference
### SYBEX Prompter Series
**Alan Simpson**
471pp. Ref. 484-4; 4 ¾" × 8"

Comprehensive information at a glance: a brief explanation of syntax and usage for every dBASE command, with step-by-step instructions and exact keystroke sequences. Commands are grouped by function in twenty precise categories.

### Understanding R:BASE
### Alan Simpson/Karen Watterson
609pp. Ref.503-4

This is the definitive R:BASE tutorial, for use with either OS/2 or DOS. Hands-on lessons cover every aspect of the software, from creating and using a database, to custom systems. Includes Fast Track speed notes.

### Power User's Guide to R:BASE
### Alan Simpson/Cheryl Currid/Craig Gillett
446pp. Ref. 354-6

Supercharge your R:BASE applications with this straightforward tutorial that covers system design, structured programming, managing multiple data tables, and more. Sample applications include ready-to-run mailing, inventory and accounts receivable systems. Through Version 2.11.

### Understanding Oracle
### James T. Perry/Joseph G. Lateer
634pp. Ref. 534-4

A comprehensive guide to the Oracle database management system for administrators, users, and applications developers. Covers everything in Version 5 from database basics to multi-user systems, performance, and development tools including SQL∗Forms, SQL∗Report, and SQL∗Calc. Includes Fast Track speed notes.

## SPREADSHEETS AND INTEGRATED SOFTWARE

### Visual Guide to Lotus 1-2-3
### Jeff Woodward
250pp. Ref. 641-3

Readers match what they see on the screen with the book's screen-by-screen action sequences. For new Lotus users, topics include computer fundamentals, opening and editing a worksheet, using graphs, macros, and printing typeset-quality reports. For Release 2.2.

### The ABC's of 1-2-3 Release 2.2
### Chris Gilbert/Laurie Williams
340pp. Ref. 623-5

New Lotus 1-2-3 users delight in this book's step-by-step approach to building trouble-free spreadsheets, displaying graphs, and efficiently building databases. The authors cover the ins and outs of the latest version including easier calculations, file linking, and better graphic presentation.

### The ABC's of 1-2-3 Release 3
### Judd Robbins
290pp. Ref. 519-0

The ideal book for beginners who are new to Lotus or new to Release 3. This step-by-step approach to the 1-2-3 spreadsheet software gets the reader up and running with spreadsheet, database, graphics, and macro functions.

### The ABC's of 1-2-3 (Second Edition)
### Chris Gilbert/Laurie Williams
245pp. Ref. 355-4

*Online Today* recommends it as "an easy

and comfortable way to get started with the program." An essential tutorial for novices, it will remain on your desk as a valuable source of ongoing reference and support. For Release 2.

## Mastering 1-2-3 Release 3
**Carolyn Jorgensen**
682pp. Ref. 517-4
For new Release 3 and experienced Release 2 users, "Mastering" starts with a basic spreadsheet, then introduces spreadsheet and database commands, functions, and macros, and then tells how to analyze 3D spreadsheets and make high-impact reports and graphs. Lotus add-ons are discussed and Fast Tracks are included.

## Mastering 1-2-3 (Second Edition)
**Carolyn Jorgensen**
702pp. Ref. 528-X
Get the most from 1-2-3 Release 2 with this step-by-step guide emphasizing advanced features and practical uses. Topics include data sharing, macros, spreadsheet security, expanded memory, and graphics enhancements.

## The Complete Lotus 1-2-3 Release 2.2 Handbook
**Greg Harvey**
750pp. Ref. 625-1
This comprehensive handbook discusses every 1-2-3 operating with clear instructions and practical tips. This volume especially emphasizes the new improved graphics, high-speed recalculation techniques, and spreadsheet linking available with Release 2.2.

## The Complete Lotus 1-2-3 Release 3 Handbook
**Greg Harvey**
700pp. Ref. 600-6
Everything you ever wanted to know about 1-2-3 is in this definitive handbook. As a Release 3 guide, it features the design and use of 3D worksheets, and improved graphics, along with using Lotus under DOS or OS/2. Problems, exercises, and helpful insights are included.

## Lotus 1-2-3 Desktop Companion SYBEX Ready Reference Series
**Greg Harvey**
976pp. Ref. 501-8
A full-time consultant, right on your desk. Hundreds of self-contained entries cover every 1-2-3 feature, organized by topic, indexed and cross-referenced, and supplemented by tips, macros and working examples. For Release 2.

## Advanced Techniques in Lotus 1-2-3
**Peter Antoniak/E. Michael Lunsford**
367pp. Ref. 556-5
This guide for experienced users focuses on advanced functions, and techniques for designing menu-driven applications using macros and the Release 2 command language. Interfacing techniques and add-on products are also considered.

## The ABC's of Quattro
**Alan Simpson/Douglas J. Wolf**
286pp. Ref. 560-3
Especially for users new to spreadsheets, this is an introduction to the basic concepts and a guide to instant productivity through editing and using spreadsheet formulas and functions. Includes how to print out graphs and data for presentation. For Quattro 1.1.

## Mastering Quattro
**Alan Simpson**
576pp. Ref. 514-X
This tutorial covers not only all of Quattro's classic spreadsheet features, but also its added capabilities including extended graphing, modifiable menus, and the macro debugging environment. Simpson brings out how to use all of Quattro's new-generation-spreadsheet capabilities.

## Mastering Framework III
**Douglas Hergert/Jonathan Kamin**
613pp. Ref. 513-1
Thorough, hands-on treatment of the latest Framework release. An outstanding introduction to integrated software applications, with examples for outlining, spreadsheets, word processing, databases, and more; plus an introduction to FRED programming.

# MASTERING Q&A

If you would like to use the sample database files and macros in this book, but you don't want to type them in yourself, you can send for a disk containing all of the examples in this book. To get this disk in a 5¼ inch format, complete the order form and return to the address shown below, along with a check or money order for $15.00 in U.S. currency. To get a copy of this disk in 3½ inch format, send a check or money order for $17.00 in U.S. currency. California residents add 6% sales tax.

**Greg Harvey**
**P.O. Box 1175**
**Point Reyes Station, CA   94956-1175**

Name _____

Company _____

Address _____

City/State/Zip _____

5¼ inch disk ☐          3½ inch disk ☐

**Enclosed is my check or money order.     Make check payable to Greg Harvey.**

**SYBEX** is not affiliated with Greg Harvey and assumes no responsibility for any defect in the disk or programs it contains.

## SYBEX Computer Books are different.

## Here is why . . .

At SYBEX, each book is designed with you in mind. Every manuscript is carefully selected and supervised by our editors, who are themselves computer experts. We publish the best authors, whose technical expertise is matched by an ability to write clearly and to communicate effectively. Programs are thoroughly tested for accuracy by our technical staff. Our computerized production department goes to great lengths to make sure that each book is well-designed.

In the pursuit of timeliness, SYBEX has achieved many publishing firsts. SYBEX was among the first to integrate personal computers used by authors and staff into the publishing process. SYBEX was the first to publish books on the CP/M operating system, microprocessor interfacing techniques, word processing, and many more topics.

Expertise in computers and dedication to the highest quality product have made SYBEX a world leader in computer book publishing. Translated into fourteen languages, SYBEX books have helped millions of people around the world to get the most from their computers. We hope we have helped you, too.

## For a complete catalog of our publications:

SYBEX, Inc. 2021 Challenger Drive, #100, Alameda, CA 94501
Tel: (415) 523-8233/(800) 227-2346   Telex: 336311
Fax: (415) 523-2373

# Cursor Movement in Q&A Write

| | | | |
|---|---|---|---|
| ↑ | Up a line | Ctrl-Home | To the beginning of the document |
| ↓ | Down a line | End | 1st time—To the end of the line |
| → | One character to the right | | 2nd time—To the bottom of the screen |
| ← | One character to the left | | 3rd time—To the bottom of the page |
| Ctrl-→ | One word to the right | | 4th time—To the end of the document |
| Ctrl-← | One word to the left | Ctrl-End | To the end of the document |
| Home | 1st time—To the beginning of the line | PgUp | To the top of the previous screen |
| | 2nd time—To the top of the screen | Ctrl-PgUp | To the top of the previous page |
| | 3rd time—To the top of the page | PgDn | To the top of the next screen |
| | 4th time—To the beginning of the document | Ctrl-PgDn | To the top of the next page |

# Function Key Assignments in Q&A Write

## Function keys used alone:

| | |
|---|---|
| F1 | Get on-line help |
| F2 | Print document |
| F3 | Delete a block of text (by marking with cursor highlight) |
| F4 | Delete an entire word and trailing space if cursor is at the first letter; otherwise, delete from cursor position to word's end and leave trailing space |
| F5 | Copy a block of text within a document (by marking with cursor highlight) |
| F6 | Set a temporary indented left or right margin or clear temporary indent |
| F7 | Search-and-replace text in a document. Press PgDn for advanced search options |
| F8 | Access the Options Menu to add headers or footers, center or uncenter a line, set tabs on ruler, insert text from a separate document file, add a page break, or use the line drawing set (draw mode) |
| F9 | Scroll down document window |
| F10 | Confirm command selection |

## Function keys used with Shift

| | |
|---|---|
| Shift-F1 | Spell-check the entire document |
| Shift-F2 | Define a macro sequence, record keystrokes or word processing commands, or save or load a new macro file |
| Shift-F4 | Delete the line containing the cursor |
| Shift-F5 | Move a block of text (by marking with cursor highlight) |
| Shift-F6 | Define print enhancements such as underlining, boldface, italics, and superscripts and subscripts, or return text to normal |
| Shift-F7 | Undo key to bring back just-deleted text before making further deletions or copying or moving a block of text |
| Shift-F8 | Save document in memory |
| Shift-F9 | Scroll up document window |

## Function keys used with Ctrl:

| | |
|---|---|
| Ctrl-F1 | Spell-check the word containing the cursor |
| Ctrl-F2 | Print only the block of text defined with the cursor highlight |
| Ctrl-F3 | Display document statistics |
| Ctrl-F4 | Delete from the cursor to the end of the line |
| Ctrl-F5 | Copy a block of text defined with the cursor highlight into a new document file |
| Ctrl-F6 | Define a page |
| Ctrl-F7 | Go to a specified page or line |
| Ctrl-F8 | Export the document to ASCII text |
| Ctrl-F9 | Assign fonts to the current document |

## Function keys used with Alt:

| | |
|---|---|
| Alt-F5 | Move a block of text defined with the cursor highlight into a new document file |
| Alt-F6 | Add a soft hyphen |
| Alt-F7 | List the field names of the associated merge data file |
| Alt-F8 | Print mailing labels |
| Alt-F9 | Calculate a row or column of numbers |